Computational Methods for Engineers

Modeling, Algorithms and Analysis

J.P. Mmbaga
Department of Chemical & Materials Engineering
University of Alberta

K. Nandakumar
Cain Department of Chemical Engineering
Louisiana State University

R.E. Hayes
Department of Chemical & Materials Engineering
University of Alberta

M.R. Flynn
Department of Mechanical Engineering
University of Alberta

Published by:

    ALPHA Education Press
    A division of ALPHA Fluidic Associates Inc.
    717 173B Street SW
    Edmonton, AB T6W 0N1

2nd printing

Library and Archives Canada Cataloguing in Publication

Mmbaga, J. P. (Joseph Philemon), 1961-, author
    Computational methods for engineers : modeling, algorithms and analysis
/ J.P. Mmbaga, K. Nandakumar, R.E. Hayes, M.R. Flynn.

Includes bibliographical references and index.
ISBN 978-0-9938764-7-9 (paperback)

    1. Engineering mathematics. I. Hayes, R. E. (Robert E.), author II. Nandakumar, K. (Krishnaswamy), 1951-, author III. Flynn, M. R. (Morris Robert), 1977-, author
IV. Title.

TA330.M63 2016   620.001'51   C2016-900720-0

Digitally printed in Canada by

www.pagemaster.ca

$$\underline{\qquad\qquad\qquad\qquad\qquad\qquad}\text{CONTENTS}$$

Contents

PREFACE

Revolutionary advances in hardware and software technology have made computer aided design and analysis a standard tool in engineering practice. This obviously puts a lot of power in the hands of the end user, in order to use these tools wisely and interpret the results correctly, users are expected to have a sound knowledge of the relationship between the physical world and the mathematical model and that between the mathematical model and the numerical approximation.

The text is intended for both senior level undergraduate and first year graduate students without a comprehensive numerical background. Motivation for the text has grown from the authors' need to provide a text which covers both advanced features of numerical methods and specific applications in process and mechanical engineering.

An important complement to the text are the MATLAB* algorithms that appear throughout. Soft copies of these algorithms are available at `https://sites.ualberta.ca/~mrflynn/mnhf_mfiles/`. Students are encouraged to download, run and modify the .m files in question so as to accelerate their understanding of both MATLAB and numerical methods more generally. Also, for students who are new to MATLAB, the material of Appendix A is designed to highlight key features associated with this powerful computational tool.

---

*MATLAB is a trademarked product of MathWorks (Natick, Massachusetts).

ACKNOWLEDGEMENTS

No major work can be developed in vacuum. It is necessary to acknowledge previous published works which have influenced the development of this text. A number of authors have influenced our learning in this field, including Amundson (1966), Finlayson (1980), Hoffman (1992), Rao (2002) and Chapra (2005).

Previous course instructors who have taught the subject, specifically Dr. Carolina Diaz-Goano and Dr. Jos Derksen, are acknowledged. Special thanks to Dr. Petr Nikrityuk for giving useful and insightful comments on the manuscript. We would also like to thank Dr. Rajab Litto for redrawing some of the graphs and all the assistants and TAs who have guided our delivery of this material before many classes of students.

The original manuscript for this book was developed from lecture notes written by KN. This material was later expanded and elaborated upon by JPM, REH and MRF.

Notwithstanding any efforts made by others, all errors and omissions in this text remain the sole responsibility of the authors.

JPM   KN   REH   MRF

607102

To see a World in a Grain of Sand, And a Heaven in a
Wild Flower, Hold Infinity in the palm of your hand,
And Eternity in an hour

— WILLIAM BLAKE

CHAPTER 1

INTRODUCTION

1.1 Introduction

Engineers have no greater responsibility and opportunity than to explore and understand those physical and chemical processes associated
with converting raw materials into a useful final product. In so doing,
they must invariably use mathematics to develop detailed models that
describe the process(es) of interest. Such models are oftentimes far too
complicated to solve analytically and therefore numerical techniques
must be brought to bear as documented schematically in Figure 1.1.
The objective of this book is to provide, using a combination of theory
and example, a foundational knowledge in numerical analysis that can,
in turn, be adapted in solving real engineering problems, many of which
will not doubt bear only a modest resemblance to those problems we
have room to discuss in the pages to follow.

1

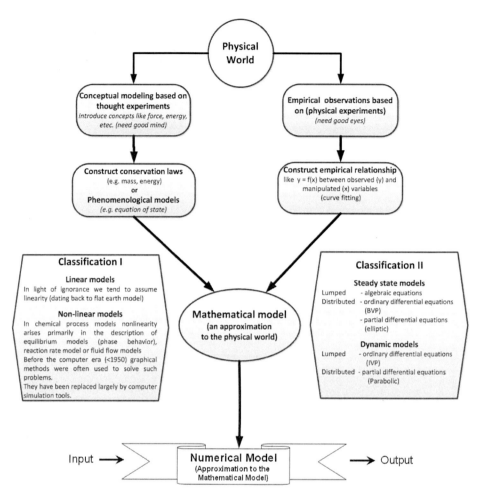

Figure 1.1: The relationship between the physical world and mathematical and numerical models.

A mathematical model is, at best, an approximation of the physical world. Such models are constructed based on certain conservation principles and/or empirical observations.* As a matter of convenience, mathematical models can be classified as *linear* or *nonlinear*, *steady-state* or *dynamic*, *lumped* or *distributed*. Examples pertaining to each of these categories are provided later in this chapter. Nonlinearity is found to occur quite frequently in nature; indeed the difficulty of solving nonlinear problems by hand was surely one of the principal drivers for the development of sophisticated numerical algorithms that accomplish this task, and many others, with aplomb.

A numerical model is an approximation of the mathematical model.

---

*Those curious about the nature of the physical laws should read the delightful book by Feynman (1967) on the character of such laws.

Although the importance of mathematical modelling in engineering has been recognized for centuries, it was the 1960 text by Bird et al. on *transport phenomena* that proved to be a major inspiration in exploring the link between the physical/industrial world and the mathematical one, at least insofar as processes governed by transfers of mass, momentum and heat. Six decades after the publication of Bird et al.'s seminal work, we find ourselves at a new threshold: computers are pervasive and monumental advances have been made in our ability to analyze difficult mathematical problems, nonlinear and otherwise. These advances could not have occurred without revolutionary developments in computer hardware and software. As a result, computer aided design and analysis (e.g. using COMSOL Multiphysics, SolidWorks, etc.) has become a standard facet of undergraduate curriculums. Moreover, general purpose mathematical tools such as MATLAB (for matrix linear algebra operations) or Mathematika and MAPLE (for symbolic computation) provide easy access to a vast array of mathematical functions and operations. These and other software packages help to

1. Codify advanced algorithms,

2. Assemble vast databases of information covering everything from material properties to mathematical functions, and,

3. Make all of the above accessible to the end user through an intuitive interface.

The end user is therefore given access to a plethora of helpful tools, however, in order to use these wisely and to interpret simulation output correctly, he or she must possess sound engineering judgement and the ability to differentiate between realistic and unrealistic model predictions. One is well served to remember the cliché *garbage in, garbage out.*

In this text we examine the link between mathematical and numerical models. Before delving too deeply into this relationship, it is helpful to first develop a better appreciation for the types of models most frequently encountered in engineering practice.

1.2 Model classification

In modelling engineering processes, one is often interested in tracking material and energy of process streams from the raw material stage to the finished product state. The state of a given stream is characterized by the relative concentrations of its constituent chemical species as well as its temperature, pressure and flow rate. Applying the laws of conservation of mass, momentum and energy allows us to track changes in the state of the stream. Typically we subject raw material streams to either physical treatments to add or remove select phases or species *e.g.* by exploiting such property differences as density, solubility, volatility, diffusivity etc. (transport and equilibrium processes) or to chemical treatment to alter chemical structures (reaction processes).

If the state (or dependent) variables are assumed to be independent of time and spatial position, then we often have a lumped parameter, steady state model resulting in a set of coupled algebraic equations. If, on the other hand, the state variables are assumed to have no spatial variation, but are time dependent, then we have lumped parameter, dynamic models that result in ordinary differential equations of the initial value type. If there is no temporal dependence, but there is a spatial variation , then we have ordinary differential equations of the boundary value type. If both spatial and temporal dependence are important, then we have partial differential equations, which are further classified as parabolic, elliptic or hyperbolic equations. In the sections to follow, the classification outlined above is illustrated with concrete examples drawn, somewhat arbitrarily, from electrical circuit theory and heat transfer. Our objective is to familiarize the reader with the process, often highly undervalued, of model development. The hope is that you will begin to appreciate the relationship between the physical world and the mathematical model(s) used to represent it.

1.3   Lumped parameter, steady state models

Figure 1.2 shows a canonical four-loop electrical circuit. We suppose that the voltages V_1, V_2, V_3 and V_4 are known and likewise for the resistances R_1, R_2, R_3, R_4 and R_5. Our objective is to compute the electrical currents i_1, i_2, i_3 and i_4. This task is achieved by recalling that

1. The sum of the voltage drops around any one of the four closed loops is zero; and

2. The voltage drop across a resistor is the product of the net current and the resistance.

The former result is an example of a *conservation law*; it follows from first principles in much the same way that, at macroscopic scales, mass can neither be created nor destroyed. The latter result, credited to the German physicist Georg Ohm, is an example of a *phenomenological law.* Phenomenological laws are based not first principles but rather on some judicious combination of empirical evidence and physical intuition. Although they lack some of the *gravitas* of conservation laws, phenomenological laws are nonetheless extremely helpful in describing processes in nature or industry.

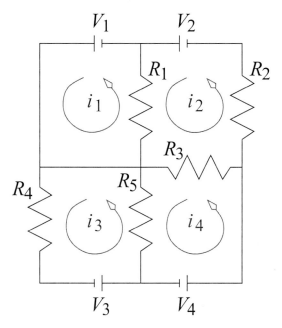

Figure 1.2: A four-loop electrical circuit. We regard the voltages and resistances as known and the currents as unknown.

For reasons of analytical expediency, many phenomenological laws are linear and Ohm's Law is no exception. It states that $V = iR$, i.e. the voltage drop is supposed to vary with R^1 and i^1, not R^2 or $\sqrt{i}$. (Other examples of linear phenomenological laws include Hooke's Law, the ideal gas law and Fick's Law of mass diffusion).

Applying the above ideas to Loop 1 of the circuit shown in Figure 1.2 leads to the following relationship:

$$V_1 = (i_1 - i_2)R_1 \Rightarrow V_1 = i_1 R_1 - i_2 R_1 \,. \tag{1.1}$$

Similar equations can be written in case of Loops 2, 3 and 4. After some elementary algebra, we find that

$$V_2 = -i_1 R_1 + i_2(R_1 + R_2 + R_3) - i_4 R_3 \,, \tag{1.2}$$

$$V_3 = i_3(R_4 + R_5) - i_4 R_5 \,, \tag{1.3}$$

$$V_4 = -i_2 R_3 - i_3 R_5 + i_4(R_3 + R_5) \,. \tag{1.4}$$

```
function i=mnhf_cct()
%MNHF_CCT solves for the currents in a four—loop electrical circuit. The
% problem is lumped and steady; currents can be determined by solving a
% 4x4 system of (linear) algebraic equations.
%
% i — column vector containing i1, i2, i3 and i4.

% Parameter input (voltages in volts, resistances in Ohms).
V1 = 60.0;
V2 = 110.0;
V3 = 200.0;
V4 = 60.0;
R1 = 22.0;
R2 = 9.0;
R3 = 10.0;
R4 = 32.0;
R5 = 41.0;
% End of parameter input.

A = [R1 —R1 0.0 0.0; —R1 R1+R2+R3 0.0 —R3; 0.0 0.0 R4+R5 —R5; ...
   0.0 —R3 —R5 R3+R5];
V = [V1; V2; V3; V4];
i = A\V;  % MATLAB's \ operator is an efficient way of solving matrix eqns.

% Print results.
fprintf('i1 (Amps) = %4.2f, i2 (Amps) = %4.2f\n',i(1),i(2))
fprintf('i3 (Amps) = %4.2f, i4 (Amps) = %4.2f\n',i(3),i(4))
```

Figure 1.3: A MATLAB function that solves for the currents defined schematically in Figure 1.2.

Equations (1.1-1.4) are four equations in the four unknowns i_1, i_2, i_3 and i_4. Because the equations are linear, they may be written using compact matrix notation as

$$\boldsymbol{Ai} = \boldsymbol{V}\,, \tag{1.5}$$

where

$$\boldsymbol{A} = \begin{bmatrix} R_1 & -R_1 & 0 & 0 \\ -R_1 & R_1 + R_2 + R_3 & 0 & -R_3 \\ 0 & 0 & R_4 + R_5 & -R_5 \\ 0 & -R_3 & -R_5 & R_3 + R_5 \end{bmatrix}.$$

$\boldsymbol{i} = (i_1, i_2, i_3, i_4)'$ and $\boldsymbol{V} = (V_1, V_2, V_3, V_4)'$ in which $'$ indicates vector transpose.

Once the values of V_1 to V_4 and R_1 to R_5 are specified, it is straightforward to solve for i_1 to i_4 either by hand-calculation or using MATLAB. Here, of course, we favor the latter approach and show in Figure 1.3 a simple MATLAB function that serves this purpose.

Because the function shown in Figure 1.3 is the first to be presented and discussed in this book, several explanatory comments are in order.

Firstly, the name of the function is `mnhf_cct` and the corresponding file name for this function is `mnhf_cct.m`*. The function does not accept any input variables; if it did, these would have to be listed within the parentheses that follow the function name. There is one (vector) output variable, `i`, whose value is computed within the function. Beginning on line 2 there appear preamble comments, which describe the problem to which this function will be applied. Thereafter follows the parameter input in which numerical values are assigned to the four voltages and five resistances. Although MATLAB, unlike more primitive programming languages, understands that `60` and `60.0` are one and the same, we nonetheless recommend writing `V1 = 60.0` to emphasize that `V1` is not an integer quantity. Note also that the values assigned to the variables `V1` to `V4` and `R1` to `R5` are arbitrary; other values could have just as easily been applied.

Following the parameter input, the matrix `A` and the column vector `V` are defined. We then solve the matrix equation (1.5) using MAT-LAB's backslash (\) operator. We will have more to say about this built-in function and its underpinnings in Chapter 3. Suffice it to say for now that \ offers a highly-optimized way of solving matrix equations of the generic form $Ax = b$. The individual elements of the column vector `i` are then printed to MATLAB's Command Window. By construction, these elements correspond, in sequential order, to i_1, i_2, i_3 and i_4.

Note finally that the easiest way to run the function `mnhf_cct` is to simply enter the name of the function (without the `.m` suffix) in the Command Window. Try, for instance, typing

```
>>current = mnhf_cct
```

MATLAB then helpfully produces the following output:

```
i1 (amps) = 17.74, i2 (amps) = 15.01
i3 (amps) = 9.21, i4 (amps) = 11.53

current =

17.7422
15.0149
9.2146
11.5284
```

---

*The prefix `mnhf` identifies this particular function as having been written by M̲mbaga, N̲andakumar, H̲ayes and F̲lynn.

However, if you type

    >>A

MATLAB complains that the variable A is undefined. How can this be if A is so clearly defined within mnhf_cct? The answer is that A is a variable that is *local* to the function. To make use of A within the Command Window, this variable must be defined either as a global variable or else included as an output variable along with i. If you find confusing the dichotomy between global variables (accessible to all functions and within the Command Window) and local variables (accessible only within the function where the variable in question is defined), an alternative is to solve the above problem using a MATLAB script instead of a MATLAB function – see Figure 1.4. The sequence of arithmetic operations is here identical to that outlined in Figure 1.3. A key difference is that mnhf_cct_script, like all MATLAB scripts, automatically adds all the variables defined within the script to MATLAB's Workspace. This feature has both advantages and disadvantages. We can, for instance, more readily determine the elements of the matrix A. On the other hand, if we define a scalar, vector or matrix variable A before running the script, its value is overwritten without warning as soon as we type

    >>mnhf_cct_script

in the Command Window.

Because MATLAB functions must explicitly define their input and output variables, they are generally considered to be more secure and also more flexible than MATLAB scripts. As a result, most of the programs presented in this book will be of the function variety. Note, however, that MATLAB scripts remain useful, in particular when they are employed as the "master program" that calls a number of MATLAB functions one after the other.

1.4   Lumped parameter, dynamic models

Lumped parameter, dynamic models typically arise when the spatial variation of the state variables can be ignored, but the time variation cannot. We illustrate such models with reference to a problem from heat transfer.

A sample of molten metal at an initial temperature of T_i is placed in a crucible (at an initial temperature of T_∞) and allowed to cool by convection. A schematic is shown in Figure 1.5. Let $T_1(t)$ be the tem-

```
%MNHF_CCT_SCRIPT solves for the currents in a four-loop electrical circuit.
% The problem is lumped and steady; currents can be determined by solving
% a 4x4 system of (linear) algebraic equations.

% Parameter input (voltages in volts, resistances in Ohms).
V1 = 60.0;
V2 = 110.0;
V3 = 200.0;
V4 = 60.0;
R1 = 22.0;
R2 = 9.0;
R3 = 10.0;
R4 = 32.0;
R5 = 41.0;
% End of parameter input.

A = [R1 -R1 0.0 0.0; -R1 R1+R2+R3 0.0 -R3; 0.0 0.0 R4+R5 -R5; ...
    0.0 -R3 -R5 R3+R5];
V = [V1; V2; V3; V4];
i = A\V;  % MATLAB's \ operator is an efficient way of solving matrix eqns.

% Print results.
fprintf('i1 (Amps) = %4.2f, i2 (Amps) = %4.2f\n',i(1),i(2))
fprintf('i3 (Amps) = %4.2f, i4 (Amps) = %4.2f\n',i(3),i(4))
```

Figure 1.4: A MATLAB script that solves for the currents defined schematically in Figure 1.2.

perature of the molten metal at any time, t, and $T_2(t)$ be the temperature of the crucible. The argument used to justify neglecting spatial variation is that the thermal conductivities of the two materials are sufficiently large to keep the temperature of each material uniform within its boundaries. The conservation law statement is:

$$\{\text{rate of accumulation}\} = \{\text{rate in}\} - \{\text{rate out}\} + \{\text{rate of generation}\}.$$

Applying this result this first to the molten metal,

$$\frac{\mathrm{d}}{\mathrm{d}t}(m_1 C_{p1} T_1) = \underbrace{-h_1 A_1 (T_1 - T_2)}_{\text{heat loss from 1 to 2}}. \tag{1.6}$$

Meanwhile, an energy balance on the crucible results in

$$\frac{\mathrm{d}}{\mathrm{d}t}(m_2 C_{p2} T_2) = \underbrace{h_1 A_1 (T_1 - T_2)}_{\text{heat gain by 2 from 1}} - \underbrace{h_2 A_2 (T_2 - T_\infty)}_{\text{heat loss from 2 to } \infty}. \tag{1.7}$$

Equations (1.6) and (1.7) can be rewritten using matrix notation as follows:

$$\frac{\mathrm{d}\underline{\theta}}{\mathrm{d}t} = \boldsymbol{A}\underline{\theta} + \boldsymbol{b}, \tag{1.8}$$

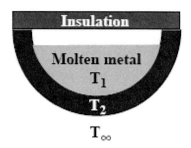

Figure 1.5: Heat transfer from a molten metal.

where

$$\underline{\theta} = \begin{bmatrix} T_1 \\ T_2 \end{bmatrix} \qquad \boldsymbol{A} = \begin{bmatrix} -\frac{h_1 A_1}{m_1 C_{P1}} & \frac{h_1 A_1}{m_1 C_{P1}} \\ \frac{h_1 A_1}{m_2 C_{P2}} & -\frac{h_1 A_1 + h_2 A_2}{m_2 C_{P2}} \end{bmatrix} \qquad \boldsymbol{b} = \begin{bmatrix} 0 \\ \frac{h_2 A_2 T_\infty}{m_2 C_{P2}} \end{bmatrix}.$$

The initial condition reads

$$\underline{\theta}(t=0) = \begin{bmatrix} T_1(0) \\ T_2(0) \end{bmatrix}.$$

The above problem depends on several parameters which are assumed to be known. A_1 is the heat transfer area at the metal-crucible interface and A_2 is the area at the crucible-air interface. h_1 and h_2 are the convective heat transfer coefficients, m_1 and m_2 are the masses of the materials and C_{p1} and C_{p2} are the specific heats of the materials. Because all of these are assumed to be known constants, the problem is linear. The numerical solution to equations (1.6) and (1.7) will be examined in Chapter 6.

1.5   Distributed parameter, steady state models

Let us now examine an example from *transport processes*. Consider the use of a fin to enhance the rate of heat transfer. Basically, a fin provides a large heat transfer surface in a compact design. In the performance analysis of fins one might be interested in a variety of questions such as "What is the efficiency of the fin?", "How many fins are required to dissipate a certain heat load?", "What is the optimal shape of the fin that maximizes the heat dissipation for minimum weight of fin material?" or "How long does it take for the fin to reach a steady state?" You will learn to develop answers to these questions in a heat transfer course. Our interest at this stage is to develop an intuition

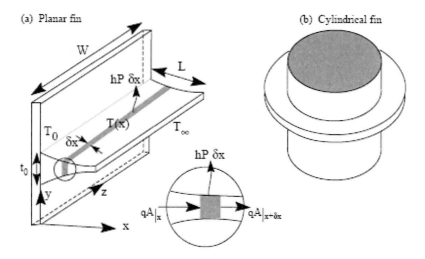

Figure 1.6: Heat transfer through a cooling fin. (a) Planar geometry, (b) cylindrical geometry

for the model building process. A sketch of two representative fins is shown in Figure 1.6. Let us examine the steady state behavior of the planar fin shown in Figure 1.6 a.

The base of the fin is maintained at a uniform temperature T_0 and the ambient temperature is T_∞. The state variable that we are interested in predicting is the temperature, T, of the fin. In general, T will be a function of all three spatial variables i.e., $T = T(x, y, z)$. (Note time, t is eliminated by assuming steady state). If we know something about the length scales and material properties of the fin, we can make further assumptions that will reduce the complexity of the problem. For instance, the thermal conductivity, k, of the fin might be independent of position. If the length, L, of the fin is much larger than the thickness, t_0, then we might argue that the temperature variation in the y direction will be smaller than that in the x direction. Thus we can assume T to be uniform in the y direction. Next, we examine what happens in the z direction. This argument is somewhat subtle as it is based on symmetries in the system. The basic premise is that symmetric causes produce symmetric effects. First we assume that the ends of the fin in the z direction are at infinity (or $W \gg L$) so that the end effects can be neglected. Because the temperature gradient within the fin is caused by the difference between T_0 and T_∞, which are independent of z, we can expect the fin to respond in a similar way - viz. T to be independent of z. Note that the end effect, however

small it may be, is always present in a planar fin. By making W large
compared to L, we reduce the error caused by the two-dimensional
effect near the ends. On the other hand the azimuthal symmetry in the
circular fin (Figure 1.6 b) make the problem truly one dimensional with
temperature varying only in the radial direction. Now that we have
a better feel for what kinds of arguments or assumptions make this
problem one-dimensional, let us proceed with constructing the model
equation.

Take an elemental control volume of thickness δx and identify the
input and output sources of energy into this control volume. Energy
enters by conduction at a rate of $(qA)|_x$ through the left boundary at x
and leaves at a rate of $(qA)|_{x+\delta x}$ through the right boundary at $x + \delta x$.
Heat is also lost by convection through the upper and lower boundaries,
which is represented by $hP\delta x(T - T_\infty)$. Here q is the conductive heat
flux (W/m^2) and is given by another phenomenological model called
Fourier's Law: $q = -k\frac{dT}{dx}$. Here k denotes a material property called
the thermal conductivity, measured in W/(m·K). Moreover, A is the
cross-sectional area which is allowed to be a function of x (tapered fin)
and h, measured in $\text{W/(m}^2\text{K)}$, is the convective heat transfer coefficient.
Finally, $P = 2w$ is the fin perimeter. As before, the conservation law
statement reads

$$\{\text{rate of accumulation}\} = \{\text{rate in}\} - \{\text{rate out}\} + \{\text{rate of generation}\},$$

or, using symbols,

$$0 = (qA)|_x - (qA)|_{x+\delta x} - hP\delta x(T - T_\infty).$$

Dividing by δx and taking the limit as $\delta x \to 0$, we obtain

$$0 = -\frac{d(qA)}{dx} - hP(T - T_\infty).$$

Finally, using Fourier's Law to replace q in terms of T, it can be shown
that

$$\frac{d}{dx}\left[kA\frac{dT}{dx}\right] - hP(T - T_\infty) = 0. \tag{1.9}$$

Equation (1.9) is a second order ordinary differential equation. The
physical description dictates that two conditions be specified at the
two ends of the fin, for instance, $T(x = 0) = T_0$ and $T(x = L) = T_\infty$.

As we illustrate in Chapter 7, the above problem can be solved to
obtain $T(x)$ provided the geometrical parameters $A(x)$, P, the material
property k and the heat transfer environment h, T_∞, T_0 are known.
The problem is nonlinear if the thermal conductivity is a function of
temperature, $k(T)$. In order to determine the fin effectiveness, one is

interested in the total rate of heat transfer, Q, through the fin. This is can be computed in one of two ways as given by

$$Q = \int_0^L hP[T(x) - T_\infty]\mathrm{d}x = -kA\frac{\mathrm{d}T}{\mathrm{d}x}\bigg|_{x=0}.$$

1.6 Distributed parameter, dynamic models

As an example of a distributed, dynamic model let us revisit the fin problem, but during the early transient phase so that $T = T(x, t)$. Let the fin have an initial temperature equal to the ambient temperature, T_∞. At time $t = 0$ suppose the base of the fin at $x = 0$ is brought to a temperature T_0. One might ask questions like "How long will it take for the fin to reach a steady state?", "What will be the temperature at the fin tip at a given time?", etc. We can represent the rate of accumulation within a control volume symbolically as $\frac{\partial(\rho A\delta x C_p T)}{\partial t}$ where the term in parentheses is the thermal energy, measured in J, C_p is the specific heat of the fin material $(\mathrm{J}/(\mathrm{kg\,K})$ and ρ is the density of the material $(\mathrm{kg/m^3})$. Thus the transient energy balance becomes

$$\frac{\partial(\rho A\delta x C_p T)}{\partial t} = (qA)|_x - (qA)|_{x+\delta x} - hP\delta x(T - T_\infty).$$

Dividing by δx and taking the limit of $\delta x \to 0$, we obtain

$$\frac{\partial(\rho A C_p T)}{\partial t} = -\frac{\partial(qA)}{\partial x} - hP(T - T_\infty).$$

Finally using Fourier's Law to replace q in terms of T, it can be shown that

$$\frac{\partial(\rho A C_p T)}{\partial t} = \frac{\partial}{\partial x}\left[kA\frac{\partial T}{\partial x}\right] - hP(T - T_\infty) \qquad (1.10)$$

Note that we have switched to partial derivatives because T is a function of both space and time. In addition to the previously-specified boundary conditions, we require an initial condition to complete the problem specification. In symbols, this initial condition is represented as $T(x, t = 0) = T_\infty$.

The numerical solution of partial differential equations such as equation (1.10) is covered in Chapter 8.

1.7 Putting it all together

1.7.1 Mathematical models and physical laws

The previous discussion may give the impression that each physical system is associated with one, or at most two, mathematical representations. Thus electrical circuits only yield lumped parameter, steady state models, cooling fins only yield distributed parameter, steady state or dynamic models, etc. In fact, and as we illustrate below with reference to a cooling spherical body, model complexity depends strongly on the number and severity of the simplifying assumptions that are made.

Let us consider a spherical object with mass m, density ρ, and a temperature T_i suspended in a medium (environment) that has a different temperature T_∞ (Figure 1.7).

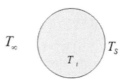

Figure 1.7: A sphere suspended in an environment at T_∞.

Linear algebraic equation

Suppose the conditions are such that the temperature inside the sphere is the same as the temperature at the surface. If the surface temperature is T_S, the heat loss by convection from the surface of the sphere to the environment is governed by Newton's Law of Cooling, which states

$$q = h(T_S - T_\infty),$$

where q heat loss per unit area (W/m^2) and h is the heat transfer coefficient (W/(m^{2}K)). Hence we have a direct (linear) relationship between heat loss and the surface temperature. For any given T_S, it is straightforward to compute q.

Nonlinear algebraic equation

Suppose we allow for other modes of heat transfer, namely heat loss by radiation. In this case, the heat loss is determined by another physical relationship namely the Stefan-Boltzman Law. When applied to a body which is in the presence of large surroundings, the law takes the form

$$q_{rad} = \epsilon\sigma(T_S^4 - T_{surr}^4),$$

where q_{rad} is the heat loss per unit area due to radiation, ϵ is the emissivity of the surface and σ is a prescribed constant. This is a nonlinear relationship because the temperature is raised to the fourth power. The total heat loss from the sphere becomes

$$q = h(T_S - T_\infty) + \epsilon\sigma(T_S^4 - T_{surr}^4).$$

In the above two cases, the heat loss will continue until the surface temperature is equal to the temperature of the environment. If this is to be prevented, some mechanism for generating energy inside the sphere must be accommodated to compensate for the heat loss.

Lumped parameter, dynamic model

Suppose we wish to monitor how the temperature of the sphere is changing with time. (We are not yet concerned about temperature gradients within the sphere.) In this case, energy balance involves a rate component, namely the rate of change of the internal energy of the sphere, given by $\frac{d}{dt}(\rho C_P T)$. The energy balance equation becomes

$$\frac{d}{dt}(\rho C_P T) = -h(T - T_\infty).$$

In order to solve the above differential equation, the initial temperature must be specified. Ours is therefore an initial value problem.

Distributed model, partial differential equation

Suppose the conditions in our model sphere are such that we cannot ignore the temperature variations inside the sphere. (In heat transfer jargon Bi > 0.1 where Bi is a Biot number.) The model has to be formulated to include temperature gradients. Assuming that the other properties are independent of temperature, and using Fourier's Law for heat conduction inside the sphere, we can rewrite our energy balance equations in spherical coordinates as

$$\rho C_P \frac{\partial T}{\partial t} = \frac{1}{r^2} \frac{\partial}{\partial r}\left(r^2 k \frac{\partial T}{\partial r}\right),$$

or, using the chain rule and setting $\alpha = k/\rho C_P$,

$$\frac{\partial^2 T}{\partial r^2} + 2r \frac{\partial T}{\partial r} = \frac{1}{\alpha}\frac{\partial T}{\partial t}.$$

What was previously an ordinary differential equation is now a partial differential equation because there are two independent variables, namely r and t. In order to solve this problem, it is no longer sufficient to know only the initial value, we also need the boundary conditions. This is because the above equation does not say anything about the boundaries, *i.e.* the surface or center of the sphere. Initial conditions *e.g.* $T(r,0) = T_i$ must therefore be specified along with boundary conditions *e.g.*

$$-k\frac{\partial T}{\partial r}\bigg|_{r=r_0} = h(T - T_\infty), \qquad \frac{\partial T}{\partial r}\bigg|_{r=0} = 0.$$

The above examples show how we can end up with very different models simply because of the different conditions/assumptions applied as well as the desired results.

1.7.2 Mathematical models, numerical approximations and errors

A mathematical model is an equation which expresses the essential features of a physical system in mathematical terms. Symbolically, we can write the functional relationship as

$$Y = f(X; p; F), \tag{1.11}$$

where Y is a dependent variable which describes the state or behaviour of the system. X represents the independent variables in the system (space dimensions or time) and p represents parameters that describe the properties of the system. The extra term, F, represents all other external influences which may act on the system.

Throughout history, mathematical models have been developed to describe physical phenomena. For instance, Newton's Laws accurately describe many everyday, macroscopic phenomena. In order to demonstrate the concept of numerical modelling, let us consider Newton's Second Law of Motion, which states that "The time rate of change of the momentum of a body is equal to the resultant force acting on it." The mathematical expression of the Second Law is

$$ma = F, \tag{1.12}$$

where F is the net force acting on the body, and m and a are the mass and acceleration of the body, respectively. We can write this law in the form of equation (1.11) by dividing by m to give

$$a = \frac{F}{m}, \tag{1.13}$$

where a is the dependent variable, m is a parameter representing a property of the system and F is the forcing function. Equation (1.13) is a mathematical model because it describes a natural process in mathematical terms, it represents an idealization and simplification of reality and finally because it can be used for predictive purposes.

Figure 1.8: Force balance on a falling sphere.

The majority of problems encountered in engineering involve differential equations. Differential equations are expressions which involve the derivative of the dependent variable. From physics, we know that acceleration is the time rate of change of velocity, v, *i.e.*

$$a = \frac{dv}{dt} \,.$$

Therefore, if we wish to use v as the dependent variable, equation (1.13) must be written in differential form as

$$\frac{dv}{dt} = \frac{F}{m} \,. \tag{1.14}$$

To solve equation (1.14) for a particular situation, more information obviously needs to be provided. Suppose we wish to determine the terminal velocity of a spherical ball of given diameter and mass that is falling in a large medium of fluid as shown in Figure 1.8. If the fluid density is negligible, a force balance requires the gravitational force, mg, to be balanced by the drag (or resistance) force, F_R. This latter force will depend on v and on body properties such as shape and surface roughness, so a further relationship is needed. Suppose, for the sake or argument, that $F_R = -kv$ where k is a known quantity. The negative sign implies that the force is acting in the opposite direction of motion. Performing a force balance on the body, we obtain

$$F = F_D - F_R = mg - kv \,.$$

Equation (1.14) can now be written in terms of the given parameters as

$$\frac{dv}{dt} = \frac{mg - kv}{m} \tag{1.15}$$

where g is the gravitational acceleration.

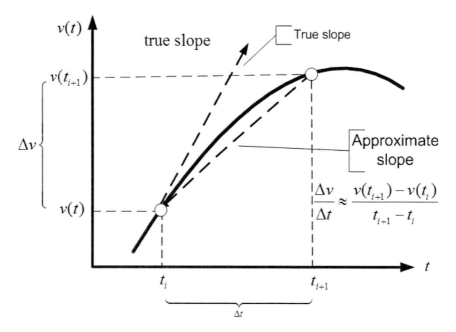

Figure 1.9: Approximation of the first derivative.

We use models to understand and predict physical phenomena and must therefore find the model equation solution in order to be resolve the dependent parameter. If one can solve the mathematical equation without need of further simplifications and obtain an exact description of the dependent variable, the model is said to have an *analytical* solution. For instance, in order to solve equation (1.15), calculus may be used to obtain velocity as a function of time

$$v(t) = \frac{mg}{k} \left[1 - e^{(-k/m)t} \right] . \tag{1.16}$$

Many mathematical models of interest in engineering do not have analytical solutions. The alternative is to develop a numerical solution that approximates the exact solution. In this respect, we seek to reformulate the problem so that it can be solved by arithmetic operations on a computer. For the above example, we need to replace the first derivative with its approximate representation. Let us reexamine the model equation again

$$\frac{dv}{dt} = \frac{mg - kv}{m} .$$

We note that the true derivative, which is a point slope, can be approximated by the secant (or two point slope) as shown in Figure 1.9. Thus we can replace the continuous derivative at point i, with the derivative based on the two points, i and $i + 1$, *i.e.*

$$\frac{v(t_{i+1}) - v(t_i)}{t_{i+1} - t_i} = \frac{mg - kv}{m} \approx \text{Slope}.\qquad (1.17)$$

The above equation can now be rearranged to yield the value of velocity at time t_{i+1} where it is assumed that the velocity is known at t_i. Thus

$$v(t_{i+1}) = v(t_i) + \left[g - \frac{k}{m}v(t_i)\right](t_{i+1} - t_i).\qquad (1.18)$$

The differential equation has been transformed into a recursive algebraic equation that may be applied at different discrete points in time. We can therefore use the above formula to compute the velocity at different times starting from the known initial value. The outcome of carrying out this procedure with a sphere of mass 20 mg falling in a fluid with a flow resistance coefficient $k = 0.015\,\text{kg/s}$ is shown in Figure 1.10 together with the analytical solution.

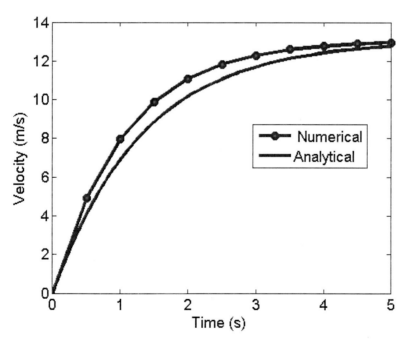

Figure 1.10: Comparison of the solutions of Equations (1.16) and (1.18) where $t_{i+1} - t_i = 0.5\,\text{s}$.

The main difference between Equations (1.18) and (1.16) is that the analytical solution is continuous, thus one can plug in any value of t to obtain the velocity at that time. On the other hand, Equation (1.18) is a recursive formula in discrete form. It has to be applied at the discrete

points repeatedly in order to arrive at a full solution. The application
of Equation (1.18), if carried out on a computer, requires a specific set
of instructions to be communicated in order to accomplish the task as
desired. These instructions constitute what we call *algorithms*.

1.7.3   Algorithms

Although we have already seen two examples of MATLAB programs,
it is necessary to more carefully define an algorithm because these are
so central to numerical analysis. An algorithm is a precise sequence of
steps for performing a specified function. For instance, in order to compute the velocity at different times, we might implement the following
set of operations given in the form of pseudo-code:

```
Set t = t_0 and v = v_0
Set t_f
Set h
Set the parameters k, g and m
Repeat while t < t_f
{
Evaluate slope=f(t,v,k,g,m)
Evaluate v = v + h*slope
Store t and v
Increment t = t + h
}
Print t and v
```

   The above set of instructions need to be put in a specific form in
order for the computer to understand and implement the different steps.
We also need to determine the conditions under which an algorithm
is expected to work and how accurately the solution produced by an
algorithm approximates the exact solution.

1.7.4   Errors in numerical computation

Numerical methods yield approximate results. With such approximations, more questions come to mind such as "How good is the approximation?", "How confident we are in our approximate result?" or "How
much error can we tolerate in our calculation?" We need to know how
errors arise when we implement an approximation which involves a
number of assumptions and simplifications. Only then can we devise

measures to determine how each point estimate deviates from the exact solution.

Sources and types of errors

1. Model errors

   Errors resulting from approximations and assumptions in representing the physical system. In our most recent model problem, we have, for instance, assumed a linear relationship between flow resistance force and velocity.

2. Machine errors

   Errors resulting from round-off and/or the chopping of numbers due to limited representation of real numbers on the computer.

3. Truncation errors

   Errors caused by use of truncated approximations to infinite series solutions.

4. User and programming errors

   Errors caused by human oversight or mistakes in code implementation.

5. Data uncertainty

   Errors resulting from the inaccuracy of measurement data, *e.g.*, for our model parameters, the constant k is obtained experimentally, so our final result will have large errors if the data are inaccurate.

In order to quantify the above discussion, we provide below more formal error definitions.

True error:
$$e = \text{exact value - approximate value}.$$

Absolute error:
$$|e| = |\text{exact value - approximate value}|.$$

Relative error:
$$e_r = \left| \frac{\text{exact value - approximate value}}{\text{exact value}} \right|.$$

Percent error:
$$e_\% = \left| \frac{\text{exact value - approximate value}}{\text{exact value}} \right| \times 100\%.$$

Approximate error:

$$e_a = \left| \frac{\text{current approximation - previous approximation}}{\text{current approximation}} \right| .$$

An expanded description of error definitions and also computer number representation and significant figures is provided in Appendix B.

Stopping criterion

In computations, we are mostly concerned with whether the approximate error is less than some specified number, which we call the tolerance, ϵ_S. In symbols, the condition to be satisfied reads $e_a < \epsilon_S$. Scarborough (1966) has shown that we can be certain of a numerical approximation to at least n significant figures where n is the largest positive number for which

$$\epsilon_S < 0.5 \times 10^{-n} .$$

For instance, in the above example, if one calculation gives a value of $v(t_{i+1}) = 12.0133$ and the previous calculation gave $v(t_i) = 12.0345$, the approximate error is

$$e_a = \left| \frac{12.0133 - 12.0345}{12.0133} \right| = 0.00176 = 0.176 \times 10^{-2} < 0.5 \times 10^{-2} ,$$

and the solution is therefore accurate to two significant figures.

1.8   Summary

In this chapter, various concepts related to the translation of a physical problem into a mathematical expression have been introduced. The mathematical expression is then simplified and approximated in order to be solved on a computer.

The numerical techniques to be implemented in the solution of such equations will be discussed in different chapters of this book. Particular attention is paid to conceptual understanding of the underlying mathematical principles as well as the solution methods. The accuracy and applicability of each approximation method is also discussed. In order to fully grasp the concepts introduced, opportunities for both hand calculations as well as implementation of numerical algorithms in the MATLAB programming environment will be presented.

CHAPTER 2

SINGLE NONLINEAR ALGEBRAIC EQUATIONS

2.1 Introduction

This chapter considers the problem of finding the root of a single nonlinear algebraic equation of the form

$$f(x) = 0, \tag{2.1}$$

where $f(x)$ is a continuous function of x and the equation is satisfied
only at selected values of $x = r$, called the *roots*. The equation can be
a simple polynomial or a more complicated function. If the equation
depends on other parameters, as is often the case, we will represent it
as

$$f(x; p) = 0, \tag{2.2}$$

where p represents a set of known parameter values. Clearly, we can
graph f vs. x for a range of values of x. The objective of such an
exercise is to graphically locate the values of $x = r$ where the function
crosses the x axis. While such a graphical approach has an intuitive
appeal, it is difficult to extend such an approach to higher-dimensional
systems. Hence we seek to construct computational algorithms that
can be generalized and successively refined to handle a large class of
nonlinear problems.

Before embarking on this task, some potential problems are illustrated with specific examples. In the general case, there is no way to
know *a priori* the number of roots, particularly if the entire range of
x in $(-\infty, \infty)$ is considered. For example, $f(x) = \sin x$ has infinitely
many solutions given by $r = n\pi$ where n is an integer. Often, the
physical description of the problem that gave rise to the mathematical

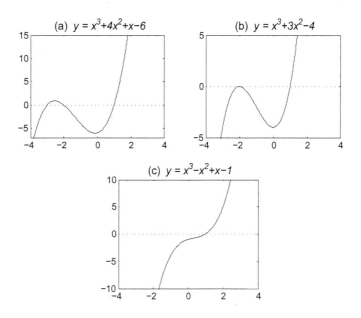

Figure 2.1: Graphs of some simple polynomial functions.

function will also provide information on the range of values of x that are of interest. Although the mathematical equation may have many other roots, outside of this range they lack physical meaning and hence would not be of interest.

Algebraic theory tells us that the total number of roots of a polynomial equals the degree of the polynomial, but not all of the roots may be real. Furthermore, if the coefficients of the polynomial are all real, then any complex roots must appear as complex conjugate pairs. Consider the three cubic equations given below

$$
\begin{aligned}
f(x) &= x^3 + 4x^2 + x - 6 = 0 & r &= -3, -2, 1, \\
f(x) &= x^3 + 3x^2 - 4 = 0, & r &= -2, -2, 1, \\
f(x) &= x^3 - x^2 + x - 1 = 0 & r &= 1.
\end{aligned}
\tag{2.3}
$$

These functions are plotted in Figures 2.1 a,b,c, respectively. In the first case there are three distinct roots. The function has a non-zero slope at each root; such roots are called *simple* roots. In the second case we have a *non-simple* (or multiple) root at $r = -2$. Thus f has a slope of zero when $x = -2$. If the coefficients of the polynomial were slightly different, the curve could have moved slightly upward giving rise to two distinct roots or downwards yielding no roots in this region. Algebraically, we can see that the root at $x = -2$ is a multiple root with a multiplicity of two by factoring the function into $(x+2)(x+2)(x-1)$.

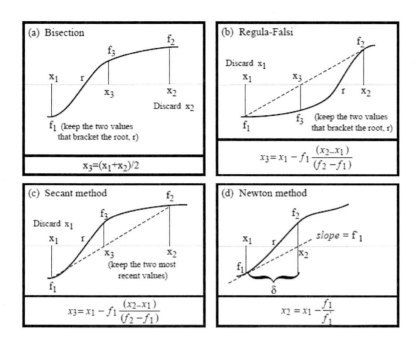

Figure 2.2: Graphical representation of some simple root finding algorithms.

In the third case there is only a single *real* root.

We begin by constructing some simple algorithms that have an intuitive appeal. They are easy to represent graphically and symbolically so that one can appreciate the connection between the two representations. Subsequently we can refine the computational algorithms to meet the challenges posed by more difficult problems, while keeping the graphical representation as a visual aid.

There are essentially three key steps in any root finding algorithm.

step 1: **Guess** one or more initial values for x.

step 2: **Iterate** using a scheme to improve the initial guess.

step 3: **Check convergence** - *i.e.*, has the improvement scheme of step 2 produced a result of desired accuracy?

The crux of the algorithm is often in the second step and the objective in devising various clever schemes is to get from the initial guess to the final result as quickly as possible.

2.2   Bisection method

The bisection algorithm is quite intuitive. A graphical illustration of this algorithm is shown in Figure 2.2 a. In step 1, we make two guesses x_1 and x_2 and calculate the function values $f_1 = f(x_1)$ and $f_2 = f(x_2)$. If the function values have opposite signs, it implies that f passes through zero somewhere between x_1 and x_2 and hence we can proceed to the second step of producing a better estimate of the root, x_3. If there is no sign change, it might imply that there is no root between (x_1, x_2). So we have to make a set of alternate guesses. The scheme for producing a better estimate is also an extremely simple one of using the average of the two previous guesses, *i.e.*,

$$x_3 = \tfrac{1}{2}(x_1 + x_2). \tag{2.4}$$

In Figure 2.2 a, (x_1, x_3) bracket the root, r; hence we discard x_2, or better still, store the *value* of x_3 in the *variable* x_2 so that we are poised to straightaway repeat step 2. If the situation were such as the one shown in Figure 2.2 b, then we would discard x_1 or better still, store the *value* of x_3 in the *variable* x_1 and repeat step 2. In either case, (x_1, x_2) represent better guesses than the original values.

The final step is to check if we are close enough to the desired root r so that we can terminate the repeated application of step 2. One test might be to check if the absolute difference between two successive values of x is smaller than a specified tolerance*, *i.e.*,

$$|x_i - x_{i-1}| \leq \epsilon.$$

When comparing values with different magnitudes, the percent relative error defined as

$$\left|\frac{x_i - x_{i-1}}{x_i}\right| \leq \epsilon, \qquad x_i \neq 0.$$

may be more useful. Another test might be to check if the absolute value of the function at the end of every iteration is below a prescribed tolerance, *i.e.*,

$$|f(x_i)| \leq \epsilon.$$

A MATLAB function that implements the above steps is given in Figure 2.3. Note that the `for` loop is executed a maximum of 100 times. If the convergence criterion `abs(f3) < tol` is not satisfied within this number of `for` loop executions, the MATLAB function does not return a solution suggesting that different initial guesses ought to be attempted.

---

*ϵ is a small number *e.g.* 10^{-3} or 10^{-6}, selected for tight tolerance

```
function r=mnhf_bisect(Fun,x,tol,trace)
%MNHF_BISECT finds root of "Fun" using bisection scheme.
%
% Fun — name of the external function
% x — vector of length 2, (initial guesses)
% tol — tolerance
% trace — print intermediate results
%
% Usage  mnhf_bisect(@poly1,[−0.5 2.0],1e−8,1)
%         poly1 is the name of the external function.
%         [−0.5 2.0] are initial guesses for the root.

% Check inputs.
if nargin < 4, trace = 1;  end
if nargin < 3, tol = 1e−8; end
if (length(x) ~= 2)
 error('Please provide two initial guesses')
end

f = feval(Fun,x); % Fun is assumed to accept a vector

if prod(sign(f)) > 0.0
 error('No sign change — no roots')
end

for i = 1:100
 x3 = 0.5*(x(1)+x(2));    % Update the guess.
 f3 = feval(Fun,x3);      % Function evaluation.
 if trace, fprintf(1,'%3i %12.5f %12.5f\n', i,x3,f3); end
 if abs(f3) < tol % Check for convergenece.
  r = x3;
  return
 else % Reset values for x(1), x(2), f(1) and f(2).
  if sign(f3*f(1)) < 0.0
   x(2) = x3;
  else
   x(1) = x3;
  end
  f = feval(Fun,x);  % Fun is assumed to accept a vector.
 end
end
```

Figure 2.3: MATLAB implementation of the bisection algorithm.

```
function f=poly1(x)
% Polynomial function of x.

f = x.^3.0-x.^2.0+x-1.0;
```

Figure 2.4: The cubic polynomial function $f(x) = x^3 - x^2 + x - 1$, defined as a MATLAB function.

To develop a heuristic sense for the relative performance of the bisection algorithm with others to be outlined later in this chapter, it is helpful to reconsider the cubic polynomial function exhibited in Figure 2.1 c. The (unique, simple) root of this function obviously occurs at $x = 1$. Two questions that remain to be answered are "Can the bisection algorithm shown in Figure 2.3 recover this root?" and, if so, "How many iterations are required?" We may address these questions by defining a second MATLAB function, `poly1.m`, as in Figure 2.4. Note that the terms proportional to x^3 and x^2 are specified using `.^` rather than `^`, i.e. `poly1` can accept either scalar or vector input. Selecting as our two initial guesses -0.5 and 2 and typing either `mnhf_bisect(@poly1,[-0.5 2.0],1e-8,1)` or `mnhf_bisect('poly1',[-0.5 2.0],1e-8,1)` in the MATLAB Command Window shows that 27 iterations are needed to converge to the root. This outcome combines good and bad news: convergence to the correct answer does occur, in fact will always occur provided an acceptable pair of initial guesses are selected. This is a general advantage of the bisection algorithm. On the other hand, the rate of convergence seems rather slow, which is an obvious disadvantage, particularly if many root finding operations need to be performed in sequence. The development of less computationally-intensive root finding schemes is a major objective of the rest of this chapter.

2.3   Regula-Falsi method

Instead of using the average of the two initial guesses as we did with the bisection scheme, we can attempt to approximate the function $f(x)$ by a straight line (a *linear* approximation) because we know two points of the function $f(x)$. This is illustrated graphically in Figure 2.2 b with the dashed line approximating the function. We can then determine the root, x_3, of this linear function, $\tilde{f}(x)$. The equation for the dashed line in Figure 2.2b can be determined from

$$\frac{x - x_1}{\tilde{f} - f_1} = \frac{x_2 - x_1}{f_2 - f_1}.$$

It is then straightforward to determine the value $x = x_3$ where $\tilde{f} = 0$. After some algebra, we find that

$$x_3 = x_1 - f_1 \left(\frac{x_2 - x_1}{f_2 - f_1} \right), \tag{2.5}$$

which is used as the iterative equation in step 2. When we evaluate the original function at x_3, $f(x_3)$ clearly will not be zero (unless f is itself linear) – see Figure 2.2 b. However, x_3 will be closer to r than either x_1 or x_2. We can then retain x_3 and one of x_1 or x_2 in such a manner that the root r remains bracketed. This is achieved by following the same logic as in the bisection algorithm to discard the x value that does not bracket the root. Figure 2.5 gives a graphical depiction of the iterative steps associated with the Regula-Falsi method.

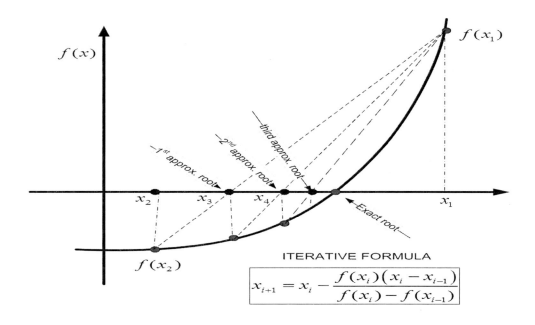

Figure 2.5: Regula-Falsi iterative steps

From the above figure, it might be supposed that the rate of convergence grinds to a crawl in the neighborhood of the root, r. This suspicion is confirmed by running `mnhf_regula_falsi` – see Figure

```
function r=mnhf_regula_falsi(Fun,x,tol,trace)
%MNHF_REGULA_FALSI finds the root of "Fun" using Regula—Falsi scheme.
%
% Fun — name of the external function
% x — vector of length 2, (initial guesses)
% tol — tolerance
% trace — print intermediate results
%
% Usage  mnhf_regula_falsi(@poly1,[−0.5 2.0],1e-8,1)
%        poly1 is the name of the external function.
%        [−0.5 2.0] are the initial guesses for the root.

% Check inputs.
if nargin < 4, trace = 1;  end
if nargin < 3, tol = 1e—8; end
if (length(x) ~= 2)
 error('Please provide two initial guesses')
end

f = feval(Fun,x); % Fun is assumed to accept a vector

for i = 1:100
 x3 = x(1)—f(1)*(x(2)—x(1))/(f(2)—f(1));  % Update guess
 f3 = feval(Fun,x3);  % Function evaluation.
 if trace, fprintf(1,'%3i %12.5f %12.5f\n', i,x3,f3); end
 if abs(f3) < tol % Check for convergenece.
  r = x3;
  return
 else % Reset values for x(1), x(2), f(1) and f(2).
  if sign(f3*f(1)) < 0.0
   x(2) = x3;
  else
   x(1) = x3;
  end
  f = feval(Fun,x);  % Fun is assumed to accept a vector.
 end
end
```

Figure 2.6: MATLAB implementation of the Regula-Falsi method.

2.6. Indeed, typing `mnhf_regula_falsi(@poly1,[-0.5 2.0],1e-8,1)` in the MATLAB Command Window indicates that no fewer than 39 iterations are needed for convergence. Therefore, despite the best of intentions, Regula-Falsi cannot be considered an improvement over the bisection algorithm, which enjoys the twin advantages of computational efficiency and conceptual simplicity. In fact, we will see shortly that a very minor change in the implementation of Regula-Falsi can lead to a significant decrease in the number of iterations required.*

---

*Of course, when assessing the efficiency of a particular algorithm, it is not the number of iterations that is most important, but rather the number of floating point operations. Even using this other yardstick, however, the Regula-Falsi scheme must be regarded as computationally inefficient.

2.4   Newton's method

Newton's method is arguably the most powerful and widely used algorithm for finding the roots of nonlinear equations. A graphical representation of the algorithm is shown in Figure 2.2 d. This algorithm also relies on constructing a linear approximation of the function; but this is achieved by taking the tangent to the function at a given point. Hence this scheme requires only one initial guess, x_1. The linear function $\tilde{f}(x)$ shown by the dashed line in Figure 2.2 d is given by

$$\tilde{f}(x) = \left(\frac{f_2 - f_1}{x_2 - x_1}\right)(x - x_1) + f_1 \,. \tag{2.6}$$

The root, $x = x_2$, of the above equation is

$$x_2 = x_1 - \frac{f_1}{f_1'} \tag{2.7}$$

which constitutes the iterative equation for step 2.

   While we have relied on the geometrical interpretation so far in constructing the algorithms, we can also derive (2.7) from a Taylor series expansion of a function. This is an instructive exercise, for it will enable us to generalize Newton's scheme to higher dimensional systems consisting of two or more equations. It will also provide helpful information on the rate of convergence of the iterative scheme.

   The Taylor series representation of a function about a reference point, x_i is,

$$f(x_i + \delta) = \sum_{k=0}^{\infty} \frac{f^{(k)}(x_i)}{k!} \delta^k \,, \tag{2.8}$$

where $f^{(k)}(x_i)$ is the kth derivative of the function at x_i and δ is a small displacement from x_i. Whereas the infinite series expansion is an exact representation of the function, it requires all the higher order derivatives of f at the reference point. We can construct various levels of approximation by *truncating* the series at a finite number of terms. For example a three-term expansion reads

$$\tilde{f}(x_i + \delta) = f(x_i) + f'(x_i)\delta + f''(x_i)\frac{\delta^2}{2!} + \mathcal{O}(\delta^3) \,,$$

where the symbol $\mathcal{O}(\delta^3)$ stands as a reminder of the higher order terms ($k \geq 3$) that have been neglected. The error introduced by such omission of higher order terms is called the *truncation error*. In fact to derive Newton's scheme, we neglect the quadratic term $\mathcal{O}(\delta^2)$ also. In Figure 2.2 d, taking the reference point to be $x_i = x_1$, the displacement to be $\delta = x_{i+1} - x_i$, and recognizing that $\tilde{f}(x_i + \delta) = 0$ we can rewrite the truncated two-term series as

$$0 = f(x_i) + f'(x_i)(x_{i+1} - x_i) + \mathcal{O}(\delta^2),$$

which can be rearranged as

$$x_{i+1} = x_i - \frac{f(x_i)}{f'(x_i)}. \tag{2.9}$$

This is a very similar equation to (2.7). The iterative steps associated with Newton's scheme are shown in Figure 2.7.

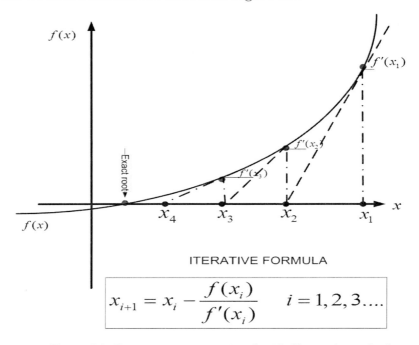

Figure 2.7: Iterative steps associated with Newton's method.

An ostensible drawback of Newton's method is that it requires at each iteration the evaluation of f', suggesting that not one but two auxiliary MATLAB functions must be defined, one for the function, f, and one for its derivative, f'. We can avoid this computational overhead if we evaluate f' numerically* i.e.

$$f'(x) \simeq \frac{f(x + \varepsilon) - f(x - \varepsilon)}{2\varepsilon},$$

where ε is a real number of small magnitude. The MATLAB function mnhf_newton, which is illustrated in Figure 2.8, employs exactly this

---

*We shall consider the numerical evaluation of derivatives more carefully in Chapter 5.

```
function r=mnhf_newton(Fun,x1,tol,trace)
%MNHF_NEWTON finds the root of "Fun" using Newton scheme.
%
% Fun — name of the external function
% x1 — vector of length 1, (initial guess)
% tol — tolerance
% trace — print intermediate results
%
% Usage  mnhf_newton(@poly1,0.5,1e—8,1)
%         poly1 is the name of the external function.
%         0.5 is the initial guess for the root, r.

% Check inputs.
if nargin < 4, trace = 1; end
if nargin < 3, tol = 1e—8; end
if (length(x1) ~= 1)
 error('Please provide one initial guess')
end

small = 1e—6;  % Small number used in estimating f'(x).

xold = x1;
for i = 1:100
 % Update the guess.
 xnew = xold—feval(Fun,xold)/(0.5*(feval(Fun,xold+small) ...
                         —feval(Fun,xold—small))/small);
 fnew = feval(Fun,xnew);   % Function evaluation.

 if trace, fprintf(1,'%3i %12.5f %12.5f\n', i,xnew,fnew); end
 if abs(fnew) < tol % Check for convergenece.
  r = xnew;
  return
 else % Prepare for next iteration.
  xold = xnew;
 end

end
error('Exceeded maximum number of iterations');
```

Figure 2.8: MATLAB implementation of Newton's method.

approach. If we return to the cubic polynomial shown in Figure 2.2 c, we find by typing `mnhf_newton(@poly1,0.5,1e-8,1)` in the MATLAB Command Window that only five iterations are required to converge to the root. Changing the initial guess from 0.5 to 100.5, it can be shown that the number of iterations increases to 16, which is still 11 less than were needed with the bisection algorithm `mnhf_bisect`. Unfortunately, one cannot conclude that Newton's method is preferable to bisection under all circumstances. Figure 2.9 shows a case where $|x_3 - r| > |x_1 - r|$, i.e. we move further away from the root as the iterations proceed. For this particular choice of initial guess, therefore, Newton's algorithm will not converge. As noted earlier, the bisection method does not share this type of pitfall.

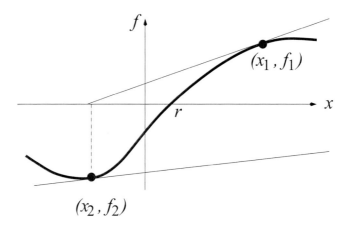

Figure 2.9: An example where Newton's method fails to converge.

2.5   Secant method

In the secant method, the two most recent estimates of the root are used to estimate the derivative of the function f. Given two estimates x_2 and x_1, the derivative is computed as $f_1' \simeq \frac{f_2 - f_1}{x_2 - x_1}$. Replacing the derivative in equation (2.7) with this expression and denoting the new root as x_3 we obtain

$$x_3 = x_1 - f_1 \left(\frac{x_2 - x_1}{f_2 - f_1} \right). \tag{2.10}$$

Equation (2.10) specifies the iterative procedure for the secant method.

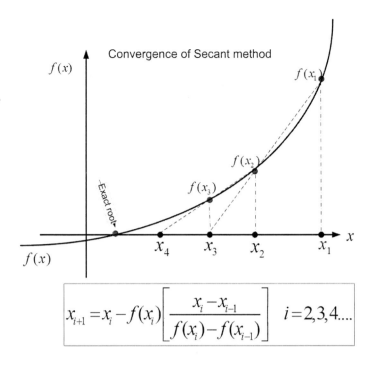

$$x_{i+1} = x_i - f(x_i) \left[\frac{x_i - x_{i-1}}{f(x_i) - f(x_{i-1})} \right] \quad i = 2,3,4....$$

Figure 2.10: Iterative steps for the secant method.

The secant formula looks exactly like the Regula-Falsi formula in form. As is clear by comparing Figures 2.5 and 2.10, however, the two methods differ in implementation. For the secant method, the oldest root estimate, x_1, is always discarded while the most recent values of x viz. x_2 and x_3 are retained. This simple change from the Regula-Falsi scheme yields a dramatic improvement in the rate of convergence. Typing `mnhf_secant(@poly1,[-0.5 2.0],1e-8,1)` in the MATLAB Command Window, where `mnhf_secant` is given in Figure 2.11, shows that only 10 iterations are needed, a nearly fourfold decrease as compared to `mnhf_regula_falsi`, which was introduced earlier in this chapter. Not surprisingly, this added computational efficiency comes at a price: for instance, the secant algorithm may fall victim to a similar type of degeneracy as that illustrated in Figure 2.9. With both Newton's method and the secant method, one must therefore choose the initial guess or guesses for r with care.

```
function r=mnhf_secant(Fun,x,tol,trace)
%MNHF_SECANT finds the root of "Fun" using secant scheme.
%
% Fun — name of the external function
% x — vector of length 2, (initial guesses)
% tol — tolerance
% trace — print intermediate results
%
% Usage  mnhf_secant(@poly1,[−0.5 2.0],1e−8,1)
%        poly1 is the name of the external function.
%        [−0.5 2.0] are the initial guesses for the root.

% Check inputs.
if nargin < 4, trace = 1;  end
if nargin < 3, tol = 1e−8; end
if (length(x) ~= 2)
 error('Please provide two initial guesses')
end

f = feval(Fun,x); % Fun is assumed to accept a vector

for i = 1:100
 x3 = x(1)−f(1)*(x(2)−x(1))/(f(2)−f(1));  % Update the guess.
 f3 = feval(Fun,x3);  % Function evaluation.
 if trace, fprintf(1,'%3i %12.5f %12.5f\n', i,x3,f3); end
 if abs(f3) < tol % Check for convergenece.
  r = x3;
  return
 else % Reset values for x(1), x(2), f(1) and f(2).
  x(1) = x(2); f(1) = f(2); x(2) = x3; f(2) = f3;
 end
end
```

Figure 2.11: MATLAB implementation of the secant method.

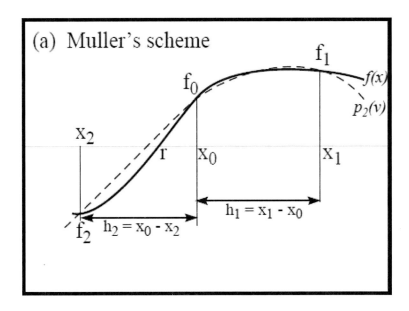

Figure 2.12: Graphical representation of Müller's method.

2.6 Müller's method

Müller's scheme can be thought of as an attempt to extend the secant method and is important at least from the point of illustrating such generalizations. Instead of making two guesses and constructing an approximate linear function as we did with the secant method, we choose three initial guesses and construct a quadratic approximation to the original function and find the roots of the quadratic. A graphical representation of this is approach shown in Figure 2.12. The three initial guesses are (x_0, x_1, x_2) and the corresponding function values are represented by (f_0, f_1, f_2) respectively. Thus we construct the following second degree polynomial:

$$p_2(v) = av^2 + bv + c,$$

where $v \equiv x - x_0$. Note that the polynomial is represented as a function of a new independent variable v, which is merely a translation of the original independent variable x by x_0. An alternate view is to regard v as the distance measured from the reference point x_0, so that $v = 0$ at this new origin. Obviously a, b and c are the coefficients of the quadratic and must be determined in such a way that $p_2(v)$ passes through the three data points (x_0, f_0), (x_1, f_1) and (x_2, f_2). Defining $h_1 = x_1 - x_0$

and $h_2 = x_0 - x_2$, we get

$$
\begin{aligned}
p_2(0) = a(0)^2 + b(0) + c &= f_0 \qquad \Rightarrow \qquad c = f_0 \\
p_2(h_1) = ah_1^2 + bh_1 + c &= f_1 \\
p_2(-h_2) = ah_2^2 - bh_2 + c &= f_2
\end{aligned}
$$

The reason for coordinate translation should now be clear. Such a shift allows c to be computed directly. Solving the remaining two equations, it can be shown that

$$
a = \frac{\gamma f_1 - f_0(1 + \gamma) + f_2}{\gamma h_1^2(1 + \gamma)} ,
$$

$$
b = \frac{f_1 - f_0 - ah_1^2}{h_1} ,
$$

where $\gamma = h_2/h_1$. So far we have only constructed an approximate representation of the original function, $f(x) \approx p_2(v)$. The next step is to find the roots of this approximating function by solving $p_2(v) = 0$. These roots are given by,

$$
v = \tilde{r} - x_0 = \frac{-b \pm \sqrt{b^2 - 4ac}}{2a}
$$

The above equation can be rearranged as

$$
\tilde{r} = x_0 - \frac{2c}{b \pm \sqrt{b^2 - 4ac}} . \tag{2.11}
$$

Because $p_2(v)$ is a quadratic function, there are clearly two roots to consider. In order to take the root closer to x_0 we choose the larger denominator in equation (2.11). Thus if $b \geq 0$, we consider the positive branch of the square root function whereas if $b < 0$, we instead consider the negative branch. In summary, the sequential procedure for implementing Müller's scheme is as follows:

1. Specify x_0, x_1 and x_2,

2. Compute $f_0 = f(x_0)$, $f_1 = f(x_1)$ and $f_2 = f(x_2)$,

3. Compute $h_1 = x_1 - x_0$, $h_2 = x_0 - x_2$ and $\gamma = h_2/h_1$,

4. Compute $c = f(x_0)$,

5. Compute $a = [\gamma f_1 - f_0(1 + \gamma) + f_2]/[\gamma h_1^2(1 + \gamma)]$,

6. Compute $b = (f_1 - f_0 - ah_1^2)/h_1$,

7. Compute, depending on the sign of b, the appropriate root from equation (2.11),

8. From x_0, x_1 and x_2 discard the point farthest from $\tilde{r}$, substitute the new root in its place and repeat.

Note that Müller's method converges almost quadratically (as does Newton's scheme), but requires only one additional function evaluation at every iteration which is comparable to the computational load of the secant method. In particular, derivative evaluation is not required, which is a major advantage as compared to Newton's method.

Whereas Müller's algorithm can, in principle, converge to complex roots, this is an unnecessary distraction in many engineering problems where we prefer to restrict attention to real roots. This is the approach taken in `mnhf_muller`, which is illustrated in Figure 2.13. Here, the built-in function `max` is used to replace the discriminant, $b^2 - 4ac$, with 0 whenever $b^2 < 4ac$. Of course, if this substitution is required, the likelihood of convergence is reduced.

Typing `mnhf_muller(@poly1,[-0.5 0.75 2.0],1e-8,1,100)` in the MATLAB Command Window indicates that only five iterations are needed to converge to the root of the function shown in Figure 2.2 c. This is the same number of iterations required by `mnhf_newton` (choosing as the initial guess the value 0.5) and one-half the number required by `mnhf_secant` (choosing as the initial guesses the values -0.5 and 2).

2.7 Fixed point iteration

Another approach to construct an update scheme (for step 2) is to rearrange the equation $f(x) = 0$ into a form

$$x = g(x).$$

Then, starting with a guess x_i, we can evaluate $g(x_i)$ from the right hand side of the above equation and the result itself is regarded as a better estimate of the root, *i.e.*

$$x_{i+1} = g(x_i) \qquad i = 0, 1 \cdots \tag{2.12}$$

Given $f(x) = 0$ it is not difficult rewrite it in the form $x = g(x)$; nor is this process unique. For example, we can always let $g(x) = x + f(x)$. Such an iterative scheme need not always converge. Let us examine the possible behavior of the iterates with a specific example. In particular we will illustrate that different choices of $g(x)$ lead to different behavior. Consider the function

$$f(x) = x^2 - x - 6,$$

```matlab
function r=mnhf_muller(Fun,x,tol,trace,Nmax)
%MNHF_MULLER finds the root of a function "Fun" using Muller scheme
%
% Fun — name of the external function
% x — vector of length 3, (inital guesses)
% tol — error criterion
% trace — print intermediate results
% Nmax — maximum number of iterations
%
% Usage  mnhf_muller(@poly1,[−0.5 0.75 2.0],1e−8,1,100)
%         poly1 is the name of the external function.
%         [−0.5 0.75 2.0] are the initial guesses for the root.

% Check inputs.
if nargin < 5, Nmax = 100; end
if nargin < 4, trace = 1;  end
if nargin < 3, tol = 1e−8; end
if (length(x) ~= 3)
 error('Please provide three initial guesses')
end

frtil=1.0; % Can select any value with |frtil| > tol.
count=1;    % Initialize counter.
while abs(frtil)>tol
 x  = sort(x);          % Ascending order.
 x2 = x(1); x0 = x(2); x1 = x(3); h2 = x0−x2; h1 = x1−x0; gamma = h2/h1;
 f0 = feval(Fun,x0);   % Function evaluations.
 f1 = feval(Fun,x1);
 f2 = feval(Fun,x2);
 % Compute coefficients a, b and c.
 c = f0;
 a = (gamma*f1−f0*(1.0+gamma)+f2)/(gamma*h1^2.0*(1.0+gamma));
 b = (f1−f0−a*h1^2.0)/h1;
 % Evaluate discriminant; if < 0, set to 0.
 discrim = max(b^2.0−4.0*a*c,0.0);
 % Select the appropriate root of the parabola.
 if b >= 0.0
  rtil = x0−2.0*c/(b+sqrt(discrim));
 else
  rtil = x0−2.0*c/(b−sqrt(discrim));
 end
 frtil = feval(Fun,rtil);
 if trace
  fprintf(1,'%3i %12.5f %12.5f\n', count,rtil,frtil);
 end
 % Decide which estimates to keep and which to discard.
 if abs(rtil−x2) < abs(x1−rtil)
  x=[x0 x2 rtil]; % Discard x1.
 else
  x=[x0 x1 rtil]; % Discard x2.
 end

 count = count+1; % Increment counter.

 if count > Nmax
  error('Maximum number of iterations exceeded.\n\n')
 end

end
r = rtil;
```

Figure 2.13: MATLAB implementation of Müller's method. For illustrative purposes, here use a `while` loop rather than a `for` loop.

Iteration Number	Iterate
x_1	5.0000000
x_2	3.3166248
x_3	3.0523147
x_4	3.0087065
x_5	3.0014507
x_6	3.0002418
x_7	3.0000403
x_8	3.0000067
x_9	3.0000011
x_{10}	3.0000002

Table 2.1: The first ten iterates of $x_{i+1} = \sqrt{x_i + 6}$ starting with $x_0 = 5$.

which has roots at $r = -2$ and $r = 3$. In the first case let us rewrite $f(x) = 0$ in the form

$$x = \sqrt{x + 6}\,.$$

A geometrical interpretation is that we are finding the intersection of two curves, $y = x$ (the left hand side) and $y = \sqrt{x+6}$ (the right hand side). See Figure 2.14 for a graphical illustration.

Starting with an initial guess, say $x_0 = 5$, we compute $x_1 = g(x_0) = \sqrt{x_0 + 6}$. This is tantamount to stepping between the $y = x$ and $y = g(x)$ curves as shown in Figure 2.14 a. It is clear that the sequence will converge monotonically to the root $r = 3$. Table 2.1 shows the first ten iterates.

Note that the slope of the function at the root is $g'(r = 3) < 1$. We will show shortly that the condition for convergence is indeed $|g'(r)| < 1$. As an alternate formulation consider rewriting equation (2.7) as $x = g(x) = 6/(x - 1)$. Now, $g(x)$ has a singularity at $x = 1$. A graphical illustration is shown in Figure 2.14b. Using this new $g(x)$, but starting at the same initial guess, $x_0 = 5$, the sequence diverges initially in an oscillatory fashion around the root $r = 3$, but eventually is attracted to the other root at $r = -2$, also in an oscillatory fashion. Observe that the slopes at the two roots are $g'(3) = -3/2$ and $g'(-2) = -2/3$. Both are negative, hence the oscillatory behavior. The root with absolute value greater than unity yields divergence whereas the root with absolute value greater than unity yields convergence. Finally consider the formulation $x = g(x) = x^2 - 6$. The behavior for this case is shown in Figure 2.14 c. For reasons indicated above, the sequence will not converge to either root. The simple function shown in Figure 2.15 presents the MATLAB implementation for generating the iterative

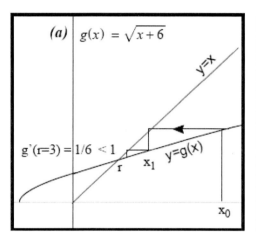

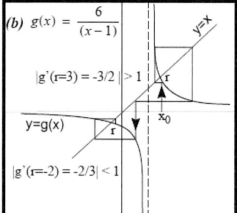

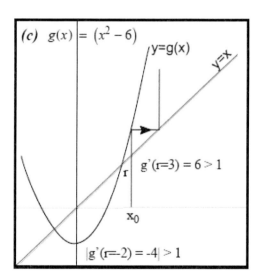

Figure 2.14: Graphical representation of the fixed point iteration scheme showing (a) convergence and (b, c) divergence.

```
function x=g(x)
for i=1:10
  fprintf(1,'%2i %12.5e\n',i,x);  % Print the iterates.
  x = sqrt(x+6);   % Try also x = 6/(x-1) and x = x^2-6.
end
```

Figure 2.15: MATLAB function for generating an iterative sequence corresponding to the function of Figure 2.14 a.

sequence for the first case.

A MATLAB function that implements the fixed point iteration algorithm is given in Figure 2.16.

2.8 Error analysis and convergence acceleration

2.8.1 Convergence of the bisection method

The speed of convergence of a given method relates to the number of iterations required to obtain a solution with desired accuracy. For the bisection method, starting with an initial interval between x_1 and x_2 which brackets the root, the next estimate is obtained by halving the interval. Defining the initial interval as $h_o = x_2 - x_1$, the error at each subsequent iteration may be obtained as

$$\text{error after the first iteration} \qquad e_1 = \frac{h_o}{2}$$

$$\text{error after the second iteration} \qquad e_2 = \frac{e_1}{2} = \frac{h_o}{2^2}$$

$$\text{error after the third iteration} \qquad e_3 = \frac{e_2}{2} = \frac{h_o}{2^3}$$

$$\vdots$$

$$\text{error after the } n^{th} \text{ iteration} \qquad e_n = \frac{e_{n-1}}{2} = \frac{h_o}{2^n},$$

where n is the number of bisections. If we desire to know the root within an interval with width ϵ, we can calculate the number of iterations (bisections) required as

$$h_o 2^{-n} < \epsilon$$

taking the logarithm of both sides yields

$$\ln h_o - n \ln 2 < \ln \epsilon.$$

```
function xnew=mnhf_fpi(Fun,xold,tol,Nmax)
%MNHF_FPI Fixed point algorithm for computing the solution to x=g(x).
%
% Fun - name of the external function, g(x).
% xold - initial estimate of the root
% tol - tolerance
% Nmax - maximum number of iterations
%
% Usage  mnhf_fpi(@poly1,1,1e-8,1000);

% Check inputs.
if nargin < 4, Nmax = 1000;  end
if nargin < 3, tol = 1e-8;   end
if (length(xold) ~= 1)
 error('Please provide one initial guess')
end

delta = 1;  % Can select any value with |delta| > tol.
count = 1;  % Initialize counter.
while abs(delta)>tol
 xnew = feval(Fun,xold); % Compute new root estimate.
 fprintf('Iteration=%2.0f\t, Current root estimate=%12.8f\n',count,xnew)
 delta = xnew-xold;

 count = count+1; % Increment counter.
 xold = xnew;

 if count > Nmax
  error('Maximum number of iterations exceeded.\n\n')
 end

end
```

Figure 2.16: MATLAB implementation of the fixed point iteration method.

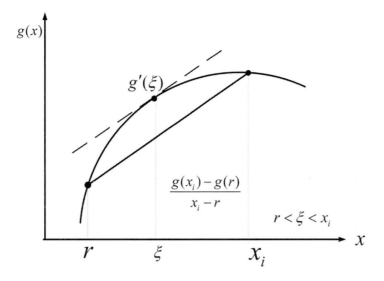

Figure 2.17: Graphical illustration of the Mean Value Theorem.

Thus we can see that the number of bisections to obtain an interval width (error) less than ϵ must be

$$n > \frac{\ln h_o - \ln \epsilon}{\ln 2} \qquad (2.13)$$

Thus for example, if the initial interval width is $h_0 = 1$ and we desire an accuracy of $\epsilon = 10^{-8}$, then $n > 26.6 = 27$ since n is an integer.

2.8.2 Convergence of the fixed point iteration method

A simple error analysis can be developed for the fixed point iteration scheme which will provide not only a criterion for convergence, but also clues for accelerating convergence with very little additional computational effort. We are clearly moving away from the realm of intuition to the realm of analysis! Consider the fixed point iteration $x_{i+1} = g(x_i)$. After convergence to the root r we will have $r = g(r)$. Subtracting the two equations we get

$$x_{i+1} - r = g(x_i) - g(r) \,.$$

Multiplying and diving the right hand side by $x_i - r$ yields

$$x_{i+1} - r = \frac{g(x_i) - g(r)}{(x_i - r)}(x_i - r) \,.$$

Now the difference $e_i = x_i - r$ is the error at iterative step i and hence the above equation can be written as

$$e_{i+1} = g'(\xi) e_i \,, \qquad (2.14)$$

where we have used the Mean Value Theorem to replace the slope of the chord by the tangent to the curve at some suitable value $x = \xi$ where $r < \xi < x_i$, *i.e.*,

$$\frac{g(x_i) - g(r)}{x_i - r} = g'(\xi).$$

A geometrical interpretation of the mean value theorem is shown in Figure 2.17. From equation (2.14), it is clear the error will decrease with every iteration if the slope $|g'(\xi)| < 1$; otherwise the error will be amplified at every iteration. Since the error in the current step is proportional to that of the previous step, we conclude that the rate of convergence of the fixed point iteration scheme is linear. The development has been reasonably rigorous so far. We now take a more pragmatic step and assume that $g'(\xi) = K$ is a constant in the neighborhood of the root r. Then we have the sequence*

$$e_2 = Ke_1, \qquad e_3 = Ke_2 = K^2e_1, \qquad e_4 = Ke_3 = K^3e_1, \qquad \cdots$$

and hence we can write a general error propagation solution as

$$e_n = K^{n-1}e_1 \qquad \text{or} \qquad x_n - r = K^{n-1}e_1. \tag{2.15}$$

It should now be clear that $e_n \to 0$ as $n \to \infty$ only if $|K| < 1^\dagger$. We refer to equation (2.15) as the error propagation equation because it provides a means of estimating the error at any step n provided the error at the first step e_1 and K are known. We can now establish a generalized method for convergence acceleration.

2.8.3 Aetkins method for convergence acceleration

One can develop a convergence acceleration scheme using the error equation (2.15) to estimate the three unknowns r, K and e_1 in the latter form of equation (2.15). Once we have generated three iterates, x_n, x_{n+1} and x_{n+2}, we can use equation (2.15) in sequence

$$\begin{aligned} x_n &= r + K^{n-1}e_1 \\ x_{n+1} &= r + K^ne_1 \\ x_{n+2} &= r + K^{n+1}e_1. \end{aligned} \tag{2.16}$$

Now we have three equations in three unknowns which can be solved to estimate r (and K, e_1 as well). If K were to remain a true constant with every iteration, r would be the correct root; since K is not a constant in general, r is only an *estimate* of the root, hopefully a better estimate

---

*Will K be the same constant at every iteration?

$\dagger$Obviously, if we know the error in the first step, none of this analysis would be necessary. Setting $r = x_1 - e_1$ would immediately return the correct value of the root!

than any of x_n, x_{n+1} or x_{n+2}). Let us then proceed to construct a solution for r from the above three equations. We will define a first order forward difference operator Δ as

$$\Delta x_n = x_{n+1} - x_n .$$

Think of the symbol Δ as defining a new rule of operation just like a derivative operator $\frac{d}{dx}$ defines a rule. When Δ operates on x_n, the result is computed using the rule shown on the right hand side of the last equation. Now, if we apply the operator Δ to x_{n+1} we should find

$$\Delta x_{n+1} = x_{n+2} - x_{n+1} .$$

By extension, if we apply the Δ operator twice (which is equivalent to defining higher order derivatives), we should get

$$\Delta(\Delta x_n) = \Delta^2 x_n = (\Delta x_{n+1}) - (\Delta x_n) = x_{n+2} - 2x_{n+1} + x_n .$$

You can verify that using equation (2.16) in the above definitions, we obtain

$$\frac{(\Delta x_n)^2}{\Delta^2 x_n} = K^{n-1} e_1 = x_n - r ,$$

and hence r is given by

$$r = x_n - \frac{(\Delta x_n)^2}{\Delta^2 x_n} = x_n - \frac{x_{n+1}^2 - 2x_n x_{n+1} + x_n^2}{x_{n+2} - 2x_{n+1} + x_n} .$$

Thus the three iterates x_n, x_{n+1} and x_{n+2} can be plugged into the right hand side of the above equation to get an improved estimate for the root, r.

EXAMPLE 2.1 (Convergence acceleration) *Let us apply the above convergence acceleration procedure to the first three iterates of Table 2.1.*

$$x_1 = 5.0000000$$
$$x_2 = 3.3166248$$
$$x_3 = 3.0523147$$
$$\Delta x_1 = x_2 - x_1 = -1.6833752$$
$$\Delta x_2 = x_3 - x_2 = -0.26431010$$
$$\Delta^2 x_1 = \Delta x_2 - \Delta x_1 = 1.41906510$$
$$r = x_1 - \frac{(\Delta x_1)^2}{\Delta^2 x_1} = 5.000000 - \frac{(-1.6833752)^2}{1.41906510} = 3.0030852$$

Compare this result with the fourth iterate from the original sequence $x_4 = 3.0087065.$

2.8.4   Convergence of Newton's scheme

The Newton scheme given by equation (2.7) can be thought of as a fixed point iteration scheme where $g(x)$ is defined as below

$$x_{n+1} = x_n - \frac{f(x_n)}{f'(x_n)} = g(x_n)\,. \tag{2.17}$$

Hence

$$g'(x) = 1 - \frac{(f')^2 - ff''}{(f')^2} = \frac{ff''}{(f')^2}\,. \tag{2.18}$$

By definition, $f(r) = 0$, therefore $g'(r) = 0$ (barring, say, a double root where $f'(r) = 0$) and the inequality $|g'(x)| < 1$ should hold near the root, r. Thus the Newton method is guaranteed to converge as long as we have a good initial guess. Having progressed this far, we can take the next step and ask questions about the rate of convergence of Newton's method. A Taylor series expansion of $g(x)$ around r gives

$$g(x_n) = g(r) + g'(r)(x_n - r) + \frac{g''(r)}{2}(x_n - r)^2 + \cdots$$

Recognizing that $e_{n+1} = x_{n+1} - r = g(x_n) - r$, $e_n = x_n - r$ and $g'(r) = 0$, the truncated Taylor series expansion can be rearranged as

$$e_{n+1} \simeq \frac{g''(r)}{2}e_n^2\,,$$

which confirms that the error at any step decreases as the square of the error at the previous step. This observation of quadratic convergence manifests itself in the form of a doubling of accuracy at every iteration.

2.9   Deflation technique

Having found a root, r, of $f(x) = 0$, if we are interested in finding additional roots of $f(x) = 0$, we can start with a different initial guess and hope that the new initial guess lies within the region of attraction of a root different from r. Choosing a different initial guess does not guarantee that the iteration scheme will not be attracted to the root already discovered. In order to ensure that we stay away from the known (presumed simple) root, r, we can choose to *deflate* the original function by constructing a modified function

$$g(x) = f(x)/(x - r)\,,$$

which does not have r as a root (in fact, $g(x)$ is undefined when $x = r$).

The above concepts are best illustrated graphically. Consider Figure 2.18 a where the original function, $f(x) = (x - 2)\sin(2x)e^{-0.8x}$, can

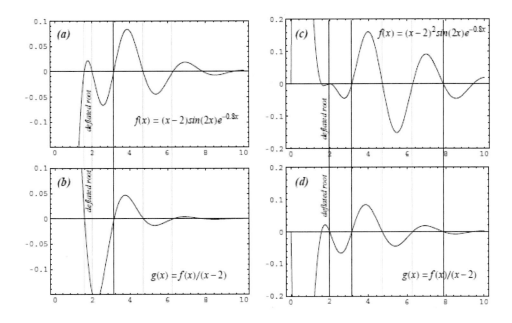

Figure 2.18: Graphical illustration the deflation technique.

be seen to have several roots including one at $r = 2$. A sketch of the deflated function, $g(x) = f(x)/(x - 2)$ is shown in Figure 2.18 b. Because $r = 2$ turns out to be a *simple root* of $f(x)$, the deflated function $g(x)$ does not contain the already discovered root at $x = 2$. Hence starting with a different initial guess and applying an iterative method like the secant or Newton scheme on the function $g(x)$ will result in convergence to another root. This process can obviously be repeated by deflating successively found roots. For example if we know two roots r_1 and r_2 then a new function can be constructed as

$$h(x) = \frac{f(x)}{(x - r_1)(x - r_2)}.$$

Note that $h(x)$ is undefined at both $x = r_1$ and $x = r_2$.

The successive application of this approach is of course susceptible to propagation of round off errors*. For example if the roots r_1, r_2 are known to only a few significant digits, then the definition of the deflated function $h(x)$ will inherit these errors and hence the roots of $h(x) = 0$ will not be as accurate as those of the original equation $f(x) = 0$.

Another aspect of the deflation technique pertains to non-simple (or multiple) roots. A sketch of the function $f(x) = (x - 2)^2 \sin(2x)e^{-0.8x}$

---

*Can you think of a way to alleviate this problem?

is shown in Figure 2.18 c. It is immediately clear that $r = 2$ is a
double root - *i.e.*, occurs with multiplicity two. Hence the deflated
function $g(x) = f(x)/(x - 2)$ still has $r = 2$ as a *simple root* as seen
in Figure 2.18 d. Multiple roots are considered in further detail in the
next example.

EXAMPLE 2.2 (Using the deflation technique) *Let us find the
roots of $y_1(x) = x(x + \sqrt{\pi})^2(e^{-x} - 2)$. For a comparatively simple
function like $y_1(x)$, which is plotted in Figure 2.19, one does necessarily require the mathematical formality of the deflation methodology to
determine the (four) roots. On the other hand, by studying this case
in a bit of detail, we may gain helpful insights into the more general
application of the deflation technique.*

*The associated MATLAB algorithm is shown in Figure 2.20. Here,
a secant root finding scheme is employed though other schemes such as
Newton or Müller could just as well have been selected. (Recall that
the bisection algorithm works only for the case of simple roots and so
would not be a suitable choice in the present context). We begin by
searching for the leftmost (double) root of y_1 and therefore select as
our initial guesses -2.5 and -1.5. Running* `mnhf_deflation_example`*,
you should find that 23 iterations are required to converge to the root
of -1.772451.... Accordingly, we define this root as the global variable*
`root1` *then deflate the function y_1 by setting*

$$y_2(x) = \begin{cases} \frac{x(x+\sqrt{\pi})^2(e^{-x}-2)}{x+1.772451...} & x \neq -1.772451... \\ \text{Undefined} & x = -1.772451... \end{cases}$$

*The dashed curve of Figure 2.19 indicates that y_2 has three simple roots.
Starting again on the lefthand side, we select as our initial guesses -2.5
and -1.5 and find, this time after 20 iterations, a root at -1.772454....
A function y_3 is then defined as*

$$y_3(x) = \begin{cases} \frac{x(x+\sqrt{\pi})^2(e^{-x}-2)}{(x+1.772451...)(x+1.772454...)} & x \neq -1.772451...,-1.772454... \\ \text{Undefined} & x = -1.772451...,-1.772454... \end{cases}$$

*The thin solid curve of Figure 2.19 indicates that y_3 has a pair of simple
roots, the latter of which appears to pass through the origin. Selecting
as our initial guesses -0.5 and 0.5 yields, after eight iterations, a root
at approximately -2×10^{-13}. Deflating one final time, we define a
function y_4 such that*

$$y_4(x) = \begin{cases} \frac{x(x+\sqrt{\pi})^2(e^{-x}-2)}{(x+1.772451...)(x+1.772454...)(x+2\times10^{-13})} & x \neq set1 \\ \text{Undefined} & x = set1 \end{cases}$$

$$set1 = -1.772451..., -1.772454..., -2 \times 10^{-13}$$

The thick dash-dotted curve of Figure 2.19 indicates that y_4 has a single simple root, whose value is -0.693147.... Five iterations are required for this final calculation starting from initial guesses of -1.0 and -0.5.

The use of global variables in mnhf_deflation_example *means that no foreknowledge of the values of the roots are needed when defining $y_2(x)$, $y_3(x)$ or $y_4(x)$. It is required, however, that we know the total number of roots (four in this case, counting the double root as two); such information can usually be determined by plotting the original function as we have done in Figure 2.19.*

Reviewing the number of iterations required to compute each of the four roots, we find, not surprisingly, that it was the double root of $y_1(x)$ that gave us the greatest difficulty. In fact, we are fortunate that problems were not also encountered when computing the leftmost root of $y_2(x)$. According to the definition of $y_2(x)$ provided above, both numerator and denominator become small in magnitude in the neighborhood of $x = -\sqrt{\pi}$. Ratios of small numbers oftentimes yield large roundoff errors, a problem that is here avoided, in part, by specifying a tight numerical tolerance of 1×10^{-10}.

2.10 MATLAB software tools

The MATLAB function for determining roots of a polynomial is called roots. You can call this function by typing

```
>>roots(c)
```

where c is a vector containing the coefficients of the polynomial in the form

$$p_n(x) = c_1 x^n + c_2 x^{n-1} + \cdots + c_n x + c_{n+1}.$$

Let us consider the factored form of the polynomial $p_3(x) = (x+2)(x+i)(x-i)$ so that we know the roots are at $(-2, \pm i)$. To check whether MATLAB can find the roots of this polynomial we need to construct the coefficients of the expanded polynomial. This can be done with the convolve function conv(f1,f2) as follows:

```
>>f1 = [1 2] % Define coeff. of (x+2) as [1 2]
>>f2 = [1 i] % Define coeff. of (x+i) as [1 i]
>>f3 = [1 -i] % Define coeff. of (x-i) as [1 -i]
```

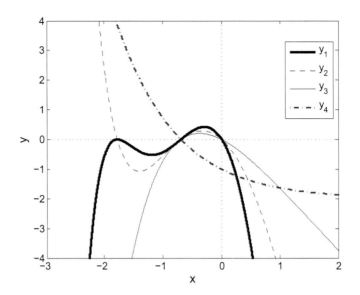

Figure 2.19: Functions defined in Example 2.2.

```
>>c=conv(conv(f1,f2),f3) % c contains polynomial coeffs.
>>r=roots(c) % Return roots of polynomial defined by c.
```

Note that the function **roots** finds all of the roots of a polynomial, including those that are complex.

The MATLAB function for finding a *real* root of any real, single nonlinear algebraic equation (not necessarily a polynomial) is called **fzero**. You can invoke it by typing

```
>>fzero('fn',x)
```

where **fn** is the name of a function specified in an external .m file and x is the initial guess for the root. Unfortunately if the function you want to solve has singularities or repeated roots, **fzero** often fails to converge, often without producing illuminating error or warning messages. Hence use with caution. After **fzero** returns an answer, it is not a bad idea to verify that it is the correct result by evaluating the function at the supposed root.

```
function mnhf_deflation_example()
%MNHF_DEFLATION_EXAMPLE illustrates the use of the deflation technique for
% finding multiple roots of the function defined in fn1. By plotting this
% function, we know that there are four roots, not necessarily all unique.

global root1 root2 root3

% Call secant root finding algorithm in succesion to determine the four
% different roots of the function defined in fn1.m.
root1 = mnhf_secant(@fn1,[-2.5 -1.5],1e-10,1)
fprintf('\n\n')
root2 = mnhf_secant(@fn2,[-2.5 -1.5],1e-10,1)
fprintf('\n\n')
root3 = mnhf_secant(@fn3,[-0.5  0.5],1e-10,1)
fprintf('\n\n')
root4 = mnhf_secant(@fn4,[-1.0 -0.5],1e-10,1)
fprintf('\n\n')

%%%%%%%%%%%%%%%%%
function y1=fn1(x)
% Function of x used in illustrating deflation technique.

y1 = x.*(x+sqrt(pi)).^2.0.*(exp(-x)-2.0);

%%%%%%%%%%%%%%%%%
function y2=fn2(x)
% Function of x used in illustrating deflation technique.

global root1

y2 = fn1(x)./(x-root1);

%%%%%%%%%%%%%%%%%
function y3=fn3(x)
% Function of x used in illustrating deflation technique.

global root1 root2

y3 = fn1(x)./(x-root1)./(x-root2);

%%%%%%%%%%%%%%%%%
function y4=fn4(x)
% Function of x used in illustrating deflation technique.

global root1 root2 root3

y4 = fn1(x)./(x-root1)./(x-root2)./(x-root3);
```

Figure 2.20: MATLAB implementation of the deflation technique as applied to the function $y_1(x) = x(x + \sqrt{\pi})^2(e^{-x} - 2)$.

2.11   Summary

The solution of nonlinear equations using a computer will generally require some sort of iterative process. In this chapter, different methods for solving nonlinear equations have been presented. The methods differ from simple to complicated, depending on the nature of the function and available information. Simple methods such as bisection require the root to be bracketed and will find it if it exists, albeit at a slower pace. On the other hand, Newton's method is quadratically convergent and will obtain the root with a minimum number iterations. However, the method may diverge if the slope of the function is close to zero.

Convergence acceleration may be applied to improve the performance of root finding techniques.

2.12 Exercise problems

P2.1. Rewrite `mnhf_bisect.m`, `mnhf_secant.m` and `mnhf_newton.m` so that they each use a `while` loop instead of a `for` loop. Hint: Carefully review `mnhf_muller.m`.

P2.2. The volume liquid methane in a spherical reactor of radius $r = 1\,\mathrm{m}$ is related to the depth of the liquid (h) by the following equation:

$$V = \frac{\pi h^2 (3r - h)}{3}$$

Determine the height of liquid (h) for a reactor with volume $V = 0.5\,\mathrm{m}^3$ using the bisection method, the secant method and the Regula-Falsi method. Perform only two iterations for each method. For all cases, start with $x_0 = 0.5\,\mathrm{m}$ and $x_1 = 0.1\,\mathrm{m}$.

P2.3. The van der Waals equation relates the pressure (P), volume (V) and temperature (T) for real gases. It reads

$$\left(P + \frac{n^2 a}{V^2}\right)(V - nb) = nRT\,,$$

where n is the number of moles of gas present, R is the universal gas constant and a and b are prescribed constants. You are required to find the volume, V, of $1\,\mathrm{mol}$ of chlorine gas at a temperature of $T = 313\,\mathrm{K}$ and pressure $P = 2\,\mathrm{atm}$ given the following parameters: $a = 6.29\,\mathrm{atm/L^2/mol^2}$, $b = 0.0562\mathrm{L/mol}$ and $R = 0.08206\,\mathrm{atm{\cdot}L/mol/K}$.

(a) Based on Figure 2.21, estimate the chlorine gas volume.

(b) Perform three iterations of the bisection method. Select a suitable bound based on Figure 2.21.

(c) Perform three iterations of Newton's method. Select an initial value based on Figure 2.21.

(d) Assuming that the value of V obtained in part (c) is the most accurate (true value), calculate the percent error for parts (a) and (b).

P2.4. The equation of state developed by Beattie and Bridgemann is an extension of the ideal gas law and can be represented as

$$P = \frac{RT}{V} + \frac{a}{V^2} + \frac{b}{V^3} + \frac{c}{V^4}\,,$$

where a, b and c are parameters specific to a given gas. Determine the specific volume (V) for a gas at $T = 293\,\mathrm{K}$, $P = 25\,\mathrm{atm}$ with $a = -0.106$, $b = 0.057$ and $c - 0.0001$

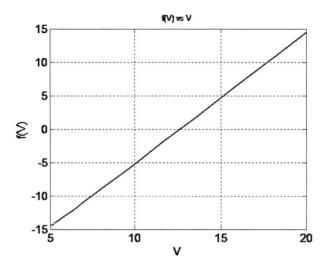

Figure 2.21: Plot of $f(V)$ vs. V for chlorine gas at $T = 313\,\mathrm{K}$ and $P = 2\,\mathrm{atm}$.

(a) Perform three iterations of the bisection method, using initial estimates of $V_1 = 0.001\,\mathrm{L/mol}$ and $V_2 = 0.01\,\mathrm{L/mol}$.

(b) Perform two iterations of Newton's method using an initial estimate of $V_1 = 0.001\,\mathrm{L/mol}$.

(c) If the exact value of the specific volume for the given parameters is $0.0018\,\mathrm{L/mol}$, calculate the percent relative errors for the results in parts (a) and (b).

P2.5. Determine the fraction of feed that goes into vapor when a multicomponent feed consisting of propane, n-butane and n-pentane with a composition if $Z_i = [0.3, 0.3, 0.4]$ is flashed at a temperature and pressure of $T = 750\,\mathrm{R}$, $P = 400\,\mathrm{psia}$. Use equilibrium data from Holland (1963) in the form $(K_i/T)^{1/3} = \sum_{j=1} a_{ij} T^{j-1}$, where the coefficients are given in the table below. Determine the liquid and vapor composition. The flash equation is given by

$$f(T, P, \psi) = \sum_{i=1}^{N} \frac{(1 - K_i) z_i}{(K_i - 1)\psi + 1} = 0$$

(a) Use the secant algorithm and Müller's scheme. Include copies of your .m files.

(b) Using only Müller's scheme, what should the temperature be in order to get 50% of the feed into vapor? (Answer: $T = 744.96\,\mathrm{R}$).

Component	a_{i1}	a_{i2}	a_{i3}	a_{i4}
Propane	-2.7980091E-1	1.1811943E-3	-1.0935041E-6	0.3518021E-9
n-Butane	-2.3203344E-1	0.83753226E-3	-0.61774360E-6	0.15243376E-9
n-Pentane	0.37103008E-1	-0.36257004E-3	0.99113800E-6	-0.54441110E-9

Table 2.2: Gas mixture data.

P2.6. Müller's algorithm is typically employed in finding the roots of "nasty" functions, but it should equally well apply when considering relatively simple functions. Suppose we were to apply Müller's algorithm in finding the root of the linear function $f(x) = \sigma_0 x + \sigma_1$ where $\sigma_0 \neq 0$. (i) For an arbitrary trio of initial guesses $(x_0, f(x_0))$, $(x_1, f(x_1))$ and $(x_2, f(x_2))$, what will be the values of a, b and c? (ii) How many iterations are necessary till we converge to the root, $r = -\sigma_1/\sigma_0$, of $f(x)$?

P2.7. The bisection algorithm is an iterative scheme for finding the *root* of an equation $f(x) = 0$. Let's apply this same methodology in finding the *minimum* of a function $y = f(x)$. Consider the function $y = f(x)$ sketched in Figure 2.22; between x_{left} and x_{right} there is a unique local minimum, x^*. We can be sure that there is a local minimum between x_{left} and x_{right} because $f(x_{\text{left}}) > f(x_{\text{mid}})$ and $f(x_{\text{right}}) > f(x_{\text{mid}})$ where $x_{\text{mid}} = \frac{1}{2}(x_{\text{left}} + x_{\text{right}})$.

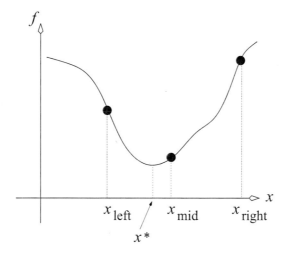

Figure 2.22: Finding the minimum of a function, f, using bisection.

From this starting point, outline the steps required to converge to the local minimum, x^*, of f. Hint: Consider the value of x

that is midway between x_{left} and x_{mid} and also the value of x that is midway between x_{mid} and x_{right}. Based on the value of the function at these points, you should be able to shrink the interval bracketing x^* and possibly update your estimate of x^* as well.

P2.8. Consider the three-loop electrical circuit shown schematically in Figure 2.23. By summing the voltage drops around each of loops 1, 2 and 3, it can be shown that

$$i_1(R_1 + R_2) - i_2 R_1 - i_3 R_2 = V_1 , \qquad (2.19)$$

$$-i_1 R_1 + i_2(R_1 + R_3 + R_4) - i_3 R_4 = V_2 , \qquad (2.20)$$

$$-i_1 R_2 - i_2 R_4 + i_3(R_2 + R_4 + R_5) = V_3 , \qquad (2.21)$$

where the i's, V's and R's denote, respectively, currents, voltages and resistances. Suppose we wanted to determine the voltage V_3 that yields $i_3 = 0$. One way to do this is to rewrite the above equations in the following form:

$$i_1(R_1 + R_2) - i_2 R_1 = V_1 , \qquad (2.22)$$

$$-i_1 R_1 + i_2(R_1 + R_3 + R_4) = V_2 , \qquad (2.23)$$

$$-i_1 R_2 - i_2 R_4 - V_3 = 0 , \qquad (2.24)$$

and solve for i_1, i_2 and V_3 (assuming V_1, V_2 and all the resistance values are known). An alternative strategy is to take a root finding approach as we illustrate below. (i) Write a MATLAB function that takes as its input V_3 then computes i_1, i_2 and i_3 from equations (2.19-2.21) using the backslash operator and returns i_3; (ii) use Newton's method to compute the root, V_3, of the Matlab function defined in (i). Assume that $V_1 = 50\,\text{V}$, $V_2 = 180\,\text{V}$, $R_1 = 20\,\Omega$, $R_2 = 10\,\Omega$, $R_3 = 35\,\Omega$, $R_4 = 15\,\Omega$ and $R_5 = 20\,\Omega$. Hint: V_3 can be negative.

P2.9. In fluid mechanics, the Weymouth equation is used for relating the pressure drop and flow rate in a pipeline carrying compressible gases. It is given by

$$Q_o = 433.54 \frac{T_o}{P_o} \left[\frac{(P_1^2 - P_2^2)}{L \sigma T} \right]^{0.5} d^{2.667} \eta , \qquad (2.25)$$

where

Q_o is the gas flow rate $= 2000000\,\text{SCFD}$
T_o is the standard temperature $= 520\,\text{R}$
P_o is the standard pressure $= 14.7\,\text{psia}$
P_1 is the upstream pressure, (?), psia

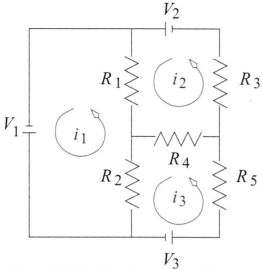

$$V_2$$

Figure 2.23: A three-loop electrical circuit.

P_2 is the downstream pressure $= 21.7\,\text{psia}$
L is the length of pipe $= 0.1894\,\text{miles}$
σ is the specific gravity of gas (air=1) $= 0.7$
T is the actual gas temperature $= 530\,\text{R}$
d is the diameter of the pipe, (?), inches
η is the efficiency $= 0.7$ (a fudge factor)

(a) If the diameter of the pipe is 4.026 inches, determine the upstream pressure using the secant algorithm and initial guesses of 5 and 45 and using `fzero` and an initial guess of 25.

(b) Suppose the maximum pressure the pipeline can withstand is only 24.7 psia. Other conditions remaining the same as in the previous part, determine the diameter of the pipe that should be employed using the secant algorithm and initial guesses of 4 and 8 and using `fzero` and an initial guess of 6.

P2.10. The phase behavior of fluids can be predicted with the help of equations of state. The one developed by Peng and Robinson is particularly well tuned, accurate and hence is widely used. The equation is given below.

$$P = \frac{RT}{(V - b)} - \frac{a(T)}{V(V + b) + b(V - b)}, \qquad (2.26)$$

where

$$a(T) = 0.45724 \frac{R^2 T_c^2}{P_c} \alpha(T_r, \omega), \qquad b = 0.0778 \frac{R T_c}{P_c},$$

$$\sqrt{\alpha} = 1 + m(1 - \sqrt{T_r}) m = 0.37464 + 1.54226\omega - 0.26992\omega^2,$$

$$T_r = T/T_c \text{and} \qquad Z = PV/RT.$$

Whenever (P, T) are given it is convenient to write equation (2.26) as a cubic equation in Z, *i.e.*

$$Z^3 - (1 - B)Z^2 + (A - 3B^2 - 2B)Z - (AB - B^2 - B^3) = 0, \quad (2.27)$$

where $A = aP/(R^2 T^2)$, $B = bP/(RT)$. Use equation (2.27) to compute the density of CO_2 in mol/L at $P = 20.684\,\text{MPa}$ and $T = 299.82\,\text{K}$. The properties required for CO_2 are $T_c = 304.2\,\text{K}$, $P_c = 7.3862\,\text{MPa}$, $\omega = 0.225$ and $R = 8314\,\text{Pa·m}^3/\text{kmol/K}$.

(a) Use the built-in function `roots` to find all the roots of the cubic equation (2.27) in terms of Z. In MATLAB, how does the function `roots` differ from the function `fzero`?

(b) Use the secant algorithm to find the real roots of the above equation.

(c) After finding the compressibility Z from each of the above methods, convert it into molar density and compare with the experimental value of 20.814 mol/L.

(d) Consider the case where you are given (P, V) and you are asked to find T. Develop and implement the Newton iteration to solve for this case. Use the above equation to compute the temperature of CO_2 in Kelvin at $P = 20.684 \times 10^6\,\text{Pa}$ and $V = 0.04783\,\text{L/mol}$. Compare the number of iterations required to obtain a solution to a tolerance of $|f| < 10^{-15}$ using an initial guess of $T = 250\,\text{K}$ by Newton's method with that required by the secant algorithm with initial guesses of 200 K and 310 K.

(e) Suppose that you are given (T, V) and you are asked to find P; which form of the equation will you choose, equation (2.26) or (2.27)? What method of solution would you recommend?

P2.11. Many engineering problems can be cast in the form of determining the roots of a nonlinear algebraic equation. One such example arises in determining the time required to cool a solid body at a given point to a predetermined temperature.

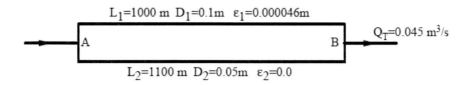

$L_1=1000$ m $D_1=0.1$m $\varepsilon_1=0.000046$m

A

B

$Q_T=0.045$ m^3/s

$L_2=1100$ m $D_2=0.05$m $\varepsilon_2=0.0$

Figure 2.24: Turbulent flow in a parallel pipe

Consider a semi-infinite solid, initially at a temperature of $T_i = 200°C$ and one side of it is suddenly exposed to an ambient temperature of $T_a = 70°C$. The heat transfer coefficient between the solid and the surroundings is $h = 525\,\mathrm{W}/(\mathrm{m}^2\,°C)$. The thermal conductivity of the solid is $k = 215\,\mathrm{W}/(\mathrm{m}°\ \mathrm{C})$ and the thermal diffusivity of the solid is $\alpha = 8.4 \times 10^{-5}\,\mathrm{m}^2/\mathrm{s}$. Determine the time required to cool the solid at a distance of $x = 4\,\mathrm{cm}$ measured from the exposed surface, to $T = 120°C$. The temperature profile as a function of time and distance is given by the following expression:

$$\theta = 1 - \mathrm{erf}(\xi) - \left[e^{(hx/k+\tau)} \right] [1 - \mathrm{erf}(\xi + \sqrt{\tau})]\,,$$

where the dimensionless temperature, $\theta = \frac{(T-T_i)}{(T_a-T_i)}$, $\xi = \frac{x}{2\sqrt{\alpha t}}$ and $\tau = \frac{h^2 \alpha t}{k^2}$ where t is the time, x is the distance and erf is the error function.

P2.12. Consider the flow of an incompressible, Newtonian fluid ($\rho = 1000\,\mathrm{kg/m}^3$, $\mu = 0.001\,\mathrm{Pa\cdot s}$) in the parallel pipeline system shown in Figure 2.24. The lengths, diameters, roughness for the pipes as well as the total flow rate are as shown in Figure 2.24. Your task is to determine the individual flow rates in each of pipe segments 1 and 2. The equation to be satisfied is obtained based on the fact that the pressure drop between points A and B is the same. The equation is

$$f_1(v_1)\frac{L_1}{D_1}\frac{v_1^2}{2} = f_2(v_2)\frac{L_2}{D_2}\frac{v_2^2}{2}\,, \qquad (2.28)$$

where v_1 and v_2 are the velocities in the two pipes and f_1 and f_2 are the corresponding friction factors given by the Churchill equation, *i.e.*

$$f_i(v_i) = 8\left[\left(\frac{8}{\mathrm{Re}_i}\right)^{12} + \frac{1}{(A+B)^{1.5}} \right]^{1/12}\,,$$

where

$$A = \left[2.457 \ln \left(\frac{1}{(1/\mathrm{Re}_i)^{0.9} + 0.27(\epsilon_i/D_i)} \right) \right]^{16},$$

$$B = \left[\frac{37530}{\mathrm{Re}_i} \right]^{16},$$

and

$$\mathrm{Re}_i = \frac{D_i v_i \rho}{\mu}.$$

Finally the mass balance equation provides another constraint

$$\frac{\pi}{4}(D_1^2 v_1 + D_2^2 v_2) = Q_T.$$

This problem can be formulated as two equation in two unknowns v_1 and v_2, but your task is to pose this as a single equation in one unknown, v_1, by rearranging equation (2.28) as

$$F(v_1) = f_1(v_1) \frac{L_1}{D_1} \frac{v_1^2}{2} - f_2(v_2) \frac{L_2}{D_2} \frac{v_2^2}{2} = 0.$$

Thus for a given guess for v_1, write an .m file that will calculate $F(v_1)$. Then carry out the following calculations:

(a) Solve the problem using the secant algorithm with initial guesses of $4.5\,\mathrm{m/s}$ and $5.5\,\mathrm{m/s}$. [Answer: $v_1 = 4.8703\,\mathrm{m/s}$]

(b) Suppose the total flow rate is increased to $0.09\,\mathrm{m^3/s}$, what are the new velocities in the pipes?

(c) Consider the case where $L_1 = 1000\,\mathrm{m}$, $L_2 = 900\,\mathrm{m}$, $D_1 = 0.1\,\mathrm{m}$ and $D_2 = 0.09\,\mathrm{m}$ all other values being the same. Is there a flow rate Q_T for which the velocities in both pipes will be the same? If so what is it? [Answer: $Q_T = 0.0017\,\mathrm{m^3/s}$]

(d) Plot v_1 vs Q_T and v_2 vs Q_T for the case above over a suitable range of Q_T.

(e) Discuss the pros and cons of implementing Newton's method for this problem.

P2.13. The velocity profile for a non-Newtonian fluid flowing in a circular pipe is given by

$$\frac{u}{u_m} = \left(\frac{3n+1}{n+1} \right) \left[1 - \left(\frac{r}{R} \right)^{\frac{n+1}{n}} \right]$$

where u_m is the mean velocity of the fluid, r is the radial position from the centre of the tube, R is the radius of the tube and n is a constant depending on the fluid properties (Newtonian fluid:

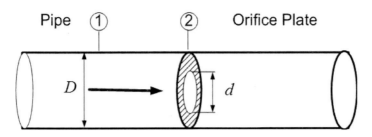

Figure 2.25: Flow through an orifice meter.

$n = 1$, dilatant fluid: $n = 3$). Determine the value of n for a fluid with $\frac{u}{u_m} = 0.8$ at $\frac{r}{R} = 0.75$. Use 0.1 and 0.9 as your initial guesses. Try the

(a) Bisection method.

(b) Regula-Falsi method.

(c) Secant method.

(d) Newton's method (start with the lower bound of 0.1).

(e) Built-in function `fzero`.

(f) Built-in function `fminsearch`.

Compare and comment on the number of iterations required for each method.

P2.14. Orifice plates are widely used flow metering devices in the process industries. A typical orifice arrangement is shown in Figure 2.25. The volumetric flow rate (m³/s) from an orifice is given by

$$Q = A_2 C_d \sqrt{\frac{2(P_1 - P_2)}{\rho(1 - \beta^4)}},$$

where A_2 is the orifice flow area, ρ (kg/m³) is the density of the fluid flowing in the pipe, $P_1 - P_2$ (kg/m·s²) is the pressure difference and C_d is the discharge coefficient defined as

$$C_d = \frac{\text{actual discharge}}{\text{ideal discharge}}.$$

A typical equation for the discharge coefficient is

$$C_d = 0.5959 + 0.031\beta^{2.1} - 0.184\beta^{8.0} + 91.71\beta^{2.5}/\text{Re}^{0.75},$$

where $\beta = d/D$ and Re is the Reynolds number for the flow. Determine the value of β that gives a discharge coefficient of $C_d = 0.615$ at Re $= 2 \times 10^4$.

(a) Solve using Müller's method choosing initial guesses of 0.1, 0.8 and 1.0.

(b) Solve using MATLAB's `fminsearch` and `fzero` functions.

P2.15. The equilibrium constant for the following third-order reversible chemical reaction given by

$$A + 2B \Leftrightarrow C$$

can be computed from

$$K = \frac{C_C}{C_A C_B^2},$$

where C_i is the concentration of species i. By performing mole balance and denoting the fractional conversion of species A as X_A and the initial molar ratio as $\varpi = \frac{C_{B0}}{C_{A0}}$, we can write

$$K = \frac{X_A}{C_{A0}^2 (1 - X_A)(\varpi - X_A)^2}.$$

Determine the fractional conversion for a system where $C_{A0} = 40 \, \text{mol/m}^3$, $C_{B0} = 25 \, \text{mol/m}^3$ and $K = 0.015$.

(a) Obtain the solution graphically.

(b) Based on your answer above, solve for the conversion to within the tolerance error of $\epsilon_s = 0.5\%$.

P2.16. The total power requirement of a natural gas compressor for a given duty is the sum of the gas power and the friction power. For a centrifugal compressor, the gas power (in horsepower) is given by

$$\text{GHP} = (0.004367)\frac{P_1}{V_1} \left(\frac{k}{k-1} \right) \left(\frac{P_2}{P_1^{(k-1)/k} - 1} \right) / \text{CE} \,.$$

where P_1 is the inlet pressure (psia), V_1 is the inlet volume (ACFM), P_2 is the discharge pressure (psia), k is the ratio of specific heats and CE is the compression efficiency.

Determine the discharge pressure when a 100 hp compressor is fed with 100 ACFM natural gas assuming a compression efficiency of 0.85 and a heat capacity ratio of 1.2. Use the

(a) Bisection method.

(b) Regula-Falsi method.

(c) Newton's method.

(d) Secant method.

Compare the results for the different methods and discuss your results.

P2.17. The specific heat capacity, c_p, of a particular substance varies with temperature, T, according to the following equation:

$$c_p = 19.86 + 5.016 \times 10^{-2}T + 1.27 \times 10^{-5}T^2 - 10.99 \times 10^{-9}T^3 \,,$$

where T is measured in K and c_p is measured in kJ/(kg·K). Construct a plot of c_p vs. T for $273\,\text{K} \leq T \leq 1500\,\text{K}$ then use the bisection algorithm to estimate the temperature corresponding to a specific heat capacity of $c_p = 62.3\,\text{kJ}/(\text{kg·K})$.

P2.18. The Colebrook equation is an implicit equation that combines experimental results for turbulent flow in smooth and rough pipes to give

$$\frac{1}{\sqrt{f}} = -2\log\left(\frac{\epsilon}{3.7D} + \frac{2.51}{\text{Re}\sqrt{f}}\right) \,,$$

where f is the Darcy friction factor, ϵ is the tube roughness, D is the inside diameter of the conduit and Re is the Reynolds number for the flow, given as

$$\text{Re} = \frac{\rho V D}{\mu} \,.$$

Here ρ is the fluid density, μ is the fluid dynamic viscosity and V is the fluid velocity. Determine the friction factor for air flowing in a tube with the following parameters: $D = 5\,\text{mm}$, $V = 35\,\text{m/s}$, $\rho = 1.52\,\text{kg/m}^3$, $\mu = 2.0\,\text{N·s/m}^2$ and $\epsilon = 0.002\,\text{mm}$.

P2.19. The function $y = \cos x - \sin[\ln(x + \pi)]$ has three roots, $r_1 < r_2 < r_3$, in the interval $0 < x < 10$. Use the deflation technique to determine the magnitude of r_1, r_2 and r_3. (Recall that in MATLAB, the natural logarithm is written as `log`.)

P2.20. We wish to use fixed point iteration to estimate the first positive root* of

$$f(x) = n - \tan\left(\frac{x - \pi/4}{5}\right) \tag{2.29}$$

by setting $g(x) = x + f(x)$. Here $n\,(> 0)$ is a free parameter, whose numerical value can be taken to be e, 2.95, 3.05 or π.

(a) Plot f as a function of x; include all four functions in the same plot. Graphically estimate the value of the root in each case.

---

*The value of this root is, of course, simply $\pi/4 + 5\tan^{-1}(n)$.

(b) Plot $g'(x)$ as a function of x; for what value of x is $g'(x) = -1$? How does this compare with your estimates from part (a)?

(c) Using `mnhf_fpi`, confirm that convergence is realized when $n = e$ or 2.95 but not when $n = 3.05$ or π. How many iterations are required when convergence does occur? In all cases, choose 7 as the initial root estimate.

(d) Mathematically-speaking, what is the range of n-values for which you expect FPI to converge?

CHAPTER 3

SYSTEMS OF LINEAR ALGEBRAIC EQUATIONS

3.1 Introduction

Topics from linear algebra form the core of numerical analysis. Almost every conceivable problem, be it curve fitting, optimization, simulation of flow sheets or simulation of distributed parameter systems necessitating solution of differential equations, require at some stage the solution of a system (often a large system) of algebraic equations. MATLAB (acronym for MATrix LABoratory) was in fact conceived as a collection of tools to aid in the interactive analysis of linear systems and was derived from a well known core of linear algebra routines written in FORTRAN called LINPACK.

In this chapter we first provide a quick review of concepts from linear algebra. We then develop ideas and algorithms related to numerical methods making frequent reference to MATLAB implementation of various concepts throughout. The reader is encouraged to try these out interactively during a MATLAB session.

3.2 Matrix notation

We have already used matrix notation to represent a system of linear algebraic equations in a compact form in Chapter 1. Whereas a matrix, as an object, is represented in boldface, its constituent elements are represented using index notation or as subscripted arrays in programming languages. For example, the following statements are equivalent:

$$\boldsymbol{A} = [a_{ij}], \qquad i = 1, \cdots, m; \quad j = 1, \cdots, n,$$

where $\boldsymbol{A}$ is an $m \times n$ matrix and a_{ij} represents the element of the matrix $\boldsymbol{A}$ in row i and column j. Thus

$$\boldsymbol{A} = [a_{ij}] = \begin{bmatrix} a_{11} & a_{12} & \cdots & a_{1,n-1} & a_{1,n} \\ a_{21} & a_{22} & \cdots & a_{2,n-1} & a_{2,n} \\ \vdots & \ddots & \ddots & \ddots & \vdots \\ a_{m-1,1} & a_{m-1,2} & \cdots & a_{m-1,n-1} & a_{m-1,n} \\ a_{m,1} & a_{m,2} & \cdots & a_{m,n-1} & a_{m,n} \end{bmatrix}.$$

A vector can be thought of as a matrix with a single row or column. A row vector is represented by

$$\boldsymbol{x} = [x_1, \ x_2 \cdots x_n],$$

while a column vector is represented by

$$\boldsymbol{y} = \begin{bmatrix} y_1 \\ y_2 \\ \vdots \\ y_m \end{bmatrix}.$$

Note that matrix/vector elements can be real or complex.

Having defined vectors and matrices, we can extend the notions of basic arithmetic operations between scalars to higher dimensional objects. The reasons for doing so are many. It not only allows us to express a large system of equations in a compact symbolic form, but a study of the properties of such objects allows us to develop and codify very efficient ways of solving and analyzing large linear systems. A package such as MATLAB presents to us a vast array of such codified algorithms. As an engineer, you should develop a conceptual understanding of the underlying principles and the skills to use such packages. But the most important task is to properly define each element of a vector or a matrix, which is tied closely to the physical description of the problem.

3.2.1   Review of basic operations

Arithmetic operations can be defined both in symbolic form and using index notation. The leads to the algorithm for implementing the rules of operation using any programming language. The syntax of these operations in MATLAB is shown with specific examples below.

The addition operation between two matrices is defined as

$$\text{addition:} \quad \boldsymbol{A} = \boldsymbol{B} + \boldsymbol{C} \quad \Rightarrow \quad a_{ij} = b_{ij} + c_{ij}.$$

This implies an element-by-element addition of the matrices $\boldsymbol{B}$ and $\boldsymbol{C}$. Clearly all the matrices involved must have the same dimension.

Note that the addition operation is *commutative* as seen with its scalar counterpart *i.e.,*

$$A + B = B + A.$$

Matrix addition is also *associative, i.e.,* independent of the order in which it is carried out. For instance,

$$A + B + C = (A + B) + C = A + (B + C).$$

The scalar multiplication of a matrix involves multiplying each element of the matrix by the scalar, *i.e.,*

$$\text{scalar multiplication:} \quad kA = B \quad \Rightarrow \quad ka_{ij} = b_{ij}.$$

Matrix subtraction can be handled by combining the rules of matrix addition and scalar multiplication .

The product of two matrices A (of dimension $n \times m$) and B (of dimension $m \times r$) is defined as*

$$\text{matrix multiplication:} \quad C = AB \quad \Rightarrow \quad c_{ij} = \sum_{k=1}^{m} a_{ik} b_{kj} \ \forall \ i, j.$$

The resultant matrix has dimension $n \times r$. The operation indicated in index notation is carried out for each value of the free indices $i = 1 \cdots n$ and $j = 1 \cdots r$. The product is defined only if the dimensions of A, B are compatible - *i.e.,* the number of *columns* in A should equal the number of *rows* in B. This implies that while the product AB may be defined, the product $B\,A$ may not be defined. By extension, even when the matrices are dimensionally compatible, in general

$$AB \neq BA$$

i.e., matrix multiplication is not *commutative.*

Other useful products can also be defined between vectors and matrices. A Hadamard (or Schur) product is defined as[†]

$$C = A \circ B \quad \Rightarrow \quad c_{ij} = a_{ij} b_{ij} \quad \forall \quad i, j.$$

Obviously, the dimensions of A and B should be the same. Meanwhile, the Kronecker product is defined as[‡]

$$C = A \otimes B \quad \Rightarrow \quad C = \begin{bmatrix} a_{11}B & a_{12}B & \cdots & a_{1m}B \\ a_{21}B & a_{22}B & \cdots & a_{2m}B \\ \vdots & & & \\ a_{n1}B & a_{n2}B & \cdots & a_{nm}B \end{bmatrix}.$$

---

[*]The MATLAB syntax for the product of two matrices is C=A*B – see also Appendix A.
[†]The MATLAB syntax for the Hadamard product of two matrices is C=A.*B.
[‡]The MATLAB syntax for the Kronecker product of two matrices is C=kron(A,B).

Multiplying a scalar by unity leaves its value unchanged. The extension of this notion to matrices results in the definition of an *identity* matrix[*]

$$\boldsymbol{I} = \begin{bmatrix} 1 & 0 & \cdots & 0 \\ 0 & 1 & \cdots & 0 \\ \vdots & 0 & 1 & 0 \\ 0 & 0 & \cdots & 1 \end{bmatrix} \qquad \Rightarrow \qquad \delta_{ij} = \begin{cases} 1 & i = j \\ 0 & i \neq j \end{cases} .$$

Multiplying any matrix $\boldsymbol{A}$ with an identity matrix $\boldsymbol{I}$ of appropriate dimension leaves the original matrix unchanged, *i.e.*,

$$\boldsymbol{AI} = \boldsymbol{A} .$$

The above concepts allow us to generalize the notion of division with scalars to matrices. Division can be thought of as the inverse of multiplication. For example, given a number, say 2, we can define its inverse, x in such a way that the product of the two numbers is unity *i.e.*, $2x = 1$ or $x = 2^{-1}$. In a similar way, given a matrix $\boldsymbol{A}$, we can define the inverse matrix $\boldsymbol{B}$ such that

$$\boldsymbol{AB} = \boldsymbol{I} \qquad \text{or} \qquad \boldsymbol{B} = \boldsymbol{A}^{-1} .$$

The task of developing an algorithm for finding the inverse of a matrix will be addressed later in this chapter.

For a square matrix, *powers* of the matrix $\boldsymbol{A}$ can be defined as

$$\boldsymbol{A}^2 = \boldsymbol{AA} \qquad \boldsymbol{A}^3 = \boldsymbol{AAA} = \boldsymbol{A}^2\boldsymbol{A} = \boldsymbol{AA}^2 .$$

Note that $\boldsymbol{A}^p\boldsymbol{A}^q = \boldsymbol{A}^{p+q}$ for positive integers p and q[†]. Having extended the definition of powers, we can extend the definition of *exponentiation* from scalars to square matrices as follows[‡]. For a scalar α

$$e^\alpha = 1 + \alpha + \frac{\alpha^2}{2} + \cdots = \sum_{k=0}^{\infty} \frac{\alpha^k}{k!} .$$

For a matrix $\boldsymbol{A}$, the analogue expression reads

$$e^{\boldsymbol{A}} = \boldsymbol{I} + \boldsymbol{A} + \frac{\boldsymbol{A}^2}{2} + \cdots = \sum_{k=0}^{\infty} \frac{\boldsymbol{A}^k}{k!} .$$

One operation that does not have a direct counterpart in the scalar world is the *transpose* of a matrix. It is defined as the result of exchanging the rows and columns, *i.e.*

$$\boldsymbol{B} = \boldsymbol{A}' \qquad \Rightarrow \qquad b_{ij} = a_{ji} .$$

---

[*]The MATLAB syntax for producing an identity matrix of size N is `I=eye(N)`.

[†]The MATLAB syntax for producing the n-th power of a matrix $\boldsymbol{A}$ is `A^n` whereas the syntax for producing element-by-element power is `A.^n`. Make sure that you understand the difference between these two operations!

[‡]The MATLAB function `exp(A)` evaluates the exponential element-by-element whereas `expm(A)` evaluates the true matrix exponential.

It is easy to verify that

$$(A + B)' = A' + B'.$$

Something that is not so easy to verify, but is nevertheless true, is

$$(AB)' = B'A'.$$

3.3   Matrices with special structure

A *diagonal* matrix D has non-zero elements only along the diagonal,

$$D = \begin{bmatrix} d_{11} & 0 & \cdots & 0 \\ 0 & d_{22} & \cdots & 0 \\ \vdots & 0 & \ddots & 0 \\ 0 & 0 & \cdots & d_{nn} \end{bmatrix}.$$

A *lower triangular* matrix L has non-zero elements on or below the diagonal,

$$L = \begin{bmatrix} l_{11} & 0 & \cdots & 0 \\ l_{21} & l_{22} & \cdots & 0 \\ \vdots & & \ddots & 0 \\ l_{n1} & l_{n2} & \cdots & l_{nn} \end{bmatrix}.$$

An *upper triangular* matrix U has non-zero elements on or above the diagonal,

$$U = \begin{bmatrix} u_{11} & u_{12} & \cdots & u_{1n} \\ 0 & u_{22} & \cdots & u_{2n} \\ 0 & 0 & \ddots & \vdots \\ 0 & 0 & \cdots & u_{nn} \end{bmatrix}.$$

A *tridiagonal* matrix T has non-zero elements on the diagonal and one off diagonal row on each side of the diagonal,

$$T = \begin{bmatrix} t_{11} & t_{12} & 0 & \cdots & & 0 \\ t_{21} & t_{22} & t_{23} & 0 & & 0 \\ 0 & \ddots & \ddots & & \ddots & 0 \\ \vdots & 0 & t_{n-1,n-2} & t_{n-1,n-1} & & t_{n-1,n} \\ 0 & \cdots & & 0 & t_{n,n-1} & t_{n,n} \end{bmatrix}.$$

A *sparse* matrix is a generic term to indicate those matrices without any specific structure such as above, but with only a small number (typically 10 to 15 %) of non-zero elements.

3.4 Matrix determinant

The determinant of a square matrix is defined in such a way that a scalar value is associated with the matrix that does not change with certain row or column operations on the matrix - *i.e.*, it is one of the scalar invariants of the matrix. In the context of solving a system of linear equations, the determinant is also useful in knowing whether the system of equations is solvable uniquely. The determinant is formed by summing *all* possible products formed by choosing *one and only one* element from each row and column of the matrix. The precise definition, taken from Amundson (1966), is

$$\det(\boldsymbol{A}) = |\boldsymbol{A}| = \sum (-1)^h (a_{1l_1} a_{2l_2} \cdots a_{nl_n}). \tag{3.1}$$

Each term in the sum consists of a product of n elements selected such that only one element appears from each row and column. The summation involves a total of $n!$ terms accounted for as follows: for the first element l_1 in the product there are n choices, followed by $n - 1$ choices for the second element l_2, $n - 2$ choices for the third element l_3 *etc.* resulting in a total of $n!$ choices for a particular product. Note that in this way of counting, the set of second subscripts $\{l_1, l_2, \cdots l_n\}$ will contain all of the numbers in the range 1 to n, but they will not be in their natural order $\{1, 2, \cdots n\}$. Hence, h is the number of permutations required to arrange $\{l_1, l_2, \cdots l_n\}$ in their natural order.

Unfortunately, the definition provided by equation (3.1) is neither intuitive nor computationally efficient. However, it is instructive in understanding the following properties of determinants:

1. The determinant of a diagonal matrix $\boldsymbol{D}$, is simply the product of all the diagonal elements, *i.e.*,

$$\det(\boldsymbol{D}) = \prod_{k=1}^{n} d_{kk}.$$

2. A little thought should convince you that it is the same scenario for lower or upper triangular matrices as well. Thus

$$\det(\boldsymbol{L}) = \prod_{k=1}^{n} l_{kk}.$$

3. It should also be clear that if all the elements of any row or column are zero, then the determinant is likewise zero.

4. If every element of a particular row or column of a matrix is multiplied by a scalar, it is equivalent to multiplying the determinant

of the original matrix by the same scalar, *i.e.*,

$$\begin{vmatrix} ka_{11} & ka_{12} & \cdots & ka_{1n} \\ a_{21} & a_{22} & \cdots & a_{2n} \\ \vdots & & \ddots & \vdots \\ a_{n1} & a_{n2} & \cdots & a_{nn} \end{vmatrix} = \begin{vmatrix} a_{11} & a_{12} & \cdots & ka_{1n} \\ a_{21} & a_{22} & \cdots & ka_{2n} \\ \vdots & & \ddots & \vdots \\ a_{n1} & a_{n2} & \cdots & ka_{nn} \end{vmatrix} = k \det(\boldsymbol{A}).$$

5. Replacing any row (or column) of a matrix with a linear combination of that row (or column) and another row (or column) leaves the determinant unchanged.

6. A consequence of rules 3 and 5 is that if two rows (or columns) of a matrix are identical the determinant is zero.

7. If any two rows (or columns) are interchanged, this results in a sign change of the determinant.

3.4.1 Laplace expansion of the determinant

A definition of the determinant that you might have seen in an earlier linear algebra course is

$$\det(\boldsymbol{A}) = |\boldsymbol{A}| = \begin{cases} \sum_{k=1}^{n} a_{ik} A_{ik} & \text{for any} \quad i \\ \sum_{k=1}^{n} a_{kj} A_{kj} & \text{for any} \quad j \end{cases} \tag{3.2}$$

Here A_{ik}, called the *cofactor*, is given by

$$A_{ik} = (-1)^{i+k} M_{ik}$$

and M_{ik}, called the *minor*, is the determinant of $(n-1) \times (n-1)$ sub-matrix of $\boldsymbol{A}$ obtained by deleting ith row and kth column of $\boldsymbol{A}$. Note that the expansion in equation (3.2) can be carried out along any row i or column j of the original matrix $\boldsymbol{A}$.

In MATLAB, matrix determinants may be computed using the built-in function `det` or, for those that prefer greater transparency, using `mnhf_determinant`, which is given in Figure 3.1. This latter algorithm provides an example of a function that calls itself. Such a strategy is necessary because, as the above discussion makes clear, calculating the determinant of an $n \times n$ matrix requires the evaluation of n minors. Thus in order to compute the determinant of a 4×4 matrix, it is necessary to first calculate four determinants for sub-matrices of size 3×3. Examining `mnhf_determinant` closely (and setting aside the trivial case of a matrix having a single row and column), function self-calls are made until the sub-matrices are of size 2×2 in which case it is very easy to evaluate the determinant. Notice also that `mnhf_determinant` makes effective use of MATLAB's colon (`:`) operator in specifying those rows and columns to be included or excluded in a given sub-matrix. Examples illustrating the use of `:` are provided in Appendix A.

```
function sum=mnhf_determinant(A)
%MNHF_DETERMINANT compute a matrix determinant.
%
% A — the (square) matrix in question
%
% Usage  mnhf_determinant(A);

[r,c] = size(A);  % Compute size of A.
if isequal(r,c)
 if c==1 % Trivial case; `matrix' is a scalar.
  sum = A(1,1);
 else
  if c==2  % Solve for determinant in 2—by—2 case.
   sum = A(1,1)*A(2,2)—A(1,2)*A(2,1);
  else
   % Call mnhf_determinant to evaluate minors. Use : notation to
   % facilitate matrix index referencing.
   for ii=1:c
    if ii==1
     sum = A(1,1)*mnhf_determinant(A(2:r,2:c));
    elseif (ii>1 && ii<c)
     sum = sum+A(1,ii)*(—1)^(ii+1)* ...
           mnhf_determinant(A(2:r,[1:ii—1,ii+1:c]));
    else
     sum = sum+A(1,c)*(—1)^(c+1)* ...
           mnhf_determinant(A(2:r,1:c—1));
    end
   end
  end
 end
else
 fprintf('A is a non—square matrix.\n\n')
end
```

Figure 3.1: MATLAB implementation of the matrix determinant algorithm.

3.5 Vector and matrix norms

Although matrices and vectors usually contain a number of elements, in some cases we may wish to allocate a single value that represents the magnitude (not the dimension) of the vector or matrix. This value is called a norm of the vector or matrix. The length (or *Euclidean norm*) of a vector is an example of a norm and is defined as

$$||\boldsymbol{x}||_2 = \sqrt{x_1^2 + x_2^2 + \cdots + x_n^2} \,. \tag{3.3}$$

This definition can be generalized to what is known as the p-norm of a vector

$$||\boldsymbol{x}||_p = L_p = (x_1^p + x_2^p + \cdots + x_n^p)^{1/p} = \left\{ \sum_{i=1}^{n} |x_i|^p \right\}^{1/p} \,. \tag{3.4}$$

Thus for $p = 1$,

$$||\boldsymbol{x}||_1 = L_1 = |x_1| + |x_2| + |x_2| + \cdots |x_n| = \left\{ \sum_{i=1}^{n} |x_i| \right\} \,. \tag{3.5}$$

Conversely, for $p \to \infty$,

$$||\boldsymbol{x}||_\infty = L_\infty \to \max|x_i| \,. \tag{3.6}$$

Matrices can be considered as a collection of column vectors or row vectors. The definition of matrix norms is therefore move involved. We can follow the analogy with vectors and define

$$||\boldsymbol{A}||_p = \max_{x \neq 0} \frac{||\boldsymbol{A}\boldsymbol{x}||_p}{||\boldsymbol{x}||_p} \,. \tag{3.7}$$

In this text we will typically limit our discussions to the 1 and ∞ norm of square matrices

$$||\boldsymbol{A}||_1 = \max_{x \neq 0} \frac{||\boldsymbol{A}\boldsymbol{x}||_1}{||\boldsymbol{x}||_1} = \max_{1 \leq j \leq n} \sum_{i=1}^{n} |a_{ij}| \,, \tag{3.8}$$

$$||\boldsymbol{A}||_\infty = \max_{1 \leq i \leq n} \sum_{j=1}^{n} |a_{ij}| \,. \tag{3.9}$$

The 1 norm is therefore the maximum column sum while the ∞ norm is the maximum row sum. Another metric that is frequently used is the spectral norm or spectral radius of a square matrix, defined as

$$\rho(\boldsymbol{A}) = \max_{1 \leq i \leq n} |\lambda_i| \,, \tag{3.10}$$

where λ_i is the largest eigenvalue of the matrix $\boldsymbol{A}$. This largest eigenvalue may be determined using a numerical technique known as *power iteration.* Alternatively, MATLAB provides a convenient built-in function for finding the eigenvalues (and associated eigenvectors) of a matrix, namely `eig`.

EXAMPLE 3.1 (✎ **Calculating norms**) *(a) Calculate L_1, L_2 and L_∞ for the following vector:*

$$x = \begin{bmatrix} 3 \\ 2 \\ -6 \end{bmatrix}.$$

Solution: applying equation (3.4) we obtain

$$L_1 = \sum_{i=1}^{3} |x_i| = |3| + |2| + |-6| = 11,$$

$$L_2 = \left\{ \sum_{i=1}^{3} x_i^2 \right\}^{1/2} = \left(3^2 + 2^2 + 6^2 \right)^{1/2} = 7,$$

$$L_\infty = \max|x_i| = \max(|3|, |2|, |-6|) = 6.$$

(b) Calculate L_1, L_∞ and the spectral radius for the matrix A given by

$$A = \begin{bmatrix} 1 & 0 & 0.306 \\ 0 & 1 & 0.702 \\ -2 & 1 & 0 \end{bmatrix}.$$

Solution:

$$||A||_1 = \max\{|1| + |0| + |-2|, |0| + |1| + |1|, |0.306| + |0.702| + |0|\}$$
$$= \max\{3, 2, 1.008\} = 3$$

$$||A||_\infty = \max\{|1| + |0| + |0.306|, |0| + |1| + |0.702|, |-2| + |1| + |0|\}$$
$$= \max\{1.306, 1.702, 3\} = 3$$

For $||A||_2$, we need to calculate the spectral radius of A. Thus

$$\rho(A) = \max(\lambda_i) \tag{3.11}$$

$$\det(A - \lambda I) = \det \left(\begin{bmatrix} 1 & 0 & 0.306 \\ 0 & 1 & 0.702 \\ -2 & 1 & 0 \end{bmatrix} - \begin{bmatrix} \lambda & 0 & 0 \\ 0 & \lambda & 0 \\ 0 & 0 & \lambda \end{bmatrix} \right) \tag{3.12}$$

$$= \det \left(\begin{bmatrix} 1-\lambda & 0 & 0.306 \\ 0 & 1-\lambda & 0.702 \\ -2 & 1 & -\lambda \end{bmatrix} \right) \tag{3.13}$$

$$= (1-\lambda)[-\lambda(1-\lambda) - 0.702] + 0 + 0.612(1-\lambda) \tag{3.14}$$

$$= \lambda^3 - 2\lambda^2 + 0.9100\lambda + 0.0900 \tag{3.15}$$

The roots of the polynomial, whence the eigenvalues, are $\lambda_1 = 1.0831$, $\lambda_2 = 1.0000$ *and* $\lambda_3 = -0.0831$, *thus*

$$||A||_2 = \max\{|1.0831|, |1.0000|, |-0.0831|\} = 1.0831\,.$$

3.6 Condition of a matrix

A matrix A is said to be *ill conditioned* if there exists a matrix B for which small changes (or perturbations) in the coefficients of A or B will produce large changes in $X = A^{-1}B$. The system of equations $AX = B$ is said to be ill conditioned when A is ill conditioned. We can quantify the degree of conditioning of a system using the condition number. To find the condition number of a matrix A, determine its inverse, A^{-1} then compute the norm of the matrix and the norm of the inverse. The product of the two may be used to determine the condition number of the matrix. Symbolically,

$$\text{cond}(A) = ||A|| \cdot ||A^{-1}||\,. \tag{3.16}$$

Here $||A||$ is the norm of the matrix A as defined in the previous section. As there are many definitions for the norm, we shall stick to the âĂŸ1âĂŹ norm or the ∞ norm in this text. If we take the condition number of an identity matrix as 1, a well-conditioned system will have a small condition number (close to 1), whereas a badly conditioned system will have a large condition number. Ill conditioning can occur when the determinant of A is close to zero suggesting that A is nearly singular.

EXAMPLE 3.2 (Demonstrating ill conditioning) *Consider two systems of equations in the two unknowns x_1 and x_2.*

System 1:

$$x_1 + x_2 = 2$$
$$x_1 + 1.0001x_2 = 2.0001$$

Solution: $x_1 = 1$, $x_2 = 1$.

System 2:

$$x_1 + x_2 = 2$$
$$x_1 + 1.0001x_2 = 2.0002$$

Solution: $x_1 = 0$, $x_2 = 2$.

Note that just a small change in the right-hand side of the second equation in the fifth decimal place causes a substantial difference in the solution to the equations. Thus small changes in the elements of $\boldsymbol{A}$ and $\boldsymbol{b}$ causes big changes in the solution $\boldsymbol{x} = \boldsymbol{A}^{-1}\boldsymbol{b}$.

For the above system we can write the coefficient matrix as

$$\boldsymbol{A} = \begin{bmatrix} 1 & 1 \\ 1 & 1.0001 \end{bmatrix},$$

and the matrix inverse as

$$\boldsymbol{A}^{-1} = 10^4 \begin{bmatrix} 1.0001 & -1 \\ -1 & 1 \end{bmatrix}.$$

The condition number based on the ∞ norm is calculated from

$$||\boldsymbol{A}||_\infty = 2.0001, ||\boldsymbol{A}^{-1}||_\infty = 10^4(2.0001)$$
$$\mathrm{cond}(\boldsymbol{A}) = ||\boldsymbol{A}||_\infty \cdot ||\boldsymbol{A}^{-1}||_\infty = 40004.0001.$$

The system is therefore ill conditioned because the condition number is quite large.

3.7   Solving a system of linear equations

3.7.1   Cramer's Rule

Consider a 2×2 system of equations

$$a_{11}x_1 + a_{12}x_2 = b_1,$$

$$a_{21}x_1 + a_{22}x_2 = b_2,$$

or, in matrix form,

$$\begin{bmatrix} a_{11} & a_{12} \\ a_{21} & a_{22} \end{bmatrix} \begin{bmatrix} x_1 \\ x_2 \end{bmatrix} = \begin{bmatrix} b_1 \\ b_2 \end{bmatrix}. \tag{3.17}$$

Direct elimination of the variable x_2 yields

$$(a_{11}a_{22} - a_{12}a_{21})\, x_1 = a_{22}b_1 - a_{12}b_2, \tag{3.18}$$

but

$$(a_{11}a_{22} - a_{12}a_{21}) = \begin{vmatrix} a_{11} & a_{12} \\ a_{21} & a_{22} \end{vmatrix} = \det(A),$$

and

$$a_{22}b_1 - a_{12}b_2 = \begin{vmatrix} b_1 & a_{12} \\ b_2 & a_{22} \end{vmatrix} = \det(A(1)).$$

Thus equation (3.18) can be written in an alternate form as
$$\det(\boldsymbol{A})\, x_1 = \det(\boldsymbol{A}(1))$$
where the matrix $\boldsymbol{A(1)}$ is obtained from $\boldsymbol{A}$ after replacing the first column with the vector $\boldsymbol{b}$ i.e.,
$$\boldsymbol{A}(1) = \begin{vmatrix} b_1 & a_{12} \\ b_2 & a_{22} \end{vmatrix}.$$

The above principles can be readily generalized to an $n \times n$ system. Cramer's Rule states that
$$x_1 = \frac{\det(\boldsymbol{A}(1))}{\det(\boldsymbol{A})}, \quad \cdots \quad x_k = \frac{\det(\boldsymbol{A}(k))}{\det(\boldsymbol{A})}, \quad \cdots \quad x_n = \frac{\det(\boldsymbol{A}(n))}{\det(\boldsymbol{A})}.$$
where $\boldsymbol{A(k)}$ is an $n \times n$ matrix obtained from $\boldsymbol{A}$ by replacing the kth column with the right-hand side vector $\boldsymbol{b}$. It should be clear from the above formulas that, in order to have a unique solution, the determinant of $\boldsymbol{A}$ must be *non-zero*. If the determinant is zero, $\boldsymbol{A}$ is referred to as a singular matrix.

A MATLAB function that implements Cramer's Rule is shown in Figure 3.2. Notice that `mnhf_cramer` leverages `mnhf_determinant`, which was introduced earlier in this chapter.

3.7.2 Matrix inverse

Previously, we defined the inverse of a matrix $\boldsymbol{A}$ as that matrix $\boldsymbol{B}$ that, when multiplied by $\boldsymbol{A}$ produces the identity matrix - *i.e.*, $\boldsymbol{AB} = \boldsymbol{I}$; but we did not develop a scheme for finding $\boldsymbol{B}$. We can do so now by combining Cramer's Rule and the Laplace expansion for a determinant. Using Laplace expansion's of the determinant of $\boldsymbol{A(k)}$ about column k yields
$$\det \boldsymbol{A(k)} = b_1 A_{1k} + b_2 A_{2k} + \cdots + b_n A_{nk} \qquad k = 1, 2, \cdots, n$$
where A_{ik} are the cofactors of $\boldsymbol{A}$ and $b_1, b_2, \ldots b_n$ are the elements of the right-hand side column vector $\boldsymbol{b}$. The components of the solution vector, $\boldsymbol{x}$ therefore read
$$x_1 = (b_1 A_{11} + b_2 A_{21} + \cdots + b_n A_{n1})/\det(\boldsymbol{A}),$$
$$x_j = (b_1 A_{1j} + b_2 A_{2j} + \cdots + b_n A_{nj})/\det(\boldsymbol{A}),$$
$$x_n = (b_1 A_{1n} + b_2 A_{2n} + \cdots + b_n A_{nn})/\det(\boldsymbol{A}).$$
The right-hand side of this system of equations can be written as a vector matrix product as follows:
$$\begin{bmatrix} x_1 \\ x_2 \\ \vdots \\ x_n \end{bmatrix} = \frac{1}{\det(\boldsymbol{A})} \begin{bmatrix} A_{11} & A_{21} & \cdots & A_{n1} \\ A_{12} & A_{22} & \cdots & A_{n2} \\ \vdots & & \ddots & \vdots \\ A_{1n} & A_{2n} & \cdots & A_{nn} \end{bmatrix} \begin{bmatrix} b_1 \\ b_2 \\ \vdots \\ b_n \end{bmatrix}.$$

```matlab
function x=mnhf_cramer(A,b)
%MNHF_CRAMER implements Cramer's Rule solution of Ax=b
%
% A — the matrix in question
% b — right—hand side vector
%
% Usage  mnhf_cramer(A,b);

tolerance = 1e—8;

[r,c] = size(A);        % Compute the size of A.
[rr,cc] = size(b);      % Compute the size of b.
if cc==1
 if isequal(r,c)
  if isequal(c,rr)

   % Initialize array, x.
   x = zeros(r,1);

   for ii=1:c
    % Define the matrix Aii as A with the appropriate column replaced
    % by b. Use : to facilitate matrix index referencing.
    if ii==1
     Aii = [b A(:,2:c)];
    elseif (ii>1 && ii<length(b))
     Aii = [A(:,1:ii—1) b A(:,ii+1:c)];
    else
     Aii = [A(:,1:c—1) b];
    end
    % Solve for x(ii) using the Cramer's rule formula.
    x(ii) = mnhf_determinant(Aii)/mnhf_determinant(A);
   end

   % Check residual.
   resid = norm(A*x—b,2);
   if resid>tolerance
    error('Residual exceeds tolerance.')
   end

  else
   fprintf('Size mismatch between matrix and vector.')
  end
 else
  fprintf('Matrix is not square.')
 end
else
 fprintf('b is not a column vector.')
end
```

Figure 3.2: MATLAB implementation of Cramer's rule.

or
$$x = Bb.$$

Premultiplying the original matrix equation $Ax = b$ by A^{-1} we find

$$A^{-1}Ax = A^{-1}b \quad \text{or} \quad x = A^{-1}b.$$

Comparing the last two equations, it is clear that

$$B = A^{-1} = \frac{1}{\det(A)} \begin{bmatrix} A_{11} & A_{21} & \cdots & A_{n1} \\ A_{12} & A_{22} & \cdots & A_{n2} \\ \vdots & & \ddots & \vdots \\ A_{1n} & A_{2n} & \cdots & A_{nn} \end{bmatrix} = \frac{\text{adj}(A)}{\det(A)}.$$

The above equation can be thought of as the definition for the matrix *adjoint*. The adjoint is obtained by simply replacing each element with its cofactor and then transposing the resulting matrix.

MATLAB functions for computing the adjoint and inverse of square matrices having r rows and $c = r$ columns are given in Figures 3.3 and 3.4, respectively. In the former case, nested `for` loops are employed to count over the row and column space. Note also that different formulas are applied when the row index is 1, an integer between 1 and r, and r. Likewise, different formulas are applied when the column index is 1, an integer between 1 and c, and c. As with `mnhf_determinant` and `mnhf_cramer`, the semicolon operator (`:`) is used to include or exclude particular rows or columns without which the length and complexity of the algorithm would be nontrivially increased.

In `mnhf_inverse`, reference is made to both `mnhf_determinant` and `mnhf_adjoint`. The solution is verified by separately computing AA^{-1} and $A^{-1}A$ and ensuring that these matrix products are sufficiently close to the identity matrix, I.

Inverse of diagonal and triangular matrices

Fortunately, the technical details of `mnhf_inverse` can be overlooked when computing the inverse of a diagonal matrix, D defined as

$$D = \begin{bmatrix} d_{11} & 0 & \cdots & 0 \\ 0 & d_{22} & \cdots & 0 \\ \vdots & 0 & \ddots & 0 \\ 0 & 0 & \cdots & d_{nn} \end{bmatrix}.$$

```
function adjA=mnhf_adjoint(A)
%MNHF_ADJOINT calculate adjoint of a (square) matrix
%
% A — the matrix in question
%
% Usage  mnhf_adjoint(A);

[r,c] = size(A);  % Compute the size of A.
if isequal(r,c)
 if r==1
  fprintf('Matrix has dimension 1—by—1.')
 else

  % Initialize array.
  adjA = zeros(r,c);

  % Evaluate minors.
  for ii=1:r
   for jj=1:c
    % Split out cases where we know the row (column) number is 1 or r
    % (c). Use : notation to facilitate matrix index referencing.
    if ii==1
     if jj==1
      adjA(ii,jj) = mnhf_determinant(A(2:r,2:c));
     elseif (jj>1 && jj<r)
      adjA(ii,jj) = mnhf_determinant(A(2:r,[1:jj—1,jj+1:c]));
     else
      adjA(ii,jj) = mnhf_determinant(A(2:r,1:c—1));
     end
    elseif (ii>1 && ii<r)
     if jj==1
      adjA(ii,jj) = mnhf_determinant(A([1:ii—1,ii+1:r],2:c));
     elseif (jj>1 && jj<r)
      adjA(ii,jj) = mnhf_determinant(A([1:ii—1,ii+1:r],[1:jj—1,jj+1:c]));
     else
      adjA(ii,jj) = mnhf_determinant(A([1:ii—1,ii+1:r],1:c—1));
     end
    else
     if jj==1
      adjA(ii,jj) = mnhf_determinant(A(1:r—1,2:c));
     elseif (jj>1 && jj<r)
      adjA(ii,jj) = mnhf_determinant(A(1:r—1,[1:jj—1,jj+1:c]));
     else
      adjA(ii,jj) = mnhf_determinant(A(1:r—1,1:c—1));
     end
    end
   end
  end

  % Turn minors into cofactors then compute matrix transpose.
  for ii=1:r
   for jj=1:c
    adjA(ii,jj) = (—1.0)^(ii+jj)*adjA(ii,jj);
   end
  end
  adjA = adjA';

 end
else
 fprintf('Can''t evaluate adjoint of non—square A.\n\n')
end
```

Figure 3.3: MATLAB implementation of the matrix adjoint.

```
function invA=mnhf_inverse(A)
%MNHF_INVERSE calculate matrix inverse
%
% A — the (square) matrix in question
%
% Usage  mnhf_inverse(A);

tolerance = 1e—8;

[r,c] = size(A);  % Compute the size of A.
if isequal(r,c)
 if r==1
  fprintf('Matrix has dimension 1—by—1.')
 else
  if abs(mnhf_determinant(A))<1e—6
   error('Matrix is singular; determinant is 0.')
  else
   invA = mnhf_adjoint(A)/mnhf_determinant(A);
  end

  % Check residuals.
  resid1 = norm(A*invA—eye(length(A)),2);
  resid2 = norm(invA*A—eye(length(A)),2);
  if max(resid1,resid2)>tolerance
   error('Residual exceeds tolerance.')
  end

 end
else
 fprintf('Can''t evaluate inverse of non—square A.\n\n')
end
```

Figure 3.4: MATLAB implementation of the matrix inverse.

It is easy to verify that $\boldsymbol{D}^{-1}$ is given by

$$
\boldsymbol{D}^{-1} =
\begin{bmatrix}
\frac{1}{d_{11}} & 0 & \cdots & 0 \\
0 & \frac{1}{d_{22}} & \cdots & 0 \\
\vdots & 0 & \ddots & 0 \\
0 & 0 & \cdots & \frac{1}{d_{nn}}
\end{bmatrix} .
$$

Similar considerations apply when computing the inverse of a tri-angular matrix, which happens to also be triangular. Suppose $\boldsymbol{U}$ is a given upper triangular matrix, then the elements of $\boldsymbol{V} = \boldsymbol{U}^{-1}$ can be found sequentially in an efficient manner by simply using the definition $\boldsymbol{UV} = \boldsymbol{I}$. This matrix equation, in expanded form, reads

$$
\begin{bmatrix}
u_{11} & u_{12} & \cdots & u_{1n} \\
0 & u_{22} & \cdots & u_{2n} \\
0 & 0 & \ddots & \vdots \\
0 & 0 & \cdots & u_{nn}
\end{bmatrix}
\begin{bmatrix}
v_{11} & v_{12} & \cdots & v_{1n} \\
v_{21} & v_{22} & \cdots & v_{2n} \\
 & & \ddots & \vdots \\
v_{n1} & v_{n2} & \cdots & v_{nn}
\end{bmatrix}
=
\begin{bmatrix}
1 & 0 & \cdots & 0 \\
0 & 1 & \cdots & 0 \\
 & & \ddots & \vdots \\
0 & 0 & \cdots & 1
\end{bmatrix} .
$$

We can develop the associated algorithm (*i.e.* determine the rules to solve for the elements of $\boldsymbol{V}$) by simply carrying out the matrix multi-plication on the left-hand side and equating it element-by-element to the right-hand side. First let us convince ourself that $\boldsymbol{V}$ is also upper triangular *i.e.*,

$$
v_{ij} = 0 \qquad i > j . \tag{3.19}
$$

Consider the element $(n, 1)$ which is obtained by summing the product of each element of n-th row of $\boldsymbol{U}$ (consisting mostly of zeros!) with the corresponding element of the first column of $\boldsymbol{V}$. The only non-zero term in this product is

$$
u_{nn} v_{n1} = 0 .
$$

Because $u_{nn} \neq 0$ it is clear that $v_{n1} = 0$. Applying similar arguments in a sequential manner and in the order $\{i = n, n - 1, \cdots j - 1, \ j = 1, 2, \cdots n\}$, it is easy to verify equation (3.19) and thus establish that $\boldsymbol{V}$ is also upper triangular.

The non-zero elements of $\boldsymbol{V}$ can also be found in a sequential man-ner. For each of the diagonal elements (i, i), summing the product of each element of the i-th row of $\boldsymbol{U}$ with the corresponding element of the i-th column of $\boldsymbol{V}$, the only non-zero term turns out to be

$$
v_{ii} = \frac{1}{u_{ii}} \qquad i = 1, \cdots, n . \tag{3.20}
$$

Next, for each of the elements above the main diagonal (i, j), summing the product of each element of the i-th row of $\boldsymbol{U}$ with the corresponding element of the j-th column of V, we get

$$u_{ii}v_{ij} + \sum_{r=i+1}^{j} u_{ir}v_{rj} = 0.$$

Therefore

$$v_{ij} = -\frac{1}{u_{ii}} \sum_{r=i+1}^{j} u_{ir}v_{rj} \quad j = 2, 3, \cdots, n; \ j > i; \ i = j-1, j-2, \cdots 1.$$

$$(3.21)$$

Note that equation (3.21) should be applied in a specific order as otherwise it may involve unknown elements v_{rj} on the right hand side. First, all of the diagonal elements of V (viz. v_{ii}) must be calculated from equation (3.20) as they are needed on the right-hand side of equation (3.21). Next the order indicated in equation (3.21), viz. increasing j from 2 to n and for each j decreasing i from $j-1$ to 1 should be obeyed to avoid having unknown values appearing on the right-hand side of (3.21).

A MATLAB implementation of the above algorithm is shown in Figure 3.5 to illustrate precisely the order of the calculations. By adapting `mnhf_invu`, it is relatively easy to write a MATLAB function that evaluates the inverse of a lower triangular matrix. Details are left as an exercise.

3.7.3 Gaussian elimination

Gaussian elimination is one of the most efficient algorithms for solving a large system of linear algebraic equations. It is based on a systematic generalization of a rather intuitive elimination process that we routinely apply to small, say, 2×2 systems. Consider, for instance,

$$10x_1 + 2x_2 = 4,$$

$$x_1 + 4x_2 = 3.$$

From the former equation, it is clear that $x_1 = (4 - 2x_2)/10$, which can be used to eliminate x_1 from the latter equation viz. $(4-2x_2)/10 + 4x_2 = 3$. On this basis, it can be shown that $x_2 = 0.6842$. This value is then back substituted into the former equation yielding $x_1 = 0.2632$. Of course, we could have reversed the order and eliminated x_1 from the former equation after first rearranging the latter equation as $x_1 = 3 - 4x_2$. Thus there are two steps to the algorithm: (i) forward elimination of one variable at a time until the last equation contains only a single unknown, and, (ii) back substitution. Note also that we have used the following two rules during the forward elimination process: (i) two

```
function V=mnhf_invu(U)
%MNHF_INVU inverts an upper triangular matrix
%
% U — the (square, upper triangular) matrix in question
%
% Usage  mnhf_invu(U);

[r,~] = size(U);  % Compute the size of U.
V = size(U);
for i=2:r
 V(i,1:i-1) = 0.0;   % Elements below main diagonal.
end

for i=1:r
 V(i,i)=1.0/U(i,i); % Diagonal elements.
end

for j=2:r
 for i=j-1:-1:1
  % Elements above main diagonal.
  V(i,j) = -1.0/U(i,i)*sum(U(i,i+1:j)*V(i+1:j,j));
 end
end
```

Figure 3.5: MATLAB implementation of the matrix inverse for an upper triangular matrix.

equations (or two rows) can be interchanged as this operation is merely a matter of bookkeeping and does not alter the problem formulation, and, (ii) an equation can be replaced with a linear combination of itself and another equation.

Developing these ideas further, consider

$$
\begin{bmatrix}
a_{11} & a_{12} & \cdots & a_{1n} \\
a_{21} & a_{22} & \cdots & a_{2n} \\
\vdots & \ddots & \ddots & \vdots \\
a_{n1} & a_{n2} & \cdots & a_{nn}
\end{bmatrix}
\begin{bmatrix}
x_1 \\ x_2 \\ \vdots \\ x_n
\end{bmatrix}
=
\begin{bmatrix}
b_1 \\ b_2 \\ \vdots \\ b_n
\end{bmatrix}.
\tag{3.22}
$$

In the solution of (3.22), it is more efficient to store all the coefficients in an augmented matrix array of dimension $n \times n + 1$ with the right-hand side column vector b occupying column $n + 1$. Each row then contains all the coefficients representing a particular equation of the linear system. If the augmented matrix is denoted by C then

$$
C = A|b =
\begin{bmatrix}
a_{11} & a_{12} & \cdots & a_{1n} & b_1 \\
a_{21} & a_{22} & \cdots & a_{2n} & b_2 \\
\vdots & \ddots & \ddots & \vdots & \vdots \\
a_{n1} & a_{n2} & \cdots & a_{nn} & b_n
\end{bmatrix}.
\tag{3.23}
$$

As we outline below, the system $Ax = b$ is solved by performing row operations on C.

EXAMPLE 3.3 (✎ **Gauss elimination**) *Consider the following 3×3 system:*

$$2x_1 - x_2 + x_3 = 4,$$
$$4x_1 + 3x_2 - x_3 = 6,$$
$$3x_1 + 2x_2 + 2x_3 = 15.$$

The coefficient matrix

$$A = \begin{bmatrix} 2 & -1 & 1 \\ 4 & 3 & -1 \\ 3 & 2 & 2 \end{bmatrix},$$

and the right-hand side vector

$$b = \begin{bmatrix} 4 \\ 6 \\ 15 \end{bmatrix},$$

can be combined to form the following augmented matrix:

$$C = \begin{bmatrix} 2 & -1 & 1 & 4 \\ 4 & 3 & -1 & 6 \\ 3 & 2 & 2 & 15 \end{bmatrix}.$$

Now consider the following algebraic manipulations:

$$C = \begin{bmatrix} 2 & -1 & 1 & 4 \\ 4 & 3 & -1 & 6 \\ 3 & 2 & 2 & 15 \end{bmatrix} \quad \begin{matrix} \\ \text{row } 2 - (4/2)\text{row } 1 \\ \text{row } 3 - (3/2)\text{row } 1 \end{matrix} \quad \begin{bmatrix} 2 & -1 & 1 & 4 \\ 0 & 5 & -3 & -2 \\ 0 & 7/2 & 1/2 & 9 \end{bmatrix}$$

$$\begin{bmatrix} 2 & -1 & 1 & 4 \\ 0 & 5 & -3 & -2 \\ 0 & 7/2 & 1/2 & 9 \end{bmatrix} \quad \text{row } 3 - (7/10)\text{row } 2 \quad \begin{bmatrix} 2 & -1 & 1 & 4 \\ 0 & 5 & -3 & -2 \\ 0 & 0 & 13/5 & 52/9 \end{bmatrix}.$$

The matrix equation then becomes

$$\begin{bmatrix} 2 & -1 & 1 \\ 0 & 5 & -3 \\ 0 & 0 & 13/5 \end{bmatrix} \begin{bmatrix} x_1 \\ x_2 \\ x_3 \end{bmatrix} = \begin{bmatrix} 4 \\ -2 \\ 52/5 \end{bmatrix}.$$

Obviously, the coefficient matrix has been converted to upper triangular form.

We can now perform back substitution to obtain the solution.

$$13/5x_3 = 52/5 \Rightarrow 13x_3 = 52 \text{ or } x_3 = 4.$$

Substituting this result into the second equation,

$$5x_2 - 3x_3 = 2 \Rightarrow x_2 - 3(3) = 10 \text{ or } x_2 = 2.$$

Now finally the first equation may be solved for x_1

$$2x_1 - x_2 + x_3 = 4 \rightarrow 2x_1 - 2 + (4) = 4 \Rightarrow 2x_1 = 2 \text{ or } x_1 = 1.$$

Thus the unknown vector $\boldsymbol{x}$ has been determined.

$$\boldsymbol{x} = \begin{bmatrix} x_1 \\ x_2 \\ x_3 \end{bmatrix} = \begin{bmatrix} 1 \\ 2 \\ 4 \end{bmatrix}.$$

A conceptual description of a naive Gaussian elimination algorithm is shown in Figure 3.6. All of the arithmetic operations needed to eliminate one variable at a time are identified in this illustration. We call the scheme naive because we have assumed that none of the diagonal elements are zero, although this is not a requirement for the existence of a solution. The reason for avoiding zeros on the diagonals is to avoid division by zero* in step 2 of Figure 3.6. If there are zeros on the diagonal, we can interchange two equations in such a way the diagonals do not contain zeros. This process is called *pivoting*. Even if we organize the equations in such a way that there are no zeros on the diagonal initially, we may end up with a zero on the diagonal during the elimination process (likely to occur in step 3). If that situation arises, we can continue to exchange that particular row with another one to avoid division by zero. If the matrix is *singular* we will eventually end up with an unavoidable zero on the diagonal. This situation will arise if the original set of equations is not *linearly independent*; in other words the *rank* of the matrix $\boldsymbol{A}$ is less than n. Due to the finite precision of computers, the floating point operation in step 3 of Figure 3.6 may not result in an exact zero, but rather a number having a small magnitude. As we shall explore shortly, loss of precision due to roundoff errors is a common problem with direct methods involving large systems of equations because any error introduced at one step corrupts all subsequent calculations.

A MATLAB implementation of the Gaussian elimination algorithm without pivoting is given in Figure 3.7. Note that we have minimized the number of `for` loops by leveraging MATLAB's colon (`:`) operator. Doing so improves the runtime efficiency of the algorithm.

To verify the accuracy of `mnhf_naiveGauss`, try the following simple exercise: returning to `mnhf_cct`, which we studied in Chapter 1, type

```
>>tic; mnhf_cct; toc
```

in MATLAB's Command Window. Then modify `mnhf_cct` by replacing

---

*In MATLAB, division by zero yields an `NaN` error where `NaN` indicates "not a number."

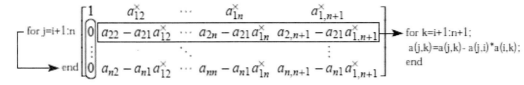

STEP 1: *Arrange A and b into an (n x n+1) matrix*

$$\begin{bmatrix} a_{11} & a_{12} & \cdots & a_{1n} & a_{1,n+1} \\ a_{21} & a_{22} & \cdots & a_{2n} & a_{2,n+1} \\ \vdots & & \ddots & & \vdots \\ a_{n1} & a_{n2} & \cdots & a_{nn} & a_{n,n+1} \end{bmatrix} \longleftarrow \left[\begin{array}{cccc|c} a_{11} & a_{12} & \cdots & a_{1n} & b_1 \\ a_{21} & a_{22} & \cdots & a_{2n} & b_2 \\ \vdots & & \ddots & & \vdots \\ a_{n1} & a_{n2} & \cdots & a_{nn} & b_n \end{array}\right]$$

for i=1:n

STEP 2: *Make diagonal elements a(i,i) into 1.0*

$$\begin{bmatrix} 1 & \frac{a_{12}}{a_{11}} & \cdots & \frac{a_{1n}}{a_{11}} & \frac{a_{1,n+1}}{a_{11}} \\ a_{21} & a_{22} & \cdots & a_{2n} & a_{2,n+1} \\ \vdots & & \ddots & & \vdots \\ a_{n1} & a_{n2} & \cdots & a_{nn} & a_{n,n+1} \end{bmatrix}$$

for j=i+1:n+1;
   a(i,j)=a(i,j)/a(i,i);
end

STEP 3 : *Make all elements in column i below diagonal into 0*

for j=i+1:n
end

$$\begin{bmatrix} 1 & a_{12}^{\times} & \cdots & a_{1n}^{\times} & a_{1,n+1}^{\times} \\ 0 & a_{22} - a_{21}a_{12}^{\times} & \cdots & a_{2n} - a_{21}a_{1n}^{\times} & a_{2,n+1} - a_{21}a_{1,n+1}^{\times} \\ \vdots & & \ddots & & \vdots \\ 0 & a_{n2} - a_{n1}a_{12}^{\times} & \cdots & a_{nn} - a_{n1}a_{1n}^{\times} & a_{n,n+1} - a_{n1}a_{1,n+1}^{\times} \end{bmatrix}$$

for k=i+1:n+1;
   a(j,k)=a(j,k)- a(j,i)*a(i,k);
end

end   *End of forward elimination. Resulting matrix structure is:*

$$\begin{bmatrix} 1 & a_{12}^{\times} & \cdots & a_{1n}^{\times} & a_{1,n+1}^{\times} \\ 0 & 1 & \cdots & a_{2n}^{\times} & a_{2,n+1}^{\times} \\ \vdots & & \ddots & & \vdots \\ 0 & 0 & \cdots & 1 & a_{n,n+1}^{\times} \end{bmatrix}$$

STEP 4: *Back substitution*

$$\begin{bmatrix} 1 & a_{12}^{\times} & \cdots & a_{1n}^{\times} & a_{1,n+1}^{\times} \\ 0 & 1 & \cdots & a_{2n}^{\times} & a_{2,n+1}^{\times} \\ \vdots & & \ddots & & \vdots \\ 0 & 0 & \cdots & 1 & a_{n,n+1}^{\times} \end{bmatrix}$$

for j=n-1:-1:1;
   a(j,n+1) = a(j,n+1) - a(j,j+1:n)*a(j+1:n,n+1);
end
a(n,n+1) = a(n,n+1)

Solution is returned in the last column a(1:n,n+1)

Figure 3.6: The naive Gaussian elimination scheme shown schematically.

```
function x=mnhf_naiveGauss(A,b)
%MNHF_NAIVEGAUSS implements Gaussian elimination
% without pivoting.
%
% A — n—by—n matrix
% b — RHS column vector of length n.
%
% Usage  mnhf_naiveGauss(A,b);

[rA,cA] = size(A);  % Compute the size of A.
[rb,cb] = size(b);  % Compute the size of b.
if cb==1
 if rA==cA
  if rA==rb
   % Step 1: form n—by—n+1 augmented matrix.
   A(:,rA+1) = b;

   for i=1:rA
    % Step 2: Make diagonal elements unity.
    A(i,i+1:rA+1) = A(i,i+1:rA+1)/A(i,i);

     % Step 3: Make elements below diagonal 0.
     for j=i+1:rA
      A(j,i+1:rA+1) = A(j,i+1:rA+1)—A(j,i)*A(i,i+1:rA+1);
     end
    end

    % Step 4: Back substitution.
    for j=rA—1:—1:1
     A(j,rA+1) = A(j,rA+1)—A(j,j+1:rA)*A(j+1:rA,rA+1);
    end
    x = A(:,rA+1);

  else
   fprintf('Rows of A ~= rows of b.')
  end
 else
  fprintf('A is not a square matrix.')
 end
else
 fprintf('b is not a column vector.')
end
```

Figure 3.7: MATLAB implementation of Gaussian elimination without pivoting.

i = A\V; with i = mnhf_naiveGauss(A,V); (if necessary, use MAT-LAB's addpath command to ensure that mnhf_cct can "see" mnhf_-naiveGauss). Is the same answer obtained in either case? Which alternative requires more computational effort?

EXAMPLE 3.4 (Loss of accuracy) *The need for pivoting can be illustrated by considering the following 2×2 system of equations:*

$$\epsilon x_1 + x_2 = 1\,,$$

$$x_1 + x_2 = 2\,,$$

where ϵ is a number small in magnitude. In matrix form, the system reads

$$\begin{bmatrix} \epsilon & 1 \\ 1 & 1 \end{bmatrix} \begin{bmatrix} x_1 \\ x_2 \end{bmatrix} = \begin{bmatrix} 1 \\ 2 \end{bmatrix}\,.$$

Using naive Gaussian elimination without rearranging the equations, we make the first diagonal element into unity, which results in

$$x_1 + \frac{1}{\epsilon}x_2 = \frac{1}{\epsilon}$$

Next we eliminate x_1 from the latter equation so that

$$\left(1 - \frac{1}{\epsilon}\right) x_2 = 2 - \frac{1}{\epsilon}\,.$$

Rearranging this expression and using back substitution, we finally get x_2 and x_1

$$x_2 = \frac{2 - \frac{1}{\epsilon}}{1 - \frac{1}{\epsilon}}\,.$$

$$x_1 = \frac{1}{\epsilon} - \frac{x_2}{\epsilon}\,.$$

The difficulty in computing x_1 as $\epsilon \to 0$ should be clear. As ϵ crosses the threshold of finite precision, taking the difference of two large numbers of comparable magnitude, can result in significant loss of numerical accuracy – see Table 3.1. Let us solve the problem once again after rearranging the equations as

$$x_1 + x_2 = 2\,,$$

$$\epsilon x_1 + x_2 = 1\,.$$

Because the diagonal element in the first equation is already unity, we can straightaway eliminate x_1 from the latter equation to obtain

$$(1 - \epsilon)x_2 = 1 - 2\epsilon \qquad or \qquad x_2 = \frac{1 - 2\epsilon}{1 - \epsilon}\,.$$

ϵ	Naive elimination without pivoting gauss(A,b)	Built-in MATLAB $A\backslash b$
1×10^{-15}	$[1.0\ldots, 1.0\ldots]$	$[1.0\ldots, 1.0\ldots]$
1×10^{-16}	$[2.0\ldots, 1.0\ldots]$	$[1.0\ldots, 1.0\ldots]$
1×10^{-17}	$[0.0\ldots, 1.0\ldots]$	$[1.0\ldots, 1.0\ldots]$

Table 3.1: Loss of precision for small ϵ.

Back substitution then yields

$$x_1 = 2 - x_2.$$

Both these computations are well behaved as $\epsilon \to 0$.

Unlike the naive Gaussian elimination algorithm presented and discussed above, MATLAB's backslash ($\backslash$) operator is clever enough to employ pivoting. The advantages of pivoting are clear from the comparison drawn in Table 3.1. Whereas `mnhf_naiveGauss` *yields unreliable output when $\epsilon = 10^{-16}$, the precision threshold for a program employing double-precision accuracy, no such difficulties are associated with the use of $\backslash$.*

This last example may seem contrived in that one usually does not explicitly include within matrices numbers that are very small in magnitude. It is important to appreciate, however, that these small numbers may arise as a result of roundoff errors from preceding arithmetic operations. Consider, for instance, an augmented matrix A defined as

$$A = \left[\begin{array}{ccc|c} 3 & 2 & -4 & 0 \\ -6 & -4 & -7 & 1 \\ 1 & 0 & -2 & -8 \end{array} \right].$$

Applying the first several steps of forward elimination, it can be shown that

$$A \sim \left[\begin{array}{ccc|c} 1 & \frac{2}{3} & -\frac{4}{3} & 0 \\ 0 & -4 + 6\left(\frac{2}{3}\right) & -15 & 1 \\ 0 & -\frac{2}{3} & -\frac{2}{3} & -8 \end{array} \right].$$

Even someone with an elementary understanding of arithmetic will realize that the diagonal element in row 2 has a value of 0 suggesting that rows 2 and 3 ought to be swapped before proceeding. Because of the roundoff error associated with the fraction $\frac{2}{3}$, however, $A(2,2)$ may be represented on the computer as a floating point number that, though very small in magnitude, is nonetheless nonzero. If this occurs and pivoting is not applied, errors of the type highlighted in this last example are not unlikely to arise. Thus, cleverly written Gaussian elimination algorithms employ pivoting not only when a given diagonal element is 0, but also when the magnitude of this diagonal element falls below some prescribed threshold. Writing such an algorithm e.g. by suitable adaptation of `mnhf_naiveGauss`, is left as an exercise.

3.7.4 Thomas's algorithm

Many problems such as the solution of boundary value problems that we will investigate in later chapters involve solving a system of linear equations $\boldsymbol{Tx} = \boldsymbol{b}$ where $\boldsymbol{T}$ has a *tridiagonal* matrix structure, *i.e.*

$$
\boldsymbol{T} = \begin{bmatrix}
d_1 & c_1 & 0 & \cdots & 0 \\
a_1 & d_2 & c_2 & \cdots & 0 \\
 & & \ddots & & \\
0 & 0 & a_{n-2} & d_{n-1} & c_{n-1} \\
0 & \cdots & 0 & a_{n-1} & d_n
\end{bmatrix}.
$$

We already know where the zero elements are, therefore we do not have to carry out the elimination steps on those entries of $\boldsymbol{T}$. However, the essential steps in the algorithm remain the same as in the Gaussian elimination scheme and are illustrated in figure 3.8. The corresponding MATLAB implementation is shown in Figure 3.9.

3.7.5 LU decomposition

Given a square matrix $\boldsymbol{A}$ of dimension $n \times n$ it is possible to write this matrix as the product of two matrices $\boldsymbol{B}$ and $\boldsymbol{C}$, *i.e.*, $\boldsymbol{A} = \boldsymbol{BC}$. This process is called *factorization* and is, in fact, not at all unique *i.e.*, there are infinitely many possibilities for $\boldsymbol{B}$ and $\boldsymbol{C}$. This is clear with a simple counting of the unknowns - viz. there are $2 \times n^2$ unknown elements in $\boldsymbol{B}$ and $\boldsymbol{C}$ while only n^2 equations can be obtained by equating each element of $\boldsymbol{A}$ with the corresponding element from the product $\boldsymbol{BC}$. These extra degrees of freedom can be used to specify a specific structure for $\boldsymbol{B}$ and $\boldsymbol{C}$. For example, we can require $\boldsymbol{B} = \boldsymbol{L}$ be a lower triangular matrix and $\boldsymbol{C} = \boldsymbol{U}$ be an upper triangular matrix. This process is called LU factorization or decomposition. Because each triangular matrix has $n \times (n+1)/2$ unknowns, we still have a total of $n^2 + n$ unknowns. The extra n degrees of freedom are often used in one of three ways as explained below.

1. The *Doolittle* method assigns the diagonal elements of $\boldsymbol{L}$ to be unity so that $l_{ii} = 1$,

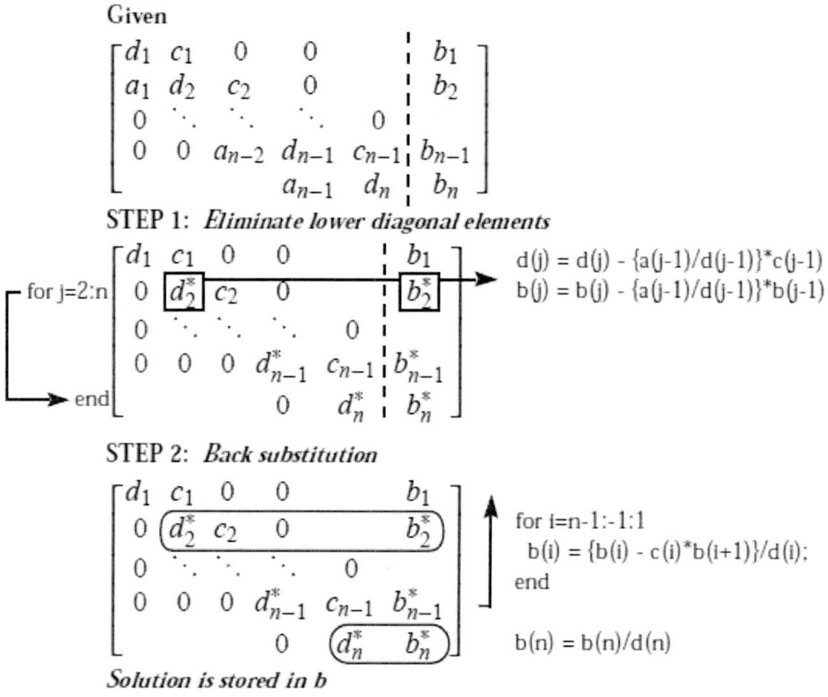

Given

$$\begin{bmatrix} d_1 & c_1 & 0 & 0 & & \vdots & b_1 \\ a_1 & d_2 & c_2 & 0 & & \vdots & b_2 \\ 0 & \ddots & \ddots & & \ddots & 0 & \vdots \\ 0 & 0 & a_{n-2} & d_{n-1} & c_{n-1} & \vdots & b_{n-1} \\ & & & a_{n-1} & d_n & \vdots & b_n \end{bmatrix}$$

STEP 1: *Eliminate lower diagonal elements*

for j=2:n

$$\begin{bmatrix} d_1 & c_1 & 0 & 0 & & \vdots & b_1 \\ 0 & \boxed{d_2^*} & c_2 & 0 & & \vdots & \boxed{b_2^*} \\ 0 & \ddots & \ddots & & \ddots & 0 & \vdots \\ 0 & 0 & 0 & d_{n-1}^* & c_{n-1} & \vdots & b_{n-1}^* \\ & & & 0 & d_n^* & \vdots & b_n^* \end{bmatrix}$$

end

$d(j) = d(j) - \{a(j-1)/d(j-1)\}^*c(j-1)$

$b(j) = b(j) - \{a(j-1)/d(j-1)\}^*b(j-1)$

STEP 2: *Back substitution*

$$\begin{bmatrix} d_1 & c_1 & 0 & 0 & & b_1 \\ 0 & \boxed{d_2^* \quad c_2 \quad 0} & & & \boxed{b_2^*} \\ 0 & \ddots & \ddots & \ddots & & 0 \\ 0 & 0 & 0 & d_{n-1}^* & c_{n-1} & b_{n-1}^* \\ & & & 0 & \boxed{d_n^*} & \boxed{b_n^*} \end{bmatrix}$$

for i=n-1:-1:1

   $b(i) = \{b(i) - c(i)^*b(i+1)\}/d(i);$

end

$b(n) = b(n)/d(n)$

Solution is stored in b

Figure 3.8: Steps involved in the Thomas algorithm.

```
function x=mnhf_thomas(A,b)
%MNHF_THOMAS implements the Thomas algorithm.
%
% A - n-by-n tridiagonal matrix
%     (do not verify tridiagonal structure)
% b - n-by-1 RHS column vector
%
% Usage  mnhf_thomas(A,b)

[r,c] = size(A);   % Compute the size of A.
[rr,cc] = size(b); % Compute the size of b.
if cc==1
 if isequal(r,c)
  if isequal(c,rr)

   % Extract elements along main/upper/lower diagonals.
   d = diag(A,0);
   a = diag(A,-1);
   c = diag(A,1);

   % Eliminate elements below the main diagonal.
   for j = 2:r
    d(j) = d(j)-a(j-1)/d(j-1)*c(j-1);
    b(j) = b(j)-a(j-1)/d(j-1)*b(j-1);
   end

   % Perform back substitution.
   b(r) = b(r)/d(r);
   for j = r-1:-1:1
    b(j) = (b(j)-c(j)*b(j+1))/d(j);
   end

   % Return solution.
   x = b;

  else
   fprintf('Size mismatch between matrix and vector.')
  end
 else
  fprint('Matrix is not square.')
 end
else
 fprint('b is not a column vector.');
end
```

Figure 3.9: MATLAB implementation of the Thomas algorithm.

2. The *Crout* method assigns the diagonal elements of U to be unity so that $u_{ii} = 1$,

3. The *Cholesky* method assigns the diagonal elements of L to be equal to those of U so that $l_{ii} = u_{ii}$.

While a simple degree of freedom analysis indicates that it is possible to factorize a matrix into a product of lower and upper triangular matrices, it does not tell us how to find out the unknown elements. For this purpose, consider the product of L and U as shown in expanded form below. All of the elements of L and U are unknown with the exception of the diagonal elements of U, which we have set to unity (Crout's method). By carrying out the matrix product on the left-hand side and equating element-by-element to the right-hand side matrix, we can develop a sufficient number of equations to evaluate all of the unknown elements. The trick is to carry out the calculations in a particular sequence so that no more than one unknown appears in each equation.

$$\begin{bmatrix} l_{11} & 0 & 0 & \cdots & 0 \\ l_{21} & l_{22} & 0 & \cdots & 0 \\ l_{31} & l_{32} & l_{33} & \cdots & 0 \\ \vdots & \vdots & \vdots & \ddots & 0 \\ l_{n1} & l_{n2} & l_{n3} & \cdots & l_{nn} \end{bmatrix} \begin{bmatrix} 1 & u_{12} & u_{13} & \cdots & u_{1n} \\ 0 & 1 & u_{23} & \cdots & u_{2n} \\ 0 & 0 & 1 & \cdots & u_{3n} \\ \vdots & \vdots & \vdots & \ddots & \vdots \\ 0 & 0 & 0 & \cdots & 1 \end{bmatrix} = \begin{bmatrix} a_{11} & a_{12} & \cdots & a_{1n} \\ a_{21} & a_{22} & \cdots & a_{2n} \\ a_{31} & a_{32} & \cdots & a_{3n} \\ \vdots & \vdots & \cdots & \vdots \\ a_{n1} & a_{n2} & \cdots & a_{nn} \end{bmatrix}$$

Let us first consider the elements in column 1 of L. Multiplying row 1 of L by column 1 of U then row 2 of L by column 1 of U, etc. yields

$$l_{i1} = a_{i1} \qquad i = 1, 2, \cdots n. \tag{3.24}$$

Next* we focus on the elements in the first row of U and multiply row 1 of L by columns 2 through n of U. We therefore find

$$u_{1j} = a_{1j}/l_{11} \qquad j = 2, 3, \cdots n. \tag{3.25}$$

Continuing in this way and alternating between columns of L and rows of U, the following general expressions can be derived:

$$l_{ij} = a_{ij} - \sum_{k=1}^{j-1} l_{ik}u_{kj} \qquad j = 2, 3, \cdots n \quad i = j, j+1, \cdots n, \tag{3.26}$$

$$u_{ji} = \frac{a_{ji} - \sum_{k=1}^{j-1} l_{jk}u_{ki}}{l_{jj}} \qquad j = 2, 3, \cdots n \quad i = j+1, j+2, \cdots n. \tag{3.27}$$

Equations (3.24-3.27) form the basic algorithm for LU decomposition. In order to illustrate the implementation of equations (3.24-3.27), a MATLAB function called `mnhf_lu` is shown in Figure 3.10. Note that MATLAB provides its own built-in function for LU decomposition called `lu`.

---

*It would be inefficient to proceed to the 2nd column of L. Why?

```
function [L,U]=mnhf_lu(A)
%MNHF_LU implements LU decomposition via the Crout Method.
%
% A — n—by—n matrix
%
% Usage  [L,U] = mnhf_lu(A)

[r,c] = size(A);   % Compute the size of A.
if isequal(r,c)
 %Step 1: first column of L.
 L(:,1) = A(:,1);

 %Step 2: first row of U.
 U(1,:) = A(1,:)/L(1,1);

 %Step 3: Alternate between columns of L and rows of U.
 for j=2:r
  for i=j:r
   L(i,j) = A(i,j)—sum(L(i,1:j—1)'.*U(1:j—1,j));
  end
  U(j,j) = 1;
  for i=j+1:r
   U(j,i) = (A(j,i)—sum(L(j,1:j—1)'.*U(1:j—1,i)))/L(j,j);
  end
 end
else
 fprintf('Can''t decompose a non—square A.\n\n')
end
```

Figure 3.10: MATLAB implementation of the LU decomposition algorithm (Crout's method).

EXAMPLE 3.5 (✎LU **factors from Gauss elimination**) *Recall Example 3.3 where the given equations were solved by Gaussian elimination. Here, we want to keep a record of all the operations that are executed when reducing the coefficient matrix to triangular form.*

The coefficient matrix reads

$$A = \begin{bmatrix} 2 & -1 & 1 \\ 4 & 3 & -1 \\ 3 & 2 & 2 \end{bmatrix}.$$

We shall construct L *from an identity matrix of the same size placed to the left of* A.

$$A = \begin{bmatrix} 1 & 0 & 0 \\ 0 & 1 & 0 \\ 0 & 0 & 1 \end{bmatrix} \begin{bmatrix} 2 & -1 & 1 \\ 4 & 3 & -1 \\ 3 & 2 & 2 \end{bmatrix}.$$

To reduce the left matrix to lower triangular form, row 2 of the right matrix is multiplied by 1/2 and then subtracted from row 1. Row 3 is then multiplied by 2/3 and subtracted from row 1. These factors are recorded in the respective positions in column 1 of the left matrix.

$$A = \begin{bmatrix} 1 & 0 & 0 \\ 2 & 1 & 0 \\ 3/2 & 0 & 1 \end{bmatrix} \begin{bmatrix} 2 & -1 & 1 \\ 0 & 5 & -3 \\ 0 & 7/2 & 1/2 \end{bmatrix}.$$

We then eliminate the element in row 3, column 2 of the right matrix take care to include the appropriate factors in the left matrix. This yields the lower and upper triangular matrices as desired.

$$A = LU = \begin{bmatrix} 1 & 0 & 0 \\ 2 & 1 & 0 \\ 3/2 & 7/10 & 1 \end{bmatrix} \begin{bmatrix} 2 & -1 & 1 \\ 0 & 5 & -3 \\ 0 & 0 & 13/5 \end{bmatrix}$$

We can, of course, verify that $A = LU$ *by multiplying* L *and* U *together to obtain* A.

Recognizing that A can be factored into the product LU, one can implement an efficient scheme for solving a system of linear algebraic equations $Ax = b$ repeatedly, particularly when the matrix A remains unchanged, but different solutions are required for different forcing terms on the right hand side, b. The equation

$$Ax = b$$

can be written as

$$LUx = b.$$

We let $\boldsymbol{U}\boldsymbol{x} = \boldsymbol{z}$ so that

$$\boldsymbol{L}\boldsymbol{z} = \boldsymbol{b}\,,$$

which can be solved for $\boldsymbol{z}$

$$\boldsymbol{z} = \boldsymbol{L}^{-1}\boldsymbol{b}\,.$$

Finally we solve for $\boldsymbol{x}$ from

$$\boldsymbol{x} = \boldsymbol{U}^{-1}\boldsymbol{z}\,.$$

The operations required for forward elimination and back substitution are stored in the LU factored matrices, which, as we have already seen, are computationally-inexpensive to invert. Hence two additional vector-matrix products provide a solution for each column vector $\boldsymbol{b}$.

3.8 Iterative algorithms for systems of linear equations

The direct methods discussed in §3.7 have the advantage of producing a solution in a finite number of calculations. They suffer, however, from loss of precision due to accumulated round off errors. This problem is particularly severe in large dimensional systems (more than 10,000 equations). Iterative methods, on the other hand, produce the result in an asymptotic manner by repeated application of a simple algorithm. Hence the number of floating point operations required to produce the final result cannot be known *a priori*. But iterative methods have the natural ability to minimize errors at every step of the iteration.

Iterative methods rely on the concepts developed in Chapter 2. They are naturally extended from a single equation (one-dimensional system) to a system of equations (n-dimensional system). The exposition parallels that of §2.7 on fixed point iteration schemes. Given an equation of the form $\boldsymbol{A}\boldsymbol{x} = \boldsymbol{b}$ we can rearrange it into the form

$$\boldsymbol{x}^{(p+1)} = \boldsymbol{G}(\boldsymbol{x}^{(p)}) \qquad p = 0, 1, \cdots \tag{3.28}$$

Here we can view the vector $\boldsymbol{x}$ as a point in a n-dimensional vector space and the above equation as an iterative map that maps a point $\boldsymbol{x}^{(p)}$ into another point $\boldsymbol{x}^{(p+1)}$ in the n-dimensional vector space*. Starting with an initial guess $\boldsymbol{x}^{(0)}$ we calculate successive iterates $\boldsymbol{x}^{(1)}$, $\boldsymbol{x}^{(2)}$...until the sequence converges. The only difference from Chapter 2 is that the above iteration is applied to a higher dimensional system of n (linear) equations. Note that $\boldsymbol{G}(\boldsymbol{x})$ is also vector. Because the system

---

*Note that we now use p rather than i as in equation (2.12); in this chapter, i is reserved for the row index of a matrix or column vector.

consists of linear equations, G will be a linear function of x which is constructed from the matrix A and the right-hand side column vector b. Generically, G can be represented as

$$x^{(p+1)} = G(x^{(p)}) = Tx^{(p)} + c. \tag{3.29}$$

(Note that, in this section, T is not supposed to represent a tridiagonal matrix.) In §2.7 we saw that a given equation $f(x) = 0$ can be rearranged into the form $x = g(x)$ in multiple ways. In a similar manner, a given equation $Ax = b$ can be rearranged into the form $x^{(p+1)} = G(x^{(p)})$ in more than one way. Different choices of G result in different iterative methods. In §2.7 we also saw that the condition for convergence of the sequence $x_{i+1} = g(x_i)$ is $g'(r) < 1$. Recognizing that the derivative of $G(x^{(p)})$ with respect to $x^{(p)}$ is a matrix, $G' = T$, a convergence condition similar to that found for the scalar case must depend on the properties of the matrix T. Another way to demonstrate this is as follows. Once the sequence $x^{(1)}$, $x^{(2)}$...converges to r, say, equation (3.29) becomes

$$r = Tr + c.$$

Subtracting equation (3.29) from the above expression yields

$$x^{(p+1)} - r = T(x^{(p)} - r).$$

Now, recognizing that $x^{(p)} - r = \epsilon^{(p)}$ is a measure of the error at iteration step p, we have

$$\epsilon^{(p+1)} = T\epsilon^{(p)}.$$

Thus, the error at step $p + 1$ depends on the error at step p. If the matrix T has the property of amplifying the error at any step, then the iterative sequence will diverge. The property of the matrix T that determines this feature is called the *spectral radius*. The spectral radius is defined as the largest eigenvalue in magnitude of T. In order for convergence to occur, the spectral radius of T should be less than one, *i.e.*

$$\rho(T) < 1. \tag{3.30}$$

Recall that eigenvalues (and eigenvectors) are most easily computed using MATLAB's built-in function `eig`.

3.8.1 Jacobi iteration

The Jacobi iteration rearranges the system of equations in the form

$$
\begin{aligned}
x_1^{(p+1)} &= \frac{1}{a_{11}}\left(b_1 - a_{12}x_2^{(p)} - a_{13}x_3^{(p)} - \cdots - a_{1n}x_n^{(p)}\right), \\
x_j^{(p+1)} &= \frac{1}{a_{jj}}\left[b_j - \sum_{k=1}^{j-1} a_{jk}x_k^{(p)} - \sum_{k=j+1}^{n} a_{jk}x_k^{(p)}\right], \\
x_n^{(p+1)} &= \frac{1}{a_{nn}}\left(b_n - a_{n1}x_1^{(p)} - a_{n2}x_2^{(p)} - \cdots - a_{n,n-1}x_{n-1}^{(p)}\right),
\end{aligned}
\tag{3.31}
$$

where the variable x_j has been extracted from the j-th equation and expressed as a function of the remaining variables. The above set of equations can be applied repetitively to update each component of the unknown column vector $\boldsymbol{x} = (x_1, x_2, \cdots x_n)'$ provided an initial guess is supplied for $\boldsymbol{x}$.

A MATLAB implementation of the Jacobi algorithm is given in Figure 3.11.

Residual form

We can obtain an equivalent and more convenient form of equation (3.31) by adding and subtracting $x_j^{(p)}$ to/from the right side of the equation to yield

$$
x_j^{(p+1)} = x_j^{(p)} + \frac{1}{a_{jj}}\left[b_j - \sum_{k=1}^{n} a_{jk}x_k^{(p)}\right]
\tag{3.32}
$$

Equation (3.32) can be written in a more general form as

$$
\begin{aligned}
x_j^{(p+1)} &= x_j^{(p)} + \frac{R_j^{(p)}}{a_{jj}} \qquad j = 1, 2, \cdots n \\
R_j^{(p)} &= b_j - \sum_{k=1}^{n} a_{jk}x_k^{(p)}
\end{aligned}
$$

Here $R_j^{(p)}$ is called the residual form of equation j. Residuals are the net values of the equations evaluated with the approximate solution vector $\boldsymbol{x}^{(p)}$.

Matrix form

Equation (3.31) can also be written* in matrix form as

$$
\boldsymbol{L}\boldsymbol{x}^{(p)} + \boldsymbol{D}\boldsymbol{x}^{(p+1)} + \boldsymbol{U}\boldsymbol{x}^{(p)} = \boldsymbol{b},
\tag{3.33}
$$

---

*The MATLAB functions `diag`, `tril` and `triu` are useful when extracting parts of a given matrix $\boldsymbol{A}$.

```matlab
function x=mnhf_Jacobi(A,b,x,tol,Nmax)
%MNHF_JACOBI Solve Ax=b using the Jacobi iterative algorithm.
%
% A — (n—by—n) matrix
% b — (n—by—1) RHS vector
% x — initial guess for the solution, x.
% tol — tolerance
% Nmax — maximum number of iterations
%
% Usage  mnhf_Jacobi(A,b,x,1e—8,1000); or
%        mnhf_Jacobi(A,b,ones(length(b),1),1e—8,1000);

[r,c] = size(A);        % Compute the size of A.
[rr,cc] = size(b);      % Compute the size of b.
if cc==1
 if isequal(r,c)
  if isequal(c,rr)

   x_new = zeros(size(x));  % Initialize x_new.
   count = 0;               % Initialize counter.

   while ( (norm(A*x—b)>tol) && (count<=Nmax) )
    % Solve for the elements of x_new.
    x_new(1) = 1.0/A(1,1)*(b(1)—A(1,2:r)*x(2:r));
    for ii=2:r—1
     x_new(ii) = 1.0/A(ii,ii)*(b(ii)—A(ii,1:ii—1)*x(1:ii—1) ...
               —A(ii,ii+1:r)*x(ii+1:r));
    end
    x_new(r) = 1.0/A(r,r)*(b(r)—A(r,1:r—1)*x(1:r—1));
    x = x_new;
    count = count+1;  % Increment counter.
   end

   if count>Nmax
    error('Maximum number of iterations exceeded.')
   end

  else
   error('Size mismatch between matrix and vector.')
  end
 else
  error('Matrix is not square.')
 end
else
 error('b is not a column vector.')
end

end
```

Figure 3.11: MATLAB implementation of the Jacobi algorithm.

where the matrices D, L and U are defined in terms of the components of A. To wit,

$$D = \begin{bmatrix} a_{11} & 0 & \cdots & 0 \\ 0 & a_{22} & \cdots & 0 \\ \vdots & 0 & \ddots & 0 \\ 0 & 0 & \cdots & a_{nn} \end{bmatrix}$$

$$L = \begin{bmatrix} 0 & 0 & \cdots & 0 \\ a_{21} & 0 & \cdots & 0 \\ \vdots & & \ddots & 0 \\ a_{n1} & a_{n2} & \cdots & 0 \end{bmatrix} \qquad U = \begin{bmatrix} 0 & a_{12} & \cdots & a_{1n} \\ 0 & 0 & \cdots & a_{2n} \\ 0 & 0 & \ddots & \vdots \\ 0 & 0 & \cdots & 0 \end{bmatrix}$$

Rearranging (3.33), it can be shown that

$$x^{(p+1)} = D^{-1}[b - (L + U)x^{(p)}], \qquad (3.34)$$

and hence $G(x^{(p)}) = -D^{-1}(L + U)x^{(p)} + D^{-1}b$ and $G' = T = -D^{-1}(L + U)$.

The Jacobi scheme has been shown to converge as long as the original matrix A is diagonally dominant such that

$$a_{ii} > \sum_{j=1, j \neq i}^{n} |a_{ij}| \qquad i = 1, 2, \cdots n. \qquad (3.35)$$

An examination of equation (3.31) reveals that none of the diagonal elements can be zero. If any are found to be zero, one can easily exchange the positions of any two equations to avoid a division by zero (or NaN) error. Equation (3.31) is used in actual computational implementations, while the matrix form of equation (3.34) is useful for conceptual descriptions and convergence analysis. Note that each element in equation (3.31) can be updated independent of all the others because the right-hand side of equation (3.31) is evaluated at the p-th level of iteration. This method requires that $x^{(p)}$ and $x^{(p+1)}$ be stored as two separate vectors until all the elements of $x^{(p+1)}$ have been updated using equation (3.31). A minor variation of the algorithm that uses a new value of the element in $x^{(p+1)}$ as soon as it is available yields a new scheme referred to as the Gauss-Seidel algorithm. As noted in the next sub-section, Gauss-Seidel has the dual advantages of faster convergence and reduced storage requirements.

3.8.2 Gauss-Seidel iteration

Now, we rearrange the system of equations in the form

$$
\begin{aligned}
x_1^{(p+1)} &= \frac{1}{a_{11}}\left(b_1 - a_{12}x_2^{(p)} - a_{13}x_3^{(p)} - \cdots - a_{1n}x_n^{(p)}\right), \\
x_j^{(p+1)} &= \frac{1}{a_{jj}}\left[b_j - \sum_{k=1}^{j-1} a_{jk}x_k^{(p+1)} - \sum_{k=j+1}^{n} a_{jk}x_k^{(p)}\right], \\
x_n^{(p+1)} &= \frac{1}{a_{nn}}\left(b_n - a_{n1}x_1^{(p+1)} - a_{n2}x_2^{(p+1)} - \cdots - a_{n,n-1}x_{n-1}^{(p+1)}\right).
\end{aligned}
\tag{3.36}
$$

Observe that known values of the elements in $x^{(p+1)}$ are used on the right-hand side of the above equation as soon as they become available. In a computer program such as that shown in Figure 3.12, there is no need to assign separate arrays for the p and $p+1$ levels of iteration. Using just a single array for x will automatically propagate the newest values as soon as they are updated.

Residual form

Equation (3.36) can be written in terms of the residuals R_j by adding and subtracting $x_j^{(p)}$ to/from the right-hand side of equation (3.36) and rearranging to obtain

$$
\begin{aligned}
x_j^{(p+1)} &= x_k^{(p)} + \frac{R_j^{(p)}}{a_{jj}} \qquad j = 1, 2, \cdots n \\
R_j^{(p)} &= b_j - \sum_{k=1}^{j-1} a_{jk}x_k^{(p+1)} - \sum_{k=1}^{n} a_{jk}x_k^{(p)}.
\end{aligned}
$$

Matrix form

The Gauss-Seidel scheme can also be written symbolically as

$$
\boldsymbol{L}x^{(p+1)} + \boldsymbol{D}x^{(p+1)} + \boldsymbol{U}x^{(p)} = \boldsymbol{b},
$$

where $\boldsymbol{D}$, $\boldsymbol{L}$ and $\boldsymbol{U}$ are defined as before. Factoring $x^{(p+1)}$ leads to

$$
x^{(p+1)} = (\boldsymbol{L} + \boldsymbol{D})^{-1}(\boldsymbol{b} - \boldsymbol{U}x^{(p)}),
\tag{3.37}
$$

and hence $\boldsymbol{G}(x^{(p)}) = -(\boldsymbol{L} + \boldsymbol{D})^{-1}\boldsymbol{U}x^{(p)} + (\boldsymbol{L} + \boldsymbol{D})^{-1}\boldsymbol{b}$ and $\boldsymbol{G}' = \boldsymbol{T} = -(\boldsymbol{L} + \boldsymbol{D})^{-1}\boldsymbol{U}$. Thus the convergence of the Gauss-Seidel scheme depends on the spectral radius of the matrix $\boldsymbol{T} = -(\boldsymbol{L} + \boldsymbol{D})^{-1}\boldsymbol{U}$. As with Jacobi, this method has also been shown to converge provided $\boldsymbol{A}$ is diagonally dominant.

```
function x=mnhf_GaussSeidel(A,b,x,tol,Nmax)
%MNHF_GAUSSSEIDEL Solve Ax=b using the Gauss-Seidel iterative algorithm.
%
% A - (n-by-n) matrix
% b - (n-by-1) RHS vector
% x - initial guess for the solution, x.
% tol - tolerance
% Nmax - maximum number of iterations
%
% Usage  mnhf_GaussSeidel(A,b,x,1e-8,1000); or
%        mnhf_GaussSeidel(A,b,ones(length(b),1),1e-8,1000);

[r,c] = size(A);        % Compute the size of A.
[rr,cc] = size(b);      % Compute the size of b.
if cc==1
 if isequal(r,c)
  if isequal(c,rr)

   count = 0;           % Initialize counter.

   while ( (norm(A*x-b)>tol) && (count<=Nmax) )
    % Solve for the elements of x.
    x(1) = 1.0/A(1,1)*(b(1)-A(1,2:r)*x(2:r));
    for ii=2:r-1
     x(ii) = 1.0/A(ii,ii)*(b(ii)-A(ii,1:ii-1)*x(1:ii-1) ...
             -A(ii,ii+1:r)*x(ii+1:r));
    end
    x(r) = 1.0/A(r,r)*(b(r)-A(r,1:r-1)*x(1:r-1));
    count = count+1;  % Increment counter.
   end

   if count>Nmax
    error('Maximum number of iterations exceeded.')
   end

  else
   error('Size mismatch between matrix and vector.')
  end
 else
  error('Matrix is not square.')
 end
else
 error('b is not a column vector.')
end

end
```

Figure 3.12: MATLAB implementation of the Gauss-Seidel algorithm. Note the similarity with the Jacobi algorithm of Figure 3.11.

EXAMPLE 3.6 (Iteration counting for Jacobi and Gauss-Seidel)
Suppose we were to apply the Gauss-Seidel algorithm in solving three linear equations in three unknowns. How many iterations would be necessary if we were to solve
  (i) $\mathbf{L}\mathbf{x} = \mathbf{b}$, $\boldsymbol{L}$ *is a diagonally dominant lower triangular matrix?*
  (ii) $\mathbf{U}\mathbf{x} = \mathbf{b}$, $\boldsymbol{U}$ *is a diagonally dominant upper triangular matrix?*
Now repeat the above calculations but consider the Jacobi algorithm rather than Gauss-Seidel.

Solution (part i):
Exploiting the fact that the entries above the main diagonal are all zero, we write the equations for x_1, x_2 and x_3 as

$$x_1^{p+1} = \frac{1}{a_{11}}\left(b_1\right),$$

$$x_2^{p+1} = \frac{1}{a_{22}}\left(b_2 - a_{21}x_1^{(\varphi)}\right),$$

$$x_3^{p+1} = \frac{1}{a_{33}}\left(b_3 - a_{31}x_1^{(\varphi)} - a_{32}x_2^{(\varphi)}\right).$$

where $\varphi = p + 1$ for Gauss-Seidel and $\varphi = p$ for Jacobi. For either method, we solve straightaway for x_1 to machine precision. Where Gauss-Seidel and Jacobi differ has to do with whether this solution for x_1 is used immediately or only after some further calculations. With Gauss-Seidel, the solution for x_1 is used immediately and by solving the second equation, we can determine x_2, again to machine precision. The solutions to x_1 and x_2 are then used in the third equation, allowing us to determine x_3. Thus only a single iteration is required. Conversely when using Jacobi, $x_2^{(1)}$ is based on $x_1^{(0)}$, an initial guess, rather than $x_1^{(1)}$, the machine-precision exact solution. Thus unless we are extremely lucky with this initial guess, $x_2^{(1)}$ will not correspond to the machine-precision exact solution for x_2. Rather, this machine-precision exact solution for x_2 would only be obtained after solving the second equation a second time. In like fashion, the machine-precision exact solution for x_3 is only obtained after solving the third equation a third time. Jacobi therefore requires three iterations.

Solution (part ii):
Exploiting the fact that the entries below the main diagonal are all zero, we write the equations for x_1, x_2 and x_3 as

$$x_1^{p+1} = \frac{1}{a_{11}}\left(b_1 - a_{12}x_2^{(\varphi)} - a_{13}x_3^{(\varphi)}\right),$$

$$x_2^{p+1} = \frac{1}{a_{22}} \left(b_2 - a_{23} x_3^{(\varphi)} \right),$$

$$x_3^{p+1} = \frac{1}{a_{33}} \left(b_3 \right).$$

It should be obvious that $x_1^{(1)}$ and $x_2^{(1)}$ do not correspond to the machine-precision exact solutions for x_1 and x_2, respectively. Conversely, $x_3^{(1)}$ does correspond to the machine-precision exact solution for x_3. Using this fact at the next iteration step gives a machine-precision exact solution for x_2 but not for x_1, whose value relies on $x_2^{(1)}$. The machine-precision exact solution for x_1 is therefore obtained only by solving the first equation a third time. Consequently three iterations are needed for both Gauss-Seidel and Jacobi.

EXAMPLE 3.7 (✎Jacobi and Gauss-Seidel) *To further illustrate the above iterative methods, let us solve the following system of equations with initial values $\boldsymbol{x}^{(0)} = [0, 0, 0]'$:*

$$\begin{aligned}
3x_1 + x_2 - 2x_3 &= 9, \\
-x_1 + 4x_2 - 3x_3 &= -8, \\
x_1 - x_2 + 4x_3 &= 1.
\end{aligned} \tag{3.38}$$

(i) Jacobi iteration:
Equations (3.38) can be rearranged to yield the following residuals:

$$\begin{aligned}
R_1 &= 9 - 3x_1 - x_2 + 2x_3, \\
R_2 &= -8 + x_1 - 4x_2 + 3x_3, \\
R_3 &= 1 - x_1 + x_2 - 4x_3.
\end{aligned} \tag{3.39}$$

Substituting the initial values $\boldsymbol{x}^{(0)} = [0, 0, 0]'$, we find that $R_1 = 9$, $R_2 = -9$ and $R_3 = 1$. Next, we apply these values into the updating equation

$$x_j^{(p+1)} = x_j^{(p)} + \frac{R_j^{(p)}}{a_{jj}}.$$

Step 1 – $p = 0$, $j = 1, 2, 3$:

$$x_1^{(1)} = x_1^{(0)} + \frac{R_1^{(0)}}{a_{11}} = 0 + \frac{9}{3} = 3.0000,$$

$$x_2^{(1)} = x_1^{(0)} + \frac{R_2^{(0)}}{a_{22}} = 0 + \frac{-8}{4} = -2.0000,$$

$$x_3^{(1)} = x_1^{(0)} + \frac{R_3^{(0)}}{a_{33}} = 0 + \frac{1}{4} = 0.2500.$$

p	x_1	x_2	x_3	L_2-norm
0	0.0000	0.0000	0.0000	-
1	3.0000	-2.0000	0.2500	3.6142
2	3.8333	-1.0625	-1.0000	1.7708
3	2.6875	-1.7917	-0.9740	1.3584
4	2.9479	-2.0586	-0.8698	0.3872
5	3.1063	-1.9154	-1.0016	0.2510
6	2.9707	-1.9746	-1.0054	0.1481
7	2.9879	-2.0114	-0.9863	0.0449
8	3.0129	-1.9928	-0.9998	0.0340
9	2.9977	-1.9966	-1.0014	0.0158
10	2.9979	-2.0016	-0.9986	0.0057

Table 3.2: Jacobi iteration results.

Step 2 – $p = 1$, $j = 1, 2, 3$ and $\boldsymbol{x}^{(1)} = [3.0000, -2.0000, 0.2500]'$ so that $R_1^{(1)} = 2.5$, $R_2^{(1)} = 3.75$ and $R_3^{(1)} = -5$. Thus

$$
\begin{aligned}
x_1^{(2)} &= 3.0000 + \frac{2.5}{3} = 3.8333\,, \\
x_2^{(2)} &= -2.0000 + \frac{3.75}{4} = -1.0025\,, \\
x_3^{(2)} &= 0.2500 + \frac{-5}{4} = -1.0000\,.
\end{aligned}
$$

The above sequence of computations can be repeated until a specified convergence criterion has been met. For instance, we might require that

$$
\left| \frac{x_j^{(p+1)} - x_j^{(p)}}{x_j^{(p+1)}} \right| \leq \epsilon_S\,,
$$

or a specified norm is realized, e.g.

$$
\left\| x_j^{(p+1)} - x_j^{(p)} \right\|_2 \leq \epsilon_S\,.
$$

Table 3.2 shows 10 iterations of the above method.

(ii) Gauss-Seidel iteration:

Table 3.3 shows 10 iterations carried out for the same problem using Gauss-Seidel. The superiority of the Gauss-Seidel algorithm over the Jacobi algorithm is plainly evident: Gauss-Seidel has converged to 1×10^{-5} in 10 iterations while Jacobi has has only reached 5.7×10^{-3}. In other words, more iterations are required for Jacobi to achieve the same level of numerical accuracy.

p	x_1	x_2	x_3	L_2-norm
0	0.0000	0.0000	0.0000	-
1	3.0000	-1.2500	-0.8125	3.3500
2	2.8750	-1.8906	-0.9414	0.6653
3	3.0026	-1.9554	-0.9895	0.1510
4	2.9921	-1.9941	-0.9966	0.0407
5	3.0003	-1.9973	-0.9994	0.0093
6	2.9995	-1.9997	-0.9998	0.0025
7	3.0000	-1.9998	-1.0000	5.7698e-4
8	3.0000	-2.0000	-1.0000	1.5805e-4
9	3.0000	-2.0000	-1.0000	3.6483e-5
10	3.0000	-2.0000	-1.0000	1.0037e-5

Table 3.3: Gauss-Seidel iteration results.

3.8.3 Successive over-relaxation (SOR)

A relaxation scheme can be thought of as a convergence acceleration strategy that can be applied to any of the basic iterative methods like the Jacobi or Gauss-Seidel algorithms. We introduce an extra parameter ω often called the *relaxation parameter* and choose its value in such a way that we can either speed up convergence by selecting $\omega > 1$ (called *over-relaxation*) or, in some difficult problems with poor initial guesses, we may enlarge the region of convergence using $\omega < 1$ (called *under-relaxation*). Let us illustrate the implementation using the Gauss-Seidel algorithm. The equation of interest reads

$$t := x_j^{(p+1)} = \frac{1}{a_{jj}} \left[b_j - \sum_{k=1}^{j-1} a_{jk} x_k^{(p+1)} - \sum_{k=j+1}^{n} a_{jk} x_k^{(p)} \right]. \qquad (3.36)$$

Instead of accepting the value of $x_j^{(p+1)}$ computed from the above formula as the current value, we instead store the right-hand side of (3.36) in a temporary variable t and form a better (or accelerated) estimate of $x_j^{(p+1)}$ via

$$x_j^{(p+1)} = x_j^{(p)} + \omega(t - x_j^{(p)}). \qquad (3.37)$$

Observe that if $\omega = 1$, the method reverts to the standard Gauss-Seidel scheme. By contrast, for $\omega > 1$ the difference between two successive iterates (the term in the brackets) is amplified leading to faster convergence, or so we hope.

The SOR equation can be written in residual form as

$$x_j^{(p+1)} = x_k^{(p)} + \omega \frac{R_j^{(p)}}{a_{jj}} \qquad j = 1, 2, \cdots n$$

$$R_j^{(p)} = b_j - \sum_{k=1}^{j-1} a_{jk} x_k^{(p+1)} - \sum_{k=1}^{n} a_{jk} x_k^{(p)},$$

and in symbolic matrix form as

$$\boldsymbol{x}^{(p+1)} = \boldsymbol{x}^{(p)} + \omega[\{\boldsymbol{D}^{-1}(\boldsymbol{b} - \boldsymbol{L}\boldsymbol{x}^{(p+1)} - \boldsymbol{U}\boldsymbol{x}^{(p)})\} - \boldsymbol{x}^{(p)}].$$

The term inside the braces is highly reminiscent of the Gauss-Seidel scheme. After extracting $\boldsymbol{x}^{(p+1)}$ from the above equation, it can be cast in the standard iterative form of equation (3.29) as

$$\boldsymbol{x}^{(p+1)} = (\boldsymbol{D} + \omega\boldsymbol{L})^{-1}[(1-\omega)\boldsymbol{D} - \omega\boldsymbol{U}]\boldsymbol{x}^{(p)} + \omega(\boldsymbol{D} + \omega\boldsymbol{L})^{-1}\boldsymbol{b}. \quad (3.38)$$

Thus the convergence of the SOR method depends on the spectral radius of the matrix $\boldsymbol{T}(\omega) = (\boldsymbol{D} + \omega\boldsymbol{L})^{-1}[(1-\omega)\boldsymbol{D} - \omega\boldsymbol{U}]$. Because $\boldsymbol{T}$ is a function of ω we have gained some measure of control over the convergence. It has been shown that the SOR method converges for $0 < \omega < 2$ and that there is an optimum value of ω which results in the maximum rate of convergence. This optimum value of ω is very problem specific and is often difficult to determine precisely. For linear problems, values in the range of $\omega \simeq 1.7 - 1.8$ are suggested.

3.9   Summary

In this chapter, we have developed methods for efficiently solving systems of linear algebraic equations. We have reviewed matrix operations and special matrices and introduced vector and matrix norms to understand matrix ill conditioning and the susceptibility of matrices to round of errors. Direct methods for solving $\boldsymbol{Ax} = \boldsymbol{b}$ including Cramer's Rule, Gaussian elimination and LU decomposition are discussed. Iterative solution schemes and their convergence characteristics are also introduced and analysed. Likewise the convergence of linear iterative schemes using an eigenvalue analysis has carried out.

3.10 Exercise Problems

P3.1. Consider a matrix A defined as
$$A = \begin{bmatrix} 4 & -1 & 2 \\ 4 & -8 & 2 \\ -2 & 1 & 6 \end{bmatrix}$$

Compute the determinant and inverse of A. Also, determine the condition number using the column sum norm.

P3.2. A continuous function is to be approximated using a fourth degree polynomial. This can be achieved by solving the following linear system:
$$Hx = b,$$
where H is the Hilbert matrix defined as
$$H_{i,j} = \frac{1}{i + j - 1},$$
and b is given by
$$b = [4.0000, 2.8400, 2.2514, 1.8771, 1.6140]'.$$

(a) Calculate the condition of H based on the ∞ norm.

(b) Solve the above matrix equation.

(c) If new measurements are made such that
$$b = [4.009, 2.8402, 2.2512, 1.8773, 1.6142]',$$
determine the new solution for x.

(d) Compute $\frac{\|\delta b\|}{\|b\|}$ and $\frac{\|\delta x\|}{\|x\|}$.

(e) How does the small perturbation in the measurements impact the solution?

P3.3. Consider the system $Hx = b$ where
$$H = \begin{bmatrix} 1 & 1/2 & 1/3 \\ 1/2 & 1/3 & 1/4 \\ 1/3 & 1/4 & 1/5 \end{bmatrix} \quad \text{and} \quad b = \begin{bmatrix} 1 \\ -1 \\ 1 \end{bmatrix},$$

where H is a Hilbert matrix that is severely ill conditioned. Solve the above system

(a) using Gaussian elimination,

(b) by pencil and paper using exact computations,

(c) by pencil and paper rounding off each number to three figures.

Now perform three iterations each using the Jacobi, Gauss-Seidel and SOR ($\omega = 1.6$) algorithms. In each case, use an initial guess $\boldsymbol{x}^{(0)} = [1, 1, 1]'$ and compare how close $\boldsymbol{x}^{(3)}$ is to the exact solution using the 2-norm for comparison.

P3.4. Consider the following system of linear equations

$$\begin{aligned}
x_1 - x_2 + 2x_3 + x_4 &= 7, \\
2x_1 - 4x_2 + x_3 + 3x_4 &= 10, \\
-x_1 + 3x_2 - 4x_3 + 2x_4 &= -14, \\
2x_1 + 4x_2 + 3x_3 - 2x_4 &= 1,
\end{aligned}$$

Solve the above system of equations using Cramer's Rule, Gaussian elimination with and without pivoting and LU factorization (Crout's method).

P3.5. Suppose that you are asked to apply Gaussian elimination to solve a 3×3 system of linear equations $\boldsymbol{Ax} = \boldsymbol{b}$ where

$$\boldsymbol{A} = \begin{bmatrix} 3 & 2 & 9 \\ 1 & 0.6666667 & 1 \\ -6 & -1 & 3 \end{bmatrix}$$

and $\boldsymbol{b} = (6, 1, 0)'$. What difficulty could be encountered if your Gaussian elimination algorithm did not employ pivoting? How does pivoting resolve this potential problem?

P3.6. Solve the following system of equations using the Gauss-Seidel algorithm:

$$\begin{aligned}
12x_1 + x_2 + 7x_3 &= 27, \\
x_1 + 12x_2 + 3x_3 &= -24, \\
7x_1 + 3x_2 + 12x_3 &= 3.
\end{aligned}$$

P3.7. Consider the following system of tridiagonal equations:

$$\begin{aligned}
2x_1 + x_2 &= 4, \\
x_1 + 2x_2 + x_3 &= 8, \\
x_2 + 2x_3 + x_4 &= 12, \\
x_3 + 2x_4 &= 11.
\end{aligned}$$

Solve the above system using the Thomas algorithm. Then repeat your calculations but use the Jacobi, Gauss-Seidel and SOR ($\omega = 1.3$) algorithms.

P3.8. Consider the following system of tridiagonal equations:

$$\begin{bmatrix} 3 & 2 & 0 & 0 \\ 2 & 3 & 2 & 0 \\ 0 & 2 & 3 & 2 \\ 0 & 0 & 2 & 3 \end{bmatrix} \begin{bmatrix} x_1 \\ x_2 \\ x_3 \\ x_4 \end{bmatrix} = \begin{bmatrix} 12 \\ 17 \\ 14 \\ 7 \end{bmatrix}.$$

Solve the above problem using the Jacobi, Gauss-Seidel and SOR ($\omega = 1.4$) algorithms.

P3.9. It is desired to solve the system $\boldsymbol{A}\boldsymbol{x} = \boldsymbol{b}$ where $\boldsymbol{A}$ is given by either

$$\boldsymbol{A} = \begin{bmatrix} 1 & 2 & 3 \\ 2 & 1 & 4 \\ 3 & 1 & 5 \end{bmatrix} \quad \text{or} \quad \boldsymbol{A} = \begin{bmatrix} 2 & 4 & -4 \\ 2 & 2 & 2 \\ 3 & 3 & 1 \end{bmatrix}.$$

If the Jacobi and Gauss-Seidel algorithms are used, will they converge? Why or why not?

P3.10. Consider a matrix $\boldsymbol{A}$ defined as

$$\boldsymbol{A} = \begin{bmatrix} 1 & 1+\epsilon \\ 1 & 1 \end{bmatrix}$$

Calculate $\boldsymbol{A}^{-1}$ and $\det(\boldsymbol{A})$ for the following values of ϵ: 0.01, 0.001 and 0.0001.

P3.11. The following equations have been obtained in the analysis of an engineering system:

$$\begin{aligned} 3x_1 - x_2 - x_4 &= -3\,, \\ -x_1 + 3x_2 - x_3 &= 2\,, \\ -x_2 + 4x_3 - x_4 &= 6\,, \\ -x_1 - x_3 + 4x_4 &= 12\,. \end{aligned}$$

Solve the above problem using

(a) Gaussian elimination,

(b) The Jacobi algorithm,

(c) The Gauss-Seidel algorithm,

(d) The SOR algorithm,

(e) MATLAB's backslash operator,

(f) MATLAB's built-in function for computing the inverse of a matrix, `inv`.

Compare the CPU execution time and/or the number of floating point operations required for each method.

P3.12. By adapting `mnhf_invu`, which is given in Figure 3.5, write a MATLAB function that computes the inverse of a lower triangular matrix.

P3.13. Consider laminar flow through the network shown in Figure 3.13. The governing equations are the pressure drop equations for each

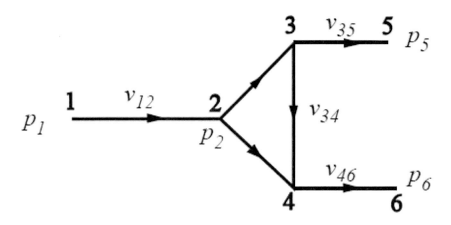

Figure 3.13: Laminar flow in a pipe network.

pipe element $i - j$ and the mass balance equation at each node. The pressure drop between nodes i and j is given by

$$p_i - p_j = \alpha_{ij} v_{ij} \qquad \text{where} \qquad \alpha_{ij} = \frac{32 \mu l_{ij}}{d_{ij}^2}.$$

Meanwhile the mass balance at $e.g.$ node 2 is given by

$$d_{12}^2 v_{12} = d_{23}^2 v_{23} + d_{24}^2 v_{24}.$$

Similar equations apply at nodes 3 and 4. Assuming pipes of known length and diameter, the vector of unknowns can be written as

$$\boldsymbol{x} = [p_2, p_3, p_4, v_{12}, v_{23}, v_{24}, v_{34}, v_{35}, v_{46}]'.$$

There will be six momentum balance equations, one for each pipe element, and three mass balance equations, one at each node. Arrange these equations as a system of nine (linear) equations in nine unknowns and solve the resulting set of equations. Assume a fluid dynamic viscosity of $\mu = 0.1$ Pa·s. Assume also pipe dimensions as given in tabular form below.

(a) Use MATLAB to solve the above problem by following the steps outlined below. Assume that the pressures p_1, p_5 and p_6 are given by $p_1 = 300$ kPa and $p_5 = p_6 = 100$ kPa. You will need to write the system of equations in the form $\boldsymbol{Ax} = \boldsymbol{b}$. Report the time for each step using the built-in functions tic and toc.

Element #	12	23	24	34	35	46
d_{ij} (m)	0.1	0.08	0.08	0.1	0.09	0.09
l_{ij} (m)	1000	800	800	900	1000	1000

Table 3.4: Pipe dimensions (diameter and length).

- Compute the determinant of $\boldsymbol{A}$.
- Compute the LU factorization of $\boldsymbol{A}$ using the built-in function `lu`. What is the structure of $\boldsymbol{L}$? Explain. Why will the function `mnhf_lu` not work in this case?
- Compute the solution using `inv(A)*b`.
- Compute the rank of $\boldsymbol{A}$.

(b) Determine the new flow velocities and pressures if p_6 is changed to 150 kPa.

(c) Comment on how you would adapt the above formulation if a valve on line 34 were shut so that there is no flow between nodes 3 and 4.

P3.14. The following system of equations is used to determine the concentration C in three coupled reactors according to the mass input to each reactor:

$$20C_1 - C_2 - C_3 = 424 \, ,$$
$$-5C_1 + 21C_2 - 2C_3 = 200 \, ,$$
$$-5C_1 - 5C_2 + 22C_3 = -24 \, .$$

(a) Write the above equations in matrix form.

(b) Manually perform two iterations of the Jacobi algorithm. Verify that the Jacobi method will converge by computing the spectral radius of the matrix.

(c) Manually perform two iterations of the Gauss-Seidel algorithm.

(d) Manually perform two iterations of the SOR algorithm with $\omega = 1.5$.

(e) Solve the above problem using MATLAB and a method of your choice.

P3.15. The mass balance for a stage extraction process can be written as follows:

$$P_1 y_{i-1} + P_2 x_{i+1} = P_1 y_i + P_2 x_i \, .$$

When equilibrium is achieved,

$$x_i = K y_i \,,$$

where K is a distribution coefficient. The above results can be combined to yield

$$y_{i-1} - \left(1 + \frac{P_2}{P_1} K\right) y_i + \frac{P_2}{P_1} K y_{i+1} = 0 \,.$$

If $P_1 = 500 \,\text{kg/h}$, $P_2 = 900 \,\text{kg/h}$, $x_{in} = 0$, $y_{in} = 0.1$ and $K = 4$, determine the values of x_{out} and y_{out} relevant to a five stage separation system by following these steps:

(a) Write the equations in matrix form.

(b) Solve the problem using the Jacobi algorithm; calculate the spectral radius of the matrix.

(c) Solve the problem using the Gauss-Seidel algorithm.

P3.16. Consider the following chemical reaction:

$$O_2 + 2H_2 \rightarrow 2H_2O \,, \tag{3.39}$$

where each atom balance can be written in matrix form as

$$\begin{matrix} O: \\ H: \end{matrix} \begin{bmatrix} 2 \\ 0 \end{bmatrix} \begin{bmatrix} 0 \\ 4 \end{bmatrix} \begin{bmatrix} 2 \\ 4 \end{bmatrix}.$$

This result can be represented as a matrix equation, *i.e.*

$$\sum \nu_i A_i = 0 \,, \tag{3.40}$$

where ν_i specify the stoichiometric coefficients (negative for products/positive for reactants) and A_i specifies the molecules present. We can therefore write reaction (3.39) in the form of (3.40) as

$$-1O_2 - 2H_2 + 2H_2O = 0 \,.$$

Rewriting the molecular formulae with the corresponding matrices yields

$$-1 \begin{bmatrix} 2 \\ 0 \end{bmatrix} - 2 \begin{bmatrix} 0 \\ 4 \end{bmatrix} + 2 \begin{bmatrix} 2 \\ 4 \end{bmatrix} = \begin{bmatrix} 0 \\ 0 \end{bmatrix}.$$

This last equation can be written in matrix form as

$$\begin{bmatrix} 2 & 0 & 2 \\ 0 & 4 & 4 \end{bmatrix} \begin{bmatrix} -1 \\ -2 \\ 2 \end{bmatrix} = \begin{bmatrix} 0 \\ 0 \end{bmatrix},$$

which can be written in compact form as $\boldsymbol{A\nu} = \boldsymbol{0}$, which is a null matrix. By solving the null matrix equation we can obtain

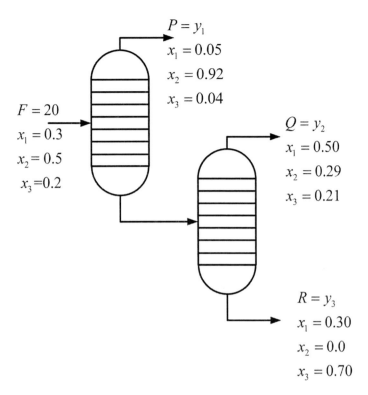

Figure 3.14: A two column distillation train.

the stoichiometric coefficients and therefore balance the chemical reactions.

Let us apply the above concepts to the catalytic hydrogenation of carbon monoxide to methane (also called the Sabatier reaction), which is an important reaction that could have future applications in astronaut life support systems in manned space colonization adventures. The process is described as

$$CO_2 + H_2 \Rightarrow CH_4 + H_2O\,.$$

What is the smallest positive integer to balance the above equation?

P3.17. Figure 3.14 shows a two column distillation train. Based on the information provided in this schematic, what are the mass flow rates P, Q and R corresponding to the column outlets?

P3.18. Consider the four loop electrical circuit illustrated schematically in figure 3.15. Derive the four (linear) equations needed to solve for i_1, i_2, i_3 and i_4. Solve this system of equations using `mnhf_Jacobi` taking as initial guesses $i_1 = i_2 = i_3 = i_4 = 1\,\text{Amp}$.

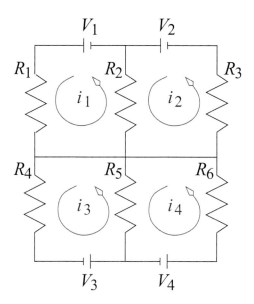

Figure 3.15: A four loop electrical circuit. Voltage and resistance values are as follows: $V_1 = 75\,\mathrm{V}$, $V_2 = 20\,\mathrm{V}$, $V_3 = 120\,\mathrm{V}$, $V_4 = 50\,\mathrm{V}$, $R_1 = 12\,\Omega$, $R_2 = 17\,\Omega$, $R_3 = 6\,\Omega$, $R_4 = 2\,\Omega$, $R_5 = 33\,\Omega$ and $R_6 = 13\,\Omega$.

Now repeat your calculation, but use instead `mnhf_GaussSeidel`. Which algorithm requires more iterations for convergence?

P3.19. In section 3.7.5, we studied LU decomposition for a generic square matrix $\boldsymbol{A}$. Let us now examine the far simpler task of LU-decomposing a *tridiagonal matrix*, $\boldsymbol{T}$, as indicated in the form of a matrix equation below.

$$
\begin{bmatrix}
\ell_{11} & 0 & 0 & \cdots & 0 \\
\ell_{21} & \ell_{22} & 0 & \cdots & 0 \\
\ell_{31} & \ell_{32} & \ell_{33} & \cdots & 0 \\
\ell_{n-1,1} & \ell_{n-1,2} & \ell_{n-1,3} & \ddots & \vdots \\
\ell_{n1} & \ell_{n2} & \ell_{n3} & \cdots & \ell_{nn}
\end{bmatrix}
\begin{bmatrix}
1 & u_{12} & u_{13} & \cdots & u_{1n} \\
0 & 1 & u_{23} & \cdots & u_{2n} \\
0 & 0 & 1 & \cdots & u_{3n} \\
0 & 0 & 0 & \ddots & \vdots \\
0 & 0 & 0 & \cdots & 1
\end{bmatrix}
$$

$$
= \begin{bmatrix}
t_{11} & t_{12} & 0 & \cdots & 0 \\
t_{21} & t_{22} & t_{23} & \cdots & 0 \\
0 & t_{32} & t_{33} & \cdots & 0 \\
0 & 0 & 0 & \ddots & \vdots \\
0 & 0 & 0 & \cdots & t_{nn}
\end{bmatrix}
$$

Starting from the above expression, come up with general expressions for the ℓ's and the u's. Then, with reference to figure 3.16, enter the missing information indicated by the ??'s.

```
function [L,U]=lu_tridiag(T)
%LU_TRIDIAG implements (Crout) LU decomposition on a tridiagonal matrix.
%
% T — square tridiagonal matrix
%
% Usage  [L,U] = lu_tridiag(T)

[r,c] = size(T);    % Compute the size of T.
if isequal(r,c)
 %% Initialize.
 L=zeros(r); L(1,1) = T(1,1);
 U=eye(r);          % Identity matrix of size r—by—r.

 for j=2:r
  L(??,??) = T(??,??);
  U(??,??) = T(??,??)/L(??,??);
  L(??,??) = T(??,??)—L(??,??)*U(??,??);
 end

else
 fprintf('Can''t decompose a non—square T.\n\n')
end
```

Figure 3.16: Matlab algorithm for LU-decomposing the tridiagonal matrix T.

Let knowledge grow from more to more, But more of reverence in us dwell; That mind and soul, according well, May make one music as before.

— ALFRED TENNYSON

CHAPTER 4

SYSTEMS OF NONLINEAR ALGEBRAIC EQUATIONS

In this chapter we extend the concepts developed in Chapters 2 and 3 by developing methods to compute the roots of a system of nonlinear algebraic equations. These equations are supposed to have the generic form

$$\boldsymbol{f}(\boldsymbol{x}) = 0\,, \tag{4.1}$$

where $\boldsymbol{f}(\boldsymbol{x})$ is a vector function of $\boldsymbol{x}$. Consequently, there are n coupled equations to consider and these can be written in expanded (or component form) as,

$$f_1(x_1, x_2, \cdots x_n) = 0\,,$$

$$f_2(x_1, x_2, \cdots x_n) = 0\,,$$

$$\vdots$$

$$f_n(x_1, x_2, \cdots x_n) = 0\,.$$

As with the scalar case, equation (4.1) is satisfied only at select values of $\boldsymbol{x} = \boldsymbol{r} = [r_1, r_2, \cdots r_n]$ called the roots. Moreover, the equations often depend on other parameters, and we may therefore rewrite (4.1) in a still more general form as

$$\boldsymbol{f}(\boldsymbol{x}; \boldsymbol{p}) = 0\,. \tag{4.2}$$

Here $\boldsymbol{p}$ represents a set of known parameter values. In such cases it may be required to construct solution families for ranges of values of $\boldsymbol{p}$ so that $\boldsymbol{x} = \boldsymbol{x}(\boldsymbol{p})$. This task is achieved most efficiently using continuation methods. Arguably the most famous of these is Newton's method, which we consider in the following section.

4.1   Newton's method

For a scalar equation, a geometrical interpretation of the Newton method
is easy to develop as shown in Figure 2.2 d. Although this process is
considerably more difficult in higher dimensions, the algorithm shown
in Figure 2.8 can readily be generalized to equations such as (4.1) or
(4.2). In particular, the basic concept of linearizing a nonlinear function
remains unchanged. Here, however, we need to make use of a multivariate form of the Taylor series expansion. To illustrate this process, let us
consider a two-dimensional system of equations written in component
form as

$$f_1(x_1, x_2) = 0\,,$$
$$f_2(x_1, x_2) = 0\,.$$

Thus the vectors $\boldsymbol{f}(\boldsymbol{x}) = [f_1(x_1, x_2), f_2(x_1, x_2)]$ and $\boldsymbol{x} = [x_1, x_2]$ each
contain two elements. Let the roots be represented by $\boldsymbol{r} = [r_1, r_2]$; by
definition, $\boldsymbol{f}(\boldsymbol{r}) = \boldsymbol{0}$ where $\boldsymbol{0} = [0, 0]$.

Suppose $\boldsymbol{x}^{(0)}$ is some known initial guess for $\boldsymbol{r}$. We suppose that
our guess is "pretty good" such that

$$\boldsymbol{r} = \boldsymbol{x}^{(0)} + \boldsymbol{\delta}\,,$$

where $\boldsymbol{\delta} = [\delta_1, \delta_2]$ denotes some small offset. If we can devise an algorithm to estimate $\boldsymbol{\delta}$ then we can apply such a scheme repeatedly to
get progressively closer to the root, $\boldsymbol{r}$. Variations in $f_1(x_1, x_2)$ can be
the result of variations in either of the independent variables, x_1 or x_2.
Recognizing this, a bivariate Taylor series expansion around $\boldsymbol{x}^{(0)}$ can
be written as

$$f_1(x_1^{(0)} + \delta_1\,,\ x_2^{(0)} + \delta_2) = f_1(x_1^{(0)}, x_2^{(0)}) +$$

$$\underbrace{\left.\frac{\partial f_1}{\partial x_1}\right|_{[x_1^{(0)}, x_2^{(0)}]} \delta_1}_{\text{variation due to } x_1} + \underbrace{\left.\frac{\partial f_1}{\partial x_2}\right|_{[x_1^{(0)}, x_2^{(0)}]} \delta_2}_{\text{variation due to } x_2} + \mathcal{O}(\boldsymbol{\delta}^2)\,.$$

In a similar fashion,

$$f_2(x_1^{(0)} + \delta_1\,,\ x_2^{(0)} + \delta_2) = f_2(x_1^{(0)}, x_2^{(0)}) +$$

$$\underbrace{\left.\frac{\partial f_2}{\partial x_1}\right|_{[x_1^{(0)}, x_2^{(0)}]} \delta_1}_{\text{variation due to } x_1} + \underbrace{\left.\frac{\partial f_2}{\partial x_2}\right|_{[x_1^{(0)}, x_2^{(0)}]} \delta_2}_{\text{variation due to } x_2} + \mathcal{O}(\boldsymbol{\delta}^2)\,.$$

Because $\boldsymbol{\delta}$ is supposed to be small, we can neglect the higher order
terms buried inside of $\mathcal{O}(\boldsymbol{\delta}^2)$; this step is the essence of the linearization

process. Recall, moreover, that $\boldsymbol{x}^{(0)} + \boldsymbol{\delta} = \boldsymbol{r}$ and $\boldsymbol{f}(\boldsymbol{r}) = \boldsymbol{0}$. The left hand sides of the above equations are therefore zero. Thus we find that

$$0 = f_1(x_1^{(0)}, x_2^{(0)}) + \left.\frac{\partial f_1}{\partial x_1}\right|_{[x_1^{(0)}, x_2^{(0)}]} \delta_1 + \left.\frac{\partial f_1}{\partial x_2}\right|_{[x_1^{(0)}, x_2^{(0)}]} \delta_2, \qquad (4.3)$$

$$0 = f_2(x_1^{(0)}, x_2^{(0)}) + \left.\frac{\partial f_2}{\partial x_1}\right|_{[x_1^{(0)}, x_2^{(0)}]} \delta_1 + \left.\frac{\partial f_2}{\partial x_2}\right|_{[x_1^{(0)}, x_2^{(0)}]} \delta_2. \qquad (4.4)$$

These are two equations in the two unknowns δ_1 and δ_2. Because equations (4.3-4.4) are *linear*, the above equations can be arranged into matrix form as

$$\begin{bmatrix} 0 \\ 0 \end{bmatrix} = \begin{bmatrix} f_1 \\ f_2 \end{bmatrix} + \begin{bmatrix} \frac{\partial f_1}{\partial x_1} & \frac{\partial f_1}{\partial x_2} \\ \frac{\partial f_2}{\partial x_1} & \frac{\partial f_2}{\partial x_2} \end{bmatrix} \begin{bmatrix} \delta_1 \\ \delta_2 \end{bmatrix}, \qquad (4.5)$$

where it is understood that the functions and partial derivatives are evaluated at $\boldsymbol{x}^{(0)} = [x_1^{(0)}, x_2^{(0)}]$. Rewriting (4.5) in symbolic form yields

$$0 = \boldsymbol{f}^{(0)} + \boldsymbol{J}^{(0)}\boldsymbol{\delta},$$

where $\boldsymbol{J}$ is called the Jacobian matrix. Thus, the displacement vector $\boldsymbol{\delta}$ is obtained by solving the linear system

$$\boldsymbol{\delta} = -[\boldsymbol{J}^{(0)}]^{-1}\boldsymbol{f}^{(0)}.$$

The above result can be generalized in an obvious way whereby

$$\boldsymbol{\delta}^{(k)} = -[\boldsymbol{J}^{(k)}]^{-1}\boldsymbol{f}^{(k)} \qquad \boldsymbol{x}^{(k+1)} = \boldsymbol{x}^{(k)} + \boldsymbol{\delta}^{(k)} \qquad k = 0, 1, \cdots \quad (4.6)$$

In light of equation (4.6), and given some initial guess, $\boldsymbol{x}^{(0)}$, Newton's method consists of the following steps:

1. Evaluating the function and the Jacobian matrix at the current iterate $\boldsymbol{x}^{(k)}$,

2. Solving the linear system for the displacement vector $\boldsymbol{\delta}^{(k)}$,

3. Computing the new estimate for the iterate $\boldsymbol{x}^{(k+1)}$, and,

4. Checking to see whether the algorithm has converged.

This latter step is described in the next subsection.

4.1.1   Convergence test

Once we are sufficient close to the desired root, the iteration suggested by equation (4.6) can be terminated. One possible convergence test is to check whether the absolute difference between two successive values of $\boldsymbol{x}$ is smaller than some specified tolerance. This can be done by computing the norm of $\boldsymbol{\delta}$, *i.e.*

$$||\boldsymbol{\delta}|| \leq \epsilon.$$

Another convergence test might be to check if the absolute value of the function f at the end of an iteration is below a prescribed tolerance. Because we are considering vectors, a norm (of f) must once again be calculated, *i.e.*

$$||f|| \leq \epsilon.$$

Finally, and in place of the above convergence tests, we might prefer to place a limit on the number of times the iteration is repeated. Equivalently, we would specify a maximum value for k in equation (4.6).

A MATLAB function that implements equation (4.6) is shown in Figure 4.1. Note that `mnhf_newton_system` requires an initial guess as well as two external functions, one each for the function and Jacobian matrix. MATLAB provides its own function for solving systems of nonlinear equations, namely `fsolve`. Whereas this function can be thought of as a higher dimensional analogue to `fzero`, which we encountered in Chapter 2, it is important to emphasize that the underlying algorithms are different. Therefore, MATLAB may, depending on how tolerances are set, converge to a slightly different value of the root when using one built-in function vs. the other.

EXAMPLE 4.1 (Chemical reactors in series) *Consider a series of continuously stirred tank reactors (CSTRs) as shown schematically below.*

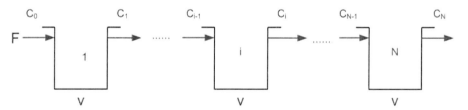

By definition, the mixing supplied to CSTRs is sufficiently vigorous that spatial variations in the chemical composition of the interior material can be ignored. Moreover, if we assume a second-order irreversible chemical reaction, the model equations can be written as

$$f_i = \beta C_i^2 + C_i - C_{i-1} = 0 \qquad i = 1, 2, \cdots N, \qquad (4.7)$$

where C_i is the exit concentration of the chemical species of interest from the i-th reactor and β is a constant of unknown magnitude that depends on the reaction rate constant, k, the reactors' volume, V, and the feed rate, F. More precisely,

$$\beta = \frac{kV}{F}.$$

```
function x=mnhf_newton_system(Fun,Jac,x,tol,trace)
%MNHF_NEWTON_SYSTEM solves a system of nonlin. eqns. using Newton's method.
%
%  Fun   - name of the external function to compute f
%  Jac   - name of the externan function to compute J
%  x     - vector of initial guesses
%  tol   - error criterion
%  trace - print intermediate results
%
%  Usage  mnhf_newton_system(@cstrF,@cstrJ,[3.0 2.0 1.0 0.75 0.5]',1e-10,1)

%Check inputs
if nargin < 5, trace = 1; end
if nargin < 4, tol = 1e-8; end

fprintf('\nCount\t Norm(f)\n')
fprintf('———————————————————————\n')

Nmax = 25;
f = 1.0;   % Can select any arbitrary value with magnitude > tol.
count = 0; % Initialize counter.

while (norm(f)  > tol && count <= Nmax)
 count = count+1;       % Increment counter.
 f = feval(Fun,x);      % Function evaluation.
 J = feval(Jac,x);      % Jacobian evaluation.
 x = x-J\f;             % Update the guess.
 if trace
  fprintf(1,'%3i %12.5f\n',count,norm(f));
 end
end

if count > Nmax
 fprintf('Maximum number of iterations reached.\n\n')
end
```

Figure 4.1: MATLAB implementation of Newton's method in higher dimensions.

By assumption, $C_{i-1} > C_i$, i.e. the species of interest is being consumed by the chemical reaction in question.

The result (4.7) can be regarded as N equations in the $N + 2$ unknowns C_0, $C_1,\ldots C_N$, β. Hence we have two degrees of freedom. Let us consider a design situation where the inlet and outlet concentrations are specified as, say, $C_0 = 5.0\, mol/L$ and $C_N = 0.5\, mol/L$. The vector of unknowns therefore consists of N elements

$$\boldsymbol{x} = (C_1, C_2 \cdots C_{N-1}, \beta)'.$$

We wish to determine the reactors' volume, V, for a given value of N. This volume can be written in terms of β as $V = \beta F/k$. The rate constant is $k = 0.125\, L/mol/min$ and the feed rate is $F = 25\, L/min$. Thus if we can solve the system of nonlinear algebraic equations for β (and also C_1, $C_2,\ldots C_{N-1}$), determining V is straightforward. Note, however, that before we can directly apply mnhf_newton_system, *we must first evaluate the entries in the Jacobian matrix from*

$$\boldsymbol{J} = \begin{bmatrix} \frac{\partial f_1}{\partial C_1} & \frac{\partial f_1}{\partial C_2} & \frac{\partial f_1}{\partial C_3} & \cdots & \frac{\partial f_1}{\partial \beta} \\ \frac{\partial f_2}{\partial C_1} & \frac{\partial f_2}{\partial C_2} & \frac{\partial f_2}{\partial C_3} & \cdots & \frac{\partial f_2}{\partial \beta} \\ \frac{\partial f_3}{\partial C_1} & \frac{\partial f_3}{\partial C_2} & \frac{\partial f_3}{\partial C_3} & \cdots & \frac{\partial f_3}{\partial \beta} \\ & & \vdots & & \\ \frac{\partial f_N}{\partial C_1} & \cdots & \frac{\partial f_N}{\partial C_{N-2}} & \frac{\partial f_N}{\partial C_{N-1}} & \frac{\partial f_N}{\partial \beta} \end{bmatrix},$$

$$= \begin{bmatrix} 2\beta C_1 + 1 & 0 & 0 & \cdots & C_1^2 \\ -1 & 2\beta C_2 + 1 & 0 & \cdots & C_2^2 \\ 0 & -1 & 2\beta C_3 + 1 & \cdots & C_3^2 \\ \vdots & 0 & & \ddots & \vdots \\ 0 & \cdots & 0 & -1 & C_N^2 \end{bmatrix}. \quad (4.8)$$

The MATLAB functions relevant to (4.7) and (4.8) are given, respectively, in Figures 4.2 and 4.3. Typing in the Command Window

```
>>mnhf_newton_system(@cstrF,@cstrJ,[3.0 2.0 1.0 0.75...
    0.5]',1e-10,1)
```

yields, as a solution for β, $\beta = 0.5597\, L/mol$. It is then easy to show that $V = 111.94\, L$.

In the above example, observe that the number of reactors, N, is defined implicitly by the length of the vector containing the initial guesses, $\boldsymbol{x}^{(0)}$. Furthermore, it can be shown that convergence is quadratic in the neighborhood of the root, much like we might anticipate from our investigation of Newton's method in one-dimension – see Chapter 2.

```
function f=cstrF(x)
% Reactor in series model, the function.
%
% x = [C(1),C(2),... C(N-1),beta]
% f(i) = beta C(i)^2 + C(i) - C(i-1)

global N CN

N = length(x); % Number of unknowns and number of reactors.
C0 = 5.0;      % Inlet concentration (mol/L).
CN = 0.5;      % Outlet concentration (mol/L).

% Initialize array (column vector format).
f = zeros(N,1);

f(1) = x(N)*x(1)^2.0+x(1)-C0;
for i=2:N-1
 f(i)= x(N)*x(i)^2.0+x(i)-x(i-1);
end
f(N) = x(N)*CN^2.0+CN-x(N-1);
```

Figure 4.2: The MATLAB function cstrF.

```
function J=cstrJ(x)
% Reactor in series model, the Jacobian.
%
% x = [C(1),C(2),... C(N-1),beta]
% f(i) = beta C(i)^2 + C(i) - C(i-1)

global N CN

% Initialize matrix.
J =  zeros(N);

% First row.
J(1,1) = 2.0*x(N)*x(1)+1.0;
J(1,N) = x(1)^2.0;

% Middle rows.
for i=2:N-1
 J(i,i) = 2.0*x(N)*x(i)+1.0;
 J(i,i-1) = -1.0;
 J(i,N) = x(i)^2.0;
end

% Last row.
J(N,N-1) = -1.0;
J(N,N) = CN^2.0;
```

Figure 4.3: The MATLAB function cstrJ.

4.2   Summary

In this chapter, we have alternatively extended the concepts of solving a single nonlinear equation to higher dimensions or of solving a system of linear equations to a system of nonlinear equations. Newton method's based on a multivariate form of the Taylor series expansion, is well suited to this task. Other techniques for solving nonlinear equations include extending the fixed point iteration (FPI) algorithm from Chapter 2, though these ideas are not pursued here. Note finally that MATLAB has a built-in function for solving nonlinear functions of several variables, namely `fsolve`. It is similar to the built-in function `fzero` encountered earlier.

4.3   Exercise Problems

P4.1. Newton's method provides a method for solving systems of non-linear equations of the form

$$f_1(x_1, x_2, \ldots x_n) = 0,$$

$$f_2(x_1, x_2, \ldots x_n) = 0,$$

$$\vdots$$

$$f_n(x_1, x_2, \ldots x_n) = 0.$$

but this algorithm should work equally well if f_1, f_2, $\ldots f_n$ are linear functions of x_1, x_2, $\ldots x_n$. Let us consider the following 2×2 system of linearly-independent equations:

$$f_1 = ax_1 + bx_2 + c, \tag{4.9}$$

$$f_2 = \alpha x_1 + \beta x_2 + \gamma, \tag{4.10}$$

where a, b, c and α, β, γ are constants.

(a) Show that the solution of (4.9) and (4.10) is given by

$$x_1 = \frac{b}{a}\left(\frac{\gamma a - \alpha c}{\beta a - \alpha b}\right) - \frac{c}{a} \qquad x_2 = \frac{\alpha c - \gamma a}{\beta a - \alpha b}.$$

(b) How is the Jacobian matrix defined given (4.9) and (4.10)?

(c) Suppose that our initial guesses for the roots of (4.9) and (4.10) are $x_1 = x_2 = 0$. Show that Newton's algorithm will converge to the solution identified in (a) in a single iteration. (You can assume that the matrix equation is solved using, say, Gaussian elimination).

P4.2. Rewrite `mnhf_newton_system` from Figure 4.1 but evaluate the partial derivatives of the Jacobian matrix numerically. Take, for example,

$$\frac{\partial f_1}{\partial x_1} \simeq \frac{f_1(x_1 + \epsilon, x_2) - f_1(x_1 - \epsilon, x_2)}{2\epsilon},$$

where ϵ is a number small in magnitude. (This is, of course, the approach that is applied in `mnhf_newton` from Figure 2.8.)

P4.3. The trajectories of two comets are given by $x^2 + 2x + 2y^2 = 26$ and $x^3 - y^2 + 4y = 19$. Use Newton's method to determine the point where the comets will collide starting with an initial guess of $(1, 1)$.

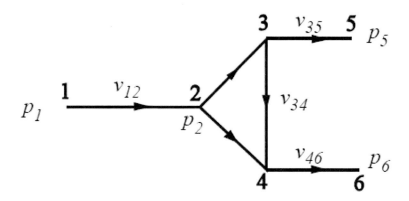

Figure 4.4: Turbulent flow in a pipe network.

P4.4. Determine the root of the following system:

$$f(x, y) = x^4 + 2x + xy - 5,$$

$$g(x, y) = x^3 - 8y^2 + 10y - 11.$$

Carry out two iterations of Newton's method starting with an initial guess of $(0, 0)$.

P4.5. Consider turbulent fluid flow through the pipe network of Figure 4.4. The governing equations consist of the pressure drop equations for each pipe element and a mass balance equation at each of nodes 2, 3 and 4. The pressure drop between nodes i and j is given by

$$p_i - p_j = \alpha_{ij} v_{ij}^2, \qquad \text{where} \qquad \alpha_{ij} = \frac{2 f \rho \ell_{ij}}{d_{ij}}. \qquad (4.11)$$

Here $\rho = 1000 \, \text{kg/m}^3$ is the fluid density and f is a friction factor. Because the flow is assumed to be fully developed and turbulent, it is reasonable to assume a constant value for f; here we shall consider $f = 0.005$. For prescribed up- and downstream pressures, the unknowns are p_2, p_3, p_4, v_{12}, v_{23}, v_{24}, v_{34}, v_{35} and v_{46}. Derive a system of nine corresponding equations and solve this system for p_2, p_3, p_4, v_{12}, v_{23}, v_{24}, v_{34}, v_{35} and v_{46}. Assume $p_1 = 352 \, \text{kPa}$, $p_5 = 161 \, \text{kPa}$ and $p_6 = 144 \, \text{kPa}$. Then repeat your calculations but set $p_6 = p_5 = 161 \, \text{kPa}$. For the same initial guess, are more or less iterations required for convergence?

Pipe element	12	23	24	34	35	46
d_{ij} (m)	0.1	0.08	0.08	0.1	0.09	0.09
ℓ_{ij} (m)	1000	800	800	900	1000	1000

Table 4.1: Pipe dimensions (diameter and length).

P4.6. The following reactions are taking place in a constant volume gas-phase batch reactor:

$$A + B \Leftrightarrow C + D \,,$$
$$B + C \Leftrightarrow R + S \,,$$
$$A + R \Leftrightarrow T \,.$$

We can solve for the equilibrium concentration of a given chemical constituent by employing the following (linear) relationships from stoichiometry:

$$C_A = C_{A0} - C_D - C_T \,,$$
$$C_B = C_{B0} - C_D - C_S \,,$$
$$C_C = C_D - C_S \,,$$
$$C_S = C_R - C_T \,,$$

coupled with the following (nonlinear) relations from kinetics:

$$K_{C1} = \frac{C_C C_D}{C_A C_D} \,,$$
$$K_{C2} = \frac{C_R C_S}{C_B C_C} \,,$$
$$K_{C2} = \frac{C_T}{C_A C_S} \,.$$

Above, C_{A0} and C_{B0} indicate the initial concentrations of species A and B. Solve for the equilibrium concentrations given only the following information: $C_{A0} = C_{B0} = 2.0 \, \mathrm{mol/L}$, $K_{C1} = 1.05$, $K_{C2} = 2.6$ and $K_{C3} = 5 \, \mathrm{L/mol}$.

> The chess-board is the world; the pieces are the phenomena of the universe; the rules of the game are what we call the laws of Nature. The player on the other side is hidden from us. We know that his play is always fair, just, and patient. But also we know, to our cost, that he never overlooks a mistake, or makes the smallest allowance for ignorance.

> — T.H. HUXLEY

CHAPTER 5

FUNCTIONAL APPROXIMATIONS

In previous chapters we have developed algorithms for solving systems of linear and nonlinear *algebraic* equations. Before undertaking the more difficult task of writing algorithms to solve *differential* equations, we must first to develop some basic concepts of *functional approximations*. In this respect, the present chapter, divided in two parts, serves as a bridge between the realms of *lumped parameter, steady state* models and *distributed* and/or *dynamic* models.

There are at least two kinds of *functional approximation* problems that we encounter frequently. In the first class of problems, a known function $f(x)$ is approximated by another function, $P_n(x)$ for reasons of computational necessity or expediency. As modellers or interpreters of physical phenomena, we often encounter a second class of problem in which we need to represent an experimentally-collected, discrete set of data of the form $\{x_i, f_i | i = 1, 2, \cdots n\}$ as a continuous function, $f(x)$. Both of the above function approximations shall be investigated below.

Part I

Approximate Representation of Functions

5.1   Approximate representation of functions

5.1.1   Series expansion

As an example of the first class of functional approximation, consider evaluating the *error function*, whose definition is given below.

$$\text{erf}(x) = \frac{2}{\sqrt{\pi}} \int_0^x e^{-\xi^2} \mathrm{d}\xi. \tag{5.1}$$

The above integral can not be written in closed form i.e. as an expression that can be evaluated using a finite number of operations, therefore, we must instead use the following series expansion for the integrand:

$$e^{-\xi^2} = \sum_{k=0}^{\infty} \frac{(-1)^k \xi^{2k}}{k!}.$$

Note that this expansion is derived about the point $\xi = 0$. According to equation (5.1), we then integrate the series expansion term-by-term to obtain

$$\text{erf}(x) = \frac{2}{\sqrt{\pi}} \sum_{k=0}^{\infty} \frac{(-1)^k x^{2k+1}}{(2k+1)k!} \tag{5.2}$$

Truncating the above series to a finite number of terms yields

$$\text{erf}(x) \simeq P_{2n+1}(x) = \frac{2}{\sqrt{\pi}} \sum_{k=0}^{n} \frac{(-1)^k x^{2k+1}}{(2k+1)k!} + R(x). \tag{5.3}$$

The error introduced by truncating the above series is of course called the *truncation error* and the magnitude of the *residual function*, $R(x)$, indicates the magnitude of this error. For x close to zero, it suffices to consider a few terms of the series (small n). The convergence of the series is demonstrated in Table 5.1. Clearly, as we migrate further from $x = 0$, more terms are required for $P_{2n+1}(x)$ to accurately represent $\text{erf}(x)$.

The error distribution, defined as $\epsilon(x, n) = |\text{erf}(x) - P_{2n+1}(x)|$, is shown in Figure 5.1. Panel (a) shows that, for a fixed number of terms,

n	$P_{2n+1}(x = 0.5)$	$P_{2n+1}(x = 1.0)$	$P_{2n+1}(x = 2.0)$
2	0.5207	0.865091	2.85856
4	0.5205	0.843449	2.09437
6	0.5205	0.842714	1.33124
8	0.5205	0.842701	1.05793
10	0.5205	0.842701	1.00318
20	0.5205	0.842701	0.995322
∞	0.5205	0.842701	0.995322

Table 5.1: Convergence of $P_{2n+1}(x)$, defined in (5.3), to $\mathrm{erf}(x)$ at selected values of x.

say $n = 8$, the error increases with x. Likewise, for larger values of x, more terms are required to keep the error small. When $x = 2.0$, for example, more than 10 terms are needed to reduce the error to an insignificant level.

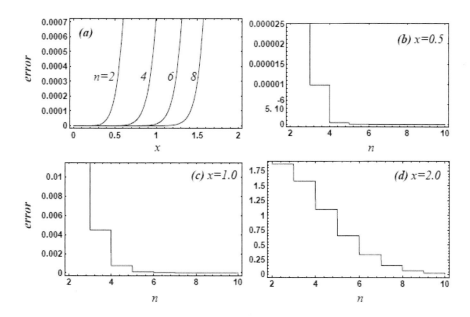

Figure 5.1: The error distribution, $\epsilon(x, n) = |\mathrm{erf}(x) - P_{2n+1}(x)|$, for different levels of truncation.

5.1.2 Polynomial collocation

In the above example, we chose to construct an approximate function to represent $f(x) = \mathrm{erf}(x)$ by integrating a Taylor series. This required that all the higher order derivatives of e^{-x^2} be available at $x = 0$. As we move further away from $x = 0$, the accuracy of the Taylor series approximation deteriorates. In another kind of functional approximation, we can attempt to get a robust representation of a given function $f(x)$ over a range $x \in [a, b]$. We do this by choosing a set of n basis functions, $\{\phi_i(x)|i = 1, 2, \cdots n\}$ that are linearly independent. The approximation is then represented as

$$f(x) \simeq P_n(x) = \sum_{i=1}^{n} a_i \phi_i(x) \,.$$

Here the basis functions $\phi_i(x)$ are known; meanwhile the coefficients a_i are unknown constants and must be determined in such a way that we can make $P_n(x)$ as good an approximation to $f(x)$ as possible. More quantitatively, and following the previous methodology, we can define an error as the difference between the exact function and its approximate representation

$$e(x; a_i) = |f(x) - P_n(x)| \,. \tag{5.4}$$

The objective is to devise a scheme for selecting a_i so that the error defined by equation (5.4) is minimized.

EXAMPLE 5.1 (Polynomial collocation) *So far we have outlined certain general concepts, but left open the choice of a specific basis functions $\phi_i(x)$. Let the basis functions be*

$$\phi_i(x) = x^{i-1} \qquad i = 1, 2, \cdots n \,,$$

which, incidentally is a poor choice, but one that is easy to understand. The approximate function will be a polynomial of degree $(n - 1)$ of the form

$$P_{n-1}(x) = \sum_{i=1}^{n} a_i x^{i-1} \,.$$

Next, let us introduce the idea of collocation *to evaluate the error at n selected points in the range of interest $x \in [a, b]$. We choose precisely n points $\{x_k | k = 1, 2, \cdots n\}$ because we have introduced n degrees of freedom (unknowns) in the coefficients a_1, a_2,...a_n. A naive choice would be to space these collocation points equally in the interval $[a, b]$ so that*

$$x_k = a + (k - 1) \frac{(b - a)}{(n - 1)} \qquad k = 1, 2, \cdots, n \,.$$

Finally we can require that the error at these points is exactly zero, i.e.

$$e(x_k; a_i) = f(x_k) - P_{n-1}(x_k) = 0 \,,$$

or

$$\sum_{i=1}^{n} a_i x_k^{i-1} = f(x_k) \qquad k = 1, 2, \cdots, n. \qquad (5.5)$$

The above constraint yields n linear equations in n unknowns a_i. In matrix form, we write

$$\boldsymbol{Pa} = \boldsymbol{f},$$

where the elements of the matrix $\boldsymbol{P}$ are given by $P_{k,i} = x_k^{i-1}$ and the vectors read $\boldsymbol{a} = (a_1, a_2, \cdots, a_n)'$ and $\boldsymbol{f} = (f(x_1), f(x_2), \cdots, f(x_n))'$. Thus we have reduced the functional approximation problem to one of solving a system of linear algebraic equations, for which the tools developed in Chapter 3 are obviously very well-suited.

Let us now be even more specific and focus on approximating the error function $f(x) = \mathrm{erf}(x)$ over the interval $x \in [0.1, 0.5]$. Let us also choose $n = 5$, i.e. a quartic polynomial. This will allow us to write out the final steps of the approximation problem explicitly. The equally spaced collocation points are

$$x_k = \{0.1, 0.2, 0.3, 0.4, 0.5\},$$

and the error function values at the collocation points are

$$\boldsymbol{f} = f(x_k) = (0.1125, 0.2227, 0.3286, 0.4284, 0.5205)'.$$

Thus equation (5.5) yields the following system:[*]

$$\boldsymbol{P} = \begin{bmatrix} 1 & x_1 & x_1^2 & x_1^3 & x_1^4 \\ 1 & x_2 & x_2^2 & x_2^3 & x_2^4 \\ 1 & x_3 & x_3^2 & x_3^3 & x_3^4 \\ 1 & x_4 & x_4^2 & x_4^3 & x_4^4 \\ 1 & x_5 & x_5^2 & x_5^3 & x_5^4 \end{bmatrix} = \begin{bmatrix} 1.0 & 0.10 & 0.010 & 0.0010 & 0.0001 \\ 1.0 & 0.20 & 0.040 & 0.0080 & 0.0016 \\ 1.0 & 0.30 & 0.090 & 0.0270 & 0.0081 \\ 1.0 & 0.40 & 0.160 & 0.0640 & 0.0256 \\ 1.0 & 0.50 & 0.250 & 0.1250 & 0.0625 \end{bmatrix}.$$

Solution of the corresponding linear system yields the unknown coefficients as

$$\boldsymbol{a} = (0.0001, 1.1262, 0.0186, -0.4503, 0.1432)'.$$

The quartic polynomial can be represented as

$$P_4(x) = \sum_{i=1}^{5} a_i x^{i-1} = a_1 x^0 + a_2 x^1 + a_3 x^2 + a_4 x^3 + a_5 x^4.$$

Making use of the above solution, we find that

$$P_4(x) = 0.0001 + 1.1262x + 0.0186x^2 - 0.4503x^3 + 0.1432x^4.$$

A MATLAB function for implementing the above procedure for a specified degree of polynomial is given in Figure 5.2.

---

[*]Also known as the Vandermonde Matrix.

```
function a=mnhf_erf_approx(n,a,b)
%MNHF_ERF_APPROX illustrates polynomial approximation of error function.
%
% n - polynomial degree
% a - lower bound of interval
% b - upper bound of interval
%
% Usage  mnhf_erf_approx(5,0.1,0.5);

% Initialize matrix.
P = zeros(n);

% Select collocation points (evenly spaced).
x = a+(0:(n-1))*(b-a)/(n-1);

% Calculate the error function at collocation points using built-in fn.
f = erf(x);

% Compute the matrix elements.
for k=1:n
 P(k,:) = x(k).^(0:n-1);
end

% Compute and print the determinant of P.
fprintf(1,'Determinant of P for deg. %2i is = %12.5e\n', n,det(P));

% Determine the unknown coefficients a_i.
a=P\f';
```

Figure 5.2: MATLAB implementation illustrating the steps associated with approximating erf(x) using a polynomial function.

T (°F)	P (psia)
220.0000	17.1860
224.0000	18.5560
228.0000	20.0150
232.0000	21.5670

Table 5.2: Steam saturation temperature vs. pressure.

How do we justify our earlier claim that the basis functions $\phi_i(x) = x^{i-1}$ $i = 1, 2, \cdots n$ represent a poor choice when approximating other functions? Consider the output returned by the MATLAB function of Figure 5.2 for approximating polynomials of progressively larger degree. The matrix P becomes poorly scaled and nearly singular as n increases; this is confirmed by recording $\det(P)$. For example, the determinant of P is 1.60000×10^{-2} for $n = 3$ and it rapidly decreases to 1.21597×10^{-12} for $n = 6$. Selecting other orthogonal polynomials such as Chebyshev polynomials and using the roots of these polynomials as the collocation points results in well-conditioned matrices and improved approximation accuracy.

5.2   Approximate representation of data

The concepts of polynomial approximation were discussed in section 5.1.2 in the context of constructing approximate representations of complicated mathematical functions such as the error function. We will further develop and apply these ideas in later chapters for solving differential equations. Let us briefly explore the problem of constructing approximate functions for representing a discrete set of m pairs of data points

$$\{(x_k, f_k) \mid k = 1, 2, \cdots, m\}.$$

Such a data set might be the output of a laboratory experiment, for instance. To be more precise, let us consider the saturation temperature vs. pressure data taken from thermodynamic steam tables that is reproduced in Table 5.2 and Figure 5.3. Here, we wish to represent pressure as a function of temperature, $P(T)$ over the temperature range $T \in [220, 232]$. A number of alternatives present themselves.

1. We can fit a cubic polynomial, $P_3(T)$ that will pass through each of the four data points over the temperature range $T \in [220, 232]$.

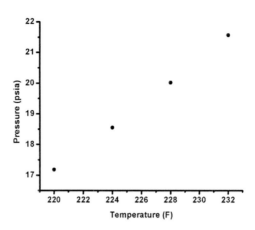

Figure 5.3: Plot of data from Table 5.2.

Such a polynomial will be considered a *global polynomial* because it covers the entire range of interest in T.

2. We can construct *piecewise polynomials* of a lower degree and possessing a limited range of applicability. For example, we might fit quadratic polynomials through the first three data points and also the last three.

3. We can fit a global polynomial of degree less < 3 that will not pass through any of the given data points, but will nonetheless produce a function that *minimizes* the error over the entire range of $T \in [220, 232]$.

The choice of method will largely depend on the nature of the data as well as the type of polynomial selected. If the data in question are known to be highly accurate, it makes sense to make the approximating polynomial able to reproduce the experimental values with good fidelity. On the other hand, if the data are inaccurate, there is no point in requiring the approximating polynomial to go through the experimental data exactly. Instead one should focus on minimizing the error over the entire range of the independent variable. These considerations lead to the following definitions:

1. **Interpolation:** Interpolation is a procedure for estimating the value of the function value between adjacent pairs of data points. This is accomplished by determining a polynomial that exactly passes through the data points in question then using this polynomial to infer one or more in-between values. Interpolation is to

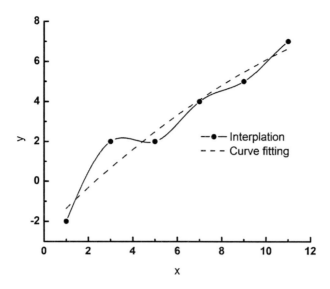

Figure 5.4: Interpolation and curve fitting.

be used when the data points are known to be precise.

2. **Curve fitting:** Curve fitting is a procedure by which a mathematical equation is used to best fit a given set of data points. This approach is most effective when the data in question are imprecise so that the aim of curve fitting is to minimize the effect of measurement uncertainty.

Figure 5.4 illustrates the difference between interpolation and curve fitting with reference to a representative data set plotted in the (x, y) plane.

The procedures developed in section 5.1.2 are directly applicable to interpolation and yield a linear system of equations that can be solved numerically. In fact, it is also possible to write the polynomial in a different fashion so that we do not solve a system of equations, *e.g.* the Lagrange polynomial or Newton polynomial. We shall explore this topic further in section 5.7. For now, we turn our attention to developing a curve fitting algorithm using the least-squares minimization concept.

5.2.1 Approximation accuracy

When a continuous function $f(x) : x \in [a, b]$ or a set of discrete data $(f_k \equiv f(x_k) : k = 1, 2, \cdots m)$ is represented by an approximate function

$\bar{f}(x)$, it is often desirable to choose $\bar{f}(x)$ such that the error between the approximate function and the real data is as small as possible. The difference between the true value of function and the model prediction can be quantified using norms. In other words, we choose the parameters for the approximating function such that

$$f(e_1, e_2, \cdots e_m) = ||f_k - \bar{f}(x_k)||_p$$

is minimized. The norms defined in Chapter 3 may be used in any one of the following contexts:

1. L_1 norm (least absolute deviation)

$$||f_k - \bar{f}(x_k)||_1 = \sum_{i=1}^{m} |f_k - \bar{f}(x_k)|.$$

Here, all deviations are weighted equally regardless of whether they are very small or very large. Thus L_1 is relatively insensitive to outliers, provided, of course, that these are few in number.

2. L_2 norm (least-squares or Euclidean norm)

$$||f_k - \bar{f}(x_k)||_2 = \sum_{i=1}^{m} \left[f_k - \bar{f}(x_k)\right]^2.$$

Statistical considerations show that the L_2 norm is the most suitable choice for smoothing data when additive errors have a normal distribution because then the influence of errors is minimized.

3. L_∞ norm (Chebyshev norm)

$$||f_k - \bar{f}(x_k)||_\infty = \max_{k=1\cdots m} \sum_{i=1}^{m} |f_k - \bar{f}(x_k)|.$$

The L_∞ norm considers only that data point or points where the maximal error appears. In practice, the L_∞ norm is used when errors are small with respect to an approximation error.

5.3   Curve fitting

5.3.1   Least-squares approximation

Suppose there are m independent experimental observations and we wish to fit a global polynomial of degree n $(n < m)$ through these date. At each observation point, an error is defined as

$$e_k = [f_k - P_{n-1}(x_k)] \qquad k = 1, \cdots, m.$$

The basis functions are still the set $\{x^{i-1} \mid i = 1, \cdots n\}$ and the polynomial approximation reads

$$P_{n-1}(x) = \sum_{i=1}^{n} a_i x^{i-1} \, .$$

The coefficients a_i are the unknowns that need to be resolved. Next we construct a scalar objective function that is the sum of squares of the error at every observation point, *i.e.*

$$S(\boldsymbol{a}) = \frac{\sum_{k=1}^{m} \epsilon_k^2}{m} = \frac{\sum_{k=1}^{m} [f_k - P_{n-1}(x_k)]^2}{m} = \frac{\sum_{k=1}^{m} (f_k - \sum_{i=1}^{n} a_i x_k^{i-1})^2}{m} \, .$$

Clearly $S(\boldsymbol{a})$ depends on the n unknowns $a_1, a_2, \ldots a_n$. From elementary calculus, the condition for the function $S(\boldsymbol{a})$ to exhibit a minimum is

$$\frac{\partial S(\boldsymbol{a})}{\partial \boldsymbol{a}} = 0 \, .$$

This last result provides n linear equations of the form $\boldsymbol{Pa} = \boldsymbol{b}$ that can be solved for $\boldsymbol{a}$. The expanded form of the equations read

$$\begin{bmatrix} \sum_{k=1}^{m} 1 & \sum_{k=1}^{m} x_k & \sum_{k=1}^{m} x_k^2 & \cdots & \sum_{k=1}^{m} x_k^{n-1} \\ \sum_{k=1}^{m} x_k & \sum_{k=1}^{m} x_k^2 & \sum_{k=1}^{m} x_k^3 & \cdots & \sum_{k=1}^{m} x_k^n \\ \sum_{k=1}^{m} x_k^2 & \sum_{k=1}^{m} x_k^3 & \sum_{k=1}^{m} x_k^4 & & \sum_{k=1}^{m} x_k^{n+1} \\ \vdots & \vdots & & \ddots & \vdots \\ \sum_{k=1}^{m} x_k^{n-1} & \sum_{k=1}^{m} x_k^n & \sum_{k=1}^{m} x_k^{n+1} & \cdots & \sum_{k=1}^{m} x_k^{2(n-1)} \end{bmatrix} \begin{bmatrix} a_1 \\ a_2 \\ a_3 \\ \vdots \\ a_n \end{bmatrix}$$

$$= \begin{bmatrix} \sum_{k=1}^{m} f_k \\ \sum_{k=1}^{m} f_k x_k \\ \sum_{k=1}^{m} f_k x_k^2 \\ \vdots \\ \sum_{k=1}^{m} f_k x_k^{n-1} \end{bmatrix} \, .$$

Observe that the equations are not only linear, but the matrix is also symmetric.

EXAMPLE 5.2 (Linear least-squares approximation) *A special well-known case of approximation is linear least squares approximation in which case we fit a linear polynomial to a given set of data. With $n = 2$ and m discrete data points, the last equation becomes*

$$\begin{bmatrix} \sum_{k=1}^{m} 1 & \sum_{k=1}^{m} x_k \\ \sum_{k=1}^{m} x_k & \sum_{k=1}^{m} x_k^2 \end{bmatrix} \begin{bmatrix} a_1 \\ a_2 \end{bmatrix} = \begin{bmatrix} \sum_{k=1}^{m} f_k \\ \sum_{k=1}^{m} f_k x_k \end{bmatrix} \, .$$

The above matrix equation can be solved using the methods of Chapter 3. More specifically, it can be shown by applying Cramer's rule that

$$a_1 = \frac{\begin{vmatrix} \sum_{k=1}^{m} f_k & \sum_{k=1}^{m} x_k \\ \sum_{k=1}^{m} f_k x_k & \sum_{k=1}^{m} x_k^2 \end{vmatrix}}{\begin{vmatrix} m & \sum_{k=1}^{m} x_k \\ \sum_{k=1}^{m} x_k & \sum_{k=1}^{m} x_k^2 \end{vmatrix}}.$$

and

$$a_2 = \frac{\begin{vmatrix} m & \sum_{k=1}^{m} f_k \\ \sum_{k=1}^{m} x_k & \sum_{k=1}^{m} f_k x_k \end{vmatrix}}{\begin{vmatrix} m & \sum_{k=1}^{m} x_k \\ \sum_{k=1}^{m} x_k & \sum_{k=1}^{m} x_k^2 \end{vmatrix}}.$$

EXAMPLE 5.3 (Linear regression) *We wish to employ linear regression to fit the data in Table 5.2. In this case $m = 4$, $f_k = P$ and $x_k = T$. Accordingly (and neglecting the units of f_k and x_k),*

$$\sum_{k=1}^{4} f_k = 17.1860 + 18.5560 + 20.0150 + 21.5670 = 77.3240$$

$$\sum_{k=1}^{4} x_k = 220.0000 + 224.0000 + 228.0000 + 232.0000 = 904.0000$$

$$\sum_{k=1}^{4} x_k^2 = 204384.0000$$

$$\sum_{k=1}^{4} f_k x_k = 1.7504 \times 10^4$$

Therefore

$$a_1 = \frac{\begin{vmatrix} 77.3240 & 904.0000 \\ 1.7504 \times 10^4 & 204384.0000 \end{vmatrix}}{\begin{vmatrix} 4 & 904.0000 \\ 904.0000 & 204384.0000 \end{vmatrix}} = -63.1703.$$

and

$$a_2 = \frac{\begin{vmatrix} 4 & 77.3240 \\ 1.7504 \times 10^4 & 1.7504 \times 10^4 \end{vmatrix}}{\begin{vmatrix} 4 & 904.0000 \\ 904.0000 & 204384.0000 \end{vmatrix}} = 0.3651.$$

```
function mnhf_normal_shock()
%MNHF_NORMAL_SHOCK plots then fits data from the normal shock table.

ms = 10;        % Markersize in figure.
fs = 16;        % Fontsize in figure.
polymax = 5;    % Maximum order of the approximating polynomial.

% Enter data from the Normal Shock Table. Ma1 gives the (supersonic)
% upstream Mach # whereas Ma2 gives the (subsonic) downstream Mach #.
Ma1 = 1.00:0.08:3.00;
Ma2 = [1.000 0.928 0.868 0.818 0.776 0.740 0.708 0.681 0.657 0.635 ...
        0.617 0.600 0.584 0.571 0.558 0.547 0.537 0.527 0.519 0.511 ...
        0.504 0.497 0.491 0.485 0.480 0.475];

% Plot the data.
figure; hold on; box on
plot(Ma1,Ma2,'k*','markersize',ms)
set(gca,'fontsize',fs)
xlabel('{\it Ma_1}, upstream Mach number')
ylabel('{\it Ma_2}, downstream Mach number')
title('Transonic flow through a normal shock')

% Show best fit curves through data up to polynomial order polymax.
for ii=1:polymax
 pf = polyfit(Ma1,Ma2,ii);
 M = linspace(min(Ma1),max(Ma1));
 plot(M,polyval(pf,M),'color',[rand, rand, rand])
end

% Add legend.
if polymax==5
 legend('tabulated data','order 1','order 2','order 3','order 4','order 5')
end
```

Figure 5.5: MATLAB function that uses `polyfit` and `polyval` to plot and fit data from the Normal Shock Table.

Thus the least-squares polynomial is

$$P_1 = a_1 T^0 + a_2 T^1 = -63.1703 + 0.3651T \,.$$

If the sums of the previous two examples are intimidating, note that MATLAB has a built-in function called `polyfit(x,y,n)` that will accept a set of pairwise data $\{x_k, y_k = f(x_k) \mid k = 1, \cdots, m\}$ and produce a polynomial fit of degree n (which can be different from m) using least-squares minimization. The use of `polyfit` (and its companion function `polyval`) is illustrated below.

EXAMPLE 5.4 (Using polyfit and polyval) *When high-velocity, supersonic flow (Mach number, $Ma > 1$) encounters a normal shock,* *it rapidly transitions to a subsonic flow (Ma < 1). Using principles from thermodynamics and fluid mechanics, it is possible to relate the upstream Mach number, $Ma_1 > 1$, to the downstream Mach number, $Ma_2 < 1$. Such data are reported in the Normal Shock Table and are reproduced in the MATLAB function illustrated in Figure 5.5. This function fits the data using polynomials of order 1 through 5 and plots the associated curves using a random color scheme. Not surprisingly, as the polynomial order increases, so too does the agreement between the curve and the data points, which are plotted as stars in Figure 5.6.*

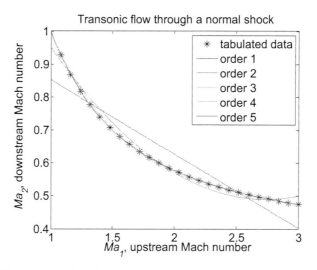

Figure 5.6: Graphical output from `mnhf_normal_shock`.

As suggested by the MATLAB commands reproduced below, we can also revisit this chapter's first example, which considered the evaluation of the error function by a collocation method.

```
>>x=[0.1:0.1:0.5]   % Define collocation points
>>y=erf(x)          % Calculate function at x
>>a=polyfit(x,y,4)  % Fit 4th degree polynomial.
>>polyval(a,x)      % Evaluate the polynomial at x
>>erf(x)            % Compare with exact values
```

EXAMPLE 5.5 (Regression accuracy) *We can determine the accuracy of the least-squares fit by computing the sum of squares of the* *deviation of the data around the mean. The mean of a function is evaluated from*

$$\bar{f} = \frac{1}{n} \sum_{i=1}^{n} f_k \, .$$

Let us define the sum of squares before application of regression as

$$S_o = \sum_{k=1}^{n} (f_k - \bar{f})^2 \, .$$

and the sum of squares after application of regression as

$$S = \sum_{i=1}^{n} \left(f_k - \sum_{i=1}^{n} a_i x^{i-1} \right)^2 \, .$$

The correlation coefficient is a normalized quantity defined as

$$r^2 = \left(\frac{S_o - S}{S_o} \right) = 1 - \frac{S}{S_o} \, .$$

In the limiting case of a perfect fit, $S = 0$ and therefore $r = 1$. In the opposite extreme where the fit is useless, $S_0 = S$ and therefore $r = 0$.

5.4 General nonlinear regression and linearization

In the previous sections, polynomials have been used as the workhorses of our functional approximations. More generally any function can be employed and the procedure for minimization remains the same.

5.4.1 Linearization

It is sometimes desirable to use linear regression, even if the function to be fitted is nonlinear. In this case, a procedure to transform the nonlinear equation to some suitable linear form may be used. For example, suppose we want to fit the exponential function $y = a_1 e^{a_2 x}$ to a data set (x_i, y_i), $i = 1, 2, \cdots m$. If we take the natural logarithm of the to-be-fitted function, we obtain an equation that is linear in the unknown parameters a_1 and a_2, *i.e.*

$$\ln y = \ln a_1 - a_2 x \, .$$

If we now designate a new dependent variable $\tilde{y} = \ln y$ and a "new" independent variable $\tilde{x} = x$, we obtain a new linear function in the transformed variables. The next step is to fit this new function $\tilde{y} = b + c\tilde{x}$ to the data set $(\tilde{x}_i, \tilde{y}_i)$, $i = 1, 2, \cdots m$ by linear regression.

Table 5.3 shows some common nonlinear functions and their equivalent transformations. Of course, at the end of the regression process, variables may be restored to their original form, i.e. $\tilde{x} \to x$, $\tilde{y} \to y$.

Original relation	Transformation and linear relation $\tilde{y} = c\tilde{x} + d$
$y = ax^b$	$\ln y = \ln a + b \ln x$ $\tilde{y} = \ln y, \ \tilde{x} = \ln x, \ c = b, \ d = \ln a$
$y = ae^{bx}$	$\ln y = \ln a + bx$ $\tilde{y} = \ln y, \ \tilde{x} = x, \ c = b, \ d = \ln a$
$y = \frac{ax}{b+x}$	$\frac{1}{y} = \frac{b+x}{ax}$ $\tilde{y} = \frac{1}{y}, \ \tilde{x} = \frac{1}{x}, \ c = \frac{b}{a}, \ d = \frac{1}{a}$
$y = \frac{a}{b+x}$	$\frac{1}{y} = \frac{b+x}{a}$ $\tilde{y} = \frac{1}{y}, \ \tilde{x} = x, \ c = \frac{1}{a}, \ d = \frac{b}{a}$
$y = a_0 x_1^{a1} x_2^{a2} x_3^{a3} \cdots x_m^{am}$	$\ln y = \ln a_0 + a_1 \ln x_1 + \cdots + a_m \ln a_m$ $\tilde{y} = c_0 + c_1 \tilde{x}_1 + c_2 \tilde{x}_2 + \cdots + c_m \tilde{x}_m$ $\tilde{y} = \ln y, \ c_0 = \ln a_0, \ c_i = a_i, \ i = 1, 2, \cdots m$ $\tilde{x}_i = \ln x_i, \ i = 1, 2, \cdots m$

Table 5.3: Some nonlinear relations and their transformed linear forms.

5.5 Difference operators

In the previous sections we developed polynomial approximation schemes in such a way that they required a solution of a system of linear algebraic equation. For uniformly spaced data, introduction of *difference operators* and difference tables, allows us to solve the same polynomial approximation problem in a more elegant manner without the need for solving a system of algebraic equations. This difference operator approach also lends itself naturally to recursive construction of higher degree polynomials with very little additional computation as well as extension to numerical differentiation and integration of discrete data as we study in Chapter 6.

Consider pairs of data $\{(x_i, f_i) \mid i = 1, 2, \cdots, m\}$ where the independent variable is uniformly-spaced so that

$$x_{i+1} = x_i + h, \qquad i = 1, 2, \cdots m \quad \text{or} \quad x_i = x_1 + (i-1)h.$$

Important difference operators are described as below.

Forward difference operator:

$$\Delta f_i = f_{i+1} - f_i. \tag{5.6}$$

Backward difference operator:

$$\nabla f_i = f_i - f_{i-1}. \tag{5.7}$$

Central difference operator:

$$\delta f_i = f_{i+1/2} - f_{i-1/2}\,. \tag{5.8}$$

Shift operator:

$$E f_i = f_{i+1}\,. \tag{5.9}$$

Differential operator:

$$D f(x) = \frac{\mathrm{d}f(x)}{\mathrm{d}x} = f'(x)\,. \tag{5.10}$$

The above difference operators are nothing but rules of calculation, just like the differential operator defines a rule for differentiation. Clearly these rules can be applied repeatedly to obtain higher order differences. For example, a second order forward difference with respect to reference point i is

$$\Delta^2 f_i = \Delta(\Delta f_i) = \Delta(f_{i+1} - f_i) = f_{i+2} - 2f_{i+1} + f_i\,.$$

5.5.1 Operator algebra

Having introduced some new definitions of operators, we can discover some interesting relationships between these operators. For instance,

$$\Delta f_i = f_{i+1} - f_i \quad \text{and} \quad E f_i = f_{i+1}\,,$$

so by combining these two equations, we can write

$$\Delta f_i = E f_i - f_i = (E - 1) f_i\,.$$

Because the operand f_i is the same on both sides of the equation, the operators (which define certain rules and hence have certain effects on the operand) must be related to one another via

$$\Delta = E - 1 \quad \text{or} \quad E = 1 + \Delta\,. \tag{5.11}$$

Equation (5.11) can then be applied on any other operand like f_{i+k}. All of the operators satisfy the distributive, commutative and associative rules of algebra. Also, repeated application of the shift operation associated with E can be represented by

$$E^\alpha = (1 + \Delta)^\alpha\,.$$

Note that $E^\alpha f(x)$ simply implies that the function f is evaluated after shifting the independent variable by α, *i.e.*

$$E^\alpha f(x) = f(x + \alpha h)\,.$$

Hence α can be an integer or any real number. Similarly, we have

$$\nabla f_i = f_i - f_{i-1} \quad , \quad E f_{i-1} = f_i \quad \text{and} \quad f_{i-1} = E^{-1} f_i \,,$$

where we have introduced the inverse of the shift operator E to indicate a shift in the backwards direction. Combining the above results, it can be shown that

$$\nabla f_i = f_i - E^{-1} f_i = (1 - E^{-1}) f_i \,.$$

Recognizing once again that the operand, f_i, is the same on both sides of the equation, the operators must themselves be related by

$$\nabla = 1 - E^{-1} \quad \text{or} \quad E^{-1} = 1 - \nabla \quad \text{or} \quad E = (1 - \nabla)^{-1} \,. \quad (5.12)$$

Yet another relation between the shift operator E and the differential operator D can be developed by considering the Taylor series expansion of $f(x + h)$, *i.e.*

$$f(x + h) = f(x) + h f'(x) + \frac{h^2}{2!} f''(x) + \cdots \,,$$

which can be written using operator notation as

$$E f(x) = \left[1 + hD + \frac{h^2 D^2}{2!} + \cdots \right] f(x)$$

The term inside the square brackets is related, of course, to the exponential function and hence

$$E = e^{hD} \,. \quad (5.13)$$

While such a game of discovering relationships between various operators can be played indefinitely, let us turn to developing some useful algorithms that may be applied in solving numerical problems of relevance to engineering.

5.5.2   Newton forward difference approximation

Our objective is to construct a polynomial representation for the discrete data set $\{(x_i, f_i) \mid i = 1, 2, \cdots, m\}$ using an alternate approach from that outlined in section 5.1.2.

Assuming there is a function $f(x)$ representing the given data*, we can express such a function as

$$f(x) = P_n(x) + R(x) \,,$$

where $P_n(x)$ is the polynomial approximation to $f(x)$ and $R(x)$ is the residual error. Given a set of m data points we know from section 5.1.2

---

*Is such an assumption always valid?

one way to can construct a corresponding polynomial of degree $m - 1$. Now let us use the power of operator algebra to develop an alternate way to construct such a polynomial. In the process, we will also learn something about the residual function, $R(x)$. Applying equation (5.11) α times on $f(x)$, we get

$$E^\alpha f(x) = (1 + \Delta)^\alpha f(x).$$

For integer values of α, $(1 + \Delta)^\alpha$ can be expressed using the binomial expansion while for any real number, it yields an infinite series. Using such an expansion, the above equation can be written as

$$
\begin{aligned}
f(x + \alpha h) \;=\; & \left[1 + \alpha\Delta + \frac{\alpha(\alpha - 1)}{2!}\Delta^2 + \frac{\alpha(\alpha - 1)(\alpha - 2)}{3!}\Delta^3 + \cdots \right. \\
& \left. \frac{\alpha(\alpha - 1)(\alpha - 2)\cdots(\alpha - n + 1)}{n!}\Delta^n + \cdots \right] f(x) \quad (5.14)
\end{aligned}
$$

Up to this point in our development we have merely used tricks of operator algebra. Now let us make a direct connection to the given set of discrete data $\{(x_i, f_i) \mid i = 1, 2, \cdots, m\}$. Taking x_1 as the reference point, the transformation $x = x_1 + \alpha h$ renders α the new independent variable. For integer values of $\alpha = 0, 1, \cdots m - 1$, we retrieve the equally-spaced data set $\{x_1, x_2, \cdots x_m\}$. Conversely, for non-integer (real) values of α we can realize the other values of $x \in (x_1, x_m)$. Splitting equation (5.14) into two parts,

$$
\begin{aligned}
f(x_1 + \alpha h) = & \left[1 + \alpha\Delta + \frac{\alpha(\alpha - 1)}{2!}\Delta^2 + \frac{\alpha(\alpha - 1)(\alpha - 2)}{3!}\Delta^3 + \cdots \right. \\
& \left. \frac{\alpha(\alpha - 1)(\alpha - 2)\cdots(\alpha - m + 2)}{(m - 1)!}\Delta^{m-1} \right] f(x_1) + R(x)
\end{aligned}
$$

The terms inside the square brackets are a polynomial of degree $m - 1$ in the transformed variable α. We still need to determine the numbers $\{\Delta f(x_1), \Delta^2 f(x_1), \cdots, \Delta^{m-1} f(x_1)\}$. These can be computed and organized as a forward difference table as shown schematically below.

Because forward differences are needed for constructing the polynomial, this polynomial is called the Newton forward difference polynomial. It is given by

$$
\begin{aligned}
P_{m-1}(x_1 + \alpha h) = & \left[1 + \alpha\Delta + \frac{\alpha(\alpha - 1)}{2!}\Delta^2 + \frac{\alpha(\alpha - 1)(\alpha - 2)}{3!}\Delta^3 \right. \\
& \left. \frac{\alpha(\alpha - 1)(\alpha - 2)\cdots(\alpha - m + 2)}{(m - 1)!}\Delta^{m-1} \right] f(x_1) \quad (5.15)
\end{aligned}
$$

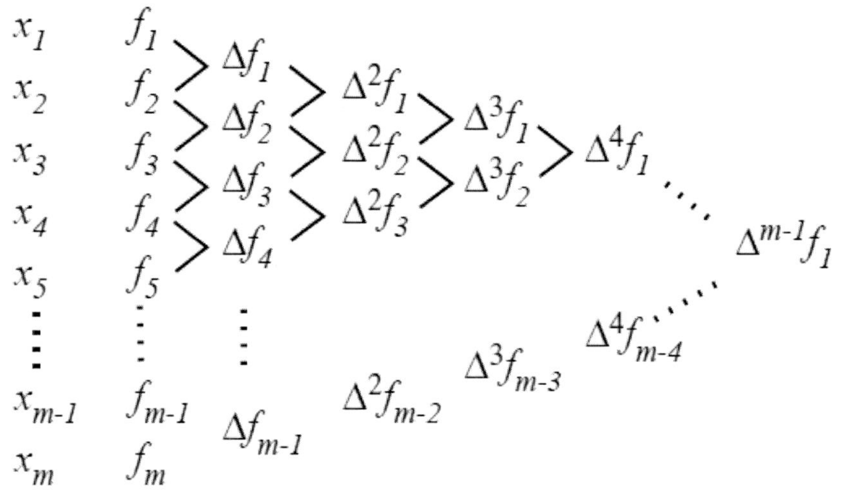

Figure 5.7: Structure of a Newton forward difference table for m equally spaced data points.

The above polynomial will pass through all the data within the data set $\{(x_i, f_i) \mid i = 1, 2, \cdots, m\}$, *i.e.* for integer values of $\alpha = 0, 1, \cdots m - 1$, the polynomial will return the values $\{f_1, f_2, \cdots f_m\}$. Thus the residual function, $R(x)$, will have roots at the data points $\{x_i \mid i = 1, 2, \cdots, m\}$. For a polynomial of degree $m - 1$, the residual at the other values of x is typically represented as $R(x) \sim \mathcal{O}(h^m)$ to suggest that the leading term in the truncated part of the series is of order m.

EXAMPLE 5.6 (Using the forward difference table) *A set of five* $(m = 5)$ *equally-spaced data points are shown in the form of a forward difference table in Figure 5.8.*

For this example, clearly $h = 1$ *and therefore* $x = x_1 + \alpha$. *We can take the reference point as* $x_1 = 2$ *and construct the following linear, quadratic and cubic polynomials, respectively:*[*]

$$P_1(2 + \alpha) = [1 + \alpha\Delta]\, f(x_1) = 8 + \alpha(19) + \mathcal{O}(h^2),$$

$$P_2(2 + \alpha) = 8 + \alpha(19) + \frac{\alpha(\alpha - 1)}{2!}(18) + \mathcal{O}(h^3),$$

$$P_3(2 + \alpha) = 8 + \alpha(19) + \frac{\alpha(\alpha - 1)}{2!}(18) + \frac{\alpha(\alpha - 1)(\alpha - 2)}{3!}(6) + \mathcal{O}(h^4)$$

You can verify easily that $P_1(2 + \alpha)$ *passes through* $\{x_1, x_2\}$, $P_2(2 + \alpha)$ *passes through* $\{x_1, x_2, x_3\}$ *and* $P_3(2 + \alpha)$ *passes through* $\{x_1, x_2, x_3, x_4\}$.

---

[*]Note that $P_4(2 + \alpha) = P_3(2 + \alpha)$ for this case. Why?

$$x_1 = 2 \quad f_1 = 8$$
$$\Delta f_1 = 19$$
$$x_2 = 3 \quad f_2 = 27 \qquad \Delta^2 f_1 = 18$$
$$\Delta f_2 = 37 \qquad \Delta^3 f_1 = 6$$
$$x_3 = 4 \quad f_3 = 64 \qquad \Delta^2 f_2 = 24 \qquad \Delta^4 f_1 = 0$$
$$\Delta f_3 = 61 \qquad \Delta^3 f_2 = 6$$
$$x_4 = 5 \quad f_4 = 125 \qquad \Delta^2 f_3 = 30$$
$$\Delta f_4 = 91$$
$$x_5 = 6 \quad f_5 = 216$$

Figure 5.8: Example of a Newton forward difference table.

For finding the interpolated value of $f(x = 3.5)$, for example, first determine the values of α at $x = 3.5$ from the equation $x = x_1 + \alpha h$. It is $\alpha = (3.5 - 2)/1 = 1.5$. Using this value in the cubic polynomial,

$$P_3(2 + 1.5) = 8 + 1.5(19) + \frac{1.5(0.5)}{2!}(18) + \frac{1.5(0.5)(-0.5)}{3!}(6) = 42.875$$

As another example, by taking $x_3 = 4$ as the reference point, we can construct the following quadratic polynomial:

$$P_2(4 + \alpha) = 64 + \alpha(61) + \frac{\alpha(\alpha - 1)}{2!}(30) \,,$$

which will pass through the data set $\{x_3, x_4, x_5\}$. This illustration should show that once the difference table is constructed, a variety of polynomials of varying degrees can be easily developed.

5.5.3 Newton backward difference approximation

An equivalent class of polynomials using the *backward difference* operator based on equation (5.12) can be constructed. Applying equation (5.12) α times on $f(x)$, we get

$$E^\alpha f(x) = (1 - \nabla)^{-\alpha} f(x) \,,$$

which can be expanded as before to yield

$$f(x + \alpha h) = \left[1 + \alpha \nabla + \frac{\alpha(\alpha + 1)}{2!} \nabla^2 + \frac{\alpha(\alpha + 1)(\alpha + 2)}{3!} \nabla^3 + \cdots \right.$$
$$\left. \frac{\alpha(\alpha + 1)(\alpha + 2) \cdots (\alpha + n - 1)}{n!} \nabla^n + \cdots \right] f(x) \quad (5.16)$$

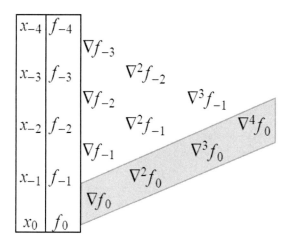

Figure 5.9: Structure of Newton backward difference table for five equally-spaced data points.

As with the Newton forward formula, equation (5.16) terminates at a finite number of terms for integer values of α and, for non-integer values, it will represent an infinite series which must be truncated, thus introducing a truncation error.

In making the connection to a discrete data set $\{(x_i, f_i) \mid i = 0, -1 \cdots , -n\}$, typically the largest value of x (say, x_0) is taken as the reference point. The transformation $x = x_0 + \alpha h$ renders α the new independent variable. For negative integer values of $\alpha = -1, -2, \cdots -n$, we retrieve the equally-spaced data set $\{x_{-1}, \cdots x_{-n}\}$. Conversely for non-integer (real) values of α, we may realize the other values of $x \in (x_{-n}, x_0)$. Moreover, splitting equation (5.16) into two parts

$$f(x_0 + \alpha h) = \left[1 + \alpha\nabla + \frac{\alpha(\alpha + 1)}{2!}\nabla^2 + \frac{\alpha(\alpha + 1)(\alpha + 2)}{3!}\nabla^3 + \cdots \right.$$
$$\left. \frac{\alpha(\alpha + 1)(\alpha + 2)\cdots(\alpha + n - 1)}{n!}\nabla^n + \cdots \right] f(x_0) + R(x)$$

we can recognize the terms inside the square brackets as a polynomial of degree n in the transformed variable α. Similar to before, we still need to determine the numbers $\{\nabla f(x_0), \nabla^2 f(x_0), \cdots , \nabla^n f(x_0)\}$. These can be computed and organized in the form of a backward difference table as shown in Figure 5.9.

Because backward differences are needed for constructing the polynomial, this polynomial is called the Newton backward difference poly-

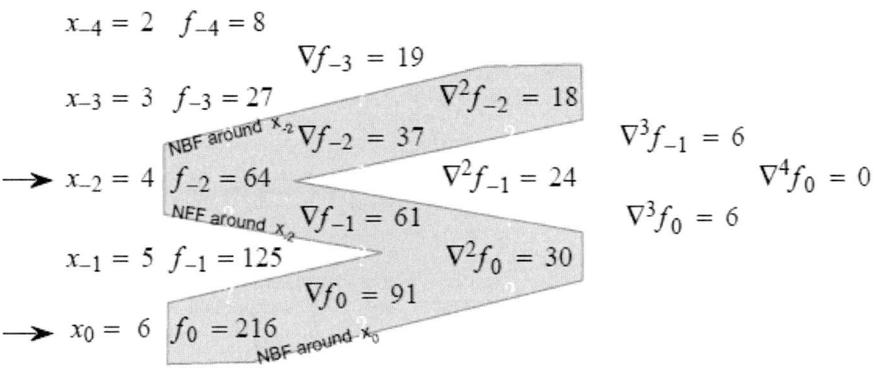

$$x_{-4} = 2 \quad f_{-4} = 8$$

$$\nabla f_{-3} = 19$$

$$x_{-3} = 3 \quad f_{-3} = 27 \qquad\qquad \nabla^2 f_{-2} = 18$$

NBF around x_{-2} $\nabla f_{-2} = 37 \qquad\qquad\qquad \nabla^3 f_{-1} = 6$

$$x_{-2} = 4 \quad f_{-2} = 64 \qquad\qquad \nabla^2 f_{-1} = 24 \qquad\qquad\qquad \nabla^4 f_0 = 0$$

NFF around x_{-2} $\nabla f_{-1} = 61 \qquad\qquad\qquad \nabla^3 f_0 = 6$

$$x_{-1} = 5 \quad f_{-1} = 125 \qquad\qquad \nabla^2 f_0 = 30$$

$$\nabla f_0 = 91$$

$$x_0 = 6 \quad f_0 = 216$$

NBF around x_0

Figure 5.10: Example of a Newton backward difference table

nomial. It is given by

$$P_n(x_0 + \alpha h) = \left[1 + \alpha\nabla + \frac{\alpha(\alpha+1)}{2!}\nabla^2 + \frac{\alpha(\alpha+1)(\alpha+2)}{3!}\nabla^3 + \cdots \right.$$
$$\left. \frac{\alpha(\alpha+1)(\alpha+2)\cdots(\alpha+n-1)}{n!}\nabla^n \right] f(x_0) + \mathcal{O}(h^{n+1}) \quad (5.17)$$

The above polynomial will pass through the data set $\{(x_i, f_i) \mid i = 0, \cdots, -n\}$, i.e. for integer values of $\alpha = 0, -1, \cdots - n$, the polynomial will return values $\{f_0, f_{-1}, \cdots f_{-n}\}$. For all other values of x, the residual error will be of order $\mathcal{O}(h^{n+1})$.

EXAMPLE 5.7 *A set of five ($n = 4$) equally-spaced data points are shown in the form of a backward difference table in Figure 5.10.*

These are the same data as used in the previous example! Again, $h = 1$ and therefore $x = x_0 + \alpha$. In the present case, let us use $x_{-2} = 4$ as the reference point. A quadratic backward difference polynomial in α is

$$P_2(4 + \alpha) = 64 + \alpha(37) + \frac{\alpha(\alpha+1)}{2!}(18) + \mathcal{O}(h^3) \,,$$

which passes through the points (x_{-2}, f_{-2}), (x_{-3}, f_{-3}) and (x_{-4}, f_{-4}) for $\alpha = 0, -1, -2$, respectively. Recall that the corresponding forward difference polynomial around the same point read

$$P_2(4 + \alpha) = 64 + \alpha(61) + \frac{\alpha(\alpha-1)}{2!}(30) \,,$$

which passes through the three forward points for $\alpha = 0, 1, 2$. Although they are based on the same reference point, these are two different polynomials passing through different sets of data points.

As a final example, let us construct a quadratic backward difference polynomial around $x_0 = 6$. It is

$$P_2(6 + \alpha) = 216 + \alpha(91) + \frac{\alpha(\alpha + 1)}{2!}(30)\,.$$

5.6   Inverse interpolation

One of the objectives in constructing an interpolating polynomial is to be able to evaluate the function $f(x)$ at values of x other than the ones within the discrete data set (x_i, f_i). The objective of *inverse interpolation* is to determine the independent variable x for a given value of f using the given data. If x_i are equally-spaced, we can combine two tools (polynomial curve fitting and root finding) to meet this objective, although this must be done with caution as we highlight below.

Consider the data shown in Figure 5.8. Suppose we wish to find the value of x where $f = 100$. Using the three data points in the neighbourhood of $f = 100$ in Figure 5.8 viz. (x_3, x_4, x_5), and using a quadratic polynomial fit, we have

$$P_2(4 + \alpha) = 64 + \alpha(61) + \frac{\alpha(\alpha - 1)}{2!}(30)\,.$$

A graph of this polynomial approximation $P_2(4 + \alpha)$ and the actual function $f(x) = x^3$ used to generate the data given in Figure 5.8 are shown in Figure 5.11.

It is clear that the polynomial approximation is quite reliable when $4 \lesssim x \lesssim 6$. Outside of this range, however, the polynomial is a comparatively poor approximation of the original function. Note, in particular, that if we solve the inverse interpolation problem by setting

$$P_2(4 + \alpha) - 100 = 0 \qquad \text{or} \qquad 64 + \alpha(61) + \frac{\alpha(\alpha - 1)}{2!}(30) - 100 = 0\,,$$

we will find two roots. One of these $(\alpha = 0.64637, \ x = 4.64637)$ is the desired root while the other $(\alpha = -3.71304, \ x = 0.286962)$ is spurious. This problem can become compounded if we use higher degree polynomials in an effort to improve accuracy.

In order to achieve high accuracy but remain close to the desired root, we can generate an initial guess from *linear interpolation* and then

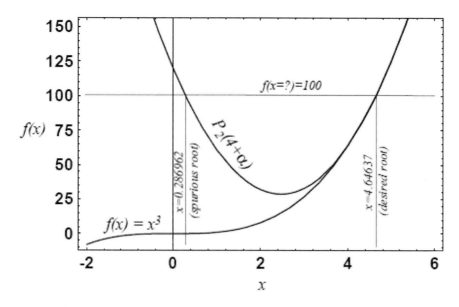

Figure 5.11: Example of a inverse interpolation (graphical form).

construct a *fixed point iteration* scheme on the polynomial approximation. Suppose, for example, that we wish to find x corresponding to
$f(x) = d$, where d indicates the desired function value. As indicated
by the next equation, we first construct a polynomial of degree $m - 1$
to represent the discrete data.

$$P_{m-1}(x_1 + \alpha h) = \left[1 + \alpha \Delta + \frac{\alpha(\alpha - 1)}{2!} \Delta^2 + \frac{\alpha(\alpha - 1)(\alpha - 2)}{3!} \Delta^3 + \cdots \right.$$
$$\left. \frac{\alpha(\alpha - 1)(\alpha - 2) \cdots (\alpha - m + 2)}{(m - 1)!} \Delta^{m-1} \right] f(x_1).$$

Then we let $f(x_1 + \alpha h) = d$ and rearrange the polynomial in the form

$$\alpha_{i+1} = g(\alpha_i) \qquad i = 0, 1, 2 \cdots,$$

where $g(\alpha)$ is obtained by rearranging the polynomial

$$g(\alpha) = \frac{1}{\Delta f_1} \left[d - f_1 - \frac{\alpha(\alpha - 1)}{2!} \Delta^2 f_1 - \frac{\alpha(\alpha - 1)(\alpha - 2)}{3!} \Delta^3 f_1 + \cdots \right].$$

The initial guess is obtained by truncating the polynomial after the
linear term, *i.e.*

$$\alpha_0 = \frac{d - f_1}{\Delta f_1}.$$

i	α_i
1	.59016393
2	.64964028
3	.64613306
4	.64638815
5	.64636980
6	.64637112
7	.64637102
8	.64637103
9	.64637103
10	.64637103

Table 5.4: Example of a inverse interpolation (tabular form).

EXAMPLE 5.8 *Continuing with the task of computing x where $f(x) = 100$ for the data shown in Figure 5.8, the fixed point iterate is*

$$\alpha_{i+1} = [100 - 64 - 15\alpha_i(\alpha_i - 1)] / 61,$$

and the initial guess is

$$\alpha_0 = \frac{d - f_1}{\Delta f_1} = \frac{100 - 64}{61} = 0.5902.$$

The first ten iterates are shown in Table 5.4.

5.7   Lagrange polynomials

Thus far we have examined ways to construct polynomial approximations using data equally-spaced in x. For a data set $\{x_i, f_i | i = 0, 1, \cdots n\}$, that contains unequally-spaced data in the independent variable, we can instead apply the following Lagrange interpolation formula:

$$P_n(x) = \sum_{i=0}^{n} f_i L_i(x) \tag{5.18}$$

where

$$L_i(x) = \prod_{j=0, j \neq i}^{n} \frac{x - x_j}{x_i - x_j}.$$

Note that

$$L_i(x_j) = \begin{cases} 0 & j \neq i \\ 1 & j = i \end{cases},$$

and each $L_i(x)$ is a polynomial of degree n. It is also clear from equation (5.18) that $P_n(x_j) = f_j$, *i.e.* the polynomial passes through the data points (x_j, f_j).

If we wish to construct a quadratic polynomial passing through (x_0, f_0), (x_1, f_1), (x_2, f_2), for example, we can employ equation (5.18) and show that

$$P_2(x) = f_0 \frac{(x - x_1)(x - x_2)}{(x_0 - x1)(x_0 - x_2)} + f_1 \frac{(x - x_0)(x - x_2)}{(x_1 - x_0)(x_1 - x_2)} + f_2 \frac{(x - x_0)(x - x_1)}{(x_2 - x_0)(x_2 - x_1)}$$
$$= 1.00 \frac{(x - 1.2)(x - 1.5)}{(1 - 1.2)(1 - 1.5)} + 1.728 \frac{(x - 1)(x - 1.5)}{(1.2 - 1)(1.2 - 1.5)} + 3.375 \frac{(x - 1)(x - 1.2)}{(1.5 - 1)(1.5 - 1.2)}$$

A MATLAB function that implements Lagrange interpolation using equation (5.18) is given in Figure 5.12. This function accepts two arrays specifying the discrete data then constructs the highest possible degree Lagrange polynomial and finally evaluates and returns the interpolated values of the function f at specified values of x.

5.8   Newton's divided difference polynomials

An alternate way to construct the approximating polynomial is based on constructing a so-called divided difference table. The polynomial itself is written in the form

$$P_n(x) = \sum_{i=0}^{n} a_i \prod_{j=0}^{i} (x - x_{j-1}) \tag{5.19}$$
$$= a_0 + a_1(x - x_0) + a_2(x - x_0)(x - x_1) + \cdots$$
$$+ a_n(x - x_0) \cdots (x - x_{n-1}).$$

The advantage of this approach is that the unknown coefficients a_i can be constructed recursively or found directly from the divided difference table. The first divided difference is defined by the equation

$$f[x_0, x_1] = \frac{f_1 - f_0}{x_1 - x_0}.$$

Similarly the second divided difference is defined as

$$f[x_0, x_1, x_2] = \frac{f[x_1, x_2] - f[x_0, x_1]}{x_2 - x_0}.$$

With these definitions to hand, we return to the task of finding the coefficients a_i in equation (5.19) The first coefficient is

$$P_n(x_0) = a_0 = f[x_0] = f_0.$$

```matlab
function f=mnhf_lagrangeP(xt,ft,x)
%MNHF_LAGRANGEP contructs a Lagrange polynomial from discrete data.
%
% (xt,ft) — discrete data (xt unequally—spaced)
% x — x—coordinate of interpolated values.
% f — y—coordinate of interpolated values.
%
% Usage:  mnhf_lagrangeP([1,2,3.5,5],[1,4,3.5^2,25],[3,4])

nx = length(xt);
ny = length(ft);
m =  length(x);

if nx~=ny
  error(' (xt,ft) do not have the same number of values')
end

% Initialize.
delt = zeros(1,nx);
f    = zeros(1,m);

for k=1:m
 sum = 0;
 for i=1:nx
  delt(i)=1;
   for j=1:nx
    if j~=i
      delt(i) = delt(i)*(x(k)—xt(j))/(xt(i)—xt(j));
    end
   end
  sum = sum + ft(i) * delt(i) ;
 end
 f(k) = sum;
end
```

Figure 5.12: MATLAB implementation of the Lagrange interpolation formula given by equation (5.18).

$x_0 = 1.0 \quad f_0 = 1.000$

$\quad\quad\quad\quad f[x_0, x_1] = 3.6400$

$x_1 = 1.2 \quad f_1 = 1.728 \quad\quad\quad\quad f[x_0, x_1, x_2] = 3.700$

$\quad\quad\quad\quad f[x_1, x_2] = 5.4900 \quad\quad\quad\quad f[x_0, x_1, x_2, x_3] = 1.000$

$x_2 = 1.5 \quad f_2 = 3.375 \quad\quad\quad\quad f[x_1, x_2, x_3] = 4.300$

$\quad\quad\quad\quad f[x_2, x_3] = 7.2100$

$x_3 = 1.6 \quad f_3 = 4.096$

Figure 5.13: Divided difference table for four unequally-spaced data points.

The second coefficient is

$$P_n(x_1) = a_0 + a_1(x_1 - x_0) = f_1,$$

which can be rearranged as

$$a_1 = \frac{f_1 - f_0}{x_1 - x_0} = f[x_0, x_1].$$

The third coefficient is obtained from,

$$P_n(x_2) = a_0 + a_1(x_2 - x_0) + a_2(x_2 - x_0)(x_2 - x_1) = f_2.$$

The only unknown here is a_2, which, after some rearrangement, can be determined from

$$a_2 = \frac{f[x_1, x_2] - f[x_0, x_1]}{x_2 - x_0} = f[x_0, x_1, x_2].$$

In general the n-th coefficient is the n-th divided difference.

$$a_n = \frac{f[x_1, x_2, \cdots x_n] - f[x_0, x_1, \cdots x_{n-1}]}{x_n - x_0} = f[x_0, x_1, \cdots, x_n].$$

EXAMPLE 5.9 *Consider the example data and the divided difference table shown in Figure 5.13.*

If we wish to construct a quadratic polynomial passing through (x_0, f_0), (x_1, f_1), (x_2, f_2) using equation (5.19) and the above difference table, then

$$\begin{aligned} P_2(x) &= f_0 + f[x_0, x_1](x - x_0) + f[x_0, x_1, x_2](x - x_0)(x - x_1), \\ &= 1.000 + 3.64(x - 1) + 3.70(x - 1)(x - 1.2). \end{aligned}$$

In order to construct a cubic polynomial by adding the additional data point (x_3, f_3), a Lagrange polynomial based on equation (5.18) requires a *complete reconstruction of the equation, whereas one based on equation (5.19) is simply*

$$
\begin{aligned}
P_2(x) &= f_0 + f[x_0, x_1](x - x_0) + f[x_0, x_1, x_2](x - x_0)(x - x_1) + \\
&\quad f[x_0, x_1, x_2, x_3](x - x_0)(x - x_1)(x - x_2)\,, \\
\\
&= 1.000 + 3.64(x - 1) + 3.70(x - 1)(x - 1.2) + \\
&\quad 1(x - 1)(x - 1.2)(x - 1.5)\,.
\end{aligned}
$$

5.9   Piecewise continuous functions - splines

In the methods outlined above, we sought to fit a single function over the entire range of data. This approach works well for low order polynomials, whereas high order polynomials may exhibit osculations. Figure 5.14 a shows a 9-th degree polynomial fit to a data set having ten points. Although the polynomial passes through all ten data points, there are unacceptable variations in the approximating polynomial between data points. To overcome the problem of large fluctuations for situations with large n ($n > 4$) we usually interpolate in a piecewise manner. In this case, each pair of data points is fitted with a low order polynomial. Figure 5.14 b shows the same data points fitted with cubic splines, which we shall describe in more detail below. The word "spline" is a legacy term that refers to a strip of metal or wood. In earlier times, curves were designed for planes and ships by mounting strips of metal or wood such that they went through desired points but were free to move.

From a computational point of view, suppose we have a set of n points through which we want to prescribe a function that can be used to determine the value of $f(x_k)$ for any x_k. With zeroth-order splines, the construction ends up looking like a step function. From Figure 5.15, it is obvious that this is not an ideal representation. Moreover, the function f is discontinuous over the range in question.

Zeroth-order splines

$$
f_i(x) = f_{i-1} \qquad \text{for } x_{i-1} \leq x \leq x_i\,.
$$

First-order splines - Linear interpolation

$$
f_i(x) = f_{i-1} + \left(\frac{f_i - f_{i-1}}{x_i - x_{i-1}} \right)(x - x_{i-1}) \qquad \text{for } x_{i-1} \leq x \leq x_i\,.
$$

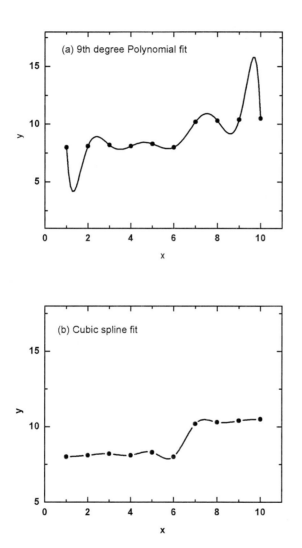

Figure 5.14: Fitting data using a single polynomial vs. using (cubic) splines.

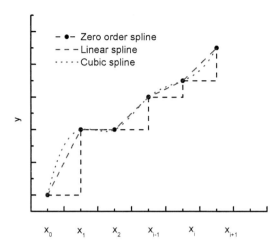

Figure 5.15: Different forms of spline interpolation.

With linear splines, straight lines are drawn between adjacent points. This approach is obviously more accurate than that of the zeroth-order spline, however, the derivatives of f remain discontinuous at the junction nodes or knots.

Second-order splines - Quadratic interpolation

The logical next step is to employ second-order splines. In this case we assume a quadratic function $(f_i(x) = a_i + b_i x + c_i x^2)$ in the interval $x_{i-1} \leq x \leq x_i$. Because there are n intervals, we need to determine $3n$ constants. This requires $3n$ conditions. Regarding points $i = 1$ to $i = n - 1$ as the interior points or knots and points $i = 0$ and $i = n$ as the end points, we develop conditions as outlined below.

1. For knot i,
$$f_i(x_i) = a_i + b_i x_i + c_i x_i^2 \,,$$
and
$$f_{i+1}(x_i) = a_{i+1} + b_{i+1} x_i + c_{i+1} x_i^2 = f_i \,.$$
The above represent $2(n - 1)$ conditions.

2. Also for knot i, the derivative approaching from the left must be the same as the derivative approaching from the right. In symbols,
$$f_i'(x_i) = f_{i+1}'(x_i) \,.$$

This implies that

$$b_i + 2c_i x_i = b_{i+1} + 2c_{i+1} x_i \,.$$

The above represent a further $n - 1$ conditions.

Obviously, this leaves $3n - 2(n - 1) - (n - 1) = 3$ conditions or degrees of freedom. Two obvious choices are to specify the start and end points, *i.e.*

$$f_i(x_0) = f_0 \qquad \text{and} \qquad f_n(x_n) = f_n \,.$$

There remains one final condition to be specified. The choice is often quite arbitrary, *e.g.* we can assume that the second derivative at one of the extrema is zero, in which case we might write

$$f_n''(x_n) = 2c_n = 0 \,.$$

Thus $3n$ conditions form a linear system in $3n$ unknowns. We can easily solve such a system using the methods of Chapter 3.

EXAMPLE 5.10 (✎ **Quadratic splines**) *Suppose the following measurements have been obtained from an experiment:*

i	0	1	2	3	4
x	5.0	7.0	12.0	15.0	20.0
y	2.0	5.0	8.0	11.0	5.0

Let us fit a second-order spline to the data and estimate the value of y at $x = 11.0$.

We begin by noting that there are five data points, thus we have four intervals for which we can fit four quadratic equations. The equation for any one of these quadratic equations is given by the following general formula:

$$f_i(x) = a_i + b_i x_i + c_i x_i^2 \,.$$

Each quadratic has three parameters, thus there are a total of $3 \times 4 = 12$ unknowns: $[a_1, b_1, c_1, a_2, b_2, c_2, a_3, b_3, c_3, a_4, b_4, c_4]$. The twelve corresponding equations are constructed as follows:

$i = 1$

$$f_1(x) = a_1 + b_1 x_0 + c_1 x_0^2 = a_1 + 5b_1 + 5^2 c_1 = 2$$
$$f_1(x) = a_1 + b_1 x_1 + c_1 x_1^2 = a_1 + 7b_1 + 7^2 c_1 = 5$$

$i = 2$

$$f_2(x) = a_2 + b_2 x_1 + c_2 x_1^2 = a_2 + 7b_2 + 7^2 c_2$$
$$f_2(x) = a_2 + b_2 x_2 + c_2 x_2^2 = a_2 + 12b_2 + 12^2 c_2$$

$i = 3$

$$f_i(x) = a_3 + b_3 x_2 + c_3 x_2^2 = a_3 + 12 b_3 + 12^2 c_3$$
$$f_i(x) = a_3 + b_3 x_3 + c_3 x_3^2 = a_3 + 15 b_3 + 15^2 c_3$$

$i = 4$

$$f_i(x) = a_4 + b_4 x_3 + c_4 x_3^2 = a_4 + 15 b_4 + 15^2 c_4$$
$$f_i(x) = a_4 + b_4 x_4 + c_4 x_4^2 = a_4 + 20 b_4 + 20^2 c_4$$

Meanwhile enforcing the continuity of the first derivatives yields

$$b_i + 2 c_i x_i = b_{i+1} + 2 c_{i+1} x_i .$$

Quadratics 1 and 2, node $i = 2$

$$b_1 + 2 c_1 x_2 = b_2 + 2 c_2 x_2 \Rightarrow b_1 + 10 c_1 - b_2 - 10 c_2 = 0$$

Quadratics 2 and 3, node $i = 3$

$$b_2 + 2 c_2 x_3 = b_3 + 2 c_3 x_3 \Rightarrow b_2 + 24 c_2 - b_3 - 24 c_3 = 0$$

Quadratics 3 and 4, node $i = 4$

$$b_3 + 2 c_3 x_4 = b_4 + 2 c_4 x_4 \Rightarrow b_3 + 30 c_2 - b_4 - 30 c_4 = 0$$

Finally, for the last condition, the second derivative at node $i = 4$ is supposed to vanish. In symbols,

$$2 c_4 = 0 \qquad \Rightarrow \qquad c_4 = 0 .$$

We have a system of 12 linear equations, which, in matrix form, may be written as

$$
\begin{bmatrix}
1 & 5 & 5^2 & 0 & 0 & 0 & 0 & 0 & 0 & 0 & 0 & 0 \\
1 & 7 & 7^2 & 0 & 0 & 0 & 0 & 0 & 0 & 0 & 0 & 0 \\
0 & 0 & 0 & 1 & 7 & 7^2 & 0 & 0 & 0 & 0 & 0 & 0 \\
0 & 0 & 0 & 1 & 12 & 12^2 & 0 & 0 & 0 & 0 & 0 & 0 \\
0 & 0 & 0 & 0 & 0 & 0 & 1 & 12 & 12^2 & 0 & 0 & 0 \\
0 & 0 & 0 & 0 & 0 & 0 & 1 & 15 & 15^2 & 0 & 0 & 0 \\
0 & 0 & 0 & 0 & 0 & 0 & 0 & 0 & 0 & 1 & 15 & 15^2 \\
0 & 0 & 0 & 0 & 0 & 0 & 0 & 0 & 0 & 1 & 20 & 20^2 \\
0 & 1 & 10 & 0 & 0 & -1 & -10 & 0 & 0 & 0 & 0 & 0 \\
0 & 0 & 0 & 0 & 0 & 1 & 24 & 0 & -1 & -24 & 0 & 0 \\
0 & 0 & 0 & 0 & 0 & 0 & 0 & 1 & 30 & 0 & -1 & 0 \\
0 & 0 & 0 & 0 & 0 & 0 & 0 & 0 & 0 & 0 & 0 & 1
\end{bmatrix}
\begin{bmatrix}
a_1 \\ b_1 \\ c_1 \\ a_2 \\ b_2 \\ c_2 \\ a_3 \\ b_3 \\ c_3 \\ a_4 \\ b_4 \\ c_4
\end{bmatrix}
=
\begin{bmatrix}
2 \\ 5 \\ 5 \\ 8 \\ 8 \\ 11 \\ 11 \\ 5 \\ 0 \\ 0 \\ 0 \\ 0
\end{bmatrix}
$$

The solution is given by

$$
\begin{bmatrix} a_1 \\ b_1 \\ c_1 \\ a_2 \\ b_2 \\ c_2 \\ a_3 \\ b_3 \\ c_3 \\ a_4 \\ b_4 \\ c_4 \end{bmatrix} = \begin{bmatrix} 66.9500 \\ -23.3400 \\ 2.0700 \\ 31.0400 \\ -6.2400 \\ 0.3600 \\ -88.0000 \\ 13.6000 \\ -0.4667 \\ 17.0000 \\ -0.4000 \\ 0.0000 \end{bmatrix} ,
$$

and thus the four quadratic equations may be written as

$$
\begin{aligned}
f_1(x) &= 66.9500 - 23.3400x + 2.0700x^2 & 5.0 \leq x \leq 7.0 \\
f_2(x) &= 31.0400 - 6.2400x + 0.3600x^2 & 7.0 \leq x \leq 12.0 \\
f_3(x) &= -88.0000 + 13.6000x - 0.4667x^2 & 12.0 \leq x \leq 15 \\
f_4(x) &= 17.0000 - 0.4000x & 15.0 \leq x \leq 20.0
\end{aligned}
$$

Note that $f_4(x)$ is, in fact, a linear function because of the particular condition imposed at node $i = 4$.

The interpolation estimate for $x = 11.0$ is obtained by using $f_2(x)$ viz.

$$
f_2(11.0) = 31.0400 - 6.2400(11.0) + 0.3600(11.0)^2 = 5.9600 .
$$

Third-order (cubic) splines

Cubic splines are the most widely used splines in numerical analysis. They are a natural extension of second-order splines and have the following general form:

$$
f_i(x) = a_i + b_i x + c_i x^2 + d_i x^3 .
$$

Here we assume a cubic function in the interval $x_{i-1} \leq x \leq x_i$, thus making the second derivative continuous over the entire length of the curve. In each of the n subintervals, there are four coefficients and hence a total of $4n$ unknowns. To develop the requisite number of equations, we require that the function and its first and second derivatives all be conditions at the knots (points $i = 1, 2, \cdots n - 1$) thus giving $2(n-1) +$

```
function mnhf_exchange_rate()
%MNHF_EXCHANGE_RATE plots then interpolates Canada—US exchange rate data.

ms = 10;   % markersize in figure.
fs = 12;   % fontsize in figure.

% Input exchange rate information. x represents the month of 2010; y gives
% the monthly average exchange rate (amount of US$ needed to buy $1 Cdn).
x = 1:1:12;
y = [0.95883 0.94623 0.97751 0.99496 0.96161 0.96345 0.95906 0.96026 ...
    0.96797 0.98234 0.98736 0.99231];

% Plot data.
figure; hold on; box on
plot(x,y,'ko','markersize',ms)
set(gca,'fontsize',fs)
xlim([1 12])
set(gca,'xtick',[1 2 3 4 5 6 7 8 9 10 11 12])
set(gca,'xticklabel',['J';'F';'M';'A';'M';'J';'J';'A';'S';'O';'N';'D'])
xlabel('Month of 2010','fontsize',fs+4)
ylabel('Monthly average exchange rate','fontsize',fs+4)
title('Canada—US exchange rate','fontsize',fs+4)

% Contrast different interpolation routines.
xi = 1:0.05:12;
yi_nearest = interp1(x,y,xi,'nearest');
plot(xi,yi_nearest,'b-.')
yi_linear = interp1(x,y,xi,'linear');
plot(xi,yi_linear,'r—')
yi_spline = interp1(x,y,xi,'spline');
plot(xi,yi_spline,'k—')

% Add legend.
legend('Raw data','Nearest neighbor','Piecewise linear','Cubic spline',...
       'location','southeast')
```

Figure 5.16: MATLAB function that applies different interpolation schemes to 2010 Canada-US exchange rate information (source: Bank of Canada).

$(n - 1) + (n - 1) = 4n - 4$ conditions. We are therefore left with four degrees of freedom. If we require that the function pass through both of the end points ($i = 0$ and $i = n$), the number of degrees of freedom is cut by half. A popular way of closing the problem is to consider so-called *natural cubic splines* for which the second derivatives at the endpoints are made to vanish, *i.e.*

$$f_1''(x_0) = 2c_1 + 6d_1x_0 = 0 \qquad \text{and} \qquad f_n''(x_n) = 2c_n + 6d_nx_n = 0\,.$$

Note that in deriving the above functions we used the standard polynomial form. We could also have used Lagrange polynomials for the splines. Such possibilities are explored in the exercises below. First, we present an example that contrasts different interpolation schemes using the built-in MATLAB function `interp1`.

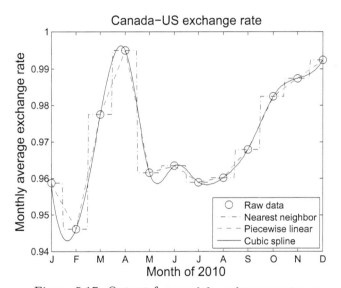

Figure 5.17: Output from `mnhf_exchange_rate.m`.

EXAMPLE 5.11 (Using `interp1` to interpolate exchange rates)
A key indicator of comparative economic performance is the exchange rate with a particular foreign currency. Using data from the Bank of Canada, the MATLAB function illustrated in Figure 5.16 shows the amount of US dollars required to purchase $1 Cdn. for each month of 2010. These data can be interpolated using a variety of schemes. In Figures 5.16 and 5.17, we consider three different possibilities, i.e. "nearest neighbor" (the analogue of the zeroth-order spline), "piecewise linear" (the analogue of the first-order spline), and "cubic spline." Only the latter scheme yields a curve that can be differentiated.

5.10   Exercise problems I

P5I.1. The power generation P in a micro-turbine depends, among other factors, on the diameter D of the pipe which conveys water to the turbine.

D (m)	0.3	0.6	0.9	1.2
P (kW)	25	60	120	250

Fit a cubic polynomial to the above data and estimate the power output for a 1 m diameter pipe.

P5I.2. The convective heat transfer coefficient, h, for flow over an exposed pipeline has been found to depend on the wind velocity. Given the data below, determine whether a linear fit is appropriate.

V (m/s)	1	2	4	8	10
h (W/m^2/K)	20	60	100	500	1000

P5I.3. The data below has been obtained from experiments on the growth of bacteria as a function of oxygen concentration in a biological treatment reactor. It is proposed to model the reactor using substrate inhibition model

$$\mu = \frac{\mu_{max} C}{k_m + k_1 C^2} ,$$

where C is the substrate concentration (g/L) and μ is the growth rate in hr^{-1}. Transform the equation into linear form and use linear regression to estimate the parameters k_m and k_1 given that $\mu_{max} = 2.1 \, \text{hr}^{-1}$.

μ (hr^{-1})	1.0	2.0	3.0	4.0
C (g/L)	0.7	0.9	1.2	1.4

P5I.4. The viscosity of gas-saturated heavy oil is highly dependent of the temperature. A typical correlation expresses this dependency in the form of an Arrhenius formula, *i.e.*

$$\mu = A e^{k/T} .$$

Here μ is the dynamic viscosity, T is the temperature and A and k are parameters to be determined. Fit the above model given the following laboratory data:

i	1	2	3	4	5
T (°F)	25	50	75	100	125
μ (cp)	5.0×10^6	5×10^3	1.0×10^2	5.0×10^1	1.0×10^1

Table 5.5: Natural gas composition (mol basis).

Component	mol%
Methane	93.74
Ethane	0.52
Propane	0.05
i-butane	0.01
n-butane	0.02
i-pentane	0.01
n-pentane	0.01
Carbon dioxide	1.54
Nitrogen	4.10

P5I.5. The heat capacity ratio, $\gamma = C_P/C_V$, is an important parameter in the design and performance evaluation of compressors. For an ideal gas, $C_V = C_P - R$ and therefore

$$\gamma = \frac{C_P}{C_P - R}.$$

Here $R = 8.314\,\text{kJ/kmol/K}$ is the universal gas constant. For a mixture of gases, the specific capacity may be found from a weighted average of the pure component values, *i.e.*

$$C_{Pm} = \sum_i C_{Pi} w_i.$$

Given natural gas with a composition prescribed in Table 5.5, determine the heat capacity ratio.

P5I.6. The rate of power dissipation from a pulp suspension mixer varies with the agitation speed. The following measurements have been obtained:

N (rpm)	15	40	60	90	110
Power, P (kW)	5	10	12	15	12

(a) Determine a fourth-order Lagrange polynomial that passes through all five measurement points.

(b) Use the polynomial obtained in (a) to estimate the power at 100 rpm.

(c) Use linear splines interpolation to estimate the power at 100 rpm.

(d) Use quadratic splines interpolation to estimate the power at 100 rpm.

(e) Determine a fourth-order Newton polynomial that passes through all five measurement points.

Table 5.6: Vapour pressure for CO_2.

Temperature (K)	Pressure (kPa)
250.00	1783.700
254.00	2024.300
256.00	2147.700
260.00	2417.300
266.00	2872.300
270.00	3201.800
273.15	3480.000
273.15	3486.590
278.15	3970.000
283.15	4500.000
287.91	5059.160
288.15	5080.000
293.15	5730.000
293.34	5753.230
296.79	6231.490
298.15	6440.000

(f) Use the polynomial obtained in (e) to estimate the power dissipation at 50 rpm.

P5I.7. Table 5.6 presents data showing vapor pressure vs. temperature for carbon dioxide. In a design problem, the data needs to be correlated using algebraic expressions which can provide the pressure P (kPa) as a function of temperature T (K). A simple polynomial could be used as an empirical modeling equation in the form

$$P = a_0 + a_1 T + a_2 T^2 + a_3 T^3 + \cdots + a_n T^n,$$

where $a_0, a_1, \cdots a_n$ are coefficients to be determined by regression and n is the degree of the polynomial. Typically, the degree of the polynomial is that which provides the best fit to the data when using a least-squares objective function.

Another useful correlation is the Antoine equation given by

$$\log(P) = A - \frac{B}{T + C},$$

where P is the pressure measured in mmHg[*] and T is the temperature measured in °C. Meanwhile A, B and C are parameters to be determined by regression.

---

[*]The coefficients of Antoine's are normally given in mmHg even today where Pascals are preferred. The usage of a pre-SI unit has only historic significance and originates directly from Antoine's seminal publication.

Extensions to Antoine's equation can be made by introducing additional parameters to increase the flexibility of the equation and allow the description of the entire vapor pressure curve. For example

$$\log(P) = A - \frac{B}{T+C} + D\ln T + ET^F .$$

(a) Regress the data with a polynomial in the form suggested above. Determine the degree of the polynomial that best represents the data.

(b) Regress the data using the nonlinear regression of Antoine's equation.

(c) Regress the data using the nonlinear regression of the modified Antoine's equation.

P5I.8. Write a MATLAB function that determines the best fit of an exponential function of the form $y = ae^{-bx}$ to a given set of data points. Name the function function [a b] = ExpFit(x,y) where the input arguments x and y are vectors containing the data points, and the output arguments a and b are the values of the fitted parameters.

P5I.9. Given the data

N (rpm)	15	40	60	90	110
Power, P (kW)	5	10	12	15	12

(a) Use the exponential function developed in problem **P5I.8.** to fit a function $P = Ae^{kN}$.

(b) Using MATLAB's built-in function.

For each of (a) and (b), plot the data points and the fitting function in the same figure.

P5I.10. Suppose (x_1, f_1) and (x_2, f_2) are given; we wish to estimate $f(x_j)$ where $x_1 < x_j < x_2$. Arguably the simplest interpolation scheme to apply is *linear* interpolation or interpolation using first-order splines, *i.e.*

$$f_j = f_1 + \left(\frac{f_2 - f_1}{x_2 - x_1}\right)(x_j - x_1).$$

Now suppose that $f = f(x, y)$ is a function of both x and y and that $f(x_1, y_1)$, $f(x_1, y_2)$, $f(x_2, y_1)$ and $f(x_2, y_2)$ are all prescribed. By generalizing the above formula, derive a linear interpolation formula for $f(x_j, y_j)$ where $x_1 < x_j < x_2$ and

$y_1 < y_j < y_2$. Write your result as a single equation. What awkward numerical problems might arise in applying your formula to a new function, $\mathcal{G}$, that depends on y but not x?

Part II

Numerical Differentiation and Integration

Having derived approximate functional representations as outlined in Part I of this chapter, we proceed to construct algorithms that approximate not the function itself, but rather its derivative or integral.

5.11 Numerical differentiation

5.11.1 Approximations for first order derivatives

Consider the Newton forward difference formula given by equation (5.15)

$$
\begin{aligned}
f(x) &\simeq P_{m-1}(x_1 + \alpha h) \\
&= \left[1 + \alpha \Delta + \frac{\alpha(\alpha - 1)}{2!} \Delta^2 + \frac{\alpha(\alpha - 1)(\alpha - 2)}{3!} \Delta^3 + \cdots \right. \\
&\quad \left. + \cdots + \frac{\alpha(\alpha - 1) \cdots (\alpha - m + 2)}{(m - 1)!} \Delta^{m-1} \right] f(x_1) + \mathcal{O}(h^m)
\end{aligned}
$$

that passes through the points of the data set $\{(x_i, f_i) \mid i = 1, 2, \cdots, m\}$. Note that the independent variable x has been transformed into α using $x = x_1 + \alpha h$, hence $\mathrm{d}x/\mathrm{d}\alpha = h$. The first derivative is obtained as

$$
\begin{aligned}
f'(x) &\simeq \frac{\mathrm{d}P_{m-1}}{\mathrm{d}x} \\
&= \frac{\mathrm{d}P_{m-1}}{\mathrm{d}\alpha} \frac{\mathrm{d}\alpha}{\mathrm{d}x} \\
&= \frac{1}{h} \left[\Delta + \frac{\alpha + (\alpha - 1)}{2} \Delta^2 + \right. \\
&\quad \frac{\{\alpha(\alpha - 1) + (\alpha - 1)(\alpha - 2) + \alpha(\alpha - 2)\}}{6} \Delta^3 + \\
&\quad \left. \cdots \right] f(x_1) \tag{5.20}
\end{aligned}
$$

Equation (5.20) forms the basis for deriving a class of approximations for first derivatives from tabular data. Note that equation (5.20) still depends on α and hence it can be used to evaluate the derivative at any value of $x = x_1 + \alpha h$. Also, the series can be truncated after any number of terms. Thus, a whole class of successively more accurate representations for the first derivative can be constructed. For example, evaluating the derivative at the reference point x_1, (*i.e.* $\alpha = 0$), it can be shown that equation (5.20) reduces to

$$f'(x_1) = \frac{1}{h}\left[\Delta - \frac{1}{2}\Delta^2 + \frac{1}{3}\Delta^3 - \frac{1}{4}\Delta^4 \cdots \pm \frac{1}{m-1}\Delta^{m-1}\right] f(x_1) + \mathcal{O}(h^{m-1}).$$

This last result can also be obtained directly using equation (5.13) as

$$E = e^{hD} \quad \text{or} \quad hD = \ln E = \ln(1 + \Delta),.$$

Expanding the logarithmic term we obtain

$$hD = \Delta - \frac{\Delta^2}{2} + \frac{\Delta^3}{3} - \frac{\Delta^4}{4} + \cdots$$

Operating both sides with $f(x_1)$ (*i.e.* again using x_1 as the reference point), we get

$$Df(x_1) = f'(x_1) = \frac{1}{h}\left[\Delta - \frac{\Delta^2}{2} + \frac{\Delta^3}{3} - \frac{\Delta^4}{4} + \cdots\right] f(x_1).$$

Truncating the above series after the first term ($m = 2$) yields

$$\begin{aligned} f'(x_1) &= \frac{1}{h}\left[\Delta f(x_1)\right] + \mathcal{O}(h), \\ &= \frac{1}{h}\left[f_2 - f_1\right] + \mathcal{O}(h), \end{aligned}$$

which is a two-point, first-order accurate, forward difference approximation for the first derivative of f at x_1. Conversely, truncating the series after the first two terms ($m = 3$) gives

$$\begin{aligned} f'(x_1) &= \frac{1}{h}\left[\Delta f(x_1) - \frac{1}{2}\Delta^2 f(x_1)\right] + \mathcal{O}(h^2), \\ &= \frac{1}{h}\left[(f_2 - f_1) - \frac{1}{2}(f_1 - 2f_2 + f_3)\right] + \mathcal{O}(h^2), \\ &= \frac{1}{2h}\left[-3f_1 + 4f_2 - f_3\right] + \mathcal{O}(h^2), \end{aligned}$$

which is a three-point, second-order accurate, forward difference approximation for this same derivative. Clearly both are approximate representations of the first derivative at x_1, but the latter is more accurate because the truncation error is of the order h^2, not h.

To reiterate, equation (5.20) is a polynomial that is constructed around the reference point x_1 but can be evaluated at any other point by choosing appropriate α values. For example, consider the first derivative of f at $x = x_2$ for which $\alpha = 1$. A two term truncation of equation (5.20) yields

$$
\begin{aligned}
f'(x_2) &= \frac{1}{h}\left[\Delta + \frac{1}{2}\Delta^2\right]f(x_1) + \mathcal{O}(h^2), \\
&= \frac{1}{2h}[f_3 - f_1] + \mathcal{O}(h^2),
\end{aligned}
$$

which is a three-point, second-order accurate, central difference approximation for the first derivative at x_2.

Going through a similar process as above with the Newton backward difference formula (5.17), truncating the series at various levels and using different reference points, one can easily develop a whole class of approximations for first order derivatives. Some of the more useful formulas are summarized in Table 5.7.

5.11.2 Approximations for second order derivatives

The second derivative of the polynomial approximation is obtained by taking a further derivative of equation (5.20) - viz.

$$
f''(x) \simeq \frac{d}{d\alpha}\left[\frac{dP_{m-1}}{d\alpha}\frac{d\alpha}{dx}\right]\frac{d\alpha}{dx} = \frac{1}{h^2}\left[\Delta^2 + \right.
$$
$$
\frac{\{\alpha + (\alpha - 1) + (\alpha - 1) + (\alpha - 2) + \alpha + (\alpha - 2)\}}{6}\Delta^3
$$
$$
\left. + \cdots\right]f(x_1) + \mathcal{O}(h^{m-2}). \tag{5.21}
$$

Evaluating this last result at $x = x_1$ (*i.e.* $\alpha = 0$), we obtain,

$$
f''(x_1) = \frac{1}{h^2}\left[\Delta^2 - \Delta^3 + \frac{11}{12}\Delta^4 - -\frac{5}{6}\Delta^5 + \frac{137}{180}\Delta^6 \cdots\right]f(x_1). \tag{5.22}
$$

This last equation can also be obtained directly using equation (5.13), *i.e.*

$$
(hD)^2 = (\ln E)^2 = [\ln(1 + \Delta)]^2.
$$

As before, we expand the logarithmic term and find that

$$
\begin{aligned}
(hD)^2 &= \left[\Delta - \frac{\Delta^2}{2} + \frac{\Delta^3}{3} - \frac{\Delta^4}{4} + \frac{\Delta^5}{5}\cdots\right]^2, \\
&= \left[\Delta^2 - \Delta^3 + \frac{11}{12}\Delta^4 - \frac{5}{6}\Delta^5 + \frac{137}{180}\Delta^6 - \frac{7}{10}\Delta^7 + \frac{363}{560}\Delta^8\cdots\right].
\end{aligned}
$$

Operating both sides on $f(x_1)$ (*i.e.* using x_1 as the reference point), it can be shown that

$$
D^2 f(x_1) = f''(x_1) = \frac{1}{h^2}\left[\Delta^2 - \Delta^3 + \frac{11}{12}\Delta^4 - \cdots\right]f(x_1).
$$

Table 5.7: Finite difference approximations for the first derivative at x_i, $f'(x_i)$.

Finite difference approximation	Truncation error	Comments
$(f_{i+1} - f_i)/h$	$\mathcal{O}(h)$	One-sided (forward), two-point
$(f_i - f_{i-1})/h$	$\mathcal{O}(h)$	One-sided (backward), two-point
$(-3f_i + 4f_{i+1} - f_{i+2})/2h$	$\mathcal{O}(h^2)$	One-sided (forward), three-point
$(3f_i - 4f_{i-1} + f_{i-2})/2h$	$\mathcal{O}(h^2)$	One-sided (backward), three-point
$(f_{i+1} - f_{i-1})/2h$	$\mathcal{O}(h^2)$	Two-sided, two-point
$(f_{i-2} - 8f_{i-1} + 8f_{i+1} - f_{i+2})/12h$	$\mathcal{O}(h^4)$	Two-sided, four-point

Truncating after a single term, we find

$$f''(x_1) = \frac{1}{h^2}\left[\Delta^2 f(x_1)\right] = \frac{1}{h^2}(f_1 - 2f_2 + f_3) + \mathcal{O}(h), \qquad (5.23)$$

whereas truncating after two terms gives

$$
\begin{aligned}
f''(x_1) &= \frac{1}{h^2}\left[\Delta^2 f(x_1) - \Delta^3 f(x_1)\right], \\
&= \frac{1}{h^2}(2f_1 - 5f_2 + 4f_3 - f_4) + \mathcal{O}(h^2). \qquad (5.24)
\end{aligned}
$$

Evaluating equation (5.21) at x_2 for which $\alpha = 1$, we get

$$f''(x_2) = \frac{1}{h^2}\left[\Delta^2 - 0 \cdot \frac{\delta^3}{6}\right] f(x_1) + \mathcal{O}(h^2).$$

Because the third-order term turns out to be zero, this formula turns out to be more accurate. This is a three-point, second-order accurate central difference approximation for the second derivative that can be rewritten as

$$f''(x_2) = \frac{1}{h^2}\left[\Delta^2 f(x_1)\right] = \frac{1}{h^2}(f_1 - 2f_2 + f_3) + \mathcal{O}(h^2). \qquad (5.25)$$

Equations similar to (5.23), (5.24) and (5.25) suitable for numerically estimating $f''(x_i)$ to various degrees of accuracy are given in Table 5.8.

5.11.3   Taylor series approach

One can also derive finite difference approximations from Taylor series expansions. Consider the following expansions around x_i:

$$f(x_i + h) = f(x_i) + hf'(x_i) + \frac{h^2}{2}f''(x_i) + \frac{h^3}{3!}f'''(x_i) + \cdots,$$

$$f(x_i - h) = f(x_i) - hf'(x_i) + \frac{h^2}{2}f''(x_i) - \frac{h^3}{3!}f'''(x_i) + \cdots.$$

Subtracting the latter from the former, it can be shown that

$$f'(x_i) = \frac{f(x_i + h) - f(x_i - h)}{2h} - \frac{h^2}{6}f''(x_i) + \cdots,$$

or

$$f'(x_i) = \frac{f_{i+1} - f_{i-1}}{2h} + \mathcal{O}(h^2),$$

which is the same central difference formula for the first derivative that we derived in section 5.11. Adding the two previous Taylor series expansions, we get

$$f_{i+1} + f_{i-1} = 2f_i + h^2 f''(x_i) + \frac{h^4}{12}f''''(x_i) + \cdots,$$

or

$$f''(x_i) = \frac{1}{h^2}\left[f_{i+1} + f_{i-1} - 2f_i\right] + \mathcal{O}(h^2),$$

which is likewise a formula familiar from section 5.11.

Table 5.8: Finite difference approximations for the second derivative at x_i, $f''(x_i)$.

Finite difference approximation	Truncation error	Comments
$(f_{i+2} - 2f_{i+1} + f_i)/h^2$	$\mathcal{O}(h)$	One-sided (forward), three-point
$(f_i - 2f_{i-1} + f_{i-2})/h^2$	$\mathcal{O}(h)$	One-sided (backward), three-point
$(f_{i+1} - 2f_i + f_{i-1})/h^2$	$\mathcal{O}(h^2)$	Two-sided, three-point
$(-f_{i+3} + 4f_{i+2} - 5f_{i+1} + 2f_i)/h^2$	$\mathcal{O}(h^2)$	One-sided (forward), four-point
$(-f_{i-3} + 4f_{i-2} - 5f_{i-1} + 2f_i)/h^2$	$\mathcal{O}(h^2)$	One-sided (backward), four-point
$(-f_{i-2} + 16f_{i-1} - 30f_i + 16f_{i+1} - f_{i+2})/12h^2$	$\mathcal{O}(h^4)$	Two-sided, five-point

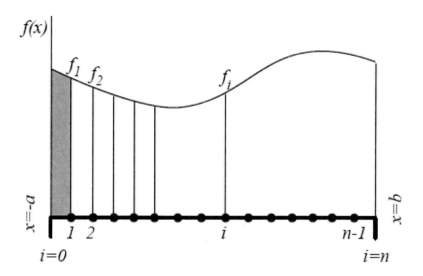

Figure 5.18: Discretizing the interval between $x = a$ and $x = b$ for purposes of estimating $\int_a^b f(x)\,\mathrm{d}x$.

5.12 Numerical integration

The ability to evaluate definite integrals numerically is useful when (i) the function in question is complicated and hence not easy (or impossible) to integrate analytically, or, (ii) the "function" actually consists of data in equally-spaced, tabular from. In either case the starting point is to use the functional approximation methods seen in earlier sections. Taking this approach, it is straightforward to derive a whole class of integration formulas. Consider, for instance,

$$\int_a^b f(x)\,\mathrm{d}x\,. \tag{5.26}$$

It is assumed that the function can be represented by a polynomial of degree n whereby

$$f(x) = P_n(x_0 + \alpha h) + \mathcal{O}(h^{n+1})\,.$$

With an error of order h^{n+1}, we can use this approximation to carry out the integration. First we divide the interval $x \in [a, b]$ into n subdivisions as shown schematically in Figure 5.18. In total, there are $n + 1$ data points and we label these as $\{x_0, x_1, \cdots x_n\}$. Moreover,

$$h = (b - a)/n\,, \qquad x = x_0 + \alpha h \qquad \text{and} \qquad \mathrm{d}x = h\mathrm{d}\alpha$$

For illustrative purposes, let us consider a first-degree polynomial and the interval $x_0 \leq x \leq x_1$. We have

$$\int_{x_0}^{x_1} f(x)\,\mathrm{d}x \simeq \int_0^1 P_1(x_0 + \alpha h)h\,\mathrm{d}\alpha + \int_0^1 \mathcal{O}(h^2)h\,\mathrm{d}\alpha\,,$$

or

$$\int_{x_0}^{x_1} f(x)\,\mathrm{d}x \simeq \int_0^1 [1 + \alpha\Delta]\,f_0 h\,\mathrm{d}\alpha + \mathcal{O}(h^3)\,,$$

which upon, completing the integration, becomes

$$\int_{x_0}^{x_1} f(x)\,\mathrm{d}x \simeq \frac{h}{2}\,[f_0 + f_1] + \underbrace{\mathcal{O}(h^3)}_{local\ error}\,. \tag{5.27}$$

This formula is the well-known trapezoidal rule for numerical integration. In contrast to numerical differentiation, which decreases the order of the truncation error by one due to the term $\mathrm{d}\alpha/\mathrm{d}x = 1/h$, numerical integration increases the order of the truncation error by one due to the term $\mathrm{d}x = h\,\mathrm{d}\alpha$. In equation (5.27), the truncation error is of order $\mathcal{O}(h^3)$. Here, we make reference to a *local truncation error* because it is the error in integrating over a single interval, *i.e.* $x \in [x_0, x_1]$. To obtain the complete integral over the interval $x \in [a, b]$, we apply equation (5.27) repeatedly so that

$$\int_a^b f(x)\,\mathrm{d}x = \sum_{i=1}^n \int_{x_{i-1}}^{x_i} f(x)\,\mathrm{d}x = \sum_{i=1}^n \frac{h}{2}\,[f_{i-1} + f_i] + \underbrace{\sum_{i=1}^n \mathcal{O}(h^3)}_{global\ error}\,.$$

Recalling that $n = (b - a)/h$, the *global truncation error* is of order $\mathcal{O}(h^2)$. On this basis, we write as the trapezoidal integration formula

$$\int_a^b f(x)\,\mathrm{d}x = \frac{h}{2}\sum_{i=1}^n [f_{i-1} + f_i] + \underbrace{\mathcal{O}(h^2)}_{global\ error}\,. \tag{5.28}$$

Fortunately, there is a straightforward alternative to using the above formula directly, i.e. the built-in MATLAB function trapz, which is illustrated in the following example.

EXAMPLE 5.12 (Trapezoidal integration) *Suppose we wish to apply trapezoidal integration to numerically evaluate $\int_0^{10} \cos(x)\,\mathrm{d}x$. The exact answer is, of course, $\sin(10)$ so it is easy to compute the global truncation error as a function of h (or n). The MATLAB function illustrated in Figure 5.19 estimates $\int_0^{10} \cos(x)\,\mathrm{d}x$ four times over using h values of 1, 0.1, 0.01 and 0.001. Notice that every time h decreases by*

```
function mnhf_trapz_example(N,subplot_index)
%MNHF_TRAPZ_EXAMPLE estimates the integral of cos(x) from x=0 to x=10
% using the built-in function trapz. The exact solution is sin(10).
%
% N - Number of grid points
% subplot_index - subplot in which graphical output is shown
%
% Usage  mnhf_trapz_example(11,1);    mnhf_trapz_example(101,2);
%        mnhf_trapz_example(1001,3); mnhf_trapz_example(10001,4);

x = linspace(0.0,10.0,N);
y = cos(x);
subplot(2,2,subplot_index); box on; hold on
plot(x,y,'ko','markersize',4); plot(x,y,'k','linewidth',1)
h = x(2)-x(1);
text(2,0.7,sprintf('h=%4.3f',x(2)-x(1)))
title(['error = ' num2str(abs(sin(10)-h*trapz(y)))])
```

Figure 5.19: MATLAB function that uses `trapz` for $\int_0^{10} \cos(x)\,\mathrm{d}x$.

a factor of 10, the global truncation error, reported in the title of each subplot of Figure 5.20, decreases by a factor of approximately 100. This is consistent with (5.28), which predicts that the global error varies as $\mathcal{O}(h^2)$.

In place of the first degree polynomial that lead us to (5.27) and (5.28), we might instead select a second-degree (or quadratic) polynomial. In this case, the integration must be performed over three, not two, points. Thus the equation associated with the integration scheme known as Simpson's 1/3 rule reads

$$\int_{x_0}^{x_2} f(x)\,\mathrm{d}x \simeq \int_0^2 P_2(x_0 + \alpha h)h\,\mathrm{d}\alpha + \int_0^2 \mathcal{O}(h^3)h\,\mathrm{d}\alpha\,,$$

or

$$\int_{x_0}^{x_2} f(x)\,\mathrm{d}x \simeq \int_0^2 \left[1 + \alpha\Delta + \frac{\alpha(\alpha-1)}{2}\Delta^2\right] f_0 h\,\mathrm{d}\alpha + \mathcal{O}(h^4)\,,$$

which upon, completing the integration, becomes

$$\int_{x_0}^{x_2} f(x)\,\mathrm{d}x \simeq \frac{h}{3}[f_0 + 4f_1 + f_2] + \underbrace{\mathcal{O}(h^4)}_{local\ error}\,. \tag{5.29}$$

Note that the next neglected term in the polynomial $P_2(x_0 + \alpha h)$ that corresponds to the order $\mathcal{O}(h^3)$ term *i.e.*

$$\int_0^2 \frac{\alpha(\alpha-1)(\alpha-2))}{3!}\Delta^3 f_0 h\,\mathrm{d}\alpha\,,$$

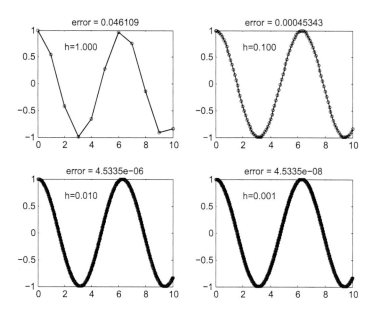

Figure 5.20: Output from `mnhf_trapz_example.m`.

turns out to be exactly zero. Thus the local truncation error associated with Simpson's 1/3 rule is actually $\mathcal{O}(h^5)$. Repeated application of (5.29) yields

$$\int_a^b f(x)\,\mathrm{d}x = \frac{h}{3}\left[f_0 + 4f_1 + 2f_2 + 4f_3 + 2f_4 + \cdots + f_n\right] + \underbrace{\mathcal{O}(h^4)}_{global\ error} .$$
(5.30)

Note that in applying Simpson's 1/3 rule repeatedly over the interval $x \in [a, b]$ we must have an even number of intervals (n even) or equivalently an odd number of points. In order to accommodate both even and odd numbers, a variation on Simpson's 1/3 rule known as Simpson's 3/8 rule has been developed. In this case, we use a cubic function to approximate f. As a result

$$\int_{x_0}^{x_3} f(x)\,\mathrm{d}x \simeq \frac{3h}{8}\left[f_0 + 3f_1 + 3f_2 + f_3\right] + \underbrace{\mathcal{O}(h^4)}_{local\ error} .$$
(5.31)

Repeated application of Simpson's 3/8 rule results in

$$\int_a^b f(x)\,\mathrm{d}x = \frac{h}{3}\left[f_0 + 3f_1 + 3f_2 + 2f_3 + 3f_4 + \cdots + f_n\right] + \underbrace{\mathcal{O}(h^4)}_{global\ error} .$$
(5.32)

This last equation is applicable only if the total number of intervals is divisible by 3; in the language of MATLAB, we must check to see whether `mod(n,3)` is or is not equal to 0. However, by clever combination of the 1/3 and 3/8 rules, we can readily estimate the integral of a given function whatever the number of intervals, i.e. n even or n odd. This idea is explored in the following pair of examples.

======

EXAMPLE 5.13 (✎ **Trapezoidal vs. Simpson 1**) *Evaluate the integral $\int_0^2 e^x \, dx$ analytically, using trapezoidal rule with one, two and four intervals, and using Simpson's rule with two and five intervals.*
Analytical solution

$$\int_a^b f(x) \, dx = \int_0^2 e^x \, dx = [e^x]_0^2 = e^2 - e^0 = 7.3891 - 1.0000 = 6.3891$$

Trapezoidal integration, one interval
$h = (b-a)/n = (2-0)/1 = 2$, *interval:* $[0,2]$ *with* $x_0 = 0$ *and* $x_1 = 2$

$$\int_a^b f(x) \, dx \simeq \frac{h}{2}[f_0 + f_1] = \frac{2}{2}[1.0000 + 7.3891] = 8.3891$$

Trapezoidal integration, two intervals
$h = (2-0)/2 = 1$, *intervals:* $[0,1]$ *and* $[1,2]$ *with* $x_0 = 0$, $x_1 = 1$ *and* $x_2 = 2$

$$\int_a^b f(x) \, dx \simeq \frac{1}{2}[1.0000 + 2.7183] + \frac{1}{2}[2.7183 + 7.3891] = 6.9128$$

Trapezoidal integration, four intervals
$h = (2-0)/4 = 0.5$, *intervals:* $[0, 0.5]$, $[0.5, 1]$, $[1, 1.5]$ *and* $[1.5, 2]$ *with* $x_0 = 0$, $x_1 = 0.5$, $x_2 = 1$, $x_3 = 1.5$ *and* $x_4 = 2$

$$\begin{aligned} \int_a^b f(x) \, dx \quad \simeq \quad & \frac{0.5}{2}[1.0000 + 1.6487] + \frac{0.5}{2}[1.6487 + 2.7183] + \cdots \\ & \frac{0.5}{2}[2.7183 + 4.4817] + \frac{0.5}{2}[4.4817 + 7.3891] \\ = \quad & 6.5216 \end{aligned}$$

Simpson's rule integration, two intervals
$h = (2-0)/2 = 1$, *intervals:* $[0,1]$ *and* $[1,2]$ *with* $x_0 = 0$, $x_1 = 1$ *and* $x_2 = 2$

$$\int_a^b f(x) \, dx \simeq \frac{h}{3}[f_0 + 4f_1 + f_2] = \frac{1}{3}[1.0000 + 4(2.7183) + 7.3891] = 6.4208$$

Simpson's rule integration, five intervals
$h = (2-0)/5 = 0.4$, *intervals:* $[0, 0.4]$, $[0.4, 0.8]$, $[0.8, 1.2]$, $[1.2, 1.6]$ *and* $[1.6, 2]$ *with* $x_0 = 0$, $x_1 = 0.4$, $x_2 = 0.8$, $x_3 = 1.2$, $x_4 = 1.6$ *and* $x_5 = 2.0$

Here, we use Simpson's 1/3 rule applied to the first three points. Meanwhile, we apply Simpson's 3/8 rule to the final four points. Thus

$$\int_a^b f(x)\,dx \; \simeq \; \frac{h}{3}[f_0 + 4f_1 + f_2] + \frac{3h}{8}[f_2 + 3f_3 + 3f_4 + f_5]$$

$$- \; \frac{0.4}{3}[1.0000 + 4(1.4918) + 2.2255] +$$

$$\frac{3 \times 0.4}{8}[2.2255 + 3(3.3201) + 3(4.9530) + 7.3891]$$

$$= \; 6.3908$$

EXAMPLE 5.14 (Trapezoidal vs. Simpson 2) *The previous example indicates the computational superiority of integration by Simpson's rule vs. the trapezoidal scheme. Here we explore this comparison in greater quantitative detail by returning to the integral first encountered in Example 5.12, namely $\int_0^{10} \cos(x)\,dx$. Running the MATLAB algorithm shown in Figure 5.21 yields the following output, printed to the Command Window:*

```
>>h=1.000, Error (trapz)=0.04610912897, Error (Simpson)=0.00342421893
>>h=0.100, Error (trapz)=0.00045342650, Error (Simpson)=0.00000030259
>>h=0.010, Error (trapz)=0.00000453352, Error (Simpson)=0.00000000003
>>h=0.001, Error (trapz)=0.00000004534, Error (Simpson)=0.00000000000
```

Observe that the global truncation error associated with Simpson's rule integration is at least an order of magnitude less than that associated with trapezoidal integration, far less in the limit of small h.

In Example 5.14, we apply our own implementation of the Simpson's rule algorithm, i.e. `mnhf_simpson` – see the sub-function in Figure 5.21. This algorithm uses the 1/3 rule when the number of intervals is odd (i.e. n is even or, in MATLAB-speak, `mod(n,2)=0`). Conversely, it uses a combination of the 1/3 and 3/8 rules when the number of intervals is even. For reference, MATLAB includes its own Simpson's rule solver, `quad`, which employs adaptive Simpson quadrature.

5.12.1   Romberg integration

An idea similar to that used in section 2.8.3 to accelerate convergence is the notion of so-called Richardson extrapolation* to improve the accuracy of numerical integration. The basic premise is to estimate the

---

*Richardson extrapolation is named after Lewis Fry Richardson (1881-1953). A talented mathematician, Richardson's greatest contributions came in the fields of fluid mechanics and meteo-

```
function mnhf_trapz_simpson_example(N)
%MNHF_TRAPZ_SIMPSON_EXAMPLE estimates the integral of cos(x) from x=0 to
% x=10 using the built-in function trapz and a Simpson's rule solver. The
% exact solution is sin(10).
%
% N - Number of grid points
%
% Usage   mnhf_trapz_simpson_example(11);
%         mnhf_trapz_simpson_example(101);
%         mnhf_trapz_simpson_example(1001);
%         mnhf_trapz_simpson_example(10001);

x = linspace(0.0,10.0,N);
y = cos(x);
h = x(2)-x(1);
fprintf('h=%4.3f, Error (trapz)=%12.11f,',h,abs(sin(10)-h*trapz(y)))
fprintf(' Error (Simpson)=%12.11f\n',abs(sin(10)-mnhf_simpson(y,h)))

function area=mnhf_simpson(g,h)
%MNHF_SIMPSON finds the Simpson's Rule integral of discrete data that is
% uniformly spaced on a grid.
%
% g - a vector containing the discrete data
% h - a scalar indicating the grid spacing

area = 0.0;         % Initialize sum.
n = length(g)-1;

if mod(n,2)==0   % Use Simpson's 1/3 rule.
 for ii=2:2:n
  area = area+4.0*g(ii);
 end
 for ii=3:2:n-1
  area = area+2.0*g(ii);
 end
 area = h/3.0*(g(1)+area+g(n+1));
else             % Use Simpson's 1/3 rule...
 for ii=2:2:n-3
  area = area+4.0*g(ii);
 end
 for ii=3:2:n-4
  area = area+2.0*g(ii);
 end
 area = h/3.0*(g(1)+area+g(n-2));
 % ... followed by Simpson's 3/8 rule.
 area = area+0.375*h*(g(n-2)+3.0*g(n-1)+3.0*g(n)+g(n+1));
end
```

Figure 5.21: MATLAB function that contrasts trapezoidal and Simpson's rule integration.

truncation error by evaluating the integral on two different grid sizes, h_1 and h_2. When applied in conjunction with the trapezoidal rule, we obtain a very powerful result known as *Romberg integration.*

Recall that trapezoidal integration has a global truncation error of $\mathcal{O}(h^2)$. Let the exact integral be represented as,

$$I = I(h_1) + E(h_1),$$

where $I(h_1)$ is the estimate of the integral obtained using a (uniform) grid spacing of h_1 and $E(h_1)$ is the error. By the same token,

$$I = I(h_2) + E(h_2).$$

For trapezoidal integration, however, $E(h_i) \propto h_i^2$ and therefore

$$\frac{E(h_1)}{E(h_2)} = \frac{h_1^2}{h_2^2}.$$

Thus

$$I = I(h_1) + E(h_1) = I(h_2) + E(h_2),$$

or

$$I(h_1) + E(h_2)\frac{h_1^2}{h_2^2} = I(h_2) + E(h_2).$$

This last equation can be solved for $E(h_2)$. To wit

$$E(h_2) = \frac{I(h_1) - I(h_2)}{1 - (h_1/h_2)^2}.$$

Hence an improved estimate for the integral is

$$I \simeq I(h_2) + \frac{I(h_2) - I(h_1)}{(h_1/h_2)^2 - 1}.$$

If $h_2 = h_1/2$, the above expression simplifies and it can be shown that

$$I \simeq \tfrac{4}{3}I(h_2) - \tfrac{1}{3}I(h_1).$$

Because we have estimated and eliminated the truncation error term of order $\mathcal{O}(h^2)$, this last equation will have a truncation error of order $\mathcal{O}(h^4)$ corresponding to the next largest term in the Taylor series expansion. By repeated application of the above approach to estimate and eliminate successively higher order terms, the following general result may be derived:

$$I_{j,k} = \frac{4^{k-1}I_{j+1,k-1} - I_{j,k-1}}{4^{k-1} - 1}. \tag{5.33}$$

rology. An ardent pacifist, Richardson was forced to abandon these disciplines, however, when he came to believe that his scientific discoveries could be used to advance chemical warfare.

To illustrate the use of equation (5.33), let us numerically estimate

$$\int_0^{0.8} (0.2 + 25x - 200x^2 + 675x^3 - 900x^4 + 400x^5)\, \mathrm{d}x\,, \qquad (5.34)$$

whose exactly value is approximately 1.64053334. A sketch of the integrand and a summary of the Romberg integration results are shown in Figure 5.22. To evaluate $I_{2,2}$, say, we substitute $j = 2$ and $k = 2$ into equation (5.33) and find that

$$I_{2,2} = \frac{4 \times I_{3,1} - I_{2,1}}{4 - 1} = \frac{4 \times 1.4848 - 1.0688}{3} = 1.6234667\,.$$

Similarly, $I_{1,3}$ is obtained by substituting $j = 1$ and $k = 3$, *i.e.*

$$I_{1,3} = \frac{4^2 \times I_{2,2} - I_{1,2}}{4^2 - 1} = \frac{4^2 \times 1.6234667 - 1.3674667}{15} = 1.64053334\,.$$

Thus by combining three relatively poor estimates of the integral computed from grids with $h = 0.8$, 0.4 and 0.2, a composite result of high accuracy can straightforwardly be obtained.

5.12.2   Gaussian quadratures

Whereas the above integration methods require the data to be evenly spaced, the Gaussian quadrature method does not. Gaussian quadrature is set up so that polynomials of degree $m \le 2n - 1$ and having the generic form

$$f(\xi) = a_1 + a_2\xi + \cdots + a_{2n}\xi^{2n-1} \qquad (5.35)$$

can be integrated exactly. Here n indicates the number of points in the interval.

The most popular Gaussian quadrature method is called the Gauss-Legendre method. For reference, and to keep the arithmetic manageable, let us define the integration in a reference space from -1 to +1. The interval $x \in [a, b]$ can be mapped onto this reference space using the coordinate transformation $x = \frac{1}{2}(b - a)\xi + \frac{1}{2}(b + a)$. We define the general Gaussian form as

$$\int_{-1}^1 f(\xi)\, \mathrm{d}\xi \simeq w_1 f_1(\xi_1) + w_2 f_2(\xi_2) + \cdots w_n f_n(\xi_n) = \sum_{i=1}^n w_i f(\xi_i)\,. \quad (5.36)$$

According to this last equation, there are n points ξ_1, $\xi_2, \ldots \xi_n$ and n weights w_1, $w_2, \ldots w_n$ and these are selected to integrate exactly polynomials of the form given by equation (5.35). Applying (5.35) into the integral of (5.36) yields

$$I = \int_{-1}^1 f(\xi)\, \mathrm{d}\xi = a_1 \int_{-1}^1 \mathrm{d}\xi + a_2 \int_{-1}^1 \xi\, \mathrm{d}\xi + \cdots + a_{2n} \int_{-1}^1 \xi^{2n-1}\, \mathrm{d}\xi\,.$$

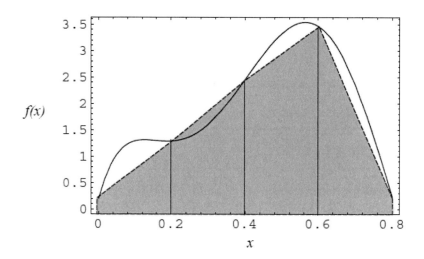

		$O(h^2)$	$O(h^4)$	$O(h^6)$
		$(k = 1)$	$(k = 2)$	$(k = 3)$
$j = 1$	$h = 0.8$	0.1728	1.3674667	1.64053334
$j = 2$	$h = 0.4$	1.0688	1.6234667	1.64053334
$j = 3$	$h = 0.2$	1.4848	1.6394667	
$j = 4$	$h = 0.1$	1.6008		

Figure 5.22: Illustration of Romberg integration.

Equivalently

$$
\begin{aligned}
I = \ & a_1(w_1 + w_2 + \cdots + w_n) + \\
& a_2(w_1\xi_1 + w_2\xi_2 + \cdots + w_n\xi_n) + \cdots \\
& a_{2n}(w_1\xi_1^{2n-1} + w_2\xi_2^{2n-1} + \cdots + w_n\xi_n^{2n-1}).
\end{aligned}
$$

For even α, therefore,

$$
\int_{-1}^{1} \xi^\alpha \, d\xi = \frac{2}{\alpha+1} = \sum_{i=1}^{n} w_i \xi_i^\alpha , \qquad (5.37)
$$

whereas for odd α,

$$
\int_{-1}^{1} \xi^\alpha \, d\xi = 0 = \sum_{i=1}^{n} w_i \xi_i^\alpha . \qquad (5.38)
$$

Equations (5.37) and (5.38) prescribe the $2n \times 2n$ system of equations to be solved. Suppose, for instance, that $n = 2$. Then

$$
I = \int_{-1}^{1} f(\xi)d\xi = w_1 f(\xi_1) + w_2 f(\xi_2) ,
$$

and

$$
\begin{aligned}
2 &= w_1 + w_2 , \\
0 &= w_1\xi_1 + w_2\xi_2 , \\
\frac{2}{3} &= w_1\xi_1^2 + w_2\xi_2^2 , \\
0 &= w_1\xi_1^3 + w_2\xi_2^3 .
\end{aligned}
$$

The solution to the above system of equations is $w_1 = w_2 = 1$ and $\xi_1 = -\xi_2 = -1/\sqrt{3}$. Comparable results can be derived for $n > 2$; when $n = 3$, for example, it can be shown that

$$
w_1 = \frac{8}{9} \quad w_2 = w_3 = \frac{5}{9} ,
$$

$$
\xi_1 = 0 \quad \xi_2 = -\xi_3 = \sqrt{\frac{3}{5}} .
$$

Likewise, when $n = 4$,

$$
w_1 = w_2 = \frac{1}{2} + \frac{1}{6\sqrt{6/5}} \qquad \xi_1 = -\xi_2 = \sqrt{\frac{3 - 2\sqrt{6/5}}{7}} ,
$$

$$
w_3 = w_4 = \frac{1}{2} - \frac{1}{6\sqrt{6/5}} \qquad \xi_3 = -\xi_4 = \sqrt{\frac{3 + 2\sqrt{6/5}}{7}} .
$$

EXAMPLE 5.15 (Gauss-Legendre method 1) *Let us illustrate the above concepts by estimating $\int_{-1}^{1} x^2 \, dx$, whose analytical solution is obviously 2/3.*

$$
\begin{aligned}
\int_{-1}^{1} x^2 \, dx &= w_1 f(\xi_1) + w_2 f(\xi_2), \\
&= 1 \left(\frac{-1}{\sqrt{3}} \right)^2 + 1 \left(\frac{1}{\sqrt{3}} \right)^2, \\
&= \frac{1}{3} + \frac{1}{3}, \\
&= \frac{2}{3}.
\end{aligned}
$$

EXAMPLE 5.16 (Gauss-Legendre method 2) *Let us apply two- and three-point Gauss quadrature in estimating $\int_{-1}^{1} \cos x \, dx$, whose analytical value is approximately 1.68294197.*

Two-point Gauss quadrature

With $n = 2$, $w_1 = w_2 = 1$ and $\xi_1 = -\xi_2 = -0.577350269$. *Therefore*

$$
\begin{aligned}
\int_{-1}^{1} \cos x \, dx &\simeq w_1 f(\xi_1) + w_2 f(\xi_2), \\
&= (1) \cos(-0.577350269) + (1) \cos(0.577350269), \\
&= 1.67582366.
\end{aligned}
$$

Two-point Gauss quadrature

With $n = 3$, $w_1 = 0.888888889$, $w_2 = w_3 = 0.555555556$; $\xi_1 = 0$, $\xi_2 = -\xi_3 = 0.774596669$. *Therefore*

$$
\begin{aligned}
\int_{-1}^{1} \cos x \, dx &= w_1 f(\xi_1) + w_2 f(\xi_2) + w_3 f(\xi_3), \\
&= 0.888888889 \cos(0) + 2 \times 0.555555556 \cos(0.774596669), \\
&= 1.683003548.
\end{aligned}
$$

Comparing these last two results with the analytical solution, we observe that, not surprisingly, the three-point method is considerably more accurate than its two-point counterpart.

5.13 Summary

In the former half of this chapter, we introduced different methods for functional approximation. For discrete data, interpolation techniques may be utilized when the data in question is known to be precise. In this case, the interpolating function is forced to pass through all the data points exactly. The Lagrange and Newton polynomials are well-suited for interpolation. In neither case do we require the solution of a system of equations. The polynomials can therefore easily be developed from the given data. The Newton polynomial is derived using difference tables and the polynomial coefficients can readily be expanded to include more data points without recalculating the existing coefficients. Thus we find that operator techniques are highly amenable for developing difference equations and polynomials.

When a given set of data derived from measurements is imprecise, it is more convenient to develop polynomials that represent the data only in the sense of a least squares approximation. Different types of polynomials as well as nonlinear functions can easily be fitted to given data by minimizing a suitably-defined objective function.

In the latter half of this chapter, we introduced various numerical techniques for differentiation and integration. For discrete data points, an approximating polynomial can be used to fit the data and then applied for either mathematical purpose. This approach can be made to work for data that are equally- or not equally-spaced.

In the case of differentiation, we have derived difference formulas for different orders of derivatives – key results are summarized in Tables 5.7 and 5.8. In the case of integration, we have presented methods ranging from simple trapezoidal integration to more complicated topics like Simpson's rules and Gaussian quadrature.

5.14   Exercise Problems II

P5II.1. Consider the function $f(x) = \sinh\left[(2 - x^3)e^{2x}\right]$.

(a) Write an .m file that will take a set of x values and return the corresponding values of f.

(b) Use the function from (a) together with the built-in function quad to evaluate the following integral:

$$\int_{-1}^{1} f(x)\,\mathrm{d}x\,.$$

Choose a tolerance of 1.0×10^{-5}.

P5II.2. Let us revisit the numerical accuracy of the MATLAB built-in function trapz, and trapezoidal integration more generally, by examining $\int_{\pi}^{29\pi/20} \tan x\,\mathrm{d}x$. Compute the global error as a function of h where

$$\text{Global error} = |\text{Exact value} - \text{Numerical value}|\,.$$

Consider as the total number of intervals 10, 20, 30,... 190, 200. Plot your results putting $\ln(\text{Global error})$ and $\ln(h)$ on the vertical and horizontal axes, respectively. Using the built-in function polyfit show that

$$\text{Global error} \propto h^{1.9858} \simeq h^2\,.$$

P5II.3. It is desired to determine the diffusion flux $j = -D\mathrm{d}C/\mathrm{d}x$ at the surface of a reservoir ($x = 0$). Concentration measurements have been collected as summarized below. If the diffusion coefficient is $D = 1 \times 10^{-4}\,\mathrm{m^2/s}$, estimate j.

x (mm)	0	1.1	4.2
C (mol/m^3)	15.5	12.3	6.1

P5II.4. We wish to calculate the mass transfer coefficient at the surface of a slab. The following measurements are available:

z	0	0.4	0.8	1.2	1.6
P_A	0.1000	0.0800	0.0701	0.0621	0.0510

z	2.0	2.4	2.8	3.2
P_A	0.0411	0.0321	0.0222	0.0201

Here, z, measured in arbitrary units, is the distance from the slab surface and P_A, also measured in arbitrary units, is the partial pressure of the gas in question. If the pressure gradient at the surface of the slab is given by $(\mathrm{d}P/\mathrm{d}z)_{z=0}$, determine the pressure gradient using the following techniques:

(a) Fit a cubic polynomial using Newton's divided difference method and evaluate the derivative of the polynomial at $z = 0$.

(b) Fit a cubic polynomial using MATLAB's `polyfit` function then use the MATLAB functions `polyder` and `polyval`.

(c) Estimate the derivative at $z = 0$ using second order accurate finite differences.

P5II.5. Evaluate the integral $\int_0^6 10e^{-2x}\,dx$

(a) Analytically.

(b) Using a single application of the trapezoidal rule.

(c) Using the trapezoidal rule with two and four intervals.

(d) Using a single application of Simpson's 1/3 rule.

(e) Using a single application of Simpson's 3/8 rule.

(f) Using Simpson's rule with five intervals.

P5II.6. Evaluate the integral

$$\int_0^{0.8} (0.2 + 25x - 200x^2 + 675x^3 - 900x^4 + 400x^5)\,dx\,,$$

(a) Using Romberg integration.

(b) Using three-point Gaussian quadrature.

P5II.7. Compressor work can be determined from measurements of pressure, p, and volume, v, using the following formula:

$$W = \int_{v_0}^{v_1} p\,dv$$

v (L)	0.5	0.55	0.6	0.65	0.70
P (kPa)	1348	1250	1160	1110	1005

v (L)	0.75	0.80	0.85	0.9	0.95	1.0
P (kPa)	995	970	950	910	890	880

Determine the work done using

(a) Simpson's rule.

(b) Three-point Gaussian Quadrature.

P5II.8. Buried pipes are frequently used to transport petroleum products in cold climates. The ground temperature, T, at various depths below the surface, assuming a semi-infinite solid, is given by

$$\frac{T(x, t) - T_S}{T_i - T_S} = \text{erf}\,\beta \equiv \frac{2}{\sqrt{\pi}} \int_0^{\beta} e^{-\xi^2}\,d\xi\,,$$

where

$$\beta = \frac{x}{2\sqrt{\alpha t}},$$

and $\alpha = 2.52 \times 10^{-5}\,\mathrm{m^2/s}$ is the thermal diffusivity of the soil, T_S is the surface temperature and T_i is the initial ground temperature. If the (uniform) ground temperature at the start of winter is $15°C$ and the surface temperature is $-18°C$,

(a) Determine the temperature of a pipe buried at a depth of 1.2 m after 21 days.

(b) Write a MATLAB script to generate a plot of temperature variation at a depth of 0.8 m for $0 \le t \le 30$ days.

P5II.9. A proposed telecommunications project has expenditures and revenues that are given by

$$\text{Expenditures} = \frac{0.2 + te^{-t}}{t + 1},$$

$$\text{Revenue} = \begin{cases} 0 & t < 3 \\ 0.15\sqrt{t - 3} & t \ge 3 \end{cases},$$

respectively, where the time t is measured in years and Expenditures and Revenue are measured in millions of dollars. Using your favorite root finding scheme, determine the point in time where Expenditures = Revenue. Then apply numerical integration to determine when the time integral of the expenditures matches the time integral of the revenue. (This is referred to as the non-discounted payback period).

P5II.10. The suspension bridge shown in Figure 5.23 features a main cable suspended between two towers. The equation describing this portion of the main cable is

$$y = A \cosh kx,$$

where $A = 3.0\,\mathrm{m}$ and $k = 0.5\,\mathrm{m^{-1}}$. If the length of the main cable between the towers is 40.0 m, use numerical integration to find the horizontal distance L. Report your answer in units of meters. Recall that the arc-length formula reads

$$\text{arc} - \text{length} = \int \sqrt{1 + \left(\frac{dy}{dx}\right)^2}\, dx.$$

P5II.11. Use Simpson's Rule to estimate the area below the function

$$y = x(\pi^2 e^{-x} - \sqrt{2})$$

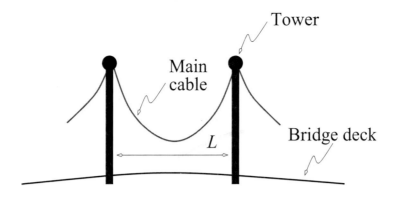

Figure 5.23: A suspension bridge.

between $x = 0$ and $x = r \simeq 1.9$, the first positive root of y. *Hint*: Before applying Simpson's Rule, use one of the root finding schemes studied previously to compute a more accurate estimate for the numerical value of r.

P5II.12. In aeronautics, reference is often made to the so-called *Prandtl-Meyer function*, ω, which is defined as

$$\omega(\text{Ma}) = \int_1^{\text{Ma}^2} \frac{\sqrt{s^2 - 1}}{2s^2 \left[1 + \frac{1}{2}(k - 1)s^2\right]} \, \mathrm{d}s^2, \qquad (5.39)$$

in which Ma is the Mach number, k is the ratio of specific heats and s is a dummy variable of integration. Using Simpson's Rule, generate a figure that shows the variation of ω with Ma. Assume $k = 1.4$ as is appropriate for air.

CHAPTER 6

LORDINARY DIFFERENTIAL EQUATIONS - INITIAL VALUE PROBLEMS

In this chapter we develop algorithms for solving systems of linear and nonlinear ordinary differential equations of *initial value type*. Such models arise in describing *lumped parameter, dynamic* models. Entire books such as Lapidus & Seinfeld (1971) and Lambert (1973) have been devoted to the development of numerical algorithms for such problems. Our treatment here will not be exhaustive; rather we shall develop elementary concepts of *single* and *multistep* methods, *implicit* and *explicit* methods and introduce concepts of numerical stability and *stiffness*.

6.1   Model equations and initial conditions

Ordinary differential equations of the initial value type are typically represented as a system of *first order* equations of the form

$$\frac{\mathrm{d}\boldsymbol{y}}{\mathrm{d}t} = \boldsymbol{f}(\boldsymbol{y}, t), \tag{6.1}$$

$$\boldsymbol{y}(t = t_0) = \boldsymbol{y}_0. \tag{6.2}$$

where $\boldsymbol{y} = \{y_1(t), y_2(t), \cdots y_n(t)\}$. The objective is to construct an approximate representation of the function $\boldsymbol{y}(t)$ over some time interval of interest $t_0 \leq t \leq t_f$ that satisfies the prescribed initial conditions $\boldsymbol{y}_0 = \{y_{1,0}, y_{2,0}, \cdots, y_{n,0}\}$. If $\boldsymbol{f}(\boldsymbol{y}, t)$ depends on t explicitly, the equations are called *non-autonomous*; otherwise they are referred to as *autonomous*.

6.1.1   Higher order differential equations

A higher order differential equation (of order n, say) can readily be converted into an equivalent system of (n) first order equations. Consider, for instance, the equation

$$a_n \frac{\mathrm{d}^n \theta}{\mathrm{d}t^n} + a_{n-1} \frac{\mathrm{d}^{n-1}\theta}{\mathrm{d}t^{n-1}} + \cdots a_1 \frac{\mathrm{d}\theta}{\mathrm{d}t} + a_0 \theta = b \,, \qquad (6.3)$$

subject to the following set of n initial conditions:

$$
\begin{aligned}
\left. \frac{\mathrm{d}^{n-1}\theta}{\mathrm{d}t^{n-1}} \right|_{t_0} &= c_{n-1} \,, \\[2mm]
\left. \frac{\mathrm{d}^{n-2}\theta}{\mathrm{d}t^{n-2}} \right|_{t_0} &= c_{n-2} \,, \\[2mm]
&\vdots \\[2mm]
\left. \frac{\mathrm{d}\theta}{\mathrm{d}t} \right|_{t_0} &= c_1 \,, \\[2mm]
\left. \theta \right|_{t_0} &= c_0 \,.
\end{aligned}
\qquad (6.4)
$$

Equation (6.3) can straightforwardly be recast as a system of n first-order equations akin to equation (6.1). Let us define θ and all of its $n-1$ successive higher derivatives as

$$y_1(t) = \theta(t) \,, \quad y_2(t) = \frac{\mathrm{d}\theta}{\mathrm{d}t} \,, \quad y_3(t) = \frac{\mathrm{d}^2\theta}{\mathrm{d}t^2} \,, \quad \cdots \quad y_n(t) = \frac{\mathrm{d}^{n-1}\theta}{\mathrm{d}t^{n-1}} \,.$$

Then we have

$$
\begin{aligned}
\frac{\mathrm{d}y_1}{\mathrm{d}t} &= y_2 \,, & y_1(t_0) &= c_0 \,, \\[2mm]
\frac{\mathrm{d}y_2}{\mathrm{d}t} &= y_3 \,, & y_2(t_0) &= c_1 \,, \\[2mm]
&\vdots \\[2mm]
\frac{\mathrm{d}y_{n-1}}{\mathrm{d}t} &= y_n \,, & y_{n-1}(t_0) &= c_{n-2} \,, \\[2mm]
\frac{\mathrm{d}y_n}{\mathrm{d}t} &= \frac{1}{a_n}(b - a_0 y_1 - a_1 y_2 - \cdots - a_{n-1} y_n) \,, & y_n(t_0) &= c_{n-1} \,,
\end{aligned}
\qquad (6.5)
$$

where the last equation has been obtained from the n-th order equation (6.3). Also shown in this last set of equations are the transformed initial conditions in terms of the new variable set $\boldsymbol{y}$.

Note that the coefficients $\{a_0, a_1, \cdots a_n, b\}$ in equation (6.3) will, in general, depend on θ and/or its derivatives in which case the differential equation (whether expressed in the form of equation 6.3 or equation 6.1) is referred to as nonlinear.

To take a more concrete example, consider the Van der Pol equation, named in honor of Balthasar Van der Pol, a Dutch electrical engineer who made one of the first discoveries of deterministic chaos whilst studying electrical circuits in the 1920s. Van der Pol's equation reads

$$\frac{\mathrm{d}^2 y}{\mathrm{d}t^2} - \mu(1 - y^2)\frac{\mathrm{d}y}{\mathrm{d}t} + y = 0 \,,$$

where μ is a damping parameter. This single second-order differential equation can be re-expressed as a pair of coupled first-order differential equations by defining a new variable $\omega \equiv \mathrm{d}y/\mathrm{d}t$. The pair of coupled equations then reads

$$\frac{\mathrm{d}y}{\mathrm{d}t} = \omega \,, \tag{6.6}$$

$$\frac{\mathrm{d}\omega}{\mathrm{d}t} = \mu(1 - y^2)\omega - y \,. \tag{6.7}$$

The initial conditions are given by $y(0) = y_0$ and $\omega(0) = \frac{\mathrm{d}y}{\mathrm{d}t}|_0$. We will return to the Van der Pol equation and its intriguing properties later in this chapter.

6.2 Taylor series-based methods

6.2.1 Explicit Euler scheme

Consider the (scalar, autonomous) initial value problem

$$\frac{\mathrm{d}y}{\mathrm{d}t} = f(y) \,, \qquad y(t_0) = y_0 \,. \tag{6.8}$$

Our task is to construct a sequence $\{y_n | n = 0, 1, \cdots\}$ that represents an approximate solution to $y(t)$ at a discrete set of points $\{t_n | n = 0, 1, \cdots\}$. This solution can be realized by constructing a Taylor series expansion for $y(t)$ around t_n with a step size of h. To wit,

$$y(t_n + h) = y(t_n) + y'(t_n)h + y''(t_n)\frac{h^2}{2} + \cdots .$$

Truncating after the linear term and noting that $y'(t_n) = f(y_n)$, we obtain the recursion relation for the so-called explicit Euler* scheme, i.e.

$$y_{n+1} = y_n + hf(y_n) + \underbrace{\mathcal{O}(h^2)}_{local\ error} \qquad n = 0, 1, \cdots , \tag{6.9}$$

---

*The explicit Euler scheme is also referred to as the forward Euler scheme in some texts.

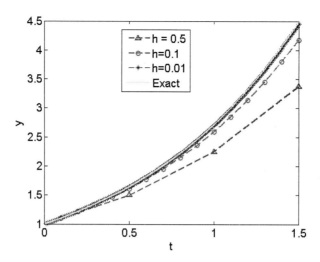

Figure 6.1: Solution of $y' = y$ using explicit Euler with different step sizes.

which is a *single-step, explicit* scheme with a local truncation error of order $\mathcal{O}(h^2)$, *i.e.* the scheme is first-order accurate. The method is called *single-step* because it requires only the value y_n to predict y_{n+1}. It is *explicit* because the right-hand side terms $y_n + hf(y_n)$ can be computed directly provided y_n is available.

EXAMPLE 6.1 (✎ Explicit Euler) *Manually solve the differential equation*

$$\frac{dy}{dt} = y, \qquad y(0) = 1, \qquad 0 \le t \le 1.5,$$

using a step size of $h = 0.5$ with the explicit Euler scheme.

Because $f(y) = y$, the calculations are straightforward, i.e.

$$y_1 = y_0 + hf(y_0) = 1 + 0.5(1) = 1.5,$$

$$y_2 = y_1 + hf(y_1) = 1.5 + 0.5(1.5) = 2.25,$$

$$y_3 = y_2 + hf(y_2) = 2.25 + 0.5(2.25) = 3.375.$$

Repeating the above calculations with smaller h does not present any conceptual difficulties, but it is tedious to do by hand. Rather, we use MATLAB and thereby generate the results shown in Figure 6.1. Consistent with the form of the truncation error shown in equation (6.9), the numerically-determined solution becomes notably more accurate as h decreases.

From an algorithmic point of view, the implementation of the explicit Euler scheme is simple, particularly for an autonomous ordinary differential equation such as that of interest here. Indeed if we examine this scheme carefully, we see that it can be rewritten as

$$y_{n+1} = y_n + hf(y_n) \Rightarrow \frac{y_{n+1} - y_n}{h} = f(y_n),$$

which brings to mind the forward difference equations e.g. from Table 5.7. The larger the step size, h, the further away is the solution from the corresponding true value. Whence we have uncovered one of the biggest weaknesses of the explicit Euler scheme: unless h is small, the solution will progressively and nontrivially deviate from the exact solution. We shall explore a further limitation of explicit Euler related not to accuracy but rather to numerical stability in section 6.2.5.

6.2.2   Midpoint method - a modification of explicit Euler

The midpoint method is a straightforward extension of the explicit Euler scheme. In this case, the slope used for calculating y_{n+1} is an estimate of the slope in the middle of, not the left-hand side of, the interval. The recursion equation is derived as follows. Explicit Euler is used to compute the slope in the middle of the interval where $t_m = t_n + h/2$ and $y_m \simeq y_n + \frac{h}{2}f(t_n, y_n)$. Thus

$$\left.\frac{dy}{dt}\right|_{t=t_m} \simeq f(t_m, y_m).$$

The above information is then used to estimate y_{n+1} from

$$y_{n+1} = y_n + hf(t_m, y_m). \tag{6.10}$$

(see Figure 6.2). If the differential equation is autonomous so that f does not, in fact, depend on t, then

$$y_{n+1} = y_n + hf(y_m).$$

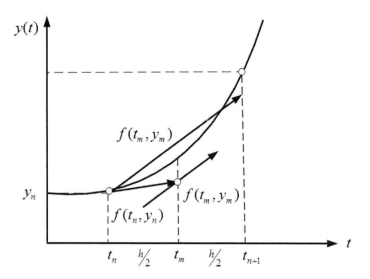

Figure 6.2: A graphical illustration of the midpoint method.

6.2.3   Modified Euler and implicit methods

Let us suppose that we were to integrate the differential equation (6.8)
such that

$$\int_{y_n}^{y_{n+1}} \mathrm{d}y = \int_{t_n}^{t_{n+1}} f(y)\,\mathrm{d}t\,. \tag{6.11}$$

Using Newton forward and backward difference polynomials to approximate the function $f(y)$ we can recover not only the explicit Euler
scheme but develop a technique for obtaining a whole class of *implicit*
and *multistep* methods. First let us adapt the m-th degree Newton
forward polynomial from equation (5.14) *i.e.*

$$f(y) \approx P_m(t_n + \alpha h) = \left[1 + \alpha\Delta + \frac{\alpha(\alpha-1)}{2!}\Delta^2 + \cdots \right.$$
$$\left. \frac{\alpha(\alpha-1)(\alpha-2)\cdots(\alpha-m+1)}{(m)!}\Delta^m \right] f_n + \mathcal{O}(h^{m+1})\,,$$

where t_n is used as the reference point and f_n stands for $f(y_n)$. Because
$t = t_n + \alpha h$ we have that $\mathrm{d}t = h\,\mathrm{d}\alpha$. Using a one-term expansion

$(m = 0)$ in equation (6.11) yields

$$y_{n+1} - y_n = \int_{t_n}^{t_{n+1}} P_0(t_n + \alpha h)\, dt + \underbrace{\int_{t_n}^{t_{n+1}} \mathcal{O}(h)\, dt}_{local\ truncation\ error} \quad,$$

$$= \int_0^1 P_0(t_n + \alpha h) h\, d\alpha + \int_0^1 \mathcal{O}(h) h\, d\alpha\,,$$

$$= \int_0^1 f_n h\, d\alpha + \mathcal{O}(h^2)\,,$$

$$= f_n h + \mathcal{O}(h^2)\,,$$

which is equivalent to equation (6.9). Meanwhile, a two-term expansion with $m = 1$ results in a second-order accurate formula of the form

$$y_{n+1} - y_n = \int_{t_n}^{t_{n+1}} P_1(t_n + \alpha h)\, dt + \underbrace{\int_{t_n}^{t_{n+1}} \mathcal{O}(h^2)\, dt}_{local\ truncation\ error} \quad,$$

$$= \int_0^1 P_1(t_n + \alpha h) h\, d\alpha + \int_0^1 \mathcal{O}(h^2) h\, d\alpha\,,$$

$$= \int_0^1 [f_n + \alpha \Delta f_n]\, h\, d\alpha + \mathcal{O}(h^3)\,,$$

$$= h \left[\alpha\, f_n + \Delta f_n \frac{\alpha^2}{2} \right]_0^1 + \mathcal{O}(h^3)\,,$$

$$= h \left[f_n + \tfrac{1}{2}(f_{n+1} - f_n) \right] + \mathcal{O}(h^3)\,.$$

Rearranging this last result yields the recursion relation for the so-called modified Euler method, *i.e.*

$$y_{n+1} = y_n + \frac{h}{2} [f_n + f_{n+1}] + \underbrace{\mathcal{O}(h^3)}_{local\ error} \qquad n = 0, 1, \cdots \qquad (6.12)$$

Both the explicit Euler method given by equation (6.9) and the modified Euler method given by equation (6.12) are *single-step*: only y_n is required to predict y_{n+1}. The modified Euler method is an implicit scheme because its recursion depends on f_{n+1}, which in turn depends on y_{n+1}. Note that implicit schemes therefore require the solution of a nonlinear algebraic equation at every time step whenever f is a nonlinear function of y. Thus in order to to calculate y_{n+1} from equation (6.12), we may need to employ one of the root finding schemes developed in Chapter 2. At a first glance, this might appear to be a significant disadvantage of implicit schemes. However, implicit schemes have the ability to anticipate sharp changes in the solution between y_n and y_{n+1} and hence are suitable (in fact required) for solving the so called *stiff*

```
function [t,y]=mnhf_modeuler(Fun,y0,h,tmax)
%MNHF_MODEULER solves an autonomous ODE using the Modified Euler scheme.
%
% Fun  - the name of the external function
% y0 - initial condition i.e. y(t_0)
% h - step size or time increment
% tmax - maximum time to which to integrate
%
% Usage  mnhf_modeuler(@odefun1,-0.5,1e-2,10.0);

tol = 1e-5; % Set tolerance.
Nmax = 1e3; % Set maximum number of iterations.

% Initialize arrays. Specify initial condition.
t = 0:h:tmax;
y = zeros(size(t)); y(1) = y0;

% Determine number of time steps, N.
N = length(t)-1;

for ij = 1:N
 count = 0;
 y(ij+1) = y(ij)+h*feval(Fun,y(ij));% Explicit Euler provides initial guess
 while abs( y(ij+1)-y(ij)-0.5*h*(feval(Fun,y(ij))+feval(Fun,y(ij+1))) )>tol
  y(ij+1) = y(ij)+0.5*h*(feval(Fun,y(ij))+feval(Fun,y(ij+1)));
  count = count+1;
  if count > Nmax
   error('Maximum number of iterations exceded.\n\n')
  end
 end
end
```

Figure 6.3: MATLAB implementation of the modified Euler scheme using a fixed point iteration method for the iterative solve with the initial guess provided by explicit Euler.

differential equations. The initial guess required for the root solve operation could be provided using explicit Euler. Such is the approach taken in `mnhf_modeuler`, which can be applied in solving autonomous ordinary differential equations; this MATLAB function is exhibited in Figure 6.3.

It should be clear that extending the Newton forward polynomial to a three-term expansion will not be fruitful because such an approach would involve not only f_{n+1}, but also f_{n+2}. We can, however, use Newton backward polynomials to develop higher-order methods; this will be the topic of section 6.4. More immediately, we shall introduce so-called predictor-corrector schemes and also discuss ideas related to the numerical stability of explicit and implicit schemes.

6.2.4 Predictor-corrector equations - Heun's Method

The preceding discussion leaves us with two alternatives, neither of which are entirely satisfactory. In solving an equation such as (6.1) we can use an explicit method provided the time step, h, is made small or we can instead use an implicit method if we are willing to perform a root solve operation at every time step. Is there a way of combining the best of both worlds *i.e.* of achieving the accuracy of an implicit method with the computational ease of an explicit method? This is the philosophy behind *predictor-corrector* schemes. Consider, for instance, the explicit Euler and modified Euler predictor-corrector pair, which reads

$$y_{n+1}^P = y_n + hf(y_n), \qquad y_{n+1}^C = y_n + \frac{h}{2}\left[f(y_n) + f(y_{n+1}^P)\right]. \quad (6.13)$$

Here the superscript P represents the predicted value for y_{n+1} (obtained from an explicit scheme) whereas C represents the corrected value (obtained from an equation that looks very much like an implicit equation). Figure 6.4 shows the corresponding schematic representation.

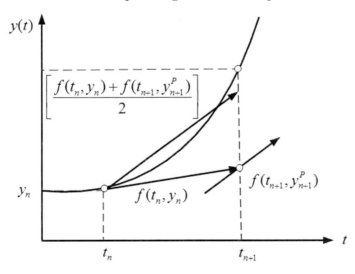

Figure 6.4: A graphical illustration of the predictor-corrector (or Heun's) method.

6.2.5 Stability limits

Let us consider a model linear equation

$$\frac{dy}{dt} = \lambda y, \qquad y(0) = 1,$$

whose analytical solution, $y(t) = e^{\lambda t}$, obviously predicts monotone decay for $\lambda < 0$. Is this behavior reproduced by the sequence $\{y_n | n =$

$0, 1, \cdots\}$ generated by either the explicit Euler scheme or the modified
Euler scheme? To address this question, we first substitute $f(y) = \lambda y$
into equation (6.9) and find

$$y_{n+1} = y_n + hf(y_n) = y_n + h\lambda y_n = [1 + h\lambda]y_n .$$

Thus the sequence giving the numerical solution is

$$
\begin{aligned}
y_1 &= [1 + h\lambda]y_0 , \\
y_2 &= [1 + h\lambda]y_1 = [1 + h\lambda]^2 y_0 , \\
y_3 &= [1 + h\lambda]y_2 = [1 + h\lambda]^3 y_0 , \ldots
\end{aligned}
$$

leading to the following general solution:

$$y_n = [1 + h\lambda]^n y_0 .$$

When the step size h is chosen to be too large (more specifically when
$1 + h\lambda > 1$ or $|h\lambda| > 2$), the sequence will diverge. This phenomenon
is called *numerical instability* and is an artifact of the discretization.
Explicit methods generally have a bound, often quite restrictive, on
the magnitude of h, which poses obvious computational frustrations
when integrating equations over a large range of t.

Do such difficulties also arise when solving the differential equation
in question using modified Euler? In this case, it can be shown that

$$y_{n+1} = y_n + \frac{h}{2}[f_n + f_{n+1}] = y_n + \frac{h}{2}[\lambda y_n + \lambda y_{n+1}] .$$

Solving for y_{n+1} yields

$$y_{n+1} = \left[\frac{1 + h\lambda/2}{1 - h\lambda/2}\right] y_n ,$$

and thus the sequence reads

$$
\begin{aligned}
y_1 &= \left[\frac{1 + h\lambda/2}{1 - h\lambda/2}\right] y_0 , \\
y_2 &= \left[\frac{1 + h\lambda/2}{1 - h\lambda/2}\right] y_1 = \left[\frac{1 + h\lambda/2}{1 - h\lambda/2}\right]^2 y_0 , \\
y_3 &= \left[\frac{1 + h\lambda/2}{1 - h\lambda/2}\right] y_2 = \left[\frac{1 + h\lambda/2}{1 - h\lambda/2}\right]^3 y_0 , \ldots
\end{aligned}
$$

leading to the general solution

$$y_n = \left[\frac{1 + h\lambda/2}{1 - h\lambda/2}\right]^n y_0 .$$

It is clear that for $\lambda < 0$, the ratio $\left[\frac{1+h\lambda/2}{1-h\lambda/2}\right] < 1$ for all positive values
of h. Thus the implicit scheme is *absolutely stable*. Summarizing the

results of these last two calculations, the choice of h is governed by both *stability* and *truncation error* considerations for explicit schemes whereas for implicit schemes only *truncation error* considerations come into play.

6.2.6 Stiff differential equations

The physical interpretation for λ in the above model problem is that it represents the *characteristic time scale* of the problem. For a second-order differential equation (or equivalently a system of two first-order equations), there exist two such time scales, λ_1 and λ_2. If the time scales are widely separated in magnitude then the associated differential equation is called *stiff*.

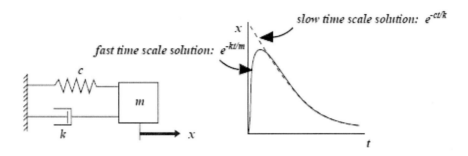

Figure 6.5: A spring and dash-pot model.

Consider, for instance, the spring and dash pot model shown in Figure 6.5. The displacement x is modelled by the force balance equation

$$m\frac{\mathrm{d}^2 x}{\mathrm{d}t^2} + k\frac{\mathrm{d}x}{\mathrm{d}t} + cx = 0\,,$$

where c is the spring constant, k is a damping factor and m is the mass of the block connected to the spring and dash-pot. The initial conditions are supposed to read $x(0) = 0$ and $x'(0) = \mathrm{constant}$. We can write the associated characteristic equation as

$$\frac{m}{k}\lambda^2 + \lambda + \frac{c}{k} = 0\,,$$

and hence the two roots are given by

$$\lambda = \frac{-1 \pm \sqrt{1 - 4mc/k^2}}{2m/k}\,.$$

In the limit $m \to 0$,

$$\lambda_1 \to -\frac{k}{m} \qquad \text{and} \qquad \lambda_2 \to -\frac{c}{k},$$

where L'Hôpital's rule has been applied in obtaining the latter root. Clearly as $m \to 0$, $\lambda_1 \gg \lambda_2$ and thus the ordinary differential equation is stiff. In general, the *stiffness ratio* is defined as the ratio of the largest to the smallest eigenvalues of the system. Here, the stiffness ratio is $k^2/(mc)$, which becomes very large in the limit of small m. The solution satisfying the initial conditions is

$$x(t) = A_1 [\underbrace{e^{-kt/m}}_{fast} - \underbrace{e^{ct/k}}_{slow}].$$

The right-hand side panel of Figure 6.5 delineates between those components of the solution that adjust rapidly and slowly. Note that if $m = 0$, the order of the differential equation drops by one and λ_1 is the only time scale for the problem. This kind of degeneracy also occurs in a number of chemical reaction systems where some of the reactions can occur on a rapid timescale while others evolve at a snail's pace.

In a system of n first-order differential equations there will be n characteristic roots or eigenvalues. If λ_{max} is the largest such eigenvalue, then explicit schemes will typically have a numerical stability restriction of the form $|h\lambda_{max}| <$ constant. Hence explicit schemes demand that punishingly small step sizes be used in regions where the system responds very rapidly. Absolutely-stable implicit schemes have no such restrictions, *i.e.* the integration sequence obtained using an implicit scheme will remain bounded. The choice of step size is determined only by the desired accuracy of the solution. Stability analyses for a variety of explicit and implicit methods are discussed in greater detail by Lapidus & Seinfeld (1971).

EXAMPLE 6.2 (Stiff differential equation and explicit Euler)
The ordinary differential equation

$$\frac{dy}{dt} = -\sin t - 200(y - \cos t), \qquad y(0) = 0 \qquad (6.14)$$

has as an exact solution

$$y = \cos t - e^{-200t},$$

as can be confirmed using integrating factors. We may write this last equation more suggestively as

$$y = \cos\left(\frac{t}{T_1}\right) - \exp\left(-\frac{t}{T_2}\right),$$

```
function mnhf_stiff1(h,Nmax)
%MNHF_STIFF1 illustrates the use of explicit Euler in solving the stiff
% non—autonomous ODE
% y'=—sin(t)—200*(y—cos(t)) with y(0)=0.
%
% h — time step
% Nmax — number of iterations
%
% Usage  mnhf_stiff1(0.01,50)

%% Initialize independent variable array.
t=linspace(0.0,h*Nmax,Nmax+1);

%% Initialize dependent variable array; specify the initial condition.
yEE=zeros(size(t));
yEE(1)=0.0;

for ij=1:Nmax
 %% Calculate solution based on explicit Euler equation.
 yEE(ij+1)=yEE(ij)+h*( —sin(t(ij))—200.0*( yEE(ij)—cos(t(ij)) ) );
end

%% Plot results.
figure(1); hold on; box on
set(gca,'fontsize',18)
plot(t,yEE,'k—','linewidth',2)
xlabel('{\it t}'); ylabel('{\it y}')
title(['time step, {\it h} = ' num2str(h)])

%% Show exact solution.
y=cos(t)—exp(—200.0*t);
plot(t,y,'k——')
legend('explicit Euler','exact','location','best')
```

Figure 6.6: MATLAB function that uses explicit Euler to solve the stiff differential equation (6.14).

where the characteristic timescales have the following values: $T_1 = 1$ and $T_2 = 0.005$. Because $T_1 \gg T_2$, equation (6.14) is evidently a stiff differential equation. Thus we expect the explicit Euler scheme (6.9) to produce reliable results only for suitably small time steps. This hypothesis is confirmed by running the MATLAB algorithm shown in Figure 6.6, which produces as graphical output figures such as those indicated in Figure 6.7.

6.3 Runge-Kutta Methods

Whereas Taylor series methods increase the solution accuracy by increasing the number of retained terms in the Taylor series expansion,

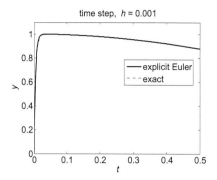 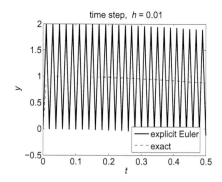

Figure 6.7: Output from `mnhf_stiff1` for two different choices of the time step, h. In the left-hand side panel, the exact and numerical solutions essentially overlap, but no so in the right-hand side panel.

so-called Runge-Kutta methods achieve the same outcome in a single step but at the expense of requiring multiple functional evaluations per step. As we document more carefully below, Runge-Kutta schemes are also classified as explicit, semi-implicit and implicit.

6.3.1   Explicit schemes

The general form of an explicit Runge-Kutta scheme reads as follows:

$$y_{n+1} \;=\; y_n + h \sum_{i=1}^{v} w_i k_i \,, \tag{6.15}$$

$$k_i \;=\; f\left(t_n + c_i, \; y_n + h \sum_{j=1}^{i-1} a_{ij} k_j\right), \quad c_1 = 0, \quad i = 1, 2, \cdots v\,.$$

In these equations, $\{c_i, w_i, a_{ij}\}$ are all parameters. The development of a specific scheme entails determining the best possible values for these constants by matching the expansion of this formula with a Taylor series expansion. Often the parameter values are given in tabular form as

0				
c_2	a_{21}			
c_3	a_{31}	a_{32}		
c_4	a_{41}	a_{42}	a_{43}	
	w_1	w_2	w_3	w_4

or

$$\frac{c \quad A}{\quad w}$$

For explicit methods, A is a lower triangular matrix.

6.3.2 Explicit Euler revisited

Let us consider $v = 1$ in equation (6.15) so that

$$
\begin{aligned}
y_{n+1} &= y_n + w_1 k_1 \,, \\
k_1 &= h f(t_n, y_n) \,,
\end{aligned}
$$

or

$$y_{n+1} = y_n + w_1 h f(t_n, y_n) \,. \tag{6.16}$$

The procedure to determine w_1 is to match the above equation with the Taylor series expansion

$$y_{n+1} = y_n + h y_n' + \frac{h^2}{2!} y_n'' + \frac{h^3}{3!} y_n''' + \cdots \tag{6.17}$$

The first term on the right-hand side of equations (6.16) and (6.17) is obviously the same. Recognizing that $y' = f$, the second term will also match if we set $w_1 = 1$ in which case we have recovered the explicit Euler scheme of equation (6.9). We cannot match any higher-order terms and hence the local truncation error is of order $\mathcal{O}(h^2)$.

6.3.3 A second-order ($v = 2$) Runge-Kutta scheme

Expanding upon the above analysis, let us now consider $v = 2$ in equation (6.15) so that

$$
\begin{aligned}
y_{n+1} &= y_n + w_1 k_1 + w_2 k_2 \,, \tag{6.18} \\
k_1 &= h f(t_n, y_n) \,, \\
k_2 &= h f(t_n + c_2 h, y_n + a_{21} h k_1) \,.
\end{aligned}
$$

The above scheme has four unknown parameters, namely w_1, w_2, c_2 and a_{21}. Again, these must be determined by matching a Taylor series expansion of equation (6.18) with equation (6.17). From equation (6.18), it can be shown that

$$
\begin{aligned}
y_{n+1} &= y_n + w_1 h f(t_n, y_n) + w_2 h f(t_n + c_2 h, y_n + a_{21} k_1) \,, \\
&= y_n + w_1 h f_n + w_2 h \left[f + c_2 h \frac{\partial f}{\partial t} + a_{21}(hf)\frac{\partial f}{\partial y} \cdots \right]_n \tag{6.19}
\end{aligned}
$$

Meanwhile substituting for y' and its higher derivatives in equation (6.17), we get

$$
\begin{aligned}
y_{n+1} &= y_n + h f_n + \frac{h^2}{2}\frac{\mathrm{d}f}{\mathrm{d}t} + \mathcal{O}(h^3)\,, \\
&= y_n + h f_n + \frac{h^2}{2}\left[\frac{\partial f}{\partial t} + \frac{\partial f}{\partial y}\frac{\partial y}{\partial t}\right] + \mathcal{O}(h^3)\,. \qquad (6.20)
\end{aligned}
$$

Comparing terms between the right-hand sides of equations (6.19) and (6.20), we require that

$$
w_1 + w_2 = 1\,, \quad w_2 c_2 = 1/2\,, \quad w_2 a_{21} = 1/2\,.
$$

Thus, we have matched all terms of order $\mathcal{O}(h^2)$ leaving a truncation error of order $\mathcal{O}(h^3)$. In so doing, we have developed three constraints on the four unknowns w_1, w_2, c_2 and a_{21} from equation (6.18). Any choice of values for w_1, w_2, c_2 and a_{21} that satisfies the above three constraints will result in a second-order Runge-Kutta scheme, so named because of its second-order accuracy. Because there are four variables but only three constraints, there exists an extra degree of freedom suggesting that the solution is not unique. One easy possibility is

$$
w_1 = 1/2\,, \quad w_2 = 1/2\,, \quad c_2 = 1\,, \quad a_{21} = 1\,.
$$

This choice is equivalent to the predictor-corrector pair discussed in connection with equation (6.13).

6.3.4   A fourth-order Runge-Kutta scheme

Obviously, the Runge-Kutta technique would be of limited value if it could only ever reproduce recursion equations that can be obtained using the more straightforward means of section 6.2. Novel, higher-order Runge-Kutta schemes can be developed by carrying out the above matching process to higher-order terms. An explicit fourth-order scheme that matches terms in the Taylor series expansion to $\mathcal{O}(h^4)$ is given, in tabular form, by

$$
\begin{array}{c|cccc}
0 & & & & \\
1/2 & 1/2 & & & \\
1/2 & 0 & 1/2 & & \\
1 & 0 & 0 & 1 & \\
\hline
 & 1/6 & 2/6 & 2/6 & 1/6
\end{array}
$$

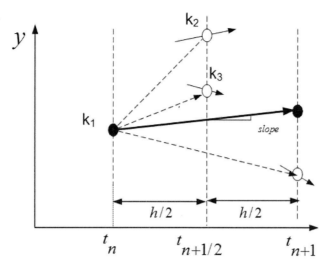

Figure 6.8: Graphical depiction of the fourth-order Runge-Kutta scheme given by equation (6.21).

Expressed in the form of an equation, having a truncation error of $\mathcal{O}(h^5)$, we write

$$
\begin{aligned}
y_{n+1} &= y_n + \frac{h}{6}\left[k_1 + 2k_2 + 2k_3 + k_4\right], & (6.21) \\
k_1 &= f(t_n, y_n), \\
k_2 &= f\left(t_n + \frac{h}{2}, y_n + \frac{h}{2}k_1\right), \\
k_3 &= f\left(t_n + \frac{h}{2}, y_n + \frac{h}{2}k_2\right), \\
k_4 &= f(t_n + h, y_n + hk_3).
\end{aligned}
$$

Figure 6.8 shows the corresponding schematic depiction. The factors $k_1 - k_4$ may be regarded as the slopes of the function at different points within the interval between t_n and t_{n+1}; obviously, these are used to obtain an improved slope for the prediction method. As with all explicit schemes, that of equation (6.21) is suitable for non-stiff differential equations.

EXAMPLE 6.3 (Runge-Kutta vs. explicit Euler) *Suppose that we wish to numerically solve*

$$
\frac{dy}{dt} = 1 + \sin(\pi y) + e^{-t}, \qquad (6.22)
$$

```matlab
function mnhf_rk4_euler(h,Nmax)
%MNHF_RK4_EULER illustrates use of RK4 in solving the non-autonomous ODE
% y'=1+sin(\pi*y)+exp(-t) with y(0)=1.
% Solution obtained by RK4 is contrasted with that obtained using explicit
% Euler.
%
% h - time step
% Nmax - number of iterations
%
% Usage  mnhf_rk4_euler(0.1,100)

%% Initialize independent variable array.
t = linspace(0.0,h*Nmax,Nmax+1);

%% Initialize dependent variable arrays; specify initial condition.
yRK4 = zeros(size(t)); yRK4(1) = 1.0;
yEE = zeros(size(t));  yEE(1) = 1.0;

for ij=1:Nmax
 %% Calculate solution based on explicit Euler.
 yEE(ij+1) = yEE(ij)+h*(1.0+sin(pi*yEE(ij))+exp(-t(ij)));
 %% Calculate solution based on RK4.
 k1 = 1.0+sin(pi*yRK4(ij))+exp(-t(ij));
 k2 = 1+sin(pi*(yRK4(ij)+0.5*h*k1))+exp(-(t(ij)+0.5*h));
 k3 = 1+sin(pi*(yRK4(ij)+0.5*h*k2))+exp(-(t(ij)+0.5*h));
 k4 = 1+sin(pi*(yRK4(ij)+h*k3))+exp(-(t(ij)+h));
 yRK4(ij+1) = yRK4(ij)+h/6.0*(k1+2.0*k2+2.0*k3+k4);
end

%% Plot results.
figure(1); hold on; box on
set(gca,'fontsize',18)
plot(t,yEE,'k--','linewidth',2)
plot(t,yRK4,'k-','linewidth',2)
xlabel('{\it t}'); ylabel('{\it y}')
legend('explicit Euler','RK4','location','best')
title(['time step, {\it h} = ' num2str(h)])
```

Figure 6.9: MATLAB function that contrasts a fourth-order Runge-Kutta (RK4) scheme with explicit Euler.

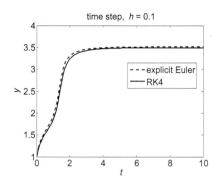 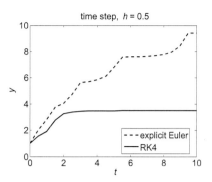

Figure 6.10: Output from `mnhf_rk4_euler` for two different choices of the time step, h.

subject to the following initial condition: $y(0) = 1$. For this purpose, we apply the MATLAB function shown in Figure 6.9, which computes the solution using both the fourth-order Runge-Kutta scheme (6.21) and the explicit Euler scheme (6.9). Graphical output is contrasted in Figure 6.10, which confirms that nearly identical numerical results are obtained for suitably small h. By contrast, quite different results are realized when h is comparatively large. In this latter case, the explicit Euler scheme is obviously numerically unstable.

Embedded forms

Embedded forms of the Runge-Kutta algorithms employ a pair of algorithms that use a common set of function evaluations to form two estimates of the solution at y_{n+1}. Typically a lower-order scheme is embedded within a higher-order scheme. In this way, we may obtain a convenient estimate of the local truncation error at every time step. This information can then be used to develop a step size control strategy. Such embedding is applied in the popular built-in function, `ode45`, which we illustrate in the next two examples.

EXAMPLE 6.4 (Lumped parameter, dynamic models) *Section 1.4 describes a heat transfer problem involving the cooling of a molten metal inside a ceramic crucible. The temperatures of the metal and crucible are assumed to be spatially-uniform but time-variable and hence*

```matlab
function mnhf_crucible()
%MNHF_CRUCIBLE solves the coupled ODEs developed as a lumped parameter,
% dynamic model in Chapter 1.

% Define global variables.
global h1 h2 A1 A2 cp1 cp2 m1 m2 Tinfty

% Parameter input (mks units where applicable with temperatures in K).
h1 = 350.6; h2 = 82.8;      %% Convective heat transfer coefficients.
A1 = 0.0020; A2 = 0.0058;   %% Areas.
cp1 = 1190.0; cp2 = 607.3;  %% Heat capacities.
m1 = 0.027; m2 = 0.009;     %% Masses.
Tinfty = 25.0+273.15;       %% Ambient temperature.
T1_init = 1000.0+273.15; T2_init = Tinfty; %% Initial temperatures.
tmax = 4e2;                 %% Final time (initial time is t=0).
% End of parameter input.

% Solve the coupled ODEs using built-in function ode45.
tint = [0.0 tmax];
init = [T1_init T2_init];
options = odeset('MaxStep',1e-1);
[t,T] = ode45(@crucible_ode,tint,init,options);

% Plot the results.
figure(1); hold on; box on
set(gca,'fontsize',16)
plot(t/60.0,T(:,1)-273.15,'k-','linewidth',2)
plot(t/60.0,T(:,2)-273.15,'k--','linewidth',2)
xlim([0.0 max(t)/60.0])

% Show the ambient temperature as its own (horizontal) line.
XX = [0.0 tmax]/60.0; YY = [Tinfty-273.15 Tinfty-273.15];
plot(XX,YY,'k:','linewidth',2)

% Add a figure title, axis labels and a legend.
title('Metal and crucible temperatures vs. time')
xlabel('Time (minutes)'); ylabel('Temperature (^oC)')
legend('{\it T}_{metal}','{\it T}_{crucible}','{\it T}_{ambient}')

function dtheta=crucible_ode(~,theta)
% Coupled ODEs corresponding to the lumped parameter, dynamical model.

global h1 h2 A1 A2 cp1 cp2 m1 m2 Tinfty

% Initialize.
dtheta = zeros(2,1);

dtheta(1) = -(h1*A1/m1/cp1)*theta(1)+(h1*A1/m1/cp1)*theta(2);
dtheta(2) = (h1*A1/m2/cp2)*theta(1)-1.0/m2/cp2*(h1*A1+h2*A2)*theta(2)+ ...
            h2*A2*Tinfty/m2/cp2;
```

Figure 6.11: MATLAB function that solves the lumped parameter, dynamic model from Chapter 1. Parameter values are chosen arbitrarily (provided, of course, that A_2>A_1, T1_init>T2_init, etc.)

the problem is classified as lumped parameter and dynamic. The coupled ordinary differential equations to be solved are given by (1.6) and (1.7). To obtain the corresponding numerical solution, we leverage the built-in function ode45 *– see the MATLAB algorithm given in Figure 6.11. Note that the equations integrated by* ode45 *must be specified in an external function; in the present case, this function is called* crucible_ode. *Other required inputs to* ode45 *are the initial conditions (here specified by* init*) and the time interval of integration (here specified by* tint*). The algorithm shown below also specifies a maximum time step of 0.1 s via the* options *flag.*

Graphical output produced by running mnhf_crucible *is shown in Figure 6.12. The metal temperature is monotone decreasing whereas the crucible gains more heat than it loses for about the first quarter-minute then loses more heat than it gains thereafter. As expected, both the metal and the crucible approach the ambient temperature in the long-time limit.*

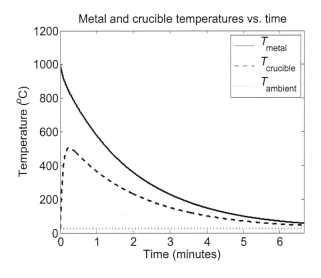

Figure 6.12: Output from mnhf_crucible.

EXAMPLE 6.5 (The Van der Pol equation revisited) *Recall from our earlier discussion that the Van der Pol equation can be written as* *a pair of coupled first-order differential equations i.e.*

$$y' = \omega,$$
$$\omega' = \mu(1 - y^2)\omega - y,$$

where μ is a damping parameter. These equations are solved for $y(0) = 0.1$, $\omega(0) = 0.1$ and $\mu = 0$, $\frac{1}{4}$ and 4 using ode45 *and the MATLAB functions exhibited in Figure 6.13. Figure 6.14 shows the graphical output produced by* mnhf_vdp*, which includes time-series solutions (y vs. t) as well as phase portraits (y' vs. y). These phase portraits provide examples of attracting limit cycles (or isolated periodic orbits). In dynamical systems theory, attractors come in numerous varieties and are classified as "strange" when they exhibit a fractal, not a periodic, structure. The Lorenz equations, named after the mathematician and meteorologist Edward Lorenz, provide perhaps the most famous example of strange attractors – see the end-of-chapter exercises below.*

6.3.5 Implicit schemes

In the general form given in equation (6.15), we fix $c_1 = 0$ and $\boldsymbol{A}$ to be lower triangular. These constraints on the parameters ensure that each k_i can be computed explicitly without the need for iteration. Let us now relax these constraints and lightly rewrite (6.15) as

$$y_{n+1} = y_n + h\sum_{i=1}^{v} w_i k_i, \tag{6.23}$$

$$k_i = f\left(t_n + c_i,\ y_n + h\sum_{j=1}^{v} a_{ij} k_j\right), \qquad i = 1, 2, \cdots v.$$

Selecting $v = 2$ then yields

$$y_{n+1} = y_n + w_1 k_1 + w_2 k_2, \tag{6.24}$$
$$k_1 = hf(t_n + c_1 h, y_n + a_{11} k_1 + a_{12} k_2),$$
$$k_2 = hf(t_n + c_2 h, y_n + a_{21} k_1 + a_{22} k_2),$$

or, in compact tabular form,

c_1	a_{11}	a_{12}
c_2	a_{21}	a_{22}
	w_1	w_2

Note that in order to compute k_1 and k_2, we now need to solve two nonlinear algebraic equations simultaneously. Readers of Chapter 4 will recall that this is not a trivial task. On the plus side, the fully implicit

```
function mnhf_vdp()
%MNHF_VDP1 solves the Van der Pol equation for \mu=0, 0.25 and 4.

global mu

fs = 18;       % Fontsize in figures.
tmax = 6e1;    % Maximum integration time.
mu_vector = [0.0 0.25 4.0]; % Vector of \mu values.

% Specify time interval and initial condition.
tint = [0.0 tmax];
init = [0.1 0.1];

for ij = 1:length(mu_vector)
 mu = mu_vector(ij);
 % Compute solution using ode45.
 options = odeset('MaxStep',1e-2);
 [t,y] = ode45(@mnhf_vdp_func1,tint,init,options);

 % Plot results, starting with y vs. t.
 if mu==0.0
  subplot(3,3,1)
 elseif mu==0.25
  subplot(3,3,4)
 elseif mu==4.0
  subplot(3,3,7)
 end
 plot(t,y(:,1),'k-'); xlim([0.0 60.0])
 set(gca,'fontsize',fs)
 xlabel('{\it t}'); ylabel('{\it y}')
 title(['Van der Pol equation, {\it \mu}=',num2str(mu)],'fontsize',fs-2)

 % Now show the phase portrait, i.e. y' vs. y.
 if mu==0.0
  subplot(3,3,2)
 elseif mu==0.25
  subplot(3,3,5)
 elseif mu==4.0
  subplot(3,3,8)
 end
 plot(y(:,1),y(:,2),'k-')
 set(gca,'fontsize',fs)
 xlabel('{\it y}'); ylabel('{\it y''}')
end

%%%%%%%%%%%%%%%%%%%%%%%%%%%%%%%%%%
function dy=mnhf_vdp_func1(~,y)

global mu

dy = zeros(2,1); % Initialize vector.
dy(1) = y(2);
dy(2) = mu*(1.0-y(1)^2.0)*y(2)-y(1);
```

Figure 6.13: MATLAB functions for solving the Van der Pol equation for various μ using the built-in function ode45.

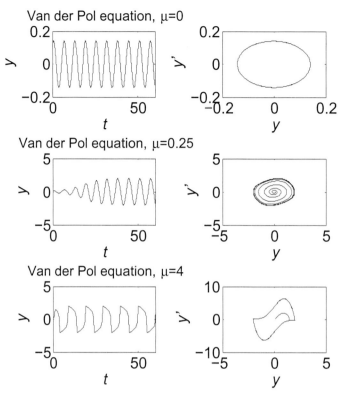

Figure 6.14: Output from `mnhf_vdp`.

nature of the above algorithm ensures numerical stability making it suitable for stiff differential equations. Also, a two-stage scheme ($v = 2$) has eight parameters. We can therefore match these equations with the corresponding Taylor series expansion to higher-order. Hence formulas of greater accuracy can be constructed. An example of an implicit two-stage, fourth-order accurate scheme is the Gauss form given by

$$
\begin{array}{c|cc}
(3 - \sqrt{3})/6 & 1/4 & (3 - 2\sqrt{3})/12 \\
(3 + \sqrt{3})/6 & (3 - 2\sqrt{3})/12 & 1/4 \\
\hline
 & 1/2 & 1/2
\end{array}
$$

6.3.6   Semi-Implicit forms of Rosenbrock

While the implicit forms of section 6.3.5 have desirable stability properties, they can be very computationally demanding. In an effort to reduce the requisite floating point operations without jeopardizing advantageous stability characteristics, Rosenbrock proposed a clever adaptation in 1963. His equations are suitable for an autonomous system of equations of the form

$$\frac{d\boldsymbol{y}}{dt} = \boldsymbol{f}(\boldsymbol{y}), \qquad \boldsymbol{y}(t = t_0) = \boldsymbol{y}_0.$$

A two-stage, third-order accurate scheme is given by

$$\begin{aligned}
\boldsymbol{y}_{n+1} &= \boldsymbol{y}_n + w_1\boldsymbol{k}_1 + w_2\boldsymbol{k}_2, \\
\boldsymbol{k}_1 &= h[\boldsymbol{I} - ha_1\boldsymbol{J}(\boldsymbol{y}_n)]^{-1}\boldsymbol{f}(\boldsymbol{y}_n), \\
\boldsymbol{k}_2 &= h[\boldsymbol{I} - ha_2\boldsymbol{J}(\boldsymbol{y}_n + c_1\boldsymbol{k}_1)]^{-1}\boldsymbol{f}(\boldsymbol{y}_n + b_1\boldsymbol{k}_1),
\end{aligned} \qquad (6.25)$$

where the parameters are

$$a_1 = 1 + \sqrt{6}/6, \qquad a_2 = 1 - \sqrt{6}/6,$$

$$w_1 = -0.41315432, \qquad w_2 = 1.41315432,$$

$$b_1 = c_1 = \frac{-6 - \sqrt{6} + \sqrt{58 + 20\sqrt{6}}}{6 + 2\sqrt{6}}.$$

Here $\boldsymbol{J} = \frac{\partial \boldsymbol{f}}{\partial \boldsymbol{y}}$ is the Jacobian matrix, which must be evaluated at every time step. Note that the main advantage of using equation (6.25) is that $\boldsymbol{k}_1$ and $\boldsymbol{k}_2$ can be computed without need for iteration, although the scheme does require two matrix inversions per time step.

6.4 Multistep methods

6.4.1 Explicit schemes

Consider approximating the function $f(y)$ in equation (6.11) using the following m-th degree Newton backward polynomial:

$$\begin{aligned}
f(y) \approx P_m(t_n + \alpha h) &= \left[1 + \alpha\nabla + \frac{\alpha(\alpha+1)}{2!}\nabla^2 + \cdots \right. \\
&\left. \frac{\alpha(\alpha+1)(\alpha+2)\cdots(\alpha+m-1)}{m!}\nabla^m \right] f_n + \mathcal{O}(h^{m+1})
\end{aligned}$$

Here, t_n has been used as the reference point. Because this polynomial involves only points at earlier times such as f_n, f_{n-1}, $f_{n-2}\ldots$, we can develop a whole class of explicit algorithms known as the Adams-Bashforth schemes. Consider a three-term expansion ($m = 2$). Equation (6.11) becomes

$$
\begin{aligned}
y_{n+1} - y_n &= \int_{t_n}^{t_{n+1}} P_2(t_n + \alpha h)\, dt + \underbrace{\int_{t_n}^{t_{n+1}} \mathcal{O}(h^3)\, dt}_{\text{local truncation error}} \\
&= \int_0^1 P_2(t_n + \alpha h)h\, d\alpha + \int_0^1 \mathcal{O}(h^3)h d\alpha\,, \\
&= \int_0^1 \left[f_n + \alpha \nabla f_n + \frac{\alpha(\alpha+1)}{2!}\nabla^2 f_n \right] h d\alpha + \mathcal{O}(h^4)\,, \\
&= h \left[\alpha f_n + \frac{\alpha^2}{2}\nabla f_n + \frac{1}{2!}\left(\frac{\alpha^3}{3} + \frac{\alpha^2}{2} \right)\nabla^2 f_n \right]_0^1 + \mathcal{O}(h^4)\,, \\
&= h \left[f_n + \frac{1}{2}(f_n - f_{n-1}) + \frac{5}{12}(f_n - 2f_{n-1} + f_{n-2}) \right] + \mathcal{O}(h^4)
\end{aligned}
$$

which can be rearranged into the form

$$
y_{n+1} = y_n + \frac{h}{12}\left[23f_n - 16f_{n-1} + 5f_{n-2} \right] + \underbrace{\mathcal{O}(h^4)}_{\text{local error}} \tag{6.26}
$$

The above recursion relation can be applied for $n = 2, 3, \dots$. A number of important points must be made in connection with equation (6.26).

1. This is an example of a *multistep scheme* that requires y_n, y_{n-1} and y_{n-2} to predict y_{n+1}.

2. Hence it is not a self-starter! Typically, in a well-posed initial value problem, we know only y_0. Therefore y_1 and y_2 must be generated using independent techniques before we can switch to the above multistep scheme. The analogy with a manual transmission automobile is a helpful one. When pulling out of a driveway, drivers do not immediately put their automobiles into their highest gear. Rather they start in first, then, after a time, shift to second, then to third, then to fourth, etc. Likewise with multistep methods. In the case of the three-term Adams-Bashforth scheme, for instance, one could use explicit Euler to solve for y_1 from y_0 then the two-term Adams-Bashforth equation to solve for y_2 from y_0 and y_1 and then finally (6.26) to solve for y_3, y_4, etc.

3. Equation (6.26) represents an explicit algorithm because y_{n+1} does not appear on the right-hand side of the equation.

4. As a consequence, equation (6.26) cannot anticipate sharp changes in y and is therefore not recommended for stiff differential equations.

5. Finally, and unlike the Runge-Kutta schemes seen in section 6.3, equation (6.26) requires only one functional evaluation per time step.

EXAMPLE 6.6 (Using the three-term Adams-Bashforth scheme)
Consider the following ordinary differential equation and initial condition:

$$\frac{dy}{dt} = 2y^2\,, \qquad y(0) = -1\,.$$

As indicated in Figure 6.15, it is straightforward to determine the numerical solution using the three-term Adams-Bashforth equation (6.26). Consistent with the above commentary, this multistep scheme is not a self-starter; we therefore begin the computations using explicit Euler and the two-term Adams-Bashforth scheme. Graphical output corresponding to `mnhf_ab3example` *is provided in Figure 6.16 where a comparison is drawn with the exact solution. Although the agreement appears to be very robust, we will see in the end-of-chapter exercises that even better agreement may be realized if explicit Euler is replaced with modified Euler and the two-term Adams-Bashforth scheme is replaced with a two-term Adams-Moulton scheme (to be discussed below).*

A fourth-order accurate Adams-Bashforth scheme can be developed from a four-term expansion of the Newton backward polynomial. Saving the derivational details as an end-of-chapter exercise, you should be able to verify that

$$y_{n+1} = y_n + \frac{h}{24}\left[55f_n - 59f_{n-1} + 37f_{n-2} - 9f_{n-3}\right] + \underbrace{\mathcal{O}(h^5)}_{local\ error} \qquad (6.27)$$

The above recursion relation can be applied for $n = 3, 4, \ldots$

6.4.2 Implicit schemes

In order to develop implicit schemes to complement the explicit schemes of section 6.4.1, we need to first construct backward polynomial approximations with t_{n+1} as the reference point, *i.e.*

$$f(y) \approx P_m(t_{n+1} + \alpha h) = \left[1 + \alpha\nabla + \frac{\alpha(\alpha+1)}{2!}\nabla^2 + \cdots \right.$$
$$\left. \frac{\alpha(\alpha+1)(\alpha+2)\cdots(\alpha+m-1)}{m!}\nabla^m\right]f_{n+1} + \mathcal{O}(h^{m+1})$$

```
function mnhf_ab3example()
%MNHF_AB3EXAMPLE example illustrating the application of the three—term
% Adams—Bashforth scheme. ODE is dy/dt = 2y^2 subject to y(0) = —1.

fs = 14; % Fontsize in figure.

% Plot exact solution, y = —1/(1+2*t).
t = linspace(0.0,20.0,1e4+1);
y = —1.0./(1.0+2.0*t);
figure; subplot(2,2,3); plot(t,y,'k—')
set(gca,'fontsize',fs—2)
xlabel('{\it t}','fontsize',fs); ylabel('{\it y}','fontsize',fs)
title('Exact solution','fontsize',fs);

clear t y

% Compute and plot numerical solution.
[t,y] = mnhf_ab3(@odefun1,—1.0,1e—2,20.0);
subplot(2,2,4); plot(t,y,'k—')
set(gca,'fontsize',fs—2)
xlabel('{\it t}','fontsize',fs); ylabel('{\it y}','fontsize',fs)
title('Numerical solution','fontsize',fs);

%%%%%%%%%%%%%%%%%%%%%%%%%%%%%%%%%%%%%%%%
function [t,y]=mnhf_ab3(Fun,y0,h,tmax)
%MNHF_AB3 three—term Adams—Bashforth algorithm for solving a single
% autonomous ODE. Uses Explicit Euler and two—term Adams—Bashforth (AB2)
% to get the integration started. Note that Adams—Bashforth is an
% explicit scheme and may therefore exhibit some numerical difficulties
% when y changes rapidly with t.
%
% Fun  — the name of the external function
% y0   — the initial condition on y, i.e. y0=y(t=0)
% h    — step size i.e. time increment (constant)
% tmax — maximum time to which to integrate
%
% Usage  mnhf_ab3(@odefun1,—1.0,1e—2,20.0);

% Initialize arrays. Specify initial condition.
t = 0:h:tmax; y = zeros(size(t)); y(1) = y0;

% Determine number of time steps, N.
N = length(t)—1;

% Explicit Euler to find y1=y(2).
y(2) = y(1)+h*feval(Fun,y(1));
% AB2 to find y2=y(3).
y(3) = y(2)+0.5*h*(3.0*feval(Fun,y(2))—feval(Fun,y(1)));
% AB3 to find y3=y(4), y4=y(5)... yN=y(N+1).
for ij=3:N
 y(ij+1) = y(ij)+h/12.0*(23.0*feval(Fun,y(ij))—16.0*feval(Fun,y(ij—1))+ ...
         5.0*feval(Fun,y(ij—2)));
end

%%%%%%%%%%%%%%%%%%%%%%
function f=odefun1(y)

f = 2.0*y^2.0;
```

Figure 6.15: MATLAB implementation of the three-term Adams-Bashforth scheme (as applied in solving $dy/dt = 2y^2$, $y(0) = -1$).

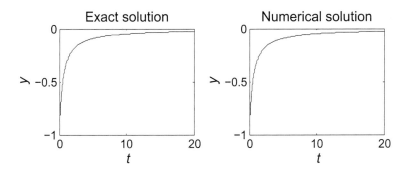

Figure 6.16: Output from `mnhf_ab3example`.

In this manner f_{n+1} is introduced on the right-hand side of the equation. The associated class of implicit algorithms are called Adams-Moulton schemes. We are still integrating from t_n to t_{n+1}. Because $t = t_{n+1} + \alpha h$, the limits of integration on α become -1 and 0. A four-term expansion results in

$$
\begin{aligned}
y_{n+1} - y_n &= \int_{t_n}^{t_{n+1}} P_3(t_{n+1} + \alpha h)\, dt + \underbrace{\int_{t_n}^{t_{n+1}} \mathcal{O}(h^4)\, dt}_{local\ truncation\ error} \\
&= \int_{-1}^{0} P_3(t_n + \alpha h) h\, d\alpha + \int_{-1}^{0} \mathcal{O}(h^4) h\, d\alpha, \\
&= \int_{-1}^{0} \Bigg[f_{n+1} + \alpha \nabla f_{n+1} + \frac{\alpha(\alpha+1)}{2!} \nabla^2 f_{n+1} + \cdots \\
&\qquad \frac{\alpha(\alpha+1)(\alpha+2)}{3!} \nabla^3 f_{n+1} \Bigg] h\, d\alpha + \mathcal{O}(h^5), \\
&= h \left[f_{n+1} - \frac{1}{2} \nabla f_{n+1} - \frac{1}{12} \nabla^2 f_{n+1} - \frac{1}{24} \nabla^3 f_{n+1} \right] + \mathcal{O}(h^5),
\end{aligned}
$$

which can be rearranged into the form

$$
y_{n+1} = y_n + \frac{h}{24} \left[9f_{n+1} + 19f_n - 5f_{n-1} + f_{n-2} \right] + \underbrace{\mathcal{O}(h^5)}_{local\ error} \tag{6.28}
$$

The above recursion relation can be applied for $n = 2, 3, \dots$ Note that the pair of explicit-implicit schemes given, respectively, by equations (6.27) and (6.28) can be combined as a predictor-corrector pair.

6.5   Summary

In this chapter we have explored different methods for solving initial value problems for first-order differential equations. Higher-order differential equations can be converted to a system of first-order equations through simple variable redefinition. Implicit and explicit schemes have both been explored; the former are shown to be unconditionally stable, whereas the latter, though easier to implement, suffer from stability limitations in the form of time step restrictions.

Single-step and multistep methods have been presented and their respective accuracies analysed. The choice of a particular method is dictated by a combination of user preference, the details of the problem at hand and the required precision.

Taylor series methods can achieve high accuracy by increasing the number of retained terms. Runge-Kutta methods can realize the accuracy of Taylor series methods at the expense of requiring multiple functional evaluations per time step. The classical fourth-order Runge-Kutta method is arguably the most versatile general purpose single-point method for solving differential equations. However, it proves unsuitable when tackling stiff differential equations, which typically demand a high-order implicit scheme such as those credited to Adams and Moulton.

6.6 Exercise Problems

P6.1. Given the initial value problem

$$\frac{dy}{dt} = 1 + \frac{y}{t}, \qquad 1 \leq t \leq 4, \qquad y(1) = 1,$$

with corresponding analytical solution $y(t) = t(1 + \ln t)$,

(a) Solve the problem with a step size of $h = 0.5$ and determine the absolute error at each iteration.

(b) By taking successively smaller steps, show that the global error associated with explicit Euler is $\mathcal{O}(h)$.

P6.2. Given the initial value problem

$$\frac{dy}{dt} = \frac{y^2 + 1}{t}, \qquad 1 \leq t \leq 4, \qquad y(1) = 0,$$

(a) Solve the problem using explicit Euler and a step size of $h = 1$; determine the absolute error at each iteration.

(b) Solve the problem with the fourth-order Runge-Kutta equation (6.21) and a step size of $h = 2$.

P6.3. Consider the autonomous differential equation $dy/dt = y^3$ with corresponding initial condition $y(0) = y_0$. Using explicit Euler, the numerical solution would be computed using the following recursion relation:

$$y_{n+1} = y_n + h y_n^3. \tag{6.29}$$

This equation is easy to implement, but may yield inaccurate results when the time step, h, is not small. Better accuracy might be expected using the modified Euler method, according to which

$$y_{n+1} = y_n + \frac{h}{2}(y_n^3 + y_{n+1}^3), \tag{6.30}$$

however this recursion relation requires the solution of a non-linear algebraic equation at each time step. Using a predictor-corrector scheme is one way to balance the benefits of an explicit algorithm (like the Euler method) and an implicit algorithm (like modified Euler). Another way is to consider the following *hybrid* recursion relation:

$$y_{n+1} = y_n + h y_n^2 y_{n+1}. \tag{6.31}$$

Note that (6.31) is *linear* in y_{n+1} and so not especially awkward to solve numerically.

Write a MATLAB program that graphically compares the solutions returned by (6.29) and (6.31) over $0 \le t \le 0.45$ for $y_0 = 0.95$ and the following step sizes: $h = 0.001, 0.01, 0.025$ and 0.05. Your figure should consist of four subplots, one for each different value of h. Be sure to include the exact solution in each subplot along with a legend and axis labels.

P6.4. Consider the differential equation

$$\frac{dy}{dt} = \lambda y^2, \qquad y(0) = 1,$$

and the hybrid recursion relation from **P6.3**. For what values of h is the scheme numerically stable?

P6.5. The general second-order explicit Runge-Kutta equations read

$$y_{n+1} = y_n + h\left[\left(1 - \frac{1}{2\alpha}\right)k_1 + \frac{1}{2\alpha}k_2\right], \qquad (6.32)$$

$$k_1 = f(t_n, y_n), \qquad (6.33)$$

$$k_2 = f(t_n + \alpha h, y_n + \alpha h k_1), \qquad (6.34)$$

where $0 < \alpha \le 1$. Consider the application of the above equations to the following differential equation:

$$\frac{dy}{dt} = \lambda y, \qquad y(t = 0) = y_0, \qquad (6.35)$$

in which $\lambda < 0$. Show that the time step restriction required for numerical stability is the same as for the explicit Euler scheme, i.e. $h < 2/|\lambda|$. In spite of this result, why might it be preferable to use (6.32) through (6.34) in place of explicit Euler?

P6.6. Given the two equations

$$\frac{dx}{dt} = y,$$

$$\frac{dy}{dt} = -x - 2y,$$

and the initial conditions $x(0) = 1$ and $y(0) = -1$,

(a) Carry out four steps of the explicit Euler method with a step size of $h = 0.25$.

(b) Carry out four steps of the predictor-corrector equation (6.13) with a step size of $h = 0.25$.

P6.7. Use the so-called *backward Euler method** to solve the following problem:

$$\frac{dy}{dt} = ty^3 - y, \qquad 0 \le t \le 1, \qquad y(0) = 0.$$

---

*$y_{n+1} = y_n + hf(t_{n+1}, y_{n+1})$

Carry out three iterations. Use Newton's method for the nonlinear algebraic equation root solve. Now repeat your calculations but used the modified Euler method.

P6.8. Use the *backward Euler method* from **P6.7.** to solve the following problem:

$$\frac{dy}{dt} = t^2 - y^2, \qquad 0 \leq t \leq 1, \qquad y(0) = 0.$$

Carry out three iterations. Use Newton's method for the nonlinear algebraic equation root solve. Now repeat your calculations but used the modified Euler method.

P6.9. The MATLAB algorithm `mnhf_ab3example` discussed earlier in this chapter uses lower-order methods (i.e. explicit Euler and a three-term Adams-Bashforth scheme) to get things started, i.e. to compute y_1 and y_2 from the initial condition, $y_0 = y(0)$. On the theory that a chain is only as strong as its weakest link, note that whatever truncation errors are introduced in calculating y_1 and, to a lesser extent, y_2 are "carried forward" to the calculation of y_3, y_4, etc. We can rectify this in a number of different ways e.g. by (i) reducing the step size for the first couple of calculations, or, (ii) by switching from explicit to implicit equations when evaluating y_1 and y_2. Here we follow the latter approach.

Rewrite `mnhf_ab3example` but replace the explicit Euler equation with the modified Euler equation. Also, replace the three-term Adams-Bashforth equation with the following three-term Adams-Moulton equation:

$$y_{n+1} = y_n + \frac{h}{12} \left(5f_{n+1} + 8f_n - f_{n-1}\right) + \mathcal{O}(h^4).$$

Thus in computing y_1 and y_2, you will have to solve a nonlinear algebraic equation using a root finding scheme of your choosing. Finally, verify that such attention to detail actually does make a difference by returning to

$$\frac{dy}{dt} = 2y^2, \qquad y(0) = -1. \tag{6.36}$$

Compute, using `mnhf_ab3example` and also your new MATLAB algorithm the numerical solution to the above equation in the interval $0 \leq t \leq 0.4$ selecting $h = 0.1$. Plot the numerical solutions against the exact solution. Which numerical solution gives better accuracy?

P6.10. Derive equation (6.27).

P6.11. Consider the differential equation

$$10x^2\frac{d^2c}{dx^2} + 2x\frac{dc}{dx} + c = 0,$$

together with the following conditions:

$$c(x = 0) = 1, \qquad \left.\frac{dc}{dx}\right|_{x=0} = -1.$$

(a) Is the equation linear or nonlinear?

(b) Convert the second-order differential equation into a system of two first-order equations.

(c) Is the resulting system autonomous or non-autonomous?

(d) Obtain the numerical solution using an algorithm of your choice.

P6.12. A chemical company produces wholesale solvent by mixing together pure benzene and pure toluene in a continuously-stirred vessel of diameter $D = 1\,\text{m}$ and height $H = 2.5\,\text{m}$ that is open to the atmosphere. The volume flux of pure benzene is $Q_b = 7.2\,\text{L/s}$ and the density of benzene is $\rho_b = 877\,\text{kg/m}^3$. The volume flux of pure toluene is $Q_t = 1.1\,\text{L/s}$ and the density of toluene is $\rho_t = 867\,\text{kg/m}^3$. Both inlet streams are "switched on" at $t = 0$ at which point the tank contains $463.8\,\text{L}$ of pure benzene. The outflow from the vessel is governed by Bernoulli's law, i.e. $Q_{\text{product}} = \sqrt{2gh} \times \frac{\pi}{4}d^2$ where $d = 1.25$ inches is the diameter of the outlet piping.

The chemical company can only market its solvent as A-grade when it contains a minimum of 6.25% toluene by mass. How much time, t_1, must elapse before this concentration is reached? Also, for the flow rates prescribed above, is there a danger that the tank will eventually overflow and, if so, when is this anticipated?

P6.13. Four perfectly-stirred tanks arranged in series as shown in Figure 6.17 are use to heat a hydrocarbon mixture before it is fed to a stripper column. The initial amount of hydrocarbon in each tank is $500\,\text{kg}$ at $300\,\text{K}$. Each tank is equipped with a heating jacket though which saturated steam at $500\,\text{K}$ is condensing. The feed rate at the first tank is $50\,\text{kg/min}$.

The heat transfer (q in kW) for a given tank is $q = UA\Delta T$ where U is the heat transfer coefficient measured in $\text{W/(m}^2\text{K}$, A is the

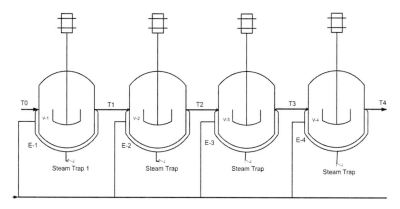

Figure 6.17: Heat exchange tank cascade.

heat transfer area for the coil measured in m^2 and ΔT is the temperature difference between the condensing steam and the tank interior.

(a) Perform an energy balance for each of the four tanks to obtain the equation for the time rate of change of temperature.

(b) Solve the four simultaneous differential equation to determine the steady state temperature in each tank.

(c) Calculate the time necessary for each tank to reach steady state.

P6.14. Figure 6.18 a shows a single pendulum swinging back and forth for which the governing equation reads

$$I\frac{d^2\theta}{dt^2} = -mg\ell\sin\theta. \tag{6.37}$$

Here I, m and ℓ are, respectively, the moment of inertia, mass and length of the pendulum, g is gravitational acceleration and the angle θ is as defined in Figure 6.18 a. Now consider the connected pendulums of Figure 6.18 b, which are attached by a spring of spring constant k. The two pendulums are equal in mass, length, etc. so that the governing equations now read

$$I\frac{d^2\alpha}{dt^2} = -mg\ell\sin\alpha - kc^2(\sin\alpha - \sin\beta), \tag{6.38}$$

$$I\frac{d^2\beta}{dt^2} = -mg\ell\sin\beta + kc^2(\sin\alpha - \sin\beta). \tag{6.39}$$

Here c is the distance between the suspension point of the pendulum and the suspension point of the spring and α and β are defined as in Figure 6.18 b.

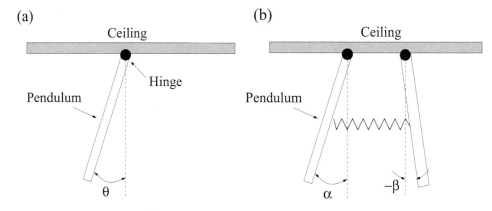

Figure 6.18: (a) A single pendulum. (b) A pair of coupled pendulums.

(a) Show that (6.38) and (6.39) can be rewritten in non-dimensional
form as follows:

$$\frac{\mathrm{d}^2\alpha}{\mathrm{d}t^{\star 2}} = -\frac{m\ell^2}{I}\sin\alpha - \frac{kc^2\ell}{Ig}(\sin\alpha - \sin\beta)\,, \qquad (6.40)$$

$$\frac{\mathrm{d}^2\beta}{\mathrm{d}t^{\star 2}} = -\frac{m\ell^2}{I}\sin\beta + \frac{kc^2\ell}{Ig}(\sin\alpha - \sin\beta)\,. \qquad (6.41)$$

Here $t^\star = t/\sqrt{\ell/g}$.

(b) Equations (6.40) and (6.41) do not admit analytical solutions, but the coupled equations can be solved numerically
provided they are expressed as first-order equations. Rewrite
the equations as such.

(c) Using one of Matlab's built-in ordinary differential equation integrators, compute the numerical solution to your
equations from above for the following choice of parame-
ters: $m\ell^2/I = 2.7$ and $kc^2\ell/(Ig) = \frac{1}{3}$. Plot your time-
series solution for α and β in the same figure over the interval $0 \le t^\star \le 30$. Assume as initial conditions $\alpha = \frac{\pi}{6}$,
$\mathrm{d}\alpha/\mathrm{d}t^\star = 0$, $\beta = -\frac{\pi}{3}$, $\mathrm{d}\beta/\mathrm{d}t^\star = 0$.

P6.15. The equation describing a nonlinear pendulum is given by

$$\ddot{\theta} + \frac{k}{m}\dot{\theta} + \frac{g}{L}\sin\theta = 0\,, \qquad (6.42)$$

where θ is the angle to the vertical, k is a damping coefficient, m
is the mass of the pendulum bob, L is the pendulum length, g is

gravitational acceleration and dots indicate time differentiation. Let us consider the solution of (6.42) for the following choice of parameters: $k = 12\,\text{g/s}$, $m = 15\,\text{g}$, $L = 50\,\text{cm}$ and $g = 980\,\text{cm/s}^2$ subject to initial conditions of *either* $\theta(0) = \pi/2$ and $\dot{\theta} = 8.0\,\text{s}^{-1}$ or $\theta(0) = \pi/2$ and $\dot{\theta} = -8.0\,\text{s}^{-1}$. Write a program that plots (a) θ and $\dot{\theta}$ vs. t for $0 \le t \le 10\,\text{s}$, and, (b) the phase plane map, i.e. θ vs. $\dot{\theta}$. Produce a separate plot for each set of initial conditions.

P6.16. The Lorenz equations read

$$\dot{x} = y - x, \qquad \dot{y} = 5x - y - xz, \qquad \dot{z} = xy - 16z, \qquad (6.43)$$

where, for example, $\dot{x} = dx/dt$. Selecting as initial conditions $x_0 = -11$, $y_0 = -15.5$ and $z_0 = 25.2$, solve the above equations over the time interval $0 \le t \le 10$ using `ode45`. Show your solutions graphically, i.e. plot y_1, y_2 and y_3 vs. t and also plot y_2 vs. y_1, y_3 vs. y_1 and y_3 vs. y_2. Let us now modify (6.43) slightly by writing

$$\dot{x} = 10(y - x), \qquad \dot{y} = 28x - y - xz, \qquad \dot{z} = xy - \tfrac{8}{3}z. \quad (6.44)$$

Plotting your solutions as before, do you observe qualitatively similar or different behavior?

P6.17. Earlier in this chapter, we used the explicit Euler method to solve a single ordinary differential equation. Let us now consider applying this scheme to the following *pair* of (autonomous) equations:

$$u' = v, \qquad v' = uv, \qquad (6.45)$$

where $u = u(t)$ and $v = v(t)$. Explicit Euler demands that we solve

$$u_{i+1} = u_i + hv_i, \qquad v_{i+1} = v_i + hu_iv_i, \qquad (6.46)$$

in which h is the time step.

(a) Supposing $h = 0.5$ and initial conditions $u(0) = 1$ and $v(0) = 2$, manually compute u_4 and v_4.

(b) As in the single equation case, numerical stability is improved by using an implicit rather than an explicit numerical method when solving (6.45). With the *backward Euler method* of **P6.7.**, (6.46) is replaced with

$$u_{i+1} = u_i + hv_{i+1}, \qquad v_{i+1} = v_i + hu_{i+1}v_{i+1}. \qquad (6.47)$$

Show, by manipulation of (6.47), that

$$u_{i+1} = \frac{1 + hu_i - \sqrt{(1 + hu_i)^2 - 4h(u_i + hv_i)}}{2h}, \qquad (6.48)$$

and

$$v_{i+1} = \frac{v_i}{1 - hu_{i+1}} \,. \tag{6.49}$$

Hint: For small h, it can be shown using Taylor series that

$$\sqrt{(1 + hu_i)^2 - 4h(u_i + hv_i)} \simeq 1 + hu_i - 2h(u_i + hv_i) \,.$$

He who can, does. He who cannot teaches.

— GEORGE BERNARD SHAW

CHAPTER 7

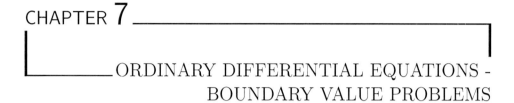

ORDINARY DIFFERENTIAL EQUATIONS - BOUNDARY VALUE PROBLEMS

In the present chapter we shall develop algorithms for solving systems of linear or nonlinear ordinary differential equations of the boundary value variety. As illustrated in Chapter 1, such equations arise in describing distributed, steady state models. The differential equations are transformed into systems of linear and nonlinear algebraic equations through a discretization process. In doing so, we use the tools and concepts developed in earlier chapters of this book. More specifically, we will develop (i) finite difference methods using the difference approximations given in Tables 5.7 and 5.8, and, (ii) shooting methods based on techniques for solving initial value problems.

For starters, let us revisit the model for heat transfer through a fin developed in section 1.5. In the coming pages, we shall examine several variations on this model problem. Before getting to these specifics, let us first scale the governing equation by introducing the following dimensionless temperature and distance variables:

$$\theta = \frac{T - T_\infty}{T_0 - T_\infty}, \qquad \xi = \frac{x}{L}.$$

Employing these definitions, equation (1.9) can be rewritten as

$$\frac{\mathrm{d}}{\mathrm{d}\xi}\left[kA\frac{\mathrm{d}\theta}{\mathrm{d}\xi}\right] - hPL^2\theta = 0, \tag{7.1}$$

with corresponding Dirichlet boundary conditions

$$\theta(\xi = 0) = 1, \qquad \theta(\xi = 1) = 0. \tag{7.2}$$

The objective is to solve the above boundary value problem over the domain $\xi \in [0, 1]$ for a prescribed k, A, h, P and L. These parameters can be constant, or they may vary with position. If the fin is tapered, for instance, then $A = A(\xi)$. Conversely, if the thermal conductivity, k, varies with temperature and temperature varies with position then k will likewise change with ξ.

For simplicity, we first examine the case of constant cross-sectional area, A, and thermal conductivity, k. Equations (7.1) and (7.2) then result in the following linear boundary value problem:

$$\frac{d^2\theta}{d\xi^2} - \frac{hPL^2}{kA}\theta = 0, \tag{7.3}$$

$$\theta(\xi = 0) = 1, \qquad \theta(\xi = 1) = 0.$$

In a variation of the above model, suppose $A = A(\xi)$ but k is constant. We then obtain a variable coefficient, linear boundary value problem of the form

$$A(\xi)\frac{d^2\theta}{d\xi^2} + \frac{dA(\xi)}{d\xi}\frac{d\theta}{d\xi} - \frac{hPL^2}{k}\theta = 0, \tag{7.4}$$

$$\theta(\xi = 0) = 1, \qquad \frac{d\theta}{d\xi}\bigg|_{\xi=1} = 0.$$

Here we have also introduced a variation on the boundary condition at $\xi = 1$. Such boundary conditions, where we specify the value of a derivative rather than of the original function, are called *Neumann boundary conditions*. The temperature at $\xi = 1$ is an unknown and must be found as part of the solution procedure.

In yet another variation, consider the case where the thermal conductivity depends upon temperature, *e.g.* $k(\theta) = \alpha + \beta\theta^2$ where α and β are experimentally determined constants. Let the area, A, be a constant. The boundary value problem now becomes nonlinear and is written as

$$k(\theta)\frac{d^2\theta}{d\xi^2} + k'(\theta)\left(\frac{d\theta}{d\xi}\right)^2 - \frac{hPL^2}{A}\theta = 0, \tag{7.5}$$

$$\theta(\xi = 0) = 1, \qquad \left[\frac{k(\theta)}{L}\frac{d\theta}{d\xi} - h\theta\right]_{\xi=1} = 0.$$

At this point, a third variation on the right-hand side boundary condition, called a mixed or *Robin boundary condition* has been utilized. Once again, the temperature at $x = L$ is an unknown and must be determined as part of the solution procedure.

All of the above problems can be represented symbolically in the following compact form:

$$\mathcal{D}\theta = f \quad \text{on} \quad \Omega, \tag{7.6}$$

$$\mathcal{B}\theta = g \quad \text{on} \quad \partial\Omega\,, \tag{7.7}$$

where $\mathcal{D}$ and $\mathcal{B}$ are differential operators, Ω is the domain of interest and $\partial\Omega$ represents its boundary. Our task is to obtain an *approximate numerical solution* expressed as $\theta = \theta(\xi)$. The solution technique consists of constructing a discrete version of the differential equation in question, which results in a system of linear or nonlinear algebraic equations. In the former and latter scenarios, respectively, the methods presented in Chapters 3 and 4 can be applied in deriving the solution. The associated numerical schemes will be developed in the sections to follow.

7.1 Finite difference method

7.1.1 Linear boundary value problem with constant coefficients

The first step in solving equation (7.3) using the so-called finite difference method is to divide the independent variable ξ into equally-spaced subdivisions as shown in Figure 7.1. The distance between two adjacent grid points is given by

$$\Delta\xi = \frac{1-0}{n+1}\,.$$

Each grid point has a unique value of ξ_i, *i.e.* $\xi_i = i\Delta\xi$ where $i = 0, 1, \cdots n+1$. Instead of attempting to find a continuous solution to (7.3), we content ourselves with finding an approximate solution at the interior nodal points *i.e.* $\bar{\theta}_i | i = 1, 2, \cdots n$, where n corresponds to the number of such interior points. Note that for the Dirichlet boundary conditions of interest here, $\bar{\theta}_0$ and $\bar{\theta}_{n+1}$ are known from (7.3), *i.e.* $\bar{\theta}_0 = 1$ and $\bar{\theta}_{n+1} = 0$. Hence, it remains to determine the n unknown interior temperatures for which purpose, we require n equations. This set of n equations is obtained by evaluating the differential equation (7.3) at each of the interior nodal points. In so doing, we replace the second derivative term by a corresponding finite difference approximation from Table 5.8. Obviously, Table 5.8 prescribes a number of alternatives. As outlined in further quantitative detail below, we recommend using the central finite difference approximation formula, which offers a good compromise between accuracy and ease of implementation.

The discrete form of (7.3) is then written as follows:

$$\left[\frac{\bar{\theta}_{i+1} - 2\bar{\theta}_i + \bar{\theta}_{i-1}}{(\Delta\xi)^2}\right] - \frac{hPL^2}{kA}\bar{\theta}_i = 0 \qquad i = 1, 2, \cdots n\,. \tag{7.8}$$

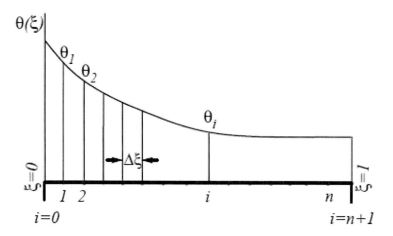

Figure 7.1: One dimensional finite difference grid consisting of equally-spaced data points.

The term in the square brackets is the $\mathcal{O}(\Delta\xi)^2$-accurate central finite difference approximation for the second derivative. Equation (7.8) prescribes a system of n linear algebraic equations. Let us write these out explicitly for $n = 4$.

$$\bar{\theta}_0 - 2\bar{\theta}_1 + \bar{\theta}_2 - \alpha\bar{\theta}_1 = 0\,,$$
$$\bar{\theta}_1 - 2\bar{\theta}_2 + \bar{\theta}_3 - \alpha\bar{\theta}_2 = 0\,,$$
$$\bar{\theta}_2 - 2\bar{\theta}_3 + \bar{\theta}_4 - \alpha\bar{\theta}_3 = 0\,,$$
$$\bar{\theta}_3 - 2\bar{\theta}_4 + \bar{\theta}_5 - \alpha\bar{\theta}_4 = 0\,.$$

For notational simplicity, we have defined $\alpha = \frac{hPL^2}{kA}(\Delta\xi)^2 = \mathrm{Bi}(\Delta\xi)^2$ in which Bi is a modified Biot number that characterizes the relative importance of convection to conduction. (We refer to Bi as a modified Biot number because here the conductive and convective heat fluxes do not both point in the surface normal direction.) When $\mathrm{Bi} \gg 1$ ($\ll 1$), we expect convection (conduction) to dominate.

The above equations can be expressed using matrix notation as $\boldsymbol{\mathcal{T}}\bar{\boldsymbol{\theta}} = \boldsymbol{b}$, or,

$$\begin{bmatrix} -(2+\alpha) & 1 & 0 & 0 \\ 1 & -(2+\alpha) & 1 & 0 \\ 0 & 1 & -(2+\alpha) & 1 \\ 0 & 0 & 1 & -(2+\alpha) \end{bmatrix} \begin{bmatrix} \bar{\theta}_1 \\ \bar{\theta}_2 \\ \bar{\theta}_3 \\ \bar{\theta}_4 \end{bmatrix} = \begin{bmatrix} -\bar{\theta}_0 \\ 0 \\ 0 \\ -\bar{\theta}_5 \end{bmatrix}$$

$$(7.9)$$

Note that the boundary values $\bar{\theta}_0$ and $\bar{\theta}_5$, which are known from the Dirichlet boundary conditions appear as forcing terms on the right-hand side of equation (7.9). Indeed, equations (7.8) and (7.9) are the *discrete* versions of equation (7.3). Once the structure is apparent, we can increase n to reduce $\Delta\xi$ and hence reduce the truncation error. In the limit of $\Delta\xi \to 0$ there will be very little difference between the numerical solution and the exact, analytical solution to equation (7.3). Obviously, increasing n also has the effect of increasing the size of the matrix $\mathcal{T}$ and thus increasing the requisite number of floating point operations.

Figure 7.2 shows the MATLAB algorithm used to numerically solve the problem in question. As can be confirmed using MATLAB's built-in function `spy`, $\mathcal{T}$ is a tridiagonal matrix. As a consequence (i) the matrix can be straightforwardly constructed using the built-in function `diag`, and, (ii) the Thomas algorithm developed in Chapter 3 can be leveraged when computing the solution, $\bar{\boldsymbol{\theta}}$. In the MATLAB function of Figure 7.2, the number of interior grid points is left as a user-defined input. So too is the value of Bi. Indeed by typing, in the MATLAB Command Window,

```
>>mnhf_fin1(100,[1e-1 1e0 1e1 1e2 1e3])
```

we generate numerical solutions for Bi spanning four orders of magnitude. Corresponding graphical output is given in Figure 7.3, which shows θ as a function of ξ.

As hinted at above, it is possible to solve (7.3) analytically. Here, however, we opt to validate our numerical solutions using a more informal (and less cumbersome) methodology. When Bi is small in magnitude, the differential equation in (7.3) is approximately equivalent to $\mathrm{d}^2\theta/\mathrm{d}\xi^2 = 0$. The solution to this equation is a straight line as anticipated by the thick solid curve of Figure 7.3. Conversely when Bi is large, the differential equation in (7.3) is approximately equivalent to $\theta = 0$. This solution is consistent with the boundary condition at $\xi = 1$, but not at $\xi = 0$. Thus there must exist a region of rapid adjustment* in the neighborhood of $\xi = 0$ where the solution abruptly changes from $\theta \simeq 1$ to $\theta \simeq 0$. Reassuringly, the left-most thin curve of Figure 7.3 displays exactly this behavior. Although the above "reality checks" do not verify with authority that the solutions computed by the algorithm of Figure 7.2 are correct, they are at least sufficient to ensure that the solutions are not obviously incorrect. Performing such checks

---

*Mathematicians refer to such regions as "boundary layers," a terminology that is also prevalent when studying external flow e.g. flow over an airfoil.

```
function mnhf_fin1(n,Bi)
%MNHF_FIN1 solves for the 1D temperature distribution in a cooling fin
% of constant cross—sectional area subject to Dirichlet BCs.
%
% n —  number of interior grid points.
% Bi — modified Biot number(s).
%
% Usage  mnhf_fin1(100,[1e—1 1e0 1e1 1e2 1e3])

% Set grid spacing, i.e. define \delta \xi.
dxi = (1.0—0.0)/(n+1);

for i = 1:length(Bi)
 fprintf('Now considering Bi=%8.2f\n',Bi(i))

 % Initialize arrays.
 maindiag = linspace(—2.0—Bi(i)*dxi^2.0,—2.0—Bi(i)*dxi^2.0,n);% Main diag.
 offdiag  = linspace(1.0,1.0,n—1);                    % Super/sub diagonals.
 T = diag(maindiag,0)+diag(offdiag,1)+diag(offdiag,—1); % Put it together.
 b = zeros(n,1);                                 % Define RHS vector.
 b(1) = —1.0;

 % Solve linear system using Thomas's algorithm then plot solution.
 theta=mnhf_thomas(T,b); theta=[1.0 theta' 0.0];
 xi = linspace(0.0,1.0,n+2);
 figure(1); hold on; box on; set(gca,'fontsize',14)
 if i==1
  plot(xi,theta,'k—','linewidth',3)
 else
  plot(xi,theta,'k—','linewidth',1)
 end
end

% Add axis labels and title.
xlabel('{\it \xi=x/L}')
ylabel('{\it \theta=(T—T_\infty)/(T_0—T_\infty)}')
title('Cooling fin (uniform cross—section, Dirichlet BCs)','fontsize',12)
```

Figure 7.2: MATLAB function that solves for the temperature distribution in a fin of constant cross-sectional area, A, and having a constant thermal conductivity, k.

is therefore quite important, particularly when the complexity of the differential equation(s) and algorithm are such that no exact solution can be derived.

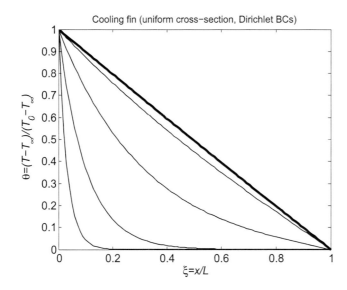

Figure 7.3: Output from `mnhf_fin1.m` for the following values of Bi: 0.1, 1, 10, 100 and 1000.

7.1.2 Linear boundary value problem with variable coefficients

We now turn our attention to equation (7.4), which is also a linear problem albeit one with a variable coefficient in $A = A(\xi)$. The discretization procedure remains the same as in the previous section with the exception that $\bar{\theta}_{n+1}$ is now included in the set of unknowns, *i.e.*

$$\bar{\theta} = [\bar{\theta}_1, \bar{\theta}_2, \cdots, \bar{\theta}_{n+1}]'.$$

Using Tables 5.7 and 5.8 and the $\mathcal{O}(\Delta\xi)^2$-accurate central finite difference approximations for both the first and second derivatives in equation (7.4), we obtain

$$A(\xi_i) \left[\frac{\bar{\theta}_{i+1} - 2\bar{\theta}_i + \bar{\theta}_{i-1}}{(\Delta\xi)^2} \right] + A'(\xi_i) \left[\frac{\bar{\theta}_{i+1} - \bar{\theta}_{i-1}}{2\Delta\xi} \right] - \frac{hPL^2}{k}\bar{\theta}_i = 0, \quad (7.10)$$

which can be applied for $i = 1, 2, \cdots n + 1$. Multiplying throughout by $(\Delta\xi)^2$ and collecting like terms yields

$$a_i\bar{\theta}_{i-1} + d_i\bar{\theta}_i + c_i\bar{\theta}_{i+1} = 0 \,, \tag{7.11}$$

where

$$a_i = A(\xi_i) - A'(\xi_i)\frac{(\Delta\xi)}{2} \,,$$

$$d_i = -2A(\xi_i) - \frac{hPL^2(\Delta\xi)^2}{k} \,,$$

$$c_i = A(\xi_i) + A'(\xi_i)\frac{(\Delta\xi)}{2} \,.$$

If the fin shape is known then it is easy to compute a_i, d_i and c_i. Unlike in equation (7.8), however, $a_i \neq c_i$. Moreover, the coefficients vary with the grid point location i. When $i = 1$, equation (7.11) yields a term proportional to $\bar{\theta}_0$, where $\bar{\theta}_0$ is know from the left-hand side Dirichlet boundary condition. Conversely when $i = n + 1$, equation (7.11) yields a term proportional to $\bar{\theta}_{n+2}$, which falls a horizontal distance $\Delta\xi$ to the right of the domain of interest. The problem therefore appears to be under-resolved: there are $n + 2$ unknowns $(\bar{\theta}_1, \bar{\theta}_2, \ldots \bar{\theta}_{n+2})$ yet equation (7.11) can only be applied $n + 1$ times. Closure is achieved by employing the right-hand side Neumann boundary condition, which states

$$\left.\frac{d\theta}{d\xi}\right|_{\xi=1} \simeq \frac{\bar{\theta}_{n+2} - \bar{\theta}_n}{2\Delta\xi} = 0 \,. \tag{7.12}$$

(Table 5.7 confirms that the above finite difference approximation is again $\mathcal{O}(\Delta\xi)^2$-order accurate). Equation (7.12) obviously implies that $\bar{\theta}_{n+2} = \bar{\theta}_n$, a fact that can be used to eliminate $\bar{\theta}_{n+2}$ from realization $n + 1$ of equation (7.11). Thus

$$(a_{n+1} + c_{n+1})\bar{\theta}_n + d_{n+1}\bar{\theta}_{n+1} = 0 \,.$$

Synthesizing the above results ultimately yields a tridiagonal system of linear equation of the form $\mathcal{T}\bar{\theta} = b$. For illustrative purposes, let us select $n = 4$ in which case the system of equations to be solved reads, in matrix form,

$$\begin{bmatrix} d_1 & c_1 & 0 & 0 & 0 \\ a_2 & d_2 & c_2 & 0 & 0 \\ 0 & a_3 & d_3 & c_3 & 0 \\ 0 & 0 & a_4 & d_4 & c_4 \\ 0 & 0 & 0 & a_5 + c_5 & d_5 \end{bmatrix} \begin{bmatrix} \bar{\theta}_1 \\ \bar{\theta}_2 \\ \bar{\theta}_3 \\ \bar{\theta}_4 \\ \bar{\theta}_5 \end{bmatrix} = \begin{bmatrix} -a_1\bar{\theta}_0 \\ 0 \\ 0 \\ 0 \\ 0 \end{bmatrix} \,. \tag{7.13}$$

Now that the matrix structure is apparent, it is straightforward to increase n and thereby decrease both $\Delta\xi$ and the truncation error. As in section 7.1.1, the Thomas algorithm provides an efficient means of solving the matrix equation.

EXAMPLE 7.1 (An example of a tapered fin) *Consider a blunt fin of length L whose base and tip heights are t_0 and $t_0/2$, respectively. The fin thickness, t, is a linear function of x so that $t = t_0[1 - x/(2L)]$. When non-dimensionalizing as before, and after lots of algebra, it can be shown that*

$$(2 - \xi)\frac{\mathrm{d}^2\theta}{\mathrm{d}\xi^2} - \frac{\mathrm{d}\theta}{\mathrm{d}\xi} - 2\,\mathrm{Bi}'\theta = 0\,, \qquad (7.14)$$

where the modified Biot number is defined as

$$\mathrm{Bi}' = \frac{2hL^2}{kt_0}\sqrt{1 + \left(\frac{t_0}{4L}\right)^2}\,.$$

By adapting `mnhf_fin1.m`, *it is straightforward to solve (7.14) using finite differences. Below, we present two algorithms;* `mnhf_fin2.m` *considers the case of a (homogeneous) Neumann right-hand side boundary condition whereas* `mnhf_fin3.m` *considers the case of a (homogeneous) Dirichlet right-hand side boundary condition. When Bi' is comparatively large (i.e. $\mathrm{Bi}' = 10$, lower pair of solid and dashed curves), the difference of right-hand side boundary condition is more-or-less insignificant especially away from the fin tip. By contrast, the difference of solution behavior is much more dramatic when Bi' is relatively small (i.e. $\mathrm{Bi}' = 0.1$, upper pair of solid and dashed curves). Note that both solid curves from Figure 7.6 have zero slope when $\xi = 1$.*

7.1.3 Nonlinear boundary value problems

Conceptually there is no difference in discretizing a linear vs. a nonlinear boundary value problem. The process of constructing a grid and replacing the differential equations with the corresponding difference equations is identical. The chief disparity lies in the choice of solution technique: as we have already seen, linear boundary value problems yield systems of linear equations, which can be solved using the algorithms of Chapter 3. By contrast, nonlinear boundary value problems yield systems of nonlinear equations and so the algorithms of Chapter 4 must instead be applied.

To illustrate this latter point, consider the nonlinear boundary value problem represented by equation (7.5). In this case, a Robin boundary condition is specified at $\Delta\xi = 1$ and hence $\bar{\theta}_{n+1}$ is unknown. Thus there

```
function mnhf_fin2(n,Bi)
%MNHF_FIN2 solves for the 1D temperature distribution in a cooling fin
% of variable cross-sectional area subject to Dirichlet/Neumann BCs.
%
% n - number of interior grid points.
% Bi - modified Biot number.
%
% Usage  mnhf_fin2(100,1e-1)

% Set grid spacing, i.e. define \delta \xi.
dxi = (1.0-0.0)/(n+1);

%% Initialize arrays.
xi = linspace(dxi,1.0,n+1);
maindiag = -2.0*(2.0-xi+Bi*dxi^2.0);                % Main diagonal.
supdiag = 2.0-xi(1:end-1)-0.5*dxi;                  % Super diagonal.
subdiag = 2.0-xi(2:end)+0.5*dxi;                    % Sub diagonal.
subdiag(end) = 2.0*(2.0-xi(end));
T = diag(maindiag,0)+diag(supdiag,1)+diag(subdiag,-1); % Put it together.
b = zeros(n+1,1);                                   % Define RHS vector.
b(1) = -1.0*(2.0-xi(1)+0.5*dxi);

% Solve linear system using Thomas's algorithm then plot solution.
theta = mnhf_thomas(T,b); theta = [1.0 theta'];
xi = linspace(0.0,1.0,n+2);
figure(1); hold on; box on; set(gca,'fontsize',14)
plot(xi,theta,'k-','linewidth',2);

%% Add axis labels and a title to the figure.
xlabel('{\it \xi=x/L}');
ylabel('{\it \theta=(T-T_\infty)/(T_0-T_\infty)}');
title('Cooling fin (variable cross-section, Dirichlet/Neumann ...
    BCs)','fontsize',12)
```

Figure 7.4: MATLAB function that solves (7.14) using finite differences and a (homogeneous) Neumann right-hand side boundary condition.

```
function mnhf_fin3(n,Bi)
%MNHF_FIN3 solves for the 1D temperature distribution in a cooling fin
% of variable cross-sectional area subject to Dirichlet BCs.
%
% n -  number of interior grid points.
% Bi - modified Biot number.
%
% Usage  mnhf_fin3(100,1e-1)

% Set grid spacing, i.e. define \delta \xi.
dxi = (1.0-0.0)/(n+1);

%% Initialize arrays.
xi = linspace(dxi,1.0-dxi,n);
maindiag = -2.0*(2.0-xi+Bi*dxi^2.0);                % Main diagonal.
supdiag = 2.0-xi(1:end-1)-0.5*dxi;                  % Super diagonal.
subdiag = 2.0-xi(2:end)+0.5*dxi;                    % Sub diagonal.
T = diag(maindiag,0)+diag(supdiag,1)+diag(subdiag,-1); % Put it together.
b = zeros(n,1);                                     % Define RHS vector.
b(1) = -1.0*(2.0-xi(1)+0.5*dxi);

% Solve linear system using Thomas's algorithm then plot solution.
theta = mnhf_thomas(T,b); theta = [1.0 theta' 0.0];
xi = linspace(0.0,1.0,n+2);
figure(1); hold on; box on; set(gca,'fontsize',14)
plot(xi,theta,'k-','linewidth',2);

%% Add axis labels and a title to the figure.
xlabel('{\it \xi=x/L}');
ylabel('{\it \theta=(T-T_\infty)/(T_0-T_\infty)}');
title('Cooling fin (variable cross-section, Dirichlet BCs)','fontsize',12)
```

Figure 7.5: MATLAB function that solves (7.14) using finite differences and a (homogeneous) Dirichlet right-hand side boundary condition.

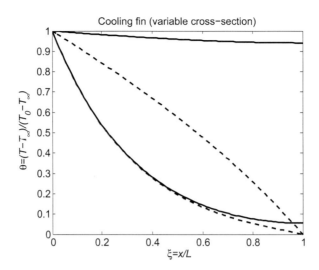

Figure 7.6: Output from `mnhf_fin2` and `mnhf_fin3` for the following values of Bi: 0.1 (upper pair of curves) and 10 (lower pair of curves).

are $n + 1$ unknowns altogether: $\bar{\theta}_1$, $\bar{\theta}_2$,... $\bar{\theta}_{n+1}$. As with the problem investigated in section 7.1.2, closure requires specification of $n+1$ equations. The vast majority of these come from equation (7.5); in discrete form, it reads

$$
f_i(\bar{\theta}_{i-1}, \bar{\theta}_i, \bar{\theta}_{i+1}) = k(\bar{\theta}_i) \left[\frac{\bar{\theta}_{i+1} - 2\bar{\theta}_i + \bar{\theta}_{i-1}}{(\Delta\xi)^2} \right] + k'(\bar{\theta}_i) \left[\frac{\bar{\theta}_{i+1} - \bar{\theta}_{i-1}}{2\Delta\xi} \right]^2 - \frac{hPL^2}{A}\bar{\theta}_i = 0 .
\tag{7.15}
$$

Equation (7.15) applies for $i = 1, 2, \ldots n + 1$. Consistent with the previous discussion, the first ($i = 1$) and last ($i = n + 1$) realization of equation (7.15) require special attention due to the influence of the boundary conditions. As before, the left-hand side boundary condition is Dirichlet suggesting that $\bar{\theta}_0 = 1$. Thus

$$
f_1(\bar{\theta}_1, \bar{\theta}_2) = k(\bar{\theta}_1) \left[\frac{\bar{\theta}_2 - 2\bar{\theta}_1 + 1}{(\Delta\xi)^2} \right] + k'(\bar{\theta}_1) \left[\frac{\bar{\theta}_2 - 1}{2\Delta\xi} \right]^2 - \frac{hPL^2}{A}\bar{\theta}_1 = 0 .
$$

Along the right-hand side boundary, it is necessary to discretize the Robin boundary condition and we do so by writing

$$
k(\bar{\theta}_{n+1}) \left[\frac{\bar{\theta}_{n+2} - \bar{\theta}_n}{2\Delta\xi} \right] + hL\bar{\theta}_{n+1} = 0 .
$$

Solving for $\bar{\theta}_{n+2}$ yields

$$\bar{\theta}_{n+2} = \bar{\theta}_n - \beta\bar{\theta}_{n+1},$$

where $\beta \equiv 2hL\Delta\xi/k(\bar{\theta}_{n+1})$. Thus

$$
\begin{aligned}
f_{n+1}(\bar{\theta}_n, \bar{\theta}_{n+1}) &= k(\bar{\theta}_{n+1})\left[\frac{2\bar{\theta}_n - (2+\beta)\bar{\theta}_{n+1}}{(\Delta\xi)^2}\right] + \\
&\quad \frac{\beta^2 k'(\bar{\theta}_{n+1})\bar{\theta}_{n+1}^2}{4(\Delta\xi)^2} - \frac{hPL^2}{A}\bar{\theta}_{n+1} = 0.
\end{aligned}
\tag{7.16}
$$

The above equations $f_1 = 0$, $f_2 = 0, \cdots f_{n+1} = 0$ can be represented symbolically as a system of $n+1$ nonlinear equations of the form $\boldsymbol{\mathcal{F}}(\bar{\boldsymbol{\theta}}) = \mathbf{0}$. Using the multidimensional Newton's method, it is straightforward to solve this set of nonlinear equations for the unknowns $\bar{\theta}_1, \bar{\theta}_2, \ldots \bar{\theta}_{n+1}$. In so doing, it is obviously necessary to evaluate the Jacobian matrix, which has a special tridiagonal structure. If $n = 4$, for instance,

$$
\boldsymbol{J} = \begin{bmatrix}
\frac{\partial f_1}{\partial \theta_1} & \frac{\partial f_1}{\partial \theta_2} & 0 & 0 & 0 \\
\frac{\partial f_2}{\partial \theta_1} & \frac{\partial f_2}{\partial \theta_2} & \frac{\partial f_2}{\partial \theta_3} & 0 & 0 \\
0 & \frac{\partial f_3}{\partial \theta_2} & \frac{\partial f_3}{\partial \theta_3} & \frac{\partial f_3}{\partial \theta_4} & 0 \\
0 & 0 & \frac{\partial f_4}{\partial \theta_3} & \frac{\partial f_4}{\partial \theta_4} & \frac{\partial f_4}{\partial \theta_5} \\
0 & 0 & 0 & \frac{\partial f_5}{\partial \theta_4} & \frac{\partial f_5}{\partial \theta_5}
\end{bmatrix}.
$$

The connection between $\boldsymbol{J}$ and the tridiagonal matrix $\boldsymbol{\mathcal{T}}$ of equation (7.9) is more than merely cosmetic. In the event that k does not, in fact, depend on θ, the nonlinear boundary value problem reduces to a linear boundary value problem, which in discrete form is represented by $\boldsymbol{\mathcal{T}}\bar{\boldsymbol{\theta}} = \boldsymbol{b}$ as we have seen already in sections 7.1.1 and 7.1.2. Note, moreover, that $\boldsymbol{J}$ contains $3n + 1$ partial derivatives, suggesting a problem of aggravating intractability when n is more than about 4 or 5. Note, however, that there are only five *independent* partial derivatives to be evaluated, i.e. $\partial f_i/\partial\bar{\theta}_{i-1}$, $\partial f_i/\partial\bar{\theta}_i$, $\partial f_i/\partial\bar{\theta}_{i+1}$ and, for the case of the Robin boundary condition studied here, $\partial f_{n+1}/\partial\bar{\theta}_n$ and $\partial f_{n+1}/\partial\bar{\theta}_{n+1}$. These five partial derivatives can, of course, be computed either manually or numerically, the preferred alternative depending on the complexity of the function $k = k(\theta)$.

Our application of finite difference techniques in solving various incarnations of the cooling fin problem risks leaving the impression that finite differences can only be employed when (i) the differential equation is posed in non-dimensional form, and/or, (ii) the underlying physical problem involves a transfer of energy, but not of, say, mass or momentum. In fact, neither assertion is true as we shall demonstrate below with reference to a new category of problem: parallel shear flow.

7.1.4   Parallel shear flow with constant dynamic viscosity (Newtonian fluid)

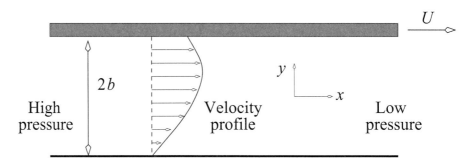

Figure 7.7: Parallel shear flow driven by a combination of a pressure gradient and a translating upper boundary.

Figure 7.7 shows a rectilinear shear flow driven by a horizontal pressure gradient and a translating upper boundary, which moves from left to right at constant speed, U. Letting u and v denote, respectively, the horizontal and vertical components of velocity, we see immediately that $v = 0$ and $u = u(y)$ where y is the vertical coordinate. Because the fluid is assumed to have a finite (and constant) dynamic viscosity, μ, we can apply the so-called no-slip condition, which stipulates that the fluid and boundary velocities must be equal at the bottom $(y = -b)$ and top $(y = b)$ of the channel. Thus, we require that $u(-b) = 0$ and $u(b) = U$. To compute the horizontal velocity distribution for $-b < y < b$, we must solve the following governing equation:

$$\mu \frac{\mathrm{d}^2 u}{\mathrm{d}y^2} = G.\tag{7.17}$$

Here, $G\,(< 0)$ is the (constant) pressure gradient, expressed in units of pressure/length.

Although it is possible to derive an analytic solution to (7.17), we seek instead a numerical solution using a familiar discretization of the second derivative term, i.e.

$$\frac{\mathrm{d}^2 u}{\mathrm{d}y^2} \simeq \frac{\bar{u}_{i+1} - 2\bar{u}_i + \bar{u}_{i-1}}{(\Delta y)^2} + \mathcal{O}(\Delta y)^2.\tag{7.18}$$

Setting $i = 1$ in equation (7.18), and neglecting the truncation error term, yields

$$\frac{\bar{u}_2 - 2\bar{u}_1 + \bar{u}_0}{(\Delta y)^2} = \frac{G}{\mu}.$$

Note, however, that $\bar{u}_0 = u(y = -b) = 0$ and hence

$$-2\bar{u}_1 + \bar{u}_2 = \frac{G(\Delta y)^2}{\mu} \,.$$

In like fashion, you should be able to convince yourself that

$$\bar{u}_1 - 2\bar{u}_2 + \bar{u}_3 = \frac{G(\Delta y)^2}{\mu} \,,$$

$$\bar{u}_2 - 2\bar{u}_3 + \bar{u}_4 = \frac{G(\Delta y)^2}{\mu} \,,$$

$$\vdots$$

$$\bar{u}_{n-2} - 2\bar{u}_{n-1} + \bar{u}_n = \frac{G(\Delta y)^2}{\mu} \,,$$

$$\bar{u}_{n-1} - 2\bar{u}_n = \frac{G(\Delta y)^2}{\mu} - U \,.$$

In this latter equation, we have exploited the fact that $\bar{u}_{n+1} = u(y = b) = U$.

As with our investigation of cooling fins, the above system of equations is linear and exhibits a tridiagonal structure. We shall therefore apply the Thomas algorithm to solve

$$
\begin{bmatrix}
-2 & 1 & 0 & 0 & 0 & \dots & 0 \\
1 & -2 & 1 & 0 & 0 & \dots & 0 \\
0 & 1 & -2 & 1 & 0 & \dots & 0 \\
\vdots & & & & & & \\
0 & \dots & 0 & 0 & 1 & -2 & 1 \\
0 & \dots & 0 & 0 & 0 & 1 & -2
\end{bmatrix}
\begin{bmatrix}
\bar{u}_1 \\
\bar{u}_2 \\
\bar{u}_3 \\
\vdots \\
\bar{u}_{n-1} \\
\bar{u}_n
\end{bmatrix}
=
\begin{bmatrix}
G(\Delta y)^2/\mu \\
G(\Delta y)^2/\mu \\
G(\Delta y)^2/\mu \\
\vdots \\
G(\Delta y)^2/\mu \\
G(\Delta y)^2/\mu - U
\end{bmatrix} .
$$

$$(7.19)$$

The corresponding MATLAB algorithm is given in Figure 7.8 with graphical output presented in Figure 7.9. As regards the latter figure, note that the numerical and analytical (or theoretical) solutions are indistinguishable from one another for all three choices of U.

7.1.5 Parallel shear flow with velocity-dependent dynamic viscosity (non-Newtonian fluid)

Whereas the problem of section 7.1.4 appears to be a straightforward extension of ideas developed in section 7.1.1, numerous complications arise if we consider so-called non-Newtonian fluids such as ketchup, synthetic motor oil or blood for which $\mu = \mu(u)$. In this circumstance,

```
function mnhf_channel1()
%MNHF_CHANNEL1 solves for the (steady) velocity distribution for parallel
% shear flow driven by a moving boundary and a (constant) pressure gradient
% using finite-differences. Boundary conditions are Dirichlet.

% Parameter input (mks units).
G = -1e1;                     % Pressure gradient (Pa/m or kg/m^2/s^2).
mu = 5e-1;                    % Dynamic viscosity (kg/m/s).
halfht = 1e-1;               % Channel half-height (m).
U = [2.5e-1 0.0 -2.5e-1];    % Upper plate velocity (m/s).
n = 1e2;                     % Number of interior grid points.
Deltay = 2.0*halfht/(n+1);   % Grid spacing.
% End of parameter input.

% Initialize arrays.
maindiag = linspace(-2.0,-2.0,n);        % Main diagonal.
offdiag = linspace(1.0,1.0,n-1);         % Super/sub diagonals.
T = diag(maindiag,0)+diag(offdiag,1)+diag(offdiag,-1); %% Put it together.

for i=1:length(U)
 b = G*Deltay^2.0/mu*ones(n,1);          % Define RHS vector.
 b(n) = b(n)-U(i);

 % Solve linear system using Thomas's algorithm then plot solution.
 u = mnhf_thomas(T,b); u=[0.0 u' U(i)];
 y = linspace(-halfht,halfht,n+2);
 figure(1); box on; hold on; set(gca,'fontsize',14)
 plot(1e2*u,1e2*y,'color',[rand, rand, rand],'linewidth',2) % Numerical.
 plot(1e2*0.5*(y+halfht).*(G/mu*(y-halfht)+U(i)/halfht),1e2*y,'k—') % Thy.
end

% Add axis labels and a title.
xlabel('{\it u} (cm/s)')
ylabel('{\it y} (cm)')
title('Velocity distribution in a channel','fontsize',14)
```

Figure 7.8: MATLAB function that solves the parallel shear flow problem specified by equation (7.19).

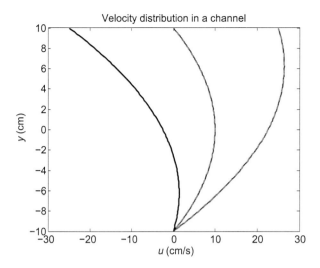

Figure 7.9: Output from `mnhf_channel1`.

the governing equation reads

$$\frac{\mathrm{d}}{\mathrm{d}y}\left(\mu(u)\frac{\mathrm{d}u}{\mathrm{d}y}\right) = G. \tag{7.20}$$

Unfortunately, we cannot now "pull out" the factor $\mu(u)$ because μ depends on u and u is a function of y, the variable of differentiation. Rather, by employing the product and chain rules, equation (7.20) becomes

$$\mu(u)\frac{\mathrm{d}^2u}{\mathrm{d}y^2} + \mu'(u)\left(\frac{\mathrm{d}u}{\mathrm{d}y}\right)^2 = G, \tag{7.21}$$

where $\mu'(u) \equiv \mathrm{d}\mu/\mathrm{d}u$. (We assume that $\mu(u)$ and hence $\mu'(u)$ are known functions.) Similar to the problem studied in section 7.1.3, this is an example of *nonlinear* boundary value problem. As such, we must again use the techniques of Chapter 4 rather than of Chapter 3 in computing the numerical solution.

Discretizing equation (7.21), it can readily be shown that

$$\mu(\bar{u}_i)\left(\frac{\bar{u}_{i+1} - 2\bar{u}_i + \bar{u}_{i-1}}{(\Delta y)^2}\right) + \mu'(\bar{u}_i)\left(\frac{\bar{u}_{i+1} - \bar{u}_{i-1}}{2\Delta y}\right)^2 = G. \tag{7.22}$$

The form of this last equation motivates us to define a series of nonlinear functions f_i as

$$f_i(\bar{u}_{i-1}, \bar{u}_i, \bar{u}_{i+1}) = \mu(\bar{u}_i)\left(\frac{\bar{u}_{i+1} - 2\bar{u}_i + \bar{u}_{i-1}}{(\Delta y)^2}\right) +$$

$$\mu'(\bar{u}_i)\left(\frac{\bar{u}_{i+1} - \bar{u}_{i-1}}{2\Delta y}\right)^2 - G. \qquad (7.23)$$

Thus

$$f_1(\bar{u}_0, \bar{u}_1, \bar{u}_2) = \mu(\bar{u}_1)\left(\frac{\bar{u}_2 - 2\bar{u}_1 + \bar{u}_0}{(\Delta y)^2}\right) + \mu'(\bar{u}_1)\left(\frac{\bar{u}_2 - \bar{u}_0}{2\Delta y}\right)^2 - G.$$

Recall, however, that $\bar{u}_0 = u(y = -b) = 0$ and therefore

$$f_1(\bar{u}_1, \bar{u}_2) = \mu(\bar{u}_1)\left(\frac{\bar{u}_2 - 2\bar{u}_1}{(\Delta y)^2}\right) + \mu'(\bar{u}_1)\left(\frac{\bar{u}_2}{2\Delta y}\right)^2 - G.$$

In like fashion, and using the boundary condition at $y = b$, it can be shown that

$$f_n(\bar{u}_{n-1}, \bar{u}_n) = \mu(\bar{u}_n)\left(\frac{U - 2\bar{u}_n + \bar{u}_{n-1}}{(\Delta y)^2}\right) + \mu'(\bar{u}_n)\left(\frac{U - \bar{u}_{n-1}}{2\Delta y}\right)^2 - G.$$

Thus the system of nonlinear equations reads

$$\begin{aligned}
f_1(\bar{u}_1, \bar{u}_2) &= 0, \\
f_2(\bar{u}_1, \bar{u}_2, \bar{u}_3) &= 0, \\
f_3(\bar{u}_2, \bar{u}_3, \bar{u}_4) &= 0, \qquad (7.24) \\
&\vdots \\
f_{n-1}(\bar{u}_{n-2}, \bar{u}_{n-1}, \bar{u}_n) &= 0, \\
f_n(\bar{u}_{n-1}, \bar{u}_n) &= 0.
\end{aligned}$$

In order to solve the above system, one first needs to compute the Jacobian matrix, $\boldsymbol{J}$, which in turn requires evaluating $\partial f_i / \partial \bar{u}_j$ for $i, j = 1, 2 \ldots n$. Fortunately, the vast majority of these partial derivatives are 0: from (7.23), we see that f_i depends only on $\bar{u}_{i-1}$, $\bar{u}_i$ and $\bar{u}_{i+1}$. Indeed, some straightforward calculations demonstrate that

$$\frac{\partial f_i}{\partial \bar{u}_{i-1}} = \frac{\mu(\bar{u}_i)}{(\Delta y)^2} - \frac{\mu'(\bar{u}_i)}{2(\Delta y)^2}(\bar{u}_{i+1} - \bar{u}_{i-1}),$$

$$\frac{\partial f_i}{\partial \bar{u}_i} = -\frac{2\mu(\bar{u}_i)}{(\Delta y)^2} + \mu'(\bar{u}_i)\left(\frac{\bar{u}_{i+1} - 2\bar{u}_i + \bar{u}_{i-1}}{(\Delta y)^2}\right) + \mu''(\bar{u}_i)\left(\frac{\bar{u}_{i+1} - \bar{u}_{i-1}}{2\Delta y}\right)^2,$$

$$\frac{\partial f_i}{\partial \bar{u}_{i+1}} = \frac{\mu(\bar{u}_i)}{(\Delta y)^2} + \frac{\mu'(\bar{u}_i)}{2(\Delta y)^2}(\bar{u}_{i+1} - \bar{u}_{i-1}).$$

Note that $\partial f_i / \partial \bar{u}_{i-1} \neq \partial f_i / \partial \bar{u}_{i+1}$ so although $\boldsymbol{J}$ is tridiagonal, the entries along the super- and sub-diagonals are different.

Of course, before any of the elements of $\boldsymbol{J}$ can be computed, we require a particular functional form for $\mu = \mu(u)$. For illustrative purposes, let us consider a shear-thinning fluid whose dynamic viscosity decreases with u according to

$$\mu = \mu_0 \left[\exp\left(-10\, \frac{\text{s}}{\text{m}} \cdot u \right) + 1 \right], \tag{7.25}$$

where μ_0 is the dynamic viscosity in the limit of large u. Note that the form of equation (7.25) encourages us to measure (though not necessarily report) velocities in units of m/s. From equation (7.25), it is straightforward to compute $\mu'(u)$ and $\mu''(u)$; details are left as an exercise.

The MATLAB algorithm used to solve the above nonlinear boundary value problem is presented in Figure 7.10. It makes judicious use of the function `mnhf_newton_system`, which we previously encountered in Chapter 4. Specification of the Jacobian matrix entries in the local function `channel2_Jac` requires careful attention to detail, in part because of the special treatment required for the first and the last row. The fact remains, however, that $\boldsymbol{J}$ is a tridiagonal matrix, which renders this problem relatively easy for MATLAB to solve.

Figure 7.11 shows the graphical output produced by `mnhf_channel2`. Note, in particular, the significant difference of solution behavior as compared to the velocity profiles reported in Figure 7.9.

7.2 Shooting method fundamentals

If the task of discretizing an interval into equal segments of length $\Delta\xi$ or Δy seems cumbersome, you may be wondering whether it is possible to solve a boundary value problem using the techniques of Chapter 6 and, more specifically, the built-in MATLAB function `ode45`. The answer is "yes," but, as will be outlined below, this approach is more helpful in some circumstances than in others.

For illustrative purposes, we firstly reconsider the cooling fin problem studied in section 7.1.1 whose governing equation and (Dirichlet) boundary conditions read

$$\frac{\mathrm{d}^2\theta}{d\xi^2} - \frac{hPL^2}{kA}\theta = 0, \qquad \theta(\xi=0) = 1, \quad \theta(\xi=1) = 0.$$

Letting $\Upsilon = \mathrm{d}\theta/\mathrm{d}\xi$, the above second-order differential equation can be

```matlab
function mnhf_channel2()
%MNHF_CHANNEL1 solves for the (steady) velocity distribution for parallel
% shear flow driven by a moving boundary and a (constant) pressure gradient
% using finite-differences. Boundary conditions are Dirichlet but viscosity
% varies with flow speed.

global G U Deltay mu0 n

% Parameter input.
G = -1e1;                       % Pressure gradient (Pa/m or kg/m^2/s^2).
halfht = 1e-1;                  % Channel half-height (m).
U = 2.5e-1;                     % Upper plate velocity (m/s).
mu0 = 5e-1;                     % Reference dynamic viscosity (kg/m/s).
n = 1e2;                        % Number of interior grid points.
Deltay = 2.0*halfht/(n+1);     % Grid spacing.
% End of parameter input.

guess = linspace(0.0,U,n+2); % Initial guess.
u = mnhf_newton_system(@channel2_Fun,@channel2_Jac,guess(2:end-1)',1e-8,1);
u = [0.0 u' U];

% Plot solution.
y = linspace(-1.0*halfht,1.0*halfht,n+2);
figure; box on; hold on; set(gca,'fontsize',14);
plot(1e2*u,1e2*y,'k','linewidth',2);

% Add axis labels and a title.
xlabel('{\it u} (cm/s)');
ylabel('{\it y} (cm)');
title('Velocity distribution in a channel','fontsize',14);

%%%%%%%%%%%%%%%%%%%%%%%%%%%%%
function f=channel2_Fun(u)

global G U Deltay n

f = zeros(n,1); % Initialize.
f(1) = mu(u(1),0)*(u(2)-2.0*u(1))/Deltay^2.0+mu(u(1),1)* ...
       (0.5*u(2)/Deltay)^2.0-G;
for i=2:n-1
 f(i) = mu(u(i),0)*(u(i+1)-2.0*u(i)+u(i-1))/Deltay^2.0+mu(u(i),1)* ...
        (0.5*(u(i+1)-u(i-1))/Deltay)^2.0-G;
end
f(n) = mu(u(n),0)*(U-2.0*u(n)+u(n-1))/Deltay^2.0+mu(u(n),1)* ...
       (0.5*(U-u(n-1))/Deltay)^2.0-G;
```

```
%%%%%%%%%%%%%%%%%%%%%%%%%%
function J=channel2_Jac(u)

global U Deltay n

J = zeros(n,n); % Initialize.
% \partial f_1/\partial u_1
J(1,1) = -2.0*mu(u(1),0)/Deltay^2.0+(u(2)-2.0*u(1))/Deltay^2.0* ...
         mu(u(1),1)+(0.5*u(2)/Deltay)^2.0*mu(u(1),2);
% \partial f_1/\partial u_2
J(1,2) = mu(u(1),0)/Deltay^2.0+0.5*u(2)/Deltay^2.0*mu(u(1),1);
for i=2:n-1
 % \partial f_{i}/\partial u_{i-1}
 J(i,i-1) = mu(u(i),0)/Deltay^2.0-0.5*(u(i+1)-u(i-1))/Deltay^2.0* ...
              mu(u(i),1);
 % \partial f_{i}/\partial u_{i}
 J(i,i) = -2.0*mu(u(i),0)/Deltay^2.0+(u(i+1)-2.0*u(i) ...
            +u(i-1))/Deltay^2.0*mu(u(i),1)+(0.5*(u(i+1) ...
            -u(i-1))/Deltay)^2.0*mu(u(i),2);
 % \partial f_{i}/\partial u_{i+1}
 J(i,i+1) = mu(u(i),0)/Deltay^2.0+0.5*(u(i+1)-u(i-1))/Deltay^2.0* ...
              mu(u(i),1);
end
% \partial f_n/\partial u_{n-1}
J(n,n-1) = mu(u(n),0)/Deltay^2.0-0.5*(U-u(n-1))/Deltay^2.0*mu(u(n),1);
% \partial f_n/\partial u_n
J(n,n) = -2.0*mu(u(n),0)/Deltay^2.0+(U-2.0*u(n)+u(n-1))/Deltay^2.0*...
         mu(u(n),1)+(0.5*(U-u(n-1))/Deltay)^2.0*mu(u(n),2);

%%%%%%%%%%%%%%%%%%%%%%%%%%
function visc=mu(u,index)
% index = 0: \mu = \mu(u)
% index = 1: \mu = \mu'(u)
% index = 2: \mu = \mu''(u)
% The formulas below assume that the velocity is measured in m/s.

global mu0

if index==0
 visc = mu0*(exp(-10.0*u)+1.0);
elseif index==1
 visc = -10.0*mu0*exp(-10.0*u);
elseif index==2
 visc = 100.0*mu0*exp(-10.0*u);
else
 fprint('Invalid entry for index.')
end
```

Figure 7.10: MATLAB function that solves the parallel shear flow problem specified by equations (7.20) and (7.25).

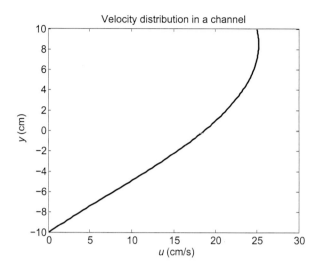

Figure 7.11: Output from mnhf_channel2.

recast as the following pair of first-order differential equations:

$$\frac{d\theta}{d\xi} = \Upsilon,$$

$$\frac{d\Upsilon}{d\xi} = \frac{hPL^2}{kA}\theta, \qquad (7.26)$$

These equations are linear and so would be very straightforward to solve except that we do not have a boundary condition for Υ e.g. at $\xi = 0$. The strategy then is to guess the value of $\Upsilon(\xi = 0)$, integrate equation (7.26) up till $\xi = 1$ (e.g. using ode45) then check whether the numerical solution for θ satisfies $\theta(\xi = 1) = 0$. If yes, the boundary condition $\Upsilon(\xi = 0)$ was chosen correctly; if no, a new guess must be selected and the process repeated. This is the essence of the "shooting method" technique.

In general, it is inelegant and computationally-inefficient to solve boundary value problems in the manner of initial value problems. There exist, however, a number of important boundary value problems in engineering that cannot readily be solved using finite differences and where shooting methods provide the only reasonable alternative. Arguably one of the most classical of these arises in the study of high-Reynolds number, but still laminar, flow over a flat plate. In this circumstance, studied originally by P.R.H. Blasius, a student of Ludwig Prandtl, a boundary layer develops whose thickness grows in the downstream direction. The boundary layer thickness is computed by solving the following ordinary differential equation for f, a function of the self-similar variable η:

$$f''' + \tfrac{1}{2}ff'' = 0\,, \qquad f(\eta = 0) = 0\,, \quad f'(\eta = 0) = 0\,, \quad f'(\eta \to \infty) = 1\,.$$
$$(7.27)$$

The fact that the third boundary condition is specified at $\eta \to \infty$ effectively rules out using finite differences because there is no way to discretize a semi-infinite interval. Instead, we recast the above third-order equation as three first-order equations, *i.e.*

$$\frac{\mathrm{d}f}{\mathrm{d}\eta} = \Omega\,, \qquad f(\eta = 0) = 0\,,$$

$$\frac{\mathrm{d}\Omega}{\mathrm{d}\eta} = \beta\,, \qquad \Omega(\eta = 0) = 0\,,$$

$$\frac{\mathrm{d}\beta}{\mathrm{d}\eta} = -\tfrac{1}{2}f\beta\,, \quad \beta(\eta = 0) \text{ chosen so } \Omega(\eta \to \infty) = 1 \ . \quad (7.28)$$

The MATLAB algorithm used to solve the above equations is given in Figure 7.12. Typing, in the MATLAB Command Window,

>>mnhf_blasius(0.1)

yields a terminal value for Ω of 0.4492. Conversely, typing

>>mnhf_blasius(0.5)

yields a terminal value of 1.3138. Finally, typing

>>mnhf_blasius(0.332)

yields a terminal value of 0.9999, which is close enough to the desired value of unity. Of course, it is possible to combine mnhf_blasius with one of the root finding algorithms studied in Chapter 2 so as to automate the iteration process outlined above. This topic is pursued in the end-of-chapter exercises (see also Example 7.2). Having determined the boundary condition on β satisfying $\Omega(\eta \to \infty) = 1$, the numerical solution for f follows directly from the graphical output produced by mnhf_blasius – see Figure 7.13.

As we illustrate with the following example, shooting methods are also extremely useful in solving ballistics problems where it is necessary to numerically analyze the trajectory of a launched projectile.

```matlab
function mnhf_blasius(beta0)
%MNHF_BLASIUS solves the Blasius boundary layer equation using a shooting
% method.
%
% beta0 - Guess for the value of \beta(\eta=0) that satisfies
% \Omega(\eta=\infty) \to 1
%
% Usage  mnhf_blasius(0.332)


%% Specify maximum value for eta, the independent variable.
eta_max = 1e1;

%% Specify initial conditions then solve ODE using ode45.
f(1) = 0.0;
Omega(1) = 0.0;
beta(1) = beta0;
[eta,y] = ode45(@blasius_func,[0.0 eta_max],[f(1) Omega(1) beta(1)]);

%% Plot/print results.
figure(1); hold on; box on; set(gca,'fontsize',18)
plot(eta,y(:,1),'k-','linewidth',2)
plot(eta,y(:,2),'k--','linewidth',2)
ylim([0.0 2.0])
xlabel('{\it \eta}'); ylabel('{\it f} (solid), {\it \Omega} (dashed)')
fprintf('Terminal value of Omega: %12.8f\n',y(end,2))

%%%%%%%%%%%%%%%%%%%%%%%%%%%%%%%%
function dy=blasius_func(~,y)
%% Specify the three first order equations that are equivalent to the third
%% order Blasius boundary layer equation.

dy = zeros(3,1); % Initialize.
dy(1) = y(2);
dy(2) = y(3);
dy(3) = -0.5*y(1)*y(3);
```

Figure 7.12: MATLAB function that solves the Blasius boundary layer equations (7.28).

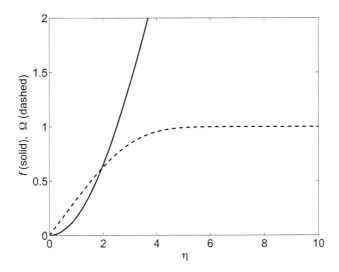

Figure 7.13: Output from `mnhf_blasius` selecting as input `beta0=0.332`.

EXAMPLE 7.2 (The trajectory of a softball) *An outfielder throws a softball from the warning track towards the infield into a 13 km/h headwind. Her (Cartesian) coordinates at the point of release are x =* 0*, y =* 0*. The ball's acceleration can be modeled using the following pair of differential equations:*

$$\frac{du}{dt} = -C_d \left(u\sqrt{u^2 + v^2} + U_{\text{wind}}^2 \right),\tag{7.29}$$

$$\frac{dv}{dt} = -C_d v\sqrt{u^2 + v^2} - g,\tag{7.30}$$

where g is gravitational acceleration, U_{wind} is the wind speed, $C_d =$ $0.037\,m^{-1}$ is a (dimensional) drag coefficient and u and v denote, respectively, the horizontal and vertical components of velocity. At the point of release, the ball makes an angle of $24.7°$ to the horizontal; the peak elevation of the ball is $5.2\,m$. We can apply a shooting method to estimate the speed of the softball as it leaves the outfielder's hand. As indicated by Figures 7.14 and 7.15, the associated MATLAB algorithm consists of a script and a series of functions. The former implements a secant-style root solve whilst leveraging `softball_function`, *which takes as input the launch speed and launch angle and returns the difference between the computed and the actual peak elevations. The function* `softball_function` *in turn calls the function* `projectile`, *where the* *equations of motion (7.29) and (7.30) are specified. Note that by using the 'Events' flag within* `options`*, the integration is executed only up till the instant in time, t', where v, the vertical velocity, becomes negative – see also the function* `vneg`*. We do not require any solution information for $t > t'$ because this portion of the motion has no bearing on the peak elevation achieved.*

Running `mnhf_softball`*, we find that, despite widely separated initial guesses, the correct final answer of 32.61 m/s is obtained after only four iterations.*

Two follow-up comments are warranted regarding this last example.

1. There is no reasonable way to solve this problem using finite differences because we lack any *a-priori* information regarding the initial values of u or v. In a similar fashion, the time of flight of the softball is unknown.

2. Ballistics problems such as that given above provide a helpful opportunity to debunk the notion, learned in high-school physics classes, that a projectile always travels the greatest horizontal distance when launched from a 45° angle. Figure 7.16 shows the trajectories associated with softballs launched from angles of 24.7° and 45° for the parameters described in Example 7.2. Notably, the horizontal distance traveled is in either case almost the same, 30.5 m. A launch angle of 45° gives the greatest horizontal distance only when drag is absent. Here, drag is an important component of the motion as evidenced by the asymmetric shape associated with the trajectories of Figure 7.16.

7.3 Shooting method – linear and nonlinear problems

7.3.1 Linear problems

For a system of linear ordinary differential equations, the shooting method does not require iteration. As an example, consider

$$\frac{dy_1}{dx} = g_1(x) + y_1 g_2(x) + y_2 g_3(x),$$

$$\frac{dy_2}{dx} = g_4(x) + y_1 g_5(x) + y_2 g_6(x), \tag{7.31}$$

with boundary conditions $y_1(a) = y_{1a}$ and $y_2(b) = y_{2b}$. First we numerically solve the above system as an initial value problem with

```
% Solve the ``softball'' problem using a shooting method combined with
% the secant algorithm. To find: the ball's launch velocity given a
% maximum elevation of ypeak.

close all
clear all
clc

global Cd Uwind g ypeak

% Variable input (mks units where appropriate).
Uwind = 13.0/3.6;
g = 9.8;
Cd = 0.037;
theta0 = 24.7*pi/180.0;
ypeak = 5.2;
% End of variable input.

% Specify initial guesses for launch speed.
U1 = 10.0;
U2 = 40.0;

% Use secant-type algorithm to find the launch velocity that gives a
% maximum elevation of ypeak.
f1 = softball_function(U1,theta0);
f2 = softball_function(U2,theta0);
delta = U2-U1;
count = 1;     % Initialize counter.
while ( (abs(delta)>1e-6) && (count<1001) )
 U3 = U1-f1*(U2-U1)/(f2-f1);
 fprintf('Iteration=%2.0f\t, Current root estimate=%12.8f\n',count,U3);
 delta = U3-U2;
 U1 = U2; f1 = softball_function(U1,theta0);
 U2 = U3; f2 = softball_function(U2,theta0);
 count = count+1;
end

if count==1000
 fprint('Maximum number of iterations reached.');
else
 fprintf('Release velocity (m/s) =%12.8f\n',U3);
end
```

Figure 7.14: MATLAB script that solves equations (7.29) and (7.30) and computes the launch speed associated with a peak softball elevation of 5.2 m.

```matlab
function elev_offset=softball_function(U,theta0)
% Perform ode45 solve of the equations of motion given in projectile.m.
%
% U — launch speed
% theta0 — launch angle (relative to the horizontal)
% elev_offset — difference between max(elevation) based on the ODE solve
%               and ypeak, which is specified in the problem statement

global ypeak

% Specify maximum integration time.
tmax = 10.0;

% Solve ODEs using ode45 taking care to terminate the integration once v
% becomes negative. The matrix y consists of a column vector for x
% (horizontal position), a column vector for u (horizontal velocity), a
% column vector for y (elevation) and a column vector for v (vertical
% velocity).
options = odeset('Events',@vneg,'MaxStep',1e-3);
[~,y] = ode45(@projectile,[0.0 tmax],[0.0 U*cos(theta0) ...
              0.0 U*sin(theta0)],options);

elev_offset = max(y(:,3))—ypeak;

%%%%%%%%%%%%%%%%%%%%%%%%%%%%%
function dy=projectile(~,y)
% The equations of motion for a projectile.
% dy(1)=x
% dy(2)=u
% dy(3)=y
% dy(4)=v

global Cd Uwind g

dy = zeros(4,1); % Initialize.

dy(1) = y(2);
dy(2) = —Cd*(y(2)*sqrt(y(2)^2.0+y(4)^2.0)+Uwind^2.0);
dy(3) = y(4);
dy(4) = —Cd*y(4)*sqrt(y(2)^2.0+y(4)^2.0)—g;

%%%%%%%%%%%%%%%%%%%%%%%%%%%%%%%%%%%%%%%%%%%%%%%%%%%
function [value,isterminal,direction]=vneg(~,y)

value = y(4);       % Focus on v, not u, x or y.
isterminal = 1;     % Stop ODE solve when v<0.
direction = —1;     % Only detect a decreasing crossing.
```

Figure 7.15: MATLAB functions associated with mnhf_softball.

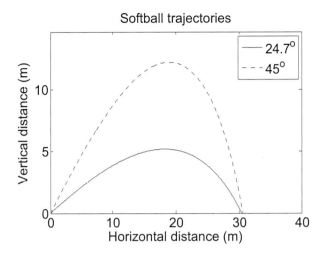

Figure 7.16: The trajectories associated with softballs launched from angles of $24.7°$ and $45°$.

$y_1(a) = y_{1a}$, $y_2(a) = 0$. Call this solution $y_1^{(1)}(x)$, $y_2^{(1)}(x)$. We then solve the corresponding homogeneous system

$$\frac{\mathrm{d}y_1}{\mathrm{d}x} = y_1 g_2(x) + y_2 g_3(x) ,$$

$$\frac{\mathrm{d}y_2}{\mathrm{d}x} = y_1 g_5(x) + y_2 g_6(x) , \tag{7.32}$$

as an initial value problem with $y_1(a) = 0$, $y_2(a) = 1$ and call this solution $y_1^{(2)}(x)$, $y_2^{(2)}(x)$. Now $y_1^{(1)}(x) + c y_1^{(2)}(x)$ and $y_2^{(1)}(x) + c y_2^{(2)}(x)$ is also a solution of equation (7.31) and it satisfies the condition $y_1(a) = y_{1a}$ for all values of the constant c. Linear interpolation can be used to determine the correct initial condition.

7.3.2   Nonlinear problems

For nonlinear problems, the methodology outlined above does not work because we cannot simply combine solutions using superposition. Instead, a different procedure must be applied as outlined below.

Consider again a second-order ordinary differential equation

$$\frac{\mathrm{d}^2\theta}{\mathrm{d}\xi^2} = f\left(\frac{\mathrm{d}\theta}{\mathrm{d}\xi}, \theta, \xi\right) ,$$

with boundary conditions $\theta(a) = \theta_a$, $\frac{d\theta}{d\xi}(b) = \theta_b'$. We shall write the above equation as a system of two first-order differential equations by introducing new variables

$$y_1 = \theta \,,$$

$$y_2 = \frac{d\theta}{d\xi} \,.$$

Therefore we can write the pair of first-order differential equations as

$$\frac{dy_1}{d\xi} = y_2 \,,$$

$$\frac{dy_2}{d\xi} = f\left(\frac{d\theta}{d\xi}, \theta, \xi\right) = f(y_2, y_1, \xi) \,,$$

with boundary conditions $y_2(a) = y_a$, $y_1(b) = y_b'$.

Let us recast the above problem as an initial value problem by assuming some initial value for y_1, e.g. $y_1^{(0)}(a)$. We now solve the initial value problem and obtain the solution $y_1^{(0)}(\xi)$ which includes $y_1^{(0)}(b)$. However, $y_1^{(0)}(b) \neq y_b'$.

At this point it should be obvious that we can use the arsenal of methods for solving nonlinear algebraic equations to get to the correct initial value for y_1. For instance and following on from the discussion of Chapter 2, we can use bracketed methods such as the bisection method if we have two initial conditions, say $y_1^{(upper)}(a)$ and $y_1^{(lower)}(a)$ with $y_1^{(upper)}(b) > y_b'$ and $y_1^{(lower)}(b) < y_b'$.

If we apply the bisection method, we would consider a new initial condition to be

$$y_1^{(mid)}(b) = \frac{y_1^{(upper)}(b) + y_1^{(lower)}(b)}{2} \,,$$

then solve the initial value problem and see if $y_1^{(mid)}(b) > y_b'$ or $y_1^{(mid)}(b) < y_b'$ and then either replace $y_1^{(upper)}(b)$ or $y_1^{(lower)}(b)$.

Alternatively, we might apply the secant method from Chapter 2 and start with solving two initial value problems, one with $y_1^{(0)}(a)$ and the other with $y_1^{(1)}(a)$. This approach yields $y_1^{(0)}(b)$ and $y_1^{(1)}(b)$. The function values are now the deviations of $y_1^{(0)}(b)$ and $y_1^{(1)}(b)$ from the desired value y_b' i.e.,

$$F^{(0)} = y_1^{(0)} - y_b' \,,$$

and

$$F^{(1)} = y_1^{(1)} - y_b' \,.$$

We can then use interpolation to find a new guess for the initial value, *i.e.*

$$y_1^{(2)}(a) = y_1^{(1)}(a) - F^{(1)} \left[\frac{y_1^{(1)}(a) - y_1^{(0)}(a)}{F^{(1)} - F^{(0)}} \right] .$$

7.4 Summary

In this chapter we have developed two different approaches for solving boundary value problems, (i) finite difference methods, and, (ii) shooting methods.

Finite difference methods are easy to implement for many types of boundary conditions. The boundary conditions are incorporated into the equations to be solved. The accuracy of finite difference methods is set by the accuracy of the corresponding finite difference approximations used when numerically estimating first and second derivatives. When applied to linear and nonlinear problems, respectively, the finite difference method requires the solution of a system of linear (Chapter 3) and nonlinear equations (Chapter 4).

Shooting methods often involve converting the boundary value problem into an initial value problem and using the methods of Chapter 6 to obtain the solution e.g. by applying the built-in function ode45. A drawback of the shooting method is that it involves guesses and iteration, which may consume significant numerical resources.

7.5   Exercise Problems

P7.1. Using a uniform grid-size with four subintervals and the central finite difference equations from Tables 5.7 and 5.8, write out the system of finite difference equations for the following equations:

(a) $\frac{d^2y}{dx^2} + 100y = 2000$, $y(0) = y(1) = 10$

(b) $\frac{d^2y}{dx^2} + x\frac{dy}{dx} = x^2$, $y(0) = 0$, $y(1) = 1$

(c) $\frac{d^2u}{dx^2} + \sin(x) = x^2$, $u(2) = 5$, $u(10) = 20$

(d) $x\frac{d^2y}{dx^2} + 8\frac{dy}{dx} = x$, $y(1) = -1$, $y(2) = 1$.

P7.2. Find the numerical solution to the following boundary value problem:

$$\frac{d^2y}{dx^2} - y = 1,   y(0) = 0, y'(1) = 1.$$

P7.3. Find the numerical solution to the following boundary value problem:

$$\frac{d^2y}{dx^2} + x\frac{dy}{dx} + y = x,   y'(0) = 0, y(1) = 1.$$

P7.4. The following equations are to be solved using the shooting method. Determine the corresponding initial value problems and the shooting method parameters.

(a) $\frac{d^2y}{dx^2} = -\frac{2}{2+x}$, $y(0) = y'(1) = 0$

(b) $\frac{d^2y}{dx^2} = \frac{1}{x}\frac{dy}{dx} = 2$, $y(0) = y(1) = 1$

P7.5. Solve the following problem using the shooting method:

$$\frac{d^2y}{dx^2} + \frac{1}{x}\frac{dy}{dx} + y = 1,   y(0) = 0, y(1) = 1.$$

P7.6. The amplitude of vibration of a string is given by the 1-dimensional Helmhotz equation

$$\frac{d^2A}{dx^2} + \frac{A}{\lambda^2} = 0,$$

with boundary conditions $A(x = 0) = 0$ and $A(x = L) = 1$. Given that $L = 400\,\text{mm}$ and $\lambda = 50\,\text{mm}$, you are required to determine the string amplitude, A, at different positions along the string.

(a) Find the amplitude using the shooting method and an initial guess of $\frac{dA}{dx}\big|_{x=0} = 0.01$. Perform only one pass using the explicit Euler method with a step size of $\Delta x = 100\,\text{mm}$. Was your initial guess correct?

(b) Repeat the above calculation but use a fourth-order Runge-Kutta method.

(c) Use the finite difference method to solve the above equation, again with $\Delta x = 100\,\mathrm{mm}$.

P7.7. Consider a thin cooling fin of uniform cross-sectional area, but now suppose that, due to ambient air currents, the convective heat transfer coefficient, h, varies with the horizontal coordinate, ξ, according to

$$h(\xi) = h_0(0.1 + 0.7\xi^2)$$

where $\xi = x/L$ and L is the fin length. The non-dimensional governing equation then reads

$$\frac{\mathrm{d}^2\theta}{\mathrm{d}\xi^2} = \mathrm{Bi}_0 \frac{h(\xi)}{h_0}\,\theta\,, \tag{7.33}$$

where $\theta = (T - T_\infty)/T_\infty$ in which T is the local fin temperature and T_∞ is the ambient temperature. Also the modified Biot number is defined as

$$\mathrm{Bi}_0 = \frac{2h_0 L^2}{kt}\,.$$

Here k and t are, respectively, the thermal conductivity and the fin thickness.

We wish to solve (7.33) numerically subject to the following Neumann and Dirichlet boundary conditions:

- Fin base: constant heat flux, i.e.

$$\left(\frac{\mathrm{d}\theta}{\mathrm{d}\xi}\right)_{\xi=0} = Q < 0\,.$$

- Fin tip: constant temperature equal to the ambient temperature, i.e.

$$\theta(\xi = 1) = 0\,.$$

(a) Is this an example of a linear or a nonlinear boundary value problem?

(b) Discretize the governing equation. How is ξ_i related to i and the (uniform) grid spacing, $\Delta\xi$?

(c) Write a MATLAB algorithm to determine the numerical solution for the following parameter values: $\mathrm{Bi}_0 = 100$, $Q = -2$. Then plot θ vs. ξ.

P7.8. The dimensionless conduction heat transfer through a fin is modelled by the equation

$$\frac{d^2\theta}{d\xi^2} - (mL)^2\theta = 0,$$

with boundary conditions

$$\theta(\xi = 0) = 1, \qquad \frac{d\theta}{d\xi}\bigg|_{\xi=1} = 0. \qquad (7.34)$$

One is interested in finding out both the temperature distribution $\theta(\xi)$ and the fin efficiency which is given by

$$\eta = -\frac{\left[\frac{d\theta}{d\xi}\right]_{\xi=0}}{(mL)^2} = \int_0^1 \theta \, d\xi. \qquad (7.35)$$

(a) Solve the above problem using finite differences and $N = 9$, 19 and 39 interior grid points. Let $mL = 2$.

(b) Compare the temperature profiles obtained in part (a) for the three different values of N.

(c) Evaluate the fin efficiency for the three different values of N.

P7.9. Consider, as in Figure 7.17, the case of parallel channel flow with *spatially-variable* dynamic viscosity, μ, i.e. μ is a prescribed function of the temperature, T, and T varies linearly over the depth of the channel. Accordingly, measurements show that

$$\mu = \mu_0\left(1.34 - \frac{y}{b}\right),$$

where $y = 0$ denotes the channel centerline. The governing equation reads

$$\frac{d}{dy}\left(\mu(y) \times \frac{du}{dy}\right) = G, \qquad (7.36)$$

where $G < 0$ is a (constant) horizontal pressure gradient. The boundary conditions are $u(y = -b) = 0$ and $u(y = b) = U$ where b is the channel half-width and U is the translational velocity of the upper plate.

(a) Is the boundary value problem linear or nonlinear?

(b) Using second-order-accurate finite-difference equations from Tables 5.7 and 5.8, discretize the differential equation (7.36).

(c) What is the matrix equation to be solved and how are the matrix and vector elements defined? Can the standard Thomas algorithm be applied in this case?

(d) Derive numerical solutions (consisting of plots of y vs. u) for the following parameter choices: $\mu_0 = 0.4\,\text{kg}/(\text{m·s})$, $G = -20\,\text{Pa/m}$, $b = 0.1\,\text{m}$ and $U = \pm 0.3\,\text{m/s}$.

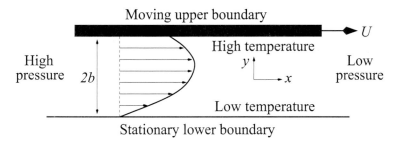

Figure 7.17: Parallel flow in a channel with a y-dependent temperature variation.

P7.10. Write a MATLAB algorithm that combines `mnhf_blasius` with a secant root finding algorithm so as to automate the process of finding the boundary condition on β that satisfies $\Omega(\eta \to \infty) = 1$.

P7.11. A disgruntled golfer hits a small stone into a 14.3 km/h headwind. The stone's acceleration can be modeled using the following pair of differential equations:

$$\frac{du}{dt} = -C_d \left(u\sqrt{u^2 + v^2} + U_{\text{wind}}^2\right),$$

$$\frac{dv}{dt} = -C_d v \sqrt{u^2 + v^2} - g,$$

where g is gravitational acceleration, U_{wind} is the wind speed, $C_d = 0.042\,\text{m}^{-1}$ is a (dimensional) drag coefficient and u and v denote, respectively, the horizontal and vertical components of velocity. When the stone (assumed to be spherical in shape) leaves the club face, it has a speed of 276.2 km/h. By the time it first strikes the ground, the stone speed is 46.1 km/h. Use `ode45` and the shooting method to estimate the angle the stone makes with respect to the horizontal as it leaves the club face. Note that more than one solution may exist.

For the range of parameters specified above, plot in the same figure and as a function of the launch angle the horizontal distance traveled before stone first strikes the ground and the speed upon impact. From the latter curve, estimate the minimum impact speed; from the former curve, estimate the maximum horizontal distance traveled.

P7.12. Consider the following system of coupled ordinary differential equations:

$$10x^2 \frac{d^2c}{dx^2} + 2x\frac{dc}{dx} + c = ce^\theta,$$

$$\theta^2 \frac{d^2\theta}{dx^2} + 3c\frac{d\theta}{dx} + \theta = ce^\theta,$$

together with the following conditions:

$$c(x = 0) = 1, \qquad \frac{dc}{dx}\bigg|_{x=1} = 1,$$

$$\theta(x = 0) = 1, \qquad \frac{d\theta}{dx}\bigg|_{x=1} = 0.$$

(a) Does the above model represent an initial value problem or a boundary value problem?

(b) Is the system linear or nonlinear? If the latter, what are the nonlinear terms.

(c) Discretize the equations with central finite difference approximations from Tables 5.7 and 5.8 to develop a set of algebraic equations over the interval $x \in [0, 1]$ with grid points $\{i|i = 0, \cdots, N+1\}$.

(d) Recommend a numerical algorithm for solving the resulting equation and outline the numerical procedure to be applied.

P7.13. The temperature distribution across a cylindrical pipe is given by the following differential equation:

$$\frac{d^2T}{dr^2} + \frac{1}{r}\frac{dT}{dr} = 0.$$

Determine the temperature distribution across a pipe wall with inner diameter 6 inches and outer diameter of 12 inches. Assume that the inner surface is maintained at a temperature of 60°C and the outer surface is at 20°C.

(a) Solve the problem using the shooting method and a fourth-order Runge-Kutta scheme.

(b) Solve the problem using finite differences.

In both cases use a step size of $\Delta r = 0.2$ Plot your results in a single graph.

CHAPTER 8

PARTIAL DIFFERENTIAL EQUATIONS

Partial differential equations are differential equations that contain more than one independent variable. Such equations may also be solved using the finite difference method, which we learned about in the previous chapter. Here, we discuss the different forms of partial differential equations, boundary conditions and techniques for their discretization. The main difference with the approach of Chapter 7 is that the discretization must now be carried out in more than one dimension or with respect to more than one variable.

8.1 Definitions

We will limit our discussion to partial differential equations of first- and second-order, typically with two independent variables (*e.g.* x and y or x and t). Just as with the ordinary differential equations seen in Chapters 6 and 7, the order of a partial differential equation is related to the highest derivative in the equation.

Partial differential equations can be linear or nonlinear. The general form of a second-order, linear partial differential equation in two independent variables x and y is

$$A\frac{\partial^2 \phi}{\partial x^2} + B\frac{\partial^2 \phi}{\partial x \partial y} + C\frac{\partial^2 \phi}{\partial y^2} + D\frac{\partial \phi}{\partial x} + E\frac{\partial \phi}{\partial y} + F\phi = H. \qquad (8.1)$$

In general A, B, C, D, E, F and H are functions of x and y. If $H = 0$ equation (8.1) is called homogeneous; otherwise it is called inhomogeneous. For linear, homogeneous partial differential equations, a superposition principle applies. It stipulates that if $\phi^{(1)}$ and $\phi^{(2)}$ are

solutions to the partial differential equation in question then so too is
$c_1\phi^{(1)} + c_2\phi^{(2)}$.

If we consider A, B, C, *etc.* to be constant, the differential equations may be classified according to the value of the discriminant, $B^2 - 4AC$

- $B^2 - 4AC < 0$: Elliptic equation
- $B^2 - 4AC = 0$: Parabolic equation
- $B^2 - 4AC > 0$: Hyperbolic equation

It should be noted that this is not just a mathematical classification but it is related to the physical processes represented by the mathematical model. Elliptic equations usually describe steady-state (time independent), distributed systems. For instance, the elliptic equation describing the two-dimensional, steady state temperature distribution in a rectangular plate reads

$$\frac{\partial^2 T}{\partial x^2} + \frac{\partial^2 T}{\partial y^2} = 0\,.$$

(The above equation is referred to as Laplace's equation.) Conversely, parabolic equations describe time-dependent diffusion problems. Such processes will evolve towards a steady state in the long time limit $t \to \infty$. Arguably the most famous example of a parabolic equation is the heat equation, which states

$$\frac{\partial T}{\partial t} = \alpha^2 \frac{\partial^2 T}{\partial x^2}\,,$$

where α^2 is a thermal diffusivity. Finally, hyperbolic equations stem from time-dependent physical processes that do not evolve towards steady state, for example the motion of a wave in the absence of dissipation. The wave equation is given by

$$\frac{\partial^2 u}{\partial t^2} = c^2 \frac{\partial^2 u}{\partial x^2}\,,$$

where $\pm c$ prescribes the wave speed.

The requirements for boundary/initial conditions necessary to solve a given partial differential equation are related to the equation type. For instance, a second-order, parabolic equation requires one initial condition and two boundary conditions. By contrast, an elliptic equation requires boundary conditions on all applicable boundaries; at least one of these boundary conditions must be of Dirichlet or Robin type in order that the solution is unique.

Analytical solutions to partial differential equations are limited to systems that may be considered "simple" either in terms of the differential equation itself, its boundary conditions, and/or the shape of the domain. In most cases, a numerical approach provides the only feasible alternative for solving a partial differential equation.

8.2 Elliptic Equations

Let us consider an elliptic equation of the form

$$\nabla^2 \phi = \frac{\partial^2 \phi}{\partial x^2} + \frac{\partial^2 \phi}{\partial y^2} = f(x, y) \tag{8.2}$$

We seek a solution on a rectangular domain extending from $0 \le x \le a$ and $0 \le y \le b$ with boundary conditions as shown in Figure 8.1.

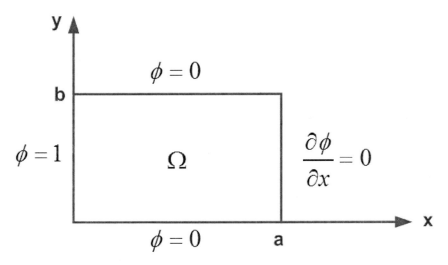

Figure 8.1: A rectangular domain with prescribed boundary conditions.

The numerical solution procedure is based on the discretization shown in Figure 8.2. Instead of determining the continuous function $\phi(x, y)$, we instead solve for a discrete version of ϕ : $\phi_{i,j}$ with $\phi_{i,j}$ being the value of ϕ at the location $x = i\Delta x$, $y = j\Delta y$. The index i increases from 1 to m whereas the index j increases from 1 to n. Thus

$$\Delta x = \frac{a}{m}, \qquad \Delta y = \frac{b}{n}.$$

We can write the discrete form of the partial differential equation as the following system of linear algebraic equations:

$$\frac{\phi_{i+1,j} - 2\phi_{i,j} + \phi_{i-1,j}}{(\Delta x)^2} + \frac{\phi_{i,j+1} - 2\phi_{i,j} + \phi_{i,j-1}}{(\Delta y)^2} = f_{i,j} \tag{8.3}$$

Here we have used central finite differences to approximate the second derivatives – see Table 5.8. From the analysis in Chapter 5, we know

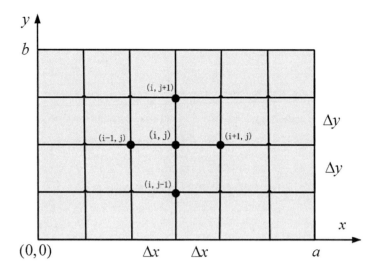

Figure 8.2: The discretized domain pertinent to Figure 8.1.

that the formula in question is second-order accurate, thus the error in discretizing the partial differential equation is then of order $\mathcal{O}(h^2)$, where $h = \Delta x = \Delta y$.

The Dirichlet boundary conditions (at $x = 0$ and $y = 0$) can be incorporated into our system of equations in a natural fashion. If in equation (8.3) $i = 1$, we need $\phi_{i-1,j}$, which is obtained from the boundary value at $x = 0$. The same procedure applies for $j = 1$, where we now make reference to the boundary condition at $y = 0$ to supply the value for $\phi_{i,j-1}$. Meanwhile, for the Neumann boundary condition at $x = a$, there are a several ways to incorporate this information *e.g.* backward differentiation or by introduction of a fictitious point outside the domain that will enable us to apply central finite differences as we first saw in Chapter 7.

8.2.1   Backward differentiation

According to this approach for incorporating the Neumann boundary condition, we determine the derivative $\frac{\partial \phi}{\partial x}$ at $x = a$ from

$$\left.\frac{\partial \phi}{\partial x}\right|_{i=m,j} \simeq \frac{\phi_{m,j} - \phi_{m-1,j}}{\Delta x}.$$

Because the right-hand side boundary condition from Figure 8.1 is homogeneous, *i.e.* $\frac{\partial \phi}{\partial x} = 0$, the backward difference formula implies

$\phi_{m,j} = \phi_{m-1,j}$. Thus for all points $i = m - 1$, equation (8.3) becomes

$$\frac{\phi_{m-2,j} - \phi_{m-1,j}}{(\Delta x)^2} + \frac{\phi_{m-1,j+1} - 2\phi_{m-1,j} + \phi_{m-1,j-1}}{(\Delta y)^2} = f_{m-1,j} \qquad (8.4)$$

One point of caution about this approach is that the two-point backward differentiation formula is only first-order accurate – see Table 5.7. The first-order accurate treatment of the boundary condition leads to a first-order accurate overall result (although we discretized the partial differential equation with second-order accuracy). This approach is therefore not recommended if one needs to preserve the second-order accuracy.

8.2.2 Central derivatives and fictitious points

An effective way to overcome the accuracy problem associated with the previous approach is to numerically compute the derivative at $x = a$ using the following second-order accurate formula:

$$\frac{\partial \phi}{\partial x}\Big|_{i=m,j} \approx \frac{\phi_{m+1,j} - \phi_{m-1,j}}{2\Delta x} \qquad (8.5)$$

In doing so we have implicitly introduced points that lie outside the domain of interest. These are referred to as fictitious points. In the case of interest, $i = m$ and $\phi_{m+1,j} = \phi_{m-1,j}$. Thus

$$\frac{2\phi_{m-1,j} - 2\phi_{m,j}}{(\Delta x)^2} + \frac{\phi_{m,j+1} - 2\phi_{m,j} + \phi_{m,j-1}}{(\Delta y)^2} = f_{m,j} . \qquad (8.6)$$

We have therefore preserved the second-order accuracy of the governing equation by using a second-order accurate formula for the Neumann boundary condition.

Note finally that an analogous numerical approach may be applied if the boundary condition is of Robin, rather than Neumann, type.

EXAMPLE 8.1 (Laplace's equation, Dirichlet boundary conditions)
Consider Laplace's equation

$$\frac{\partial^2 \phi}{\partial x^2} + \frac{\partial^2 \phi}{\partial y^2} = 0 , \qquad 0 \le x \le 3, \ 0 \le y \le 3 \qquad (8.7)$$

subject to the following boundary conditions:

$$\phi(0, y) = \phi(1, y) = \phi(x, 0) = 0 , \quad \phi(x, 1) = 20 .$$

Determine the temperature, ϕ, at the points 1, 2, 3 and 4 from Figure 8.3. Use centeral finite difference approximations.

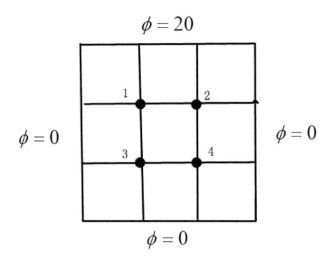

Figure 8.3: The discretized domain pertinent to Example 8.1.

Using the central finite difference approximation formula in conjunction with Laplace's equation yields

$$\frac{\phi_{i-1,j} - 2\phi_{i,j} + \phi_{i+1,j}}{(\Delta x)^2} + \frac{\phi_{i,j-1} - 2\phi_{i,j} + \phi_{i,j+1}}{(\Delta y)^2} = 0 \,.$$

The unknown nodes are interior nodes and $\Delta x = \Delta y = 1$. Rearranging the last equation, it can easily be shown that

$$\phi_{i-1,j} - 4\phi_{i,j} + \phi_{i+1,j} + \phi_{i,j-1} + \phi_{i,j+1} = 0 \,.$$

1. *Node 1:*

$$0 - 4\phi_1 + \phi_2 + 20 + \phi_3 = 0 \qquad \Rightarrow$$
$$-4\phi_1 + \phi_2 + \phi_3 = -20 \,.$$

2. *Node 2:*

$$\phi_1 - 4\phi_2 + \phi_4 + 20 + 0 = 0 \qquad \Rightarrow$$
$$\phi_1 - 4\phi_2 + \phi_3 = -20 \,.$$

3. *Node 3:*

$$0 - 4\phi_3 + \phi_4 + \phi_1 + 0 = 0 \qquad \Rightarrow$$
$$\phi_1 - 4\phi_3 + \phi_4 = 0 \,.$$

4. *Node 4:*

$$\phi_3 - 4\phi_4 + 0 + \phi_2 + 0 = 0 \qquad \Rightarrow$$
$$\phi_2 + \phi_3 - 4\phi_4 = 0 \,.$$

We have therefore to solve four equations in four unknowns, i.e.

$$\begin{bmatrix} -4 & 1 & 1 & 0 \\ 1 & -4 & 1 & 0 \\ 1 & 0 & -4 & 1 \\ 0 & 1 & 1 & -4 \end{bmatrix} \begin{Bmatrix} \phi_1 \\ \phi_2 \\ \phi_3 \\ \phi_4 \end{Bmatrix} = \begin{Bmatrix} -20 \\ -20 \\ 0 \\ 0 \end{Bmatrix} \,.$$

Solving using one of the algorithms from Chapter 3 gives

$$
\begin{Bmatrix} \phi_1 \\ \phi_2 \\ \phi_3 \\ \phi_4 \end{Bmatrix} = \begin{Bmatrix} 7.50 \\ 7.50 \\ 2.50 \\ 2.50 \end{Bmatrix} .
$$

Note that $\phi_1 = \phi_2 = 7.50$ and $\phi_3 = \phi_4 = 2.50$, suggesting an underlying symmetry to the solution. We realize in hindsight that the problem could have been solved by considering only half of the domain (left-hand side or right-hand side).

EXAMPLE 8.2 (Laplace's equation and mixed boundary conditions)
The electric potential, ϕ, in a given medium is prescribed by the elliptic equation

$$
\frac{\partial^2 \phi}{\partial x^2} + \frac{\partial^2 \phi}{\partial y^2} = 0, \qquad 0 \le x \le 1.5, \ 0 \le y \le 1.5.
$$

As shown in Figure 8.4, the associated boundary conditions read

$$
\phi(1.5, y) = phi(x, 1.5) = 0
$$
$$
\phi(0, 0.5) = \phi(0.5, 0.5) = \phi(0.5, 0) = 100
$$
$$
\frac{\partial \phi}{\partial x}(0, y) = \frac{\partial \phi}{\partial y}(x, 0) = 0
$$

Determine ϕ at points 1, 2, 3, 4 and 5 using the central finite difference equation.

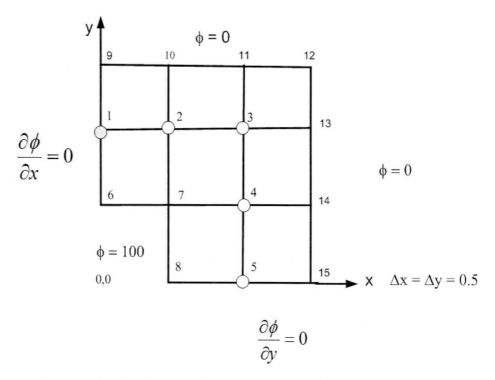

Figure 8.4: The discretized domain pertinent to Example 8.2.

Proceeding as in Example 8.1, it can be shown that

$$\frac{\phi_{i-1,j} - 2\phi_{i,j} + \phi_{i+1,j}}{(\Delta x)^2} + \frac{\phi_{i,j-1} - 2\phi_{i,j} + \phi_{i,j+1}}{(\Delta y)^2} = 0.$$

Node 1 is on the left-hand side boundary where Neumann conditions are specified. We therefore introduce a fictitious point to the left of node 1, and index ϕ at this point as ϕ_1^-. Thus

$$\frac{\phi_1^- - 2\phi_1 + \phi_2}{(0.5)^2} + \frac{\phi_6 - 2\phi_1 + \phi_9}{(0.5)^2} = 0,$$

however, for reasons outlined above, $\phi_1^- = \phi_2$ whereby

$$\phi_2 - 2\phi_1 + \phi_2 + \phi_6 - 2\phi_1 + \phi_9 = 0.$$

Consequently,

$$-4\phi_1 + 2\phi_2 = -100.$$

Meanwhile at Node 2, it can be shown that

$$\phi_1 - 2\phi_2 + \phi_3 + \phi_7 - 2\phi_2 + \phi_{10} = 0.$$

After applying the relevant boundary conditions, we obtain

$$\phi_1 - 4\phi_2 + \phi_3 + 100 + 0 = 0,$$

or

$$\phi_1 - 4\phi_2 + \phi_3 = -100.$$

Similar equations can be derived at the other nodes. We leave it as an exercise to verify that

$$
\begin{aligned}
\phi_2 - 4\phi_3 + \phi_4 &= 0 & \text{(Node 3)} \\
\phi_3 - 4\phi_4 + \phi_5 &= -100 & \text{(Node 4)} \\
2\phi_4 - 4\phi_5 &= -100 & \text{(Node 5)}
\end{aligned}
$$

We are therefore left with five equations and five unknowns, i.e.

$$
\begin{aligned}
-4\phi_1 + 2\phi_2 &= -100 \\
\phi_1 - 4\phi_2 + \phi_3 &= -100 \\
\phi_2 - 4\phi_3 + \phi_4 &= 0 \\
\phi_3 - 4\phi_4 + \phi_5 &= -100 \\
2\phi_4 - 4\phi_5 &= -100
\end{aligned}
$$

Solving e.g. using Gaussian elimination gives

$$
\begin{Bmatrix}
\phi_1 \\
\phi_2 \\
\phi_3 \\
\phi_4 \\
\phi_5
\end{Bmatrix}
=
\begin{Bmatrix}
45.83 \\
41.67 \\
20.83 \\
41.67 \\
45.83
\end{Bmatrix}.
$$

8.3   Parabolic equations

As noted above, the archetypical parabolic equation is the heat equation, which is expressed as

$$\frac{\partial \phi}{\partial t} = \alpha^2 \frac{\partial^2 \phi}{\partial x^2}, \tag{8.8}$$

where it is understood that ϕ is a function of position and time. Suppose we want to solve equation (8.8) in the interval $x \in [0, 1]$ starting at $t = 0$. The conditions needed to solve the heat equation consist of an initial condition that specifies $\phi(x, t = 0)$ and boundary conditions at $x = 0$ and $x = 1$ that apply for all $t > 0$. In symbols, we write

$$
\begin{aligned}
\phi(x, t = 0) &= h(x), & \text{(8.9a)} \\
\phi(x = 0, t) &= f(t), & \text{(8.9b)} \\
\phi(x = 1, t) &= g(t) & \text{(8.9c)}
\end{aligned}
$$

The functions h, f and g are usually constant.

Numerically-speaking, there exist two alternatives for solving equations like the heat equation: fully-discrete methods and semi-discrete methods. In the former case, we discretize both in space and time, whereas in the latter case, we only discretize the spatial variable.

8.3.1 Fully-discrete methods

To discretize in space and time, let us define a spatial step Δx and a time step Δt such that $x_i = i\Delta x$ (with i running from 0 to m with $m\Delta x = 1$), and $t_j = j\Delta t$ (with j running from 0 to whatever end time you choose). The discrete version of $\phi(x,t)$ can then be written as $\phi(x_i, t_i) = \phi_{ij}$. Accordingly, the second derivative in equation (Eq (8.8)) may be written as

$$\left.\frac{\partial^2\phi}{\partial x^2}\right|_{i,j} = \frac{\phi_{i+1,j} - 2\phi_{i,j} + \phi_{i-1,j}}{(\Delta x)^2} + \mathcal{O}\Delta x^2 \,. \tag{8.10}$$

Forward time centered space - FTCS scheme

The choice on how we discretize the first-order derivative $\frac{\partial\phi}{\partial t}$ has some far-reaching consequences as discussed below. The simplest approach is the forward difference approximation given by

$$\left.\frac{\partial\phi}{\partial t}\right|_{i,j} = \frac{\phi_{i,j+1} - \phi_{i,j}}{\Delta t} \,. \tag{8.11}$$

We now have a simple rule to update $\phi_{i,j+1}$ from the (known) solution at the previous time step $\phi_{i,j}$, *i.e.*

$$\phi_{i,j+1} = \phi_{i,j} + \left[\frac{\alpha^2\Delta t}{(\Delta x)^2}\right](\phi_{i+1,j} - 2\phi_{i,j} + \phi_{i-1,j}) \,. \tag{8.12}$$

Equation (8.12) corresponds to an *explicit* method. There are two potential problems with this approach.

1. It is not very accurate; forward differences are first-order accurate. The error is proportional to $O(h)$.

2. The method can become numerically unstable just as with explicit Euler in the case of ordinary differential equations. If we write equation (8.12) as

$$\phi_{i,j+1} = p\phi_{i+1,j} + q\phi_{i,j} + r\phi_{i-1,j} \,,$$

it can be shown that the conditions for this equation to remain stable are (i) the constants p, q and r should all be positive, and, (ii) $p + q + r \leq 1$. Because $p = \frac{\alpha^2\Delta t}{\Delta x^2}$, $q = 1 - 2\frac{\alpha^2\Delta t}{\Delta x^2}$ and $r = \frac{\alpha^2\Delta t}{\Delta x^2}$, the latter condition is always satisfied. The former condition implies that $2\frac{\alpha^2 \Delta t}{\Delta x^2} \leq 1$, which for any given Δx imposes a time step restriction of the form $\Delta t \leq \frac{1}{2}\frac{\Delta x^2}{\alpha^2}$. If we require high spatial resolution with small Δx, Δt must likewise be small, which obviously imposes significant computational demands in terms of the number of floating point operations.

Backward time centered space - BTCS scheme

A simple cure for the numerical instabilities described above is to make the method *implicit*, according to which we discretize the time derivative using

$$\left.\frac{\partial \phi}{\partial t}\right|_{i,j} = \frac{\phi_{i,j} - \phi_{i,j-1}}{\Delta t} . \tag{8.13}$$

In this instance,

$$\phi_{i,j-1} = -\frac{\alpha^2 \Delta t}{\Delta x^2}\phi_{i+1,j} + \left(1 + \frac{\alpha^2 \Delta t}{\Delta x^2}\right)\phi_{i,j} - \frac{\alpha^2 \Delta t}{\Delta x^2}\phi_{i-1,j} , \tag{8.14}$$

or, shifting one step in j and defining $\lambda = \frac{\alpha^2 \Delta t}{\Delta x^2}$,

$$\phi_{i,j} = -\lambda\phi_{i+1,j+1} + (1 + 2\lambda)\phi_{i,j+1} - \lambda\phi_{i-1,j+1} \tag{8.15}$$

The above formula prescribes an unconditionally stable method with no time step limitation in terms of numerical stability. However, the method includes multiple unknowns (*i.e.* $\phi_{.,j+1}$) and thus equation (8.15) ultimately yields a (tridiagonal) system of linear equations to be solved using the Thomas algorithm. Furthermore, the scheme is still only first-order accurate in time.

Crank-Nicolson scheme

In adapting the above results, we might also consider an intermediate time level $j + \frac{1}{2}$. At this level, $\frac{\phi_{i,j+1} - \phi_{i,j}}{\Delta t}$ is a second-order accurate estimate of $\frac{\partial \phi}{\partial t}$. In doing so, we also need to evaluate the right-hand side of equation (8.8) at time $j + \frac{1}{2}$. Thus

$$\left.\frac{\partial^2 \phi}{\partial x^2}\right|_{i,j+1/2} = \frac{\phi_{i+1,j} - 2\phi_{i,j} + \phi_{i-1,j}}{2(\Delta x)^2} + \frac{\phi_{i+1,j+1} - 2\phi_{i,j+1} + \phi_{i-1,j+1}}{2(\Delta x)^2} . \tag{8.16}$$

Here we have computed the average of time levels j and $j+1$. This expression is second-order accurate in Δx. The recursion relation places the unknowns and knowns on the left- and right-hand sides of the equation, respectively, and reads

$$
-\tfrac{1}{2}\lambda\phi_{i+1,j+1} \;+\; (1+2\lambda)\,\phi_{i,j+1} - \tfrac{1}{2}\lambda\phi_{i-1,j+1}
$$
$$
= \tfrac{1}{2}\lambda\phi_{i+1,j} + (1-2\lambda)\,\phi_{i,j} + \tfrac{1}{2}\lambda\phi_{i-1,j}\,. \qquad (8.17)
$$

This result is known as the Crank-Nicolson scheme and has the merit of being second-order accurate in both space and time. As with BTCS, the method has been shown to be stable for any time step size and it requires solving a (tridiagonal) linear system.

An extension of the above methodology to further spatial dimensions is straightforward. Let us consider a second spatial dimension y. The equivalent to equation (8.8) becomes

$$
\frac{\partial\phi}{\partial t} = \alpha^2 \left(\frac{\partial^2\phi}{\partial x^2} + \frac{\partial^2\phi}{\partial y^2} \right). \qquad (8.18)
$$

The simplest approach is to discretize in the y-direction with a step size Δy and index k such that $y_k = k\Delta y$. In discrete form, therefore,

$$
\phi_{i,k,j+1} = \phi_{i,k,j} + \alpha^2 \Delta t \frac{\phi_{i+1,k,j} - 2\phi_{i,k,j} + \phi_{i-1,k,j}}{(\Delta x)^2}
$$
$$
+\alpha^2 \Delta t \frac{\phi_{i,k+1,j} - 2\phi_{i,k,j} + \phi_{i-1,k-1,j}}{(\Delta y)^2}\,. \qquad (8.19)
$$

Note, moreover, that incorporation of initial and boundary conditions in parabolic equations is quite straightforward. The initial conditions are obviously used as the starting point for the numerical scheme. Meanwhile, boundary conditions come in the same varities as with elliptic partial differential equations, *i.e.* Dirichlet, Neumann and Robin. They are implemented in schemes for parabolic parabolic differential equations in the same way as with the elliptic equations described earlier.

8.3.2   Semi-discrete methods

In semi-discrete methods, a time-dependent partial differential equation is discretized in space, but the time variable is left to be continuous. There follows a system of ordinary differential equations, which may be solved by the techniques discussed in Chapter 6. One such semi-discrete method is the method of lines and is described below.

Method of lines (MOL)

In the method of lines (MOL), the spatial derivatives in the partial differential equation are replaced with their finite difference analogues.

This method is therefore sometimes called *the differential difference method*. Once the derivatives have been discretized, only the initial value variable, typically time in problems of physical relevance, remains. In other words, with only one remaining independent variable, we are left with a system of ordinary differential equations that approximate the original partial differential equation. The challenge then is to properly formulate the approximating system of ordinary differential equations. Once this step is complete, we can apply any integration algorithm for initial value problem to compute an approximate numerical solution to the original partial differential equation. Thus, one important aspect of the MOL technique is the use of existing, and generally well-established, numerical methods for solving the associated ordinary differential equations.

To illustrate this procedure, we apply the MOL to equation (8.8). First, we need to replace the spatial derivative $\frac{\partial^2 \phi}{\partial x^2}$ with an algebraic approximation based on finite differences, *i.e.*

$$\frac{\partial^2 \phi}{\partial x^2} = \frac{\phi_{i+1} - 2\phi_i + \phi_{i-1}}{(\Delta x)^2} + \mathcal{O}(\Delta x^2), \tag{8.20}$$

where i is an index designating a position along a grid in x and Δx is the (constant) spacing in x along the grid. Substituting equation (8.20) into equation (8.8), we obtain the MOL approximation

$$\frac{\mathrm{d}\phi_i}{\mathrm{d}t} = \alpha^2 \left(\frac{\phi_{i+1} - 2\phi_i + \phi_{i-1}}{(\Delta x)^2} \right), \qquad i = 1, 2, \cdots m. \tag{8.21}$$

Note that equation (8.21) is written as a system of m ordinary differential equation because there is now only a single independent variable, namely t. We therefore require specification of m initial conditions. The actual integration in t can be carried out using any of the methods seen in Chapter 6 that employ a fixed time step, *e.g.* explicit Euler, modified Euler, etc.

8.4 Hyperbolic equations

Consider the following first-order hyperbolic equation:

$$\frac{\partial \phi}{\partial t} + c \frac{\partial \phi}{\partial x} = 0, \tag{8.22}$$

which describes *linear advection* with speed c. The general solution to this equation is of the form $\phi(x,t) = h(x - ct)$ where the function h is determined on the basis of the initial condition as we explain below. An alternative explanation of this last result is to realize that as t

increases, the initial function $\phi(x,0)$ will advect to the right with speed c. Typically, therefore, we may say that hyperbolic equations describe wave-like phenomena. The archetypical hyperbolic equation reads

$$\frac{\partial^2 \phi}{\partial t^2} - c^2 \frac{\partial^2 \phi}{\partial x^2} = 0\,. \tag{8.23}$$

Equation (8.23) can be factored and written as a product, *i.e.*

$$\left(\frac{\partial}{\partial t} + c\frac{\partial}{\partial x}\right)\left(\frac{\partial}{\partial t} - c\frac{\partial}{\partial x}\right)\phi = 0\,. \tag{8.24}$$

On this basis, we conclude that either

$$\left(\frac{\partial}{\partial t} + c\frac{\partial}{\partial x}\right)\phi = 0\,, \quad \text{or} \quad \left(\frac{\partial}{\partial t} - c\frac{\partial}{\partial x}\right)\phi = 0\,. \tag{8.25}$$

Now suppose that the initial condition reads $\phi(x, t = 0) = h(x)$. If we disregard boundary conditions with respect to x (assuming, say, that the problem is posed over the infinite interval $-\infty < x < \infty$), solutions to the partial differential equation take the form of traveling wave solutions, *i.e.* $h(x + ct)$ and $h(x - ct)$. This claim is verified by substitution. For $h(x - ct)$, let us define the characteristic variable as $\eta = x - ct$. Thus

$$\left(\frac{\partial}{\partial t} + c\frac{\partial}{\partial x}\right)h(\eta) = \frac{dh}{d\eta}\frac{\partial \eta}{\partial t} + c\frac{dh}{d\eta}\frac{\partial \eta}{\partial x} = \frac{dh}{d\eta}(-c) + c\frac{dh}{d\eta}(1) = 0\,.$$

Conversely, for $h(x + ct)$, let us define the characteristic variable as $\eta = x + ct$. Thus

$$\left(\frac{\partial}{\partial t} - c\frac{\partial}{\partial x}\right)h(\eta) = \frac{dh}{d\eta}\frac{\partial \eta}{\partial t} - c\frac{dh}{d\eta}\frac{\partial \eta}{\partial x} = \frac{dh}{d\eta}(-c) - c\frac{dh}{d\eta}(1) = 0\,.$$

From a numerical perspective, hyperbolic partial differential equations can be solved by combination of time and space finite differencing, *e.g.* by employing the Crank-Nicolson or forward/backward time centered space schemes. These ideas are further pursued in the end-of-chapter exercises.

8.5   Summary

In this chapter, we have explored the solution of differential equations with more than one independent variable. In general, the most widely used numerical solution technique involves finite difference approximations of the derivatives in the respective space and time domains. Conditions for numerical stability have been explored. Such considerations apply most especially to parabolic and hyperbolic equations, which involve time derivatives. No time derivatives appear in the case of elliptic equations, which tend therefore to be quite stable.

Explicit methods like the forward time centered space (FTCS) scheme are conditionally stable and generally require small time steps. Implicit methods like backward time centered space (BTCS) and Crank Nicolson schemes are unconditionally stable, and are therefore allow for larger time steps, albeit at the computational expense of having to solve systems of coupled equations e.g. using the Thomas algorithm.

8.6   Exercise Problems

P8.1. Consider the following elliptic partial differential equation:

$$\frac{\partial^2 \theta}{\partial x^2} + \frac{\partial^2 \theta}{\partial y^2} = 1 \,,$$

The domain of interest is $x \in [0,1]$ and $y \in [0,1]$ and we have homogeneous conditions along each boundary. Using central finite difference approximations, discretize the above equation and write it in the form of a system of linear equations, *i.e.*

$$\boldsymbol{A\theta} = \boldsymbol{b} \,,$$

where $\{\boldsymbol{\theta} = \theta(x_i, y_j) = \theta_{i,j} \mid i = 1, 2 \cdots N, j = 1, 2, \cdots M\}$ are the interior nodal values of ϕ.

Solve the above system of linear equations using successive over-relaxation and a direct method. In either case, set $(N, M) = (19, 19)$ and $(29, 29)$.

P8.2. The governing equation for the temperature distribution in a metal wall is given by

$$\frac{\partial^2 \theta}{\partial x^2} + \frac{\partial^2 \theta}{\partial y^2} = 0 \,, \qquad 0 \le x \le 0.5, \ 0 \le y \le 1 \,,$$

with boundary conditions

$$T(0, y) = 500 \,, \quad T(x, 1) = 500 \,,$$

$$\left.\frac{\partial T}{\partial x}\right|_{(0.5, y)} = 0 \,, \quad \left.\frac{\partial T}{\partial x}\right|_{(x, 0)} = 450 \,.$$

Derive the corresponding finite difference approximation and solve the resulting system of equations using Gaussian elimination.

P8.3. Consider a metal bar with cross section $0.2\,\text{m} \times 0.3\,\text{m}$. The top and bottom of the bar are maintained at $150°\text{C}$. The left-hand side is insulated and the right side is subjected to convective heat transfer with $T_\infty = 20°\text{C}$. The governing equation reads

$$\frac{\partial^2 \theta}{\partial x^2} + \frac{\partial^2 \theta}{\partial y^2} = 0 \,, \qquad 0 \le x \le 0.2, \ 0 \le y \le 0.3 \,.$$

The boundary conditions are

$$T(x, 0) = T(x, 0.3\,\text{m}) = 150°\text{C} \,,$$

$$\left.\frac{\partial T}{\partial x}\right|_{(0, y)} = 0 \,, \quad \left. k\frac{\partial T}{\partial x}\right|_{(0.2\,\text{m}, y)} = h(T_\infty - T) \,.$$

If the thermal conductivity of the metal is $k = 2\,\mathrm{W}/(\mathrm{m{\cdot}K})$ and the heat transfer coefficient is $h = 50\,\mathrm{W}/\mathrm{m}^2\mathrm{K}$, determine the temperature distribution in the plate. Use a discretization size of $0.01\,\mathrm{m}$ for both the x and y directions.

P8.4. Consider unsteady state conductive heat transfer through a fin. The non-dimensional governing equation is

$$\frac{\partial\theta}{\partial\tau} = \frac{\partial^2\theta}{\partial\xi^2} - (mL)^2\theta\,. \tag{8.26}$$

and the initial and boundary conditions read

$$\theta(\xi,\tau=0) = 0\,,$$
$$\theta(\xi=0,\tau) = 1\,,$$
$$\left.\frac{d\theta}{d\xi}\right|_{(1,\tau)} = 0\,.$$

(a) Convert the equations into a system of *first-order ordinary differential* equations using the following procedure:

- Construct a set of uniformly spaced grid points $\{\xi_i \mid i = 0,\cdots N+1\}$ with $\xi_i = ih$ where the grid spacing $h = 1/(N+1)$. Note that τ is still treated as a continuous variable at this stage.
- Let the unknown vector be $y(\tau) = [\theta_1(\tau),\, \theta_2(\tau),\cdots,\, \theta_{N+1}(\tau)]$. Note that each element in the unknown vector y represents the temperature at a fixed spatial position and is now a function of τ only.
- At each grid point i, discretize the spatial derivatives using central finite difference equations.
- Hence rearrange equation (8.26) into a system of first order ordinary differential equations of the form

$$\frac{dy}{d\tau} = f(y)\,. \tag{8.27}$$

- Obtain the necessary initial conditions for the set of equations given by (8.27).

(b) Is the resulting system autonomous or non-autonomous?

(c) Solve the equations using `ode45` setting $mL = 1$ then $mL = 2$. Estimate the dimensionless time required to reach the steady state.

P8.5. Consider the advection equation

$$\frac{\partial\phi}{\partial t} + c\frac{\partial\phi}{\partial x} = 0\,,$$

for the particular case where the initial condition is a cosine modulated Gaussian pulse, *i.e.*

$$\phi(x,0) = \cos(kx) \exp\left(\frac{x^2}{2\sigma^2}\right),$$

with the following periodic boundary conditions:

$$\phi\left(-\frac{L}{2}, t\right) = \phi\left(\frac{L}{2}, t\right),$$

and

$$\left.\frac{\mathrm{d}\phi}{\mathrm{d}x}\right|_{x=-L/2} = \left.\frac{\mathrm{d}\phi}{\mathrm{d}x}\right|_{x=L/2}.$$

Solve the above problem for the case where $c = 1$, $L = 1$ and $\Delta x = 0.02$. Investigate the stability of the chosen method by changing the value of Δx. Use the forward time centered space (FTCS) scheme.

P8.6. Repeat **P8**.5. using the backward time centered space (BTCS) scheme.

The reasonable man adapts himself to the world: the unreasonable one persists in trying to adapt the world to himself. Therefore all progress depends on the unreasonable man.

— GEORGE BERNARD SHAW

APPENDIX A

MATLAB FUNDAMENTALS

MATLAB, in spite, or perhaps because of, its multifaceted functionality can be intimidating to use at first. If you are new to MATLAB, or require a brief refresher, we recommend working through the following set of exercises. Note that helpful tutorials can also be found at the MathWorks website: `http://www.mathworks.com`.

- Begin a new MATLAB session. The MATLAB interface consists of a Command Window, a Directory (or Current Folder) Window, a Details Window, a Workspace Window and a Command History Window. Most of our attention will be devoted to the Command Window where we enter data and commands, although we will also make use of the Workspace Window (which provides a summary of defined variables), the Edit Window (used for writing MATLAB functions and scripts) and the Graphics Window (used to display output).

- You can obtain detailed information on MATLAB's built-in functions using the `help` command. Try, for example,
  ```
  >>help help
  ```
  or
  ```
  >>help sin
  ```

- At its most basic level, think of MATLAB as a very powerful calculator, which is fully capable of the types of arithmetic operations you are used to performing with a handheld calculator. Try the following commands one after the other:
  ```
  >>5+pi;
  >>5+pi
  ```

291

```
>>format long
>>5+pi
>>log(exp(1))
```
Note that a semicolon (;) at the end of an expression suppress output, i.e. it says to MATLAB "don't bother to write the result in the Command Window." Also `log` denotes the natural logarithm[*] whereas `exp(1)` is equivalent to $e^1 \simeq 2.7182818285$.

- When we type
  ```
  >>5+pi
  ```
  or
  ```
  >>5+pi;
  ```
  the result is stored in the scratch variable `ans`. Variable assignment is achieved, as you might expect, using the equals sign (=):
  ```
  >>arith1=5+pi;
  ```
  We can keep track of variables either using the MATLAB function `who` (and its partner in crime `whos`) or, for those that prefer the GUI environment, using the Workspace Window (the tab for the Workspace Window appears just to the right of the Current Directory Window). Try, for example
  ```
  >>5+pi;
  >>arith1=5+pi;
  >>who
  >>whos
  >>clear
  >>who
  ```
  Note that `clear` deletes both `ans` and `arith1` and leaves us with an empty set of defined variables.[†] To remove only a single variable, type
  ```
  >>clear arith1
  ```
  Note also that MATLAB is case sensitive, i.e.
  ```
  >>arith1=5+pi;
  >>Arith1=5+pi;
  ```
  yields two separate variables, `arith1` and `Arith1`. Finally, we can save a variable to be used later using `save` and `load`:
  ```
  >>arith1=5+pi;
  >>save arith1
  >>whos
  >>clear
  >>whos
  ```

---

[*]Base-10 logarithms are evaluated using `log10`.
[†]What happens in the Workspace Window when you type `clear` in the Command Window?

```
>>load arith1
>>whos
```

Note that by saving the variable `arith1`, we generate a file `arith1.mat` in the current directory. The `.mat` ending reminds us that this file can only be read by MATLAB.

- Unlike spreadsheet programs, variables are not automatically updated in the MATLAB environment. Try entering the following sequence of commands:

```
>>a=2
>>b=4*a
>>a=1
>>b
>>b=4*a
>>b
```

Even though `a` has been altered, the value of `b` is only updated when the command `b=`... is executed.

- Complex variables are defined as follows:

```
>>compl1=5+1i;
```

or

```
>>compl2=5+3i;
```

MATLAB labels (and stores) real and complex numbers differently. You can verify this for yourself by leveraging `whos`, i.e.

```
>>clear
>>real1=5+pi;
>>compl1=5+1i;
>>whos
```

Also note the difference of output when you enter the following commands:

```
>>isreal(real1)
>>isreal(compl1)
```

`isreal` has some helpful affiliates, most notably `isNaN`, which can be used to find instances of division by 0 (NaN stands for "not-a-number").

- Whereas `who` and `whos` are very useful when it comes to keeping track of (real and complex) variables, they unfortunately do not provide information about built-in functions.* For this purpose, we turn instead to `which`. Some quick examples suffice:

```
>>which sin
```

---

*Try, for example, typing
```
>>who sin
```
and see what MATLAB returns.

```
>>which log
>>which lorenz
```
which tells you whether or not the particular function is defined, but it does not offer any insights into how the function is to be called, what it returns, etc. For this more detailed information, use help instead.

- The true *raison-d'etre* of MATLAB (MATrix LABoratory) is its ability to solve large systems of linear equations. Before getting into these details, let us first learn how to define vectors and matrices in MATLAB. Again, some sample exercises suffice.
```
>>vec1=[1 pi sqrt(2)]
```
defines a row vector whereas
```
>>vec2=[1; pi; sqrt(2)]
```
defines a column vector. One can access individual elements of either vector using parentheses, e.g.
```
>>vec1(3)
```
MATLAB registers the elements of vec1 and vec2 as being identical. Thus, for example,
```
>>isequal(vec1(1),vec2(1))
>>isequal(vec1(2),vec2(2))
>>isequal(vec1(3),vec2(3))
```
all return 1 for true. However, typing
```
>>isequal(vec1,vec2)
```
returns a 0 for false. Why is this? By the manner in which we defined vec1 and vec2, MATLAB recognizes the former as being a row vector (of size* 1×3) and the latter as being a column vector (of size 3×1). This may seem like a trivial difference, but you will find that inattention to such details can lead to much frustration. Conveniently, MATLAB allows you to easily transpose vectors and matrices using the apostrophe (') operator. To try this for yourself, compare
```
>>isequal(vec1,vec2)
```
and
```
>>isequal(vec1,vec2')
```
So whereas
```
>>vec1+vec2
```
complains of incompatible matrix sizes,
```
>>vec1+vec2'
```

---

*Try, for example,
```
>>size(vec1)
```

experiences no such errors.

- To enter a matrix, we borrow some ideas from the previous bullet and type, for example,

    >>mat1=[1 pi sqrt(2); 2 0 exp(1); 0 17 1]

  mat1 is a 3×3 matrix whose individual elements may be accessed by again using parenthesis. Thus

    >>mat1(2,3)

  returns 2.718281828459046, the value of the element in column 2, row 3. Alternatively, we may wish to access all the entries in a particular row or column. This is accomplished using the colon (:) operator. For instance

    >>mat1(2,:)

  returns the *row* vector of row 2 whereas

    >>mat1(:,3)

  returns the *column* vector of column 3. Taking things a step further,

    >>mat1(:,1:2)

  returns the 3×2 sub-matrix consisting of columns 1 and 2 or mat1. MATLAB's colon notation (:), though a bit confusing at first, allows for great economy when typing commands or writing MATLAB algorithms of your own.

  Having defined mat1, we can now compute matrix transposes ('), inverses (inv), etc. Special matrices that you are likely to encounter frequently include

    >>zeros(3,5)

  whose three rows and five columns consist entirely of zeros and

    >>eye(6)

  an identity matrix of size 6×6.

- We have now discussed vectors and matrices and can therefore proceed to some rudimentary problems of linear algebra. Define

    >>a=[1 1 1]

  and

    >>b=[5 3 2]

  as a pair of row vectors. Typing a*b yields familiar squabbling over incompatible matrix sizes. However, if we instead consider a*b' we are then asking MATLAB to take the product of a row vector with a column vector, which is equivalent to taking the dot product of a and b. In like fashion, mat1*a yields more errors whereas mat1*a' gives the product of a matrix and a column vector – as an exercise, make sure that you recall from your linear algebra training how the entries of the resulting column vector are determined.

- Taking things a step further, suppose we wish to solve $Ax = b$ where A is, for example, a 3×3 matrix. The following commands indicate two different solution alternatives.

  ```
  >>A=[pi -1 0; log(2) 0 4/3; 0 -8 sqrt(10)]
  >>b=[1; -1; pi]
  >>x=A\b
  >>x=inv(A)*b
  ```

  In general `x=A\b` is much faster than `x=inv(A)*b`. Use of \ basically says to MATLAB "Okay, you were designed by intelligent people... you figure out the fastest possible way of solving the system of equations be it Gaussian elimination, LU decomposition, etc." In the latter case, by contrast, we first have to compute a matrix inverse (a relatively costly operation), then we have to perform the matrix-vector multiplication. (Note that an objective of this textbook is to make you an intelligent person in your own right, i.e. to have you better understand what happens when you type `x=A\b`).

- Previously, we considered the dot product of two vectors. Suppose, however, that we have two time series, a row vector `price`, which measures, in 1 day increments, the mean oil price ($/bbl), and `volume` another row vector which measures daily production rates. To find each day's revenue, we wish form a new row vector whose elements are `price(1)*volume(1)`, `price(2)*volume(2)`,..., etc. More specifically, let us define

  ```
  >>price=[65.0 62.7 63.8 67.9 70.2 66.8]
  ```

  and

  ```
  >>volume=[1057.2 1320.7 1109.4 987.9 983.3 1017.6]
  ```

  The desired vector of revenue information is obtained using MATLAB's `.*` operator, which multiplies vectors one element at a time, i.e.

  ```
  >>revenue=price.*volume
  ```

  The difference between `.*` and `*` causes no end of confusion for students, so do yourself a favor by solidifying in your mind each operation's use. Note that this textbook will also make extensive use of the `.^` operator, i.e. `x.^2=x.*x`, `x.^3=x.*x.*x`, etc.* In addition to its linear algebraic capabilities, MATLAB is also very adept at producing graphics in the form of 2D (and even 3D) plots. This is illustrated with the following exercise which plots the function $y = x\,e^{-|x|}$

  ```
  >>x=linspace(-5,5,1001);
  ```

---

*Can one compute `x.^0.5`? Try it and find out.

```
>>y=x.*exp(-abs(x));
>>figure; set(gca,'fontsize',20)
>>plot(x,y,'r-','linewidth',2);
>>xlabel('x','fontsize',20); ylabel('y','fontsize',20)
>>title('y=x*exp(-abs(x))','fontsize',16);
>>ylim([-0.5 0.5])
```

Some useful points regarding the above set of commands:

1. We use the `linspace` command to initialize the row vector `x`. This saves us from the tedious task of having to specify each individual element of the array. Alternatively, but equivalently, you can initialize `x` by typing

   ```
   >>x=-5:0.01:5;
   ```

   which tells MATLAB to count from -5 to 5 in increments of 0.01 and assign the corresponding values to the elements of the row vector `x`.

2. Note the judicious use of `.*` in defining the row vector `y`. Omitting the dot, i.e. writing instead `*` yields the usual barrage of errors from MATLAB.

3. `'r-'` tells MATLAB to use a red, solid curve when plotting y vs. x. However, many other possibilities exist and you're encouraged to type

   ```
   >>help plot
   ```

   to investigate the gamut of possibilities.

4. Two commands can be squeezed into the same line provided they are separated by a semicolon. Such is the case, for example, when using `xlabel` and `ylabel` above.

5. `ylim` (and its partner `xlim`) can be used to change the limits of the vertical (horizontal) axis.

- From the figure generated in the previous bullet, it should be clear that `y` has a global maximum of approximately 0.37, which occurs when `x` is approximately 1. (This is especially clear if you use MATLAB's "Zoom In" tool.) Can MATLAB help us achieve greater precision? Certainly. If we are interested in finding the global maximum of `y`, we simply need to type `max(y)` in the Command Window, which returns a value of `0.367879441171442`. Finding the corresponding `x` value takes a bit more work, but not much. Try the following brief exercise:

  ```
  >>index=find(y==max(y))
  >>y(index)
  >>x(index)
  ```

In the above exercise, `index` is a scalar quantity (601), but this need not be so. To see this for yourself, try:

```
>>index=find(y>0.36)
>>x(index)
>>index=[find(y<-0.24),find(y>0.24)]
>>x(index)
```

- An apparent disadvantage of MATLAB is the need to retype everything supposing, for example, that some of the elements of a large matrix needed to be altered. Whereas the 'up' arrow alleviates some of this difficulty, MATLAB also allows users to make a record of the commands they have typed in the Command Window so that these can be revisited later on. The associated function is `diary`; its use is illustrated by the following exercise:

```
>>diary comput1
>>A=[pi -1 0; log(2) 0 4/3; 0 -8 sqrt(10)]; % Matrix
entries based on data from...
>>b=[1; -1; pi];
>>x=A\b;
>>diary off
```

Note that as soon as the first line is entered, a text file is created in the current directory that contains a sequential record of all subsequent command line input/output. Thus the file also records any error messages generated by MATLAB due, for example, to mismatched matrix sizes. Line two of the above set of commands defines the matrix `A` and also includes a comment for posterity's sake; everything following the percent sign (`%`) is ignored by MATLAB. Diary files may very easily be turned into MATLAB scripts, one of the two principal workhorses of MATLAB programming. (For further discussion of MATLAB scripts and the important difference between scripts and functions, see Chapter 1.)

APPENDIX B

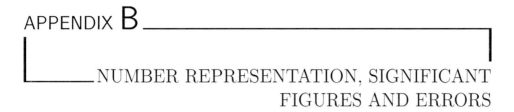

NUMBER REPRESENTATION, SIGNIFICANT FIGURES AND ERRORS

B.1 Number representation

The computer is capable of storing both numeric and non-numeric data consisting of alphabets and symbols. This information is stored in binary form, defined by several fundamental units such as bit, byte and word. A bit is a binary digit consisting of zero or one. Bits are used to form bytes, which is a larger unit consisting of 8 bits. An even larger unit is the word, consisting of several bytes. We can have words with 2 bytes (16 bits), 4 bytes (32 bits) 8 bytes (64 bits), *etc.* Numbers will therefore be stored in words according to the capability of the given computer machine. A 32 bit computer stores numbers in 32 bits while 64 bit computers store numbers in words of 64 bits.

We distinguish between integer numbers and real numbers.

- 256 is an integer number

- 1.273 is a real number

- π is a real number

- e (base of natural logarithm) is a real number

B.1.1 Fixed point system

Numbers are represented using a number system. For instance, we are commonly used to the decimal system (base 10 system). The binary system (base 2 system) is mostly used in the computer. Counting

299

numbers (whole numbers) are represented using the fixed point system. For integers numbers represented by 16 bits this means

- $1 = 0000000000000001 = 2^0$
- $2 = 0000000000000010 = 2^1$
- $3 = 0000000000000011 = 2^0 + 2^1$
- $128 = 0000000010000000 = 2^7$
- $131 = 0000000010000011 = 2^7 + 2^1 + 2^0$

B.1.2   Floating point system

Numbers such as π and e cannot be represented by a fixed number of significant figures. Fractional quantities are usually represented by a floating point form:

$$m.b^e \, ,$$

where m is the mantissa representing the fractional part and b^e represents the integer part, with b the base of the system and e the exponent. The floating point system allows both the fractions and very large numbers to be represented on the computer. However, it takes up more room and also increases the computational effort.

B.2   Significant figures

The number of significant digits in an answer to a calculation will depend on the number of significant digits in the given data, as discussed in the rules below.

   Non-zero digits should always be regarded as significant. Thus, 55 has two significant digits, and 55.2 has three significant digits. Zeros have a special consideration as outlined below.

1. Zeroes placed before other digits are not significant; 0.0054 has two significant digits.

2. Zeroes placed between other digits are always significant; 2006 km has four significant digits.

3. Zeroes placed after other digits but behind a decimal point are significant; 5.20 has three significant digits.

4. Zeroes placed at the end of a number are significant only if they are behind a decimal point. Otherwise, it is impossible to tell if they are significant. For example, in the number 3500, it is not clear if the zeroes are significant or not. The number of significant digits in 3500 is at least two, but could be three or four. To avoid

uncertainty, we use scientific notation to place significant zeroes behind a decimal point, *e.g.* 3.5000×10^{-3} has four significant digits, 3.50×10^{-3} has three and 3.5×10^{-3} has two.

B.3 Mathematical operations

B.3.1 Multiplication and division

In a calculation involving multiplication, division, trigonometric functions, *etc.*, the number of significant digits in an answer should equal the least number of significant digits in any one of the numbers being multiplied, divided *etc.* Thus when two numbers $a = 0.058$ (two significant digits) and $b = 2.67$ (three significant digits) are multiplied, the product should have two significant digits, *i.e.* $a \times b = 0.058 \times 2.67 = 0.15$.

In the case of multiplications involving *whole numbers or exact numbers* which have unlimited number of significant figures, the answer will depend on the other multiplicand. For example, if a pump uses $4.3\,\text{kW}$ of power, then two identical pumps use $8.6\,\text{kW}$: $4.3\,\text{kW}$ (two significant digits) $\times 2$ (unlimited significant digits) $= 8.6\,\text{kW}$ (two significant digits).

B.3.2 Addition and subtraction

When quantities are being added or subtracted, the number of decimal places (not significant digits) in the answer should be the same as the least number of decimal places in any of the numbers being added or subtracted. The arithmetic methodology is then

1. First perform all the operations.

2. Round off your result so that you include only one uncertain digit.

In measurements, the last digit of any is considered uncertain. When an uncertain digit is added to (or subtracted from) a certain digit, the result is an uncertain digit. For example $253\,\text{mL} + 1.8\,\text{mL} + 9.16\,\text{mL} = 263.96\,\text{mL}$, but we report the answer as $264\,\text{mL}$ (three significant digits with only one uncertain digit). In this case the answer is rounded to the same precision as the least precise measurement ($253\,\text{mL}$).

B.3.3 Multistep calculations

In multi-step calculations, we keep at least one extra significant digit in intermediate results than needed in the final answer. For example, if a final answer requires four significant digits, then carry at least five significant digits in calculations. If you round-off all your intermediate answers to only four digits, you are discarding the information contained in the fifth digit, and as a result the fourth digit in your final answer might be incorrect.

B.3.4 Multiplication/division combined with addition/subtraction

In this case we follow the order of precedence for mathematical operators (highest to lowest starting with brackets, powers and roots, multiplication and division then finally addition and subtraction). For each operation, we use the appropriate significant figures rules, as described in preceding sections.

B.4 Rounding and chopping

In order to accommodate the number of digits in a given word, chopping or rounding is employed. In chopping, any digit which is above the number of digits that can be accommodated is simply discarded. Rounding off involves more computational effort because a decision has to be made on what should be the last retained digit.

The following procedure is used to round off numbers during computations:

- If the round-off is done by retaining n digits, the last retained digit is increased by one if the first discarded digit is 6 or more.

- If the last retained digit is odd and the first discarded digit is 5 or 5 followed by zeros, the last retained digit is increased by 1.

- In all other cases, the last retained digit is unchanged.

B.5 Truncation errors

Truncation errors result from leaving out terms in the approximation of a function by a Taylor series. Consider a general function $f(x)$ which is expanded using Taylor series around a point x_i within a neighborhood $x_{i+1} - x_i = h$

$$f(x_{i+1}) = f(x_i + h) = f(x_i) + f'(x_i)h + \frac{f''(x_i)}{2!}h^2 + \cdots \quad \text{(B.1)}$$

$$\frac{f^{(n)}(x_i)}{n!}h^n + R_n .$$

Here R_n is the remainder term which represents the terms which are left out in the infinite series approximation (from $n+1$ to ∞). It is evident that the accuracy of approximation will increase with the number of terms retained. From the Mean Value Theorem, we can say that there is a point ξ between x_i and x_{i+1} such that

$$R_n = \frac{f^{(n+1)}(\xi)}{(n+1)!}h^{n+1} . \tag{B.2}$$

B.5.1 Big Oh notation

We usually do not know the derivative of the function, and thus we denote the error as $R_n = \mathcal{O}(h^{n+1})$, meaning that the truncation error is of the order of h^{n+1}. Thus the truncation error is of the order of the step size (h). The Taylor series expansion gets closer to the real value as we increase the number of terms used and/or decrease the distance between, *i.e.*, decrease h. The zeroth order approximation reads

$$f(x_{i+1}) = f(x_i) , \tag{B.3}$$

the first order approximation reads

$$f(x_{i+1}) = f(x_i) + h f'(x_i) , \tag{B.4}$$

and the second order approximation reads

$$f(x_{i+1}) = f(x_i) + h f'(x_i) + \frac{h^2}{2!} f''(x_i) . \tag{B.5}$$

B.6 Error propagation

Consider the following situation where two numbers x and y, and their approximate representation $\bar{x}$ and $\bar{y}$ are manipulated.

$$x = 1.000000 \qquad y = 1.000100 \qquad y - x = 0.000100$$
$$\bar{x} = 0.999995 \qquad \bar{y} = 1.000105 \qquad \bar{y} - \bar{x} = 0.000110$$

In subtracting these numbers we encounter a disastrous situation where the relative error changes from 0.0005% to 10%. Let us denote the error in a function when using an approximate value, $\bar{x}$, in place of a true value x as

$$\Delta f(\bar{x}) = |f(x) - f(\bar{x})| . \tag{B.6}$$

In order to calculate this error, we need to evaluate $f(x)$. Because we do not know $f(x)$, we shall approximate it using a Taylor series as

$$f(x) = f(\bar{x}) + f'(\bar{x})(x - \bar{x}) + \frac{f''(\bar{x})}{2!}(x - \bar{x})^2 + \cdots \tag{B.7}$$

Dropping the higher order terms and rearranging yields

$$f(x) - f(\bar{x}) \approx f'(\bar{x})(x - \bar{x}), \qquad \text{or} \qquad \Delta f(\bar{x}) \approx |f'(\bar{x})| \Delta \bar{x}. \quad \text{(B.8)}$$

Suppose, more generally, that we have a function f that depends on variables $x_1, x_2, \cdots, x_n$. As these variables are prone to errors, we have a set of estimates $\bar{x}_1, \bar{x}_2, \cdots \bar{x}_n$. The question is how to estimate the error in f if we know the approximate errors in $x_1, x_2, \cdots, x_n$. Using a Taylor series expansion, we can write

$$f(x_1, x_2, \cdots x_n) = f(\bar{x}_1, \bar{x}_2, \cdots \bar{x}_n) + (x_1 - \bar{x}_1)\frac{\partial f}{\partial x_1} + (x_2 - \bar{x}_2)\frac{\partial f}{\partial x_2} + \cdots$$

$$+ (x_n - \bar{x}_n)\frac{\partial f}{\partial x_n} + \text{h.o.t.}, \quad \text{(B.9)}$$

where h.o.t. stands for the *higher-order-terms*. It does not really matter where exactly we determine the partial derivatives (usually it is done at $\bar{x}_1, \bar{x}_2, \cdots \bar{x}_n$ because we know these numbers). If we neglect the higher-order-terms we can define

$$\Delta f(\bar{x}_1, \bar{x}_2, \cdots \bar{x}_n) \approx \left|\frac{\partial f}{\partial x_1}\right| \Delta \bar{x}_1 + \left|\frac{\partial f}{\partial x_2}\right| \Delta \bar{x}_2 + \cdots + \left|\frac{\partial f}{\partial x_n}\right| \Delta \bar{x}_n, \quad \text{(B.10)}$$

whence the following formula for error propagation:

$$\Delta f(\bar{x}_1, \bar{x}_2, \cdots \bar{x}_n) \approx \sum_{i=1}^{n} \left|\frac{\partial f}{\partial x_i}\right| \Delta \bar{x}_i. \quad \text{(B.11)}$$

BIBLIOGRAPHY

[1] AMUNDSON, N. R. *Mathematical methods in chemical engineering: Matrices and their application.* 1966: Englewood Cliffs: Prentice-Hall.

[2] BIRD, R. B., STEWART, W. E., & LIGHTFOOT, E. N. *Transport phenomena.* 1960: New York: John Wiley & Sons.

[3] CHAPRA, S. *Numerical methods for enginneers and scientists.* 2005: New York: McGraw-Hill.

[4] FEYNMAN, R. *The Character of Physical Law.* 1967: Cambridge, Ma.: M.I.T. Press.

[5] FINLAYSON, B. A. *Nonlinear analysis in chemical engineering.* 1980: New York: McGraw Hill.

[6] HOFFMAN, J. D. *Numerical methods for engineers and scientists.* 1992: New York: McGraw-Hill.

[7] LAMBERT, J.D. *Computational methods for ordinary differential equations.* 1973: New York: John Wiley & Sons.

[8] LAPIDUS, L., & SEINFELD, J. H. *Numerical solution of ordinary differential equations.* 1971: New York: Academic Press.

[9] RAO, S. *Numerical methods for engineers and scientists.* 2002: Englewood Cliffs, NJ: Prentice Hall.

[10] ROSENBROCK, H. H. Some general implicit processes for the numerical solution of differential equations. 1963: *Comput. J.*, **5**, 329.

[11] SCARBOROUGH, I. B. *Numerical mathematical analysis.* 1966: Baltimore : John Hopkins Press.